Staff and Research Students	Other Borrowers
Date Borrowed	Date due back

WORLD PATENT LAW AND PRACTICE

AUSTRALIA
The Law Book Company Ltd.
Sydney : Melbourne : Brisbane

INDIA
N. M. Tripathi Private Ltd.
Bombay

ISRAEL
Steimatzky's Agency Ltd.
Jerusalem : Tel Aviv : Haifa

MALAYSIA : SINGAPORE : BRUNEI
Malayan Law Journal (Pte.) Ltd.
Singapore

NEW ZEALAND
Sweet & Maxwell (N.Z.) Ltd.
Wellington

PAKISTAN
Pakistan Law House
Karachi

U.S.A. AND CANADA
Matthew Bender & Co. Inc.
New York

WORLD PATENT LAW AND PRACTICE

By

J. W. BAXTER

of the Legal Department—Patents,
Imperial Chemical Industries Limited

SECOND EDITION

LONDON
SWEET & MAXWELL
1973

First Edition 1968

Second Impression 1969

Second Edition 1973

Published by
Sweet & Maxwell Limited of
11 *New Fetter Lane, London,*
and printed in Great Britain
by The Eastern Press Limited
of London and Reading

SBN 421 17120 0

To

S. C. B.

PREFACE

In this revised edition, I have made numerous corrections, amendments and additions to bring the book up to date. Included in the new matter, apart from new legislation, are, for example, notes on the system of deferred examination, extension of term of patents, the Patent Co-operation Treaty, the current position in the United States with regard to prior foreign patenting, and the claims allowable in respect of chemical and pharmaceutical inventions.

I am grateful for the further assistance I have had from colleagues in I.C.I., and to the many correspondents and critics who have pointed out errors or suggested improvements.

This work will be kept up to date by the issue of Cumulative Supplements.

October 1, 1972

CONTENTS

Appendices

BIBLIOGRAPHY

Adams & Adams	*Patents and Designs in the Republic of South Africa*
Biesterfeld	*Patent Law*
B.I.R.P.I.	*Model Law for Developing Countries on Inventions*
Blanco-White	*Patents for Inventions (3rd Edition)*
Bodenhausen	*Guide to the Application of the Paris Convention for the Protection of Industrial Property, as revised at Stockholm in 1967*
Brink, Gipple and Hughesdon	*An Outline of United States Patent Law*
Chartered Institute of Patent Agents	*The Patents Acts 1949–1961 (2nd Edition)*
Ellis	*Patent Claims*
Falconer, Aldous and Young	*Terrell on the Law of Patents (12th Edition)*
Foster and Ono	*Translation of the Patent and Trade Mark Laws of Japan*
Fox	*Canadian Patent Law and Practice*
Humphris-Norman	*The Canadian Patent Act*
Indian Patent Office	*Hand Book (12th Edition)*
Katzaroff	*Patent Directory*
Ladas	*International Protection of Industrial Property*
McCrady	*Patent Office Practice (3rd Edition)*
Octrooibureau Los en Stigter	*Manual for the Handling of Applications for Patents, Designs and Trade Marks Throughout the World*
Pakistan Patent Office	*Hand Book (2nd Edition)*
Russell	*Patents and Trade Marks in Japan*
Schade	*Patents at a Glance*
Scheer	*International Patent, Design and Trade Mark Law (28th Edition)*

Seidman and Horwitz	*Patent Office Rules and Practice*
Simonnot, Rinuy & Blundell	*Patents and Trade Marks in West Europe and Mediterranean Countries*
Swjadosz	*Protection of Inventions in the U.S.S.R.: Basic Principles*
U.S. Department of Commerce	*Manual of Patent Examining Procedure of the United States Patent Office*
Vojacek	*A Survey of the Principal National Patent Systems*
Webster	*Patents, Trade Marks and Designs in Africa*
White and Ravenscroft	*Patents Throughout the World*

Periodicals

Decisions of the Commissioner of Patents (U.S.A.)
Fleet Street Law Reports (U.K.)
Industrial Property
Journal of the Patent Office Society (U.S.A.)
Journal of the Patent Office Society (Australia)
La Propriété Industrielle
Patent and Trade Mark Review
Reports of Patents, Designs and Trade Mark Cases (U.K.)
United States Patents Quarterly (U.S.A.)

CHAPTER 1

KINDS OF PATENTS

[*Where a section of an Act is mentioned in parentheses following a country, the section refers to the Patents Act of that country*]

ALTHOUGH patent laws vary in many respects from country to country, there are certain features which are common to all. They are all based on the grant of patent rights for a new invention capable of industrial application. This basic grant, often referred to as a patent of invention, is characterised by the fact that in duration and effect it is completely independent of any other patent.

A patentable invention has been expressed as "a creative idea of man expressed in technical terms." It must be (a) new, (b) applicable to industry, and (c) the result of the exercise of inventive ingenuity, often revealed as a technical advance effected by the invention. (See, for example, the Strasbourg "Convention on the Unification of Certain Points of Substantive Law on Patents for Invention," and the "Model Law for Developing Countries on Inventions.")

A patent of invention is granted for a limited period, and may be subject to the payment of renewal fees and/or to requirements for commercial working in the country of grant.

In many countries, however, there exist variations of the basic type of grant and descriptions of such varieties follow, namely:

- patents of addition, improvement, dependency;
- patents of importation, revalidation, confirmation and introduction;
- certificates of authorship;
- precautional patents;
- secret patents;
- reissue patents;
- plant patents;
- registrations;
- petty patents.

There are countries where no patent law exists, but where a procedure of issuing " cautionary notices " may be adopted.

Patents of Addition or Improvement

General

In most countries, notable exceptions being Brazil, Canada, Czechoslovakia, U.S.A. and U.S.S.R., the owner of a patent may obtain for an improvement, modification or alteration of his basic patented invention, a patent of addition. In some countries, this type of patent is known as a patent of improvement. The term of such a patent is limited to the unexpired term of the main patent except in Bolivia, Roumania, Uruguay and Venezuela. In Bolivia, Uruguay and Venezuela the practice is to grant a patent of addition/improvement for the same term as for a main patent. In Roumania a patent of addition is limited in term to the unexpired term of the main patent but with a minimum term of 10 years; if the term of the main patent expires before the end of the term of the patent of addition that patent becomes an independent patent. Patents of addition are not subject to renewal fees except in:

Belgium (if in name of 3rd party)	Iran	Roumania
Bolivia	Iraq	Salvador
Guatemala	Japan (if granted on or after 1/4/60)	Syria
Honduras	Lebanon	Uruguay
		Venezuela

It is generally possible to convert an application for a patent of addition into an application for an independent patent, or to convert a patent of addition into an independent patent if the main patent is revoked and if the grounds of revocation do not affect the patent of addition; but outside the British Commonwealth it is not generally possible to convert a main patent into a patent of addition.

In Albania, Bulgaria, Czechoslovakia and the U.S.S.R. the so-called " patents of addition " are, in fact, patents of dependence.

In Portugal, this type of patent is strictly an " addition to patent " and the certificate of addition (with its specification and claims) is incorporated in the main letters patent.

In Costa Rica during the first year of the patent's life only the patentee is entitled to obtain a patent of addition. Subsequently, a third party can obtain a patent of addition.

In Austria and Iceland the main patent may itself be an independent patent or a patent of dependence.

Countries not granting Patents of Addition or Improvement

These are as follows:

Albania	Grenada	St. Christopher
Antigua	Hungary	St. Vincent
Barbados	Indonesia	Seychelles
Bermuda	Mauritius	South Korea
Brazil	Mexico	Sri Lanka
Br. Honduras	Montserrat	S.W. Africa
Br. Virgin Islands	Nepal	Trinidad & Tobago
Canada	Nigeria	U.S.A.
Cuba	Panama	U.S.S.R.
Czechoslovakia	Paraguay	
Dominica	Peru	
Fiji	Philippines	

Grants to Third Parties

In the following countries the patents of addition or improvement may be granted also to third parties; but the later patentee is not allowed to work the main invention without licence from the earlier patentee, nor can the earlier patentee work an improvement without licence from the later patentee:

Argentina	Honduras	Salvador
Belgium	Iceland	Turkey
Burundi	Iran	Uruguay
Chile	Iraq	Venezuela
Costa Rica	Roumania	Zaïre
Ecuador	Rwanda	

In Chile, if there is agreement for licensing between the parties, the patent of addition may be issued to both parties jointly. If there is not agreement a patent of addition will be granted to the inventor of the improvement, but it will not be effective until expiry of the main patent, and its term will commence on that date.

Inventive Step

In the following countries the grant of a patent of addition will not be refused nor will a patent of addition be revoked solely on the ground that the invention claimed in the patent of addition does not involve any inventive step having regard to any publication or use of the main invention:

Australia	New Zealand
India	United Kingdom

In the following countries, although there are no specific references in the laws, it is believed that in practice this provision would apply:

Dominican Republic	Iceland	Spain
Greece	Italy	Yugoslavia

In the following countries the invention of the patent of addition does not require to show an inventive step over the invention of the main patent:

Colombia	Israel	South Africa
Denmark	Malawi	Sweden
Finland	Norway	Zambia
France	Rhodesia	

Status Unchallengeable

There is provision in the following countries that the validity of a patent of addition cannot be questioned on the ground that the invention ought to have been the subject of an independent patent:

Bahamas	Jordan	St. Lucia
Bangladesh	Malawi	South Africa
Guyana	New Zealand	United Kingdom
India	Pakistan	Zambia
Israel	Rhodesia	

It is believed that this provision would apply in the following countries although there are no specific references thereto in the laws:

Austria	Denmark	Finland
Belgium	Dominican Republic	Greece
Burundi		Haiti

Iceland	Norway	Switzerland
Italy	Rwanda	Yugoslavia
Luxembourg	Sweden	Zaïre
Netherlands		

Scandinavia—Limitation in Time of Filing

The application for a patent of addition must be filed before the application for the main patent has been made available to the public by the Patent Office under the early publication system in:

Denmark	Norway
Finland	Sweden

Dependent Patents

1. *Compulsory Licences and Cross-Licence*

The majority of patents granted are in respect of inventions which are improvements over the prior art, but whose *novelty* is not destroyed by the prior art; in the absence of any other factor of non-patentability they are, therefore, independently patentable. On the other hand some otherwise independent patents cannot be exercised without infringing to a greater or lesser degree an earlier patent, and in most countries it is made clear that a later patentee does not obtain by the grant the right to use an earlier patent.

In some countries there are special provisions for compulsory licensing based on the interdependence of patents. For example:

(*a*) In Algeria (s. 45) and in Israel (s. 121), if a patented invention cannot be used without risk of infringing an earlier patent, a compulsory licence may be granted to the extent necessary to enable the later patentee to use his invention. However, if both inventions relate to the same industrial purpose, the licence will be granted subject to the right of the earlier patentee to obtain a licence under the later patent.

(*b*) In Denmark, Finland, Norway and Sweden (s. 46), if a patented invention cannot be exploited without using an earlier patented invention, the junior patentee may obtain a compulsory licence to exploit the earlier invention; if this is reasonable in view of the importance of the later invention, or for other particular reasons, the senior patentee may be awarded a cross-licence.

(*c*) In France (s. 36), the owner of a patent covering an improvement in an earlier patented invention cannot work his patent without licence from the earlier patentee, nor can the latter work the patented improvement without licence from the later patentee. However, at the expiry of three years from grant, or four years from the date of application, of the earlier patent, the junior patentee may obtain a non-exclusive compulsory licence to the extent necessary to enable him to work his own patent, provided he is able to show that his invention represents an important technical advance over the earlier invention. The senior patentee may then obtain a cross-licence.

(*d*) In Hungary (s. 22), if a patented invention cannot be exploited without infringing another patent, a compulsory licence to the extent necessary for exploitation will be granted under the patent impeding exploitation. The patentee will receive adequate compensation for the compulsory licence, which will be fixed, failing agreement between the parties, by the court.

(*e*) In India (s. 96), at any time after the sealing of a patent, any person having the right to work any other patented invention which has made a substantial contribution to the establishment or development of commercial or industrial activities in India, may obtain a licence under the patent on the ground that he is prevented or hindered without such licence from working the other invention efficiently or to the best advantage possible. The applicant for licence must be in a position to grant or procure the grant of a cross-licence on reasonable terms.

(*f*) In Iraq (s. 28), if working of an invention is of great importance to industry and requires the use of another invention covered by an existing patent, a compulsory licence to exploit the earlier invention may be granted if the owner refuses to agree to such working on reasonable terms. The owner of the earlier patent may be granted a compulsory licence under the later patent if his patent is of greater importance.

(*g*) In Italy (s. 54), if a patented invention cannot be used without prejudice to rights deriving from a patent granted on an application of earlier date, a non-exclusive compulsory licence may be granted to the owner of the later patent to the extent necessary to enable him to work his own invention, provided that that invention represents a notable technical improvement over the earlier invention. If the two inventions have the same industrial aim, a licence will only be granted on condition that the owner of the earlier patent may, if he so wishes, obtain a cross-licence.

(*h*) In Japan (s. 92) if a patentee cannot work his invention without infringing someone else's prior patent, he may be granted a compulsory licence.

(*i*) In Kuwait (s. 31) the patentee of an invention of great importance to the national industry may, where working of his invention necessitates working of an earlier patented invention, be granted a compulsory licence under the earlier patent. Conversely, the earlier patentee may obtain a compulsory licence under the later patent if his invention is of greater importance.

(*j*) In the Netherlands (s. 34) a patentee is bound to grant a licence to such extent only as may be necessary to enable a subsequently patented invention to be exercised (and the person receiving the licence is bound to cross-license the holder of the earlier patent), but any such licence or cross-licence does not entitle the licensee to exercise independently the invention to which the licence relates.

(*k*) In Nigeria (s. 11) the owner of a patent which cannot be worked without infringing a patent of earlier date or priority may obtain a compulsory licence to the extent necessary for the working of his invention, provided it serves industrial purposes different from those served by the invention of the earlier patent or constitutes substantial technical progress over that invention. If the two inventions serve the same industrial purposes, the compulsory licence will be granted only if a cross-licence is granted to the patentee of the earlier patent if he so requests.

(*l*) In Peru (s. 77), the owner of a junior patent which cannot be worked without infringing an earlier patent may obtain a licence to the extent necessary to enable him to work his own patent, provided that it serves a different industrial purpose or represents an outstanding technical advance. If both inventions serve the same industrial purposes the licence will be granted only on condition that the owner of the earlier patent may, if he so wishes, obtain a cross-licence.

(*m*) In South Africa (s. 49) if a patentee cannot work his patent without infringing someone else's prior patent, the Commissioner may grant such a licence to the later patentee as will enable him to work his patent, but for no other purpose.

(*n*) In Switzerland (s. 36) if a patented invention cannot be used without infringing a prior patent, the later patentee may obtain a licence to the extent required to enable him to exercise his invention, provided that the latter serves an entirely different purpose from that of the earlier patent or that it presents considerable technical progress. This right cannot be exercised before the expiry of three years from grant of the earlier patent. If both inventions serve the same economic purpose the owner of the prior patent is entitled to obtain from the later patentee a licence to use the later invention.

(*o*) In the United Kingdom (s. 37) and in New Zealand (s. 46), after the expiration of three years from the date of sealing of a patent, any person interested may obtain a compulsory licence when, by reason of the refusal of the patentee to grant a licence on reasonable terms, the working in the U.K. (New Zealand) of any other patented invention, which makes a substantial contribution to the art, is prevented or hindered provided the other patentee is able and willing to grant a cross-licence to the first patentee.

(*p*) In Yugoslavia (s. 29) a compulsory licence may be granted to a patentee whose invention cannot be wholly or partially exploited without utilisation of a previously patented invention, if the later invention is of special importance for the economy and serves for that purpose. A request for such a licence cannot be made before the expiry of three years from registration of the earlier patent. If a compulsory licence is granted the earlier patentee may also apply for a cross-licence.

2. *Patents of Dependence*

In the following countries, namely:

Albania	Bulgaria	Poland
Austria	Czechoslovakia	U.S.S.R.

there is a special type of patent, namely, a patent of dependence, granted in those cases where an invention is patentable in itself but is incapable of being exercised without infringing an earlier patent. The later patentee cannot exercise his rights without permission of the earlier patentee. In some cases conflict between the parties is determined by the court, in others by the Patent Office. In Austria a patent of dependence may itself be the main patent from which depends a patent of addition. In Poland, the holder of a dependent patent cannot obtain a patent of addition thereto; he can, however, obtain a second dependent patent and describe the object of the first patent in the specification.

Apart from Albania, Bulgaria and U.S.S.R., a patent of dependence is not limited in term by that of the earlier patent, and with the lapse of the earlier patent it becomes independent. In all cases renewal fees are payable as for independent patents.

Patents of Importation, Revalidation, Confirmation and Introduction

The principle of invention by importation, as distinct from inspiration, was first established in the United Kingdom by the decision of the court in the case known as "*The Clothworkers of Ipswich*"; but it is one which was generally accepted in all countries where patent laws came into existence, at least in the sense that proof of inventorship is not generally required.

However, the increase in the number of countries having standards of absolute novelty caused a distinction to be drawn between inventions not previously known in any country and inventions known abroad; and this distinction led to some countries establishing a special type of patent for the latter inventions, namely, a patent of importation, sometimes referred to as a patent of revalidation or confirmation.

Within the context of this book the terms importation, revalidation and confirmation are synonymous and cover the provisions whereby the owner of a foreign patent, or his assignee, is entitled to obtain protection, comparable to that under a patent of invention, generally at any time during the life of his basic patent, for a term limited to the unexpired term of the basic patent. Particular exceptions to the general rule are:

(*a*) In Spain anyone may obtain this kind of patent, but must indicate the source, *e.g.*, foreign patent or any form of publication of the invention.

(*b*) The protection granted in Spain and Tangier (and in Uruguay in respect of process patents) is limited to manufacture, use and sale within the country and does not prevent importation and sale by third parties.

(*c*) In Barbados, Ecuador, Haiti, Spain and Tangier the term is not related to that of the basic patent.

The countries in which this kind of patent is obtainable are:

Type	*Country*	*Term*
Revalidation	Argentina	Unexpired term of basic patent, with maximum of 10 years
Confirmation	Barbados	14 years from application

Type	*Country*	*Term*
Importation	Belgium	Unexpired term of basic patent, with maximum of 20 years
Confirmation	Bolivia	Unexpired term of basic patent, with maximum of 15 years
Importation	Burundi	Unexpired term of basic patent, with maximum of 20 years
Revalidation	Chile	Unexpired term of basic patent
Confirmation	Costa Rica	Unexpired term of basic patent, with maximum of 20 years
Revalidation	Dominican Republic	Unexpired term of basic patent, with maximum of 15 years
Revalidation	Ecuador	3 to 12 years from grant
Importation	Guatemala	Unexpired term of basic patent, with maximum of 15 years
Revalidation	Haiti	5, 10 or 20 years from issue
Importation	Honduras	Unexpired term of basic patent
Importation	Iran	Unexpired term of basic patent
Importation	Iraq	Unexpired term of basic patent, with maximum of 15 years
Confirmation	Jamaica	Expires with first corresponding patent to expire
Revalidation	Panama	Unexpired term of basic patent, with maximum of 15 years
Confirmation	Paraguay	Unexpired term of basic patent, with maximum of 15 years
Importation	Rwanda	Unexpired term of basic patent, with maximum of 20 years
Importation	Spain	10 years from grant
Importation	Tangier	10 years from application
Importation	Turkey	Unexpired term of basic patent, with maximum of 15 years
Confirmation	Uruguay	15 years from date of grant of basic patent
Revalidation	Venezuela	Unexpired term of basic patent, with maximum of 10 years
Importation	Zaïre	Unexpired term of basic patent, with maximum of 20 years

Although Chile is included in the foregoing list, the patent is not termed a patent of importation, the position being that under Chilean patent law patents applied for in Chile for inventions already patented abroad will only be granted for the unexpired term of the first foreign patent granted.

It may be noted that in Ecuador revalidation is available only in respect of patents granted in any of the following countries:

Argentina	Dominican Republic	Panama
Bolivia	Guatemala	Paraguay
Brazil	Haiti	Peru
Chile	Honduras	Salvador
Colombia	Mexico	U.S.A.
Costa Rica	Nicaragua	Uruguay
Cuba		Venezuela

The application for revalidation of a patent can be filed in Ecuador at any time during the validity of that patent in any of the countries listed and it is not required that the basic patent must have been granted in its place of origin.

Further, in Ecuador there is provision for a separate type (termed a patent of importation) of protection granted in respect of the importation of machines or apparatus intended for the local manufacture of novel products or for novel methods of manufacture. The term is determined by the capital involved, and protection may cover part only of the country. Working must be effected within two years of grant and should not be interrupted for more than six months.

Application may be made at any time during the life of the basic patent except in Haiti, Paraguay and Uruguay.

Haiti: Application must be made within *one year* from the date of grant of the first foreign patent.

Paraguay: Application must be made within *one year* from the date of the first official publication of the invention.

Uruguay: Application must be filed within *three years* from the date of grant of the first foreign patent.

Mention may be made of the situation in Algeria, Nepal and Salvador, none of which appears in the list on pages 9 and 10:

(*a*) Algeria

Any patent granted in a foreign country prior to January 1, 1966, may form the subject of a patent of confirmation, but only if the importance of the invention, the industrial or agricultural advantages, and the public usefulness of its exploitation, as well as the amount of capital to be invested, justify the grant.

(*b*) Nepal

A patent will be granted in Nepal without novelty examination if the invention has already been protected by the inventor/assign by patents in the home country and in any three other countries.

(*c*) Salvador

Although the standard of absolute novelty prevails in Salvador, the prior grant of a corresponding foreign patent is excepted and a patent of invention may be obtained despite such a grant, but the patent is not tied in any way to the foreign patent.

The patent necessary to form the basis of the application for revalidation or the like differs in the various countries as follows:

First to be granted:

Argentina	Guatemala	Iran
Bolivia	Haiti	Turkey
Chile	Honduras	Uruguay
Dominican Republic		

First to be filed:

Panama (this is recommended—not a specific requirement)

Any corresponding patent:

Barbados	Iraq
Belgium	Paraguay
Burundi	Rwanda
Ecuador (but restricted to certain countries)	Spain
	Tangier
	Venezuela
	Zaïre

Home patent: Costa Rica

Patent with earliest expiry date: Jamaica

In Argentina, Belgium, Burundi, Congolese Republic, Dominican Republic and Rwanda, it is not necessary to apply for a patent of importation as such. If a patent of invention is obtained and if it subsequently forms the subject of litigation, the courts will, if they are of the opinion that the protection sought should have been by way of a patent of importation, simply treat the patent as one of importation (with a possible reduction in term). It is unlikely that such treatment could be applied in Argentina except if the applicant had obtained a five- or ten-year patent in the first instance.

Applications for this kind of patent generally require to be supported by a certified copy of the basic letters patent with specification and claims. No such support is required in:

Belgium	Paraguay	Tangier
Burundi	Rwanda	Zaïre
Jamaica	Spain	

The certified copy should carry consular legalisation for:

Bolivia	Guatemala	Panama
Costa Rica	Honduras	Uruguay
Ecuador	Iraq	Venezuela

In addition, an attested translation of the certified copy should be furnished in:

Argentina	Guatemala	Iraq
Bolivia	Honduras	Venezuela

For Chile, only a printed copy of the basic specification is called for.

For Ecuador, the certified copy comprises a copy of the basic letters patent which need not have the specification and drawings attached.

Novelty

In the following countries novelty is destroyed only by local working prior to the date of application for revalidation:

Argentina	Honduras
Dominican Republic	Tangier
	Uruguay

In Spain, novelty is destroyed by prior local user or prior local disclosure.

In Turkey novelty is destroyed by:

(i) unofficial publications disclosing the invention, that is to say all publications other than the official publications of corresponding patents or applications;

(ii) official or unofficial publications of improvements disclosing the subject-matter of the invention.

The novelty requirements for the remaining countries are the same as for patents of invention except that in each case publication resulting from grant of the basic foreign patent, or its equivalents, does not prejudice novelty.

Renewal and Working

The renewal fee requirements are the same as for patents of invention in all countries.

The working requirements are the same as for patents of invention in all countries except Spain and Tangier, as follows:

Spain: Actual working must be proved, since it is not permitted to have recourse to the Compulsory Licensing Register.

Tangier: Working must take place in Tangier.

Cuba and Venezuela each provide for a limited form of protection known as a patent of introduction which gives a right of local manufacture only, and is thus akin to the patents of importation granted in Spain and Tangier.

Cuba: A patent of introduction may be obtained by anyone irrespective of ownership of the basic foreign patent provided that the patent is more than three years old. It is granted for the unexpired portion of the foreign term, but with a maximum of ten years. Novelty is destroyed only by prior working in Cuba. No renewal fees are payable. Working in Cuba must be proved annually.

Venezuela: A patent of introduction may be obtained by one who is neither the inventor nor his assignee, and is not tied in any way to a foreign patent. It is granted for a term of five years and novelty is destroyed only if the invention is already publicly known in Venezuela. Renewal fees are payable as for patents of invention. Actual manufacture in Venezuela must be proved.

Certificates of Authorship

Countries considered under this heading are Albania, Algeria, Bulgaria, China, Czechoslovakia, East Germany, Hungary, Poland, Roumania, the U.S.S.R. and Yugoslavia.

Prior to 1917, Russian legislation in the field of industrial property followed, in the main, that of France, Germany and the United Kingdom. Subsequently, in the course of revision of the Soviet legislation two important changes appeared, namely:

(1) A broadening of the field of protection to include authorship of discoveries and of innovations (or rationalisation proposals) as well as of inventions;

(2) provision of a new and additional form of protection for inventions, known as a " certificate of authorship."

The three fields of authorship are defined in the current law (No. 435 of April 24, 1959, as amended up to 1965) and with respect to discoveries and innovations it is sufficient to say here that for the former diplomas are awarded, while for the latter attestations are awarded.

For inventions, the author (inventor) is free to choose between the grant of a patent in the normal sense and the issue of a certificate of authorship, this latter representing a radical difference in the form of protection available to inventors when it appeared for the first time in the Soviet Law of 1931.

Section 3 of the Law defines " invention " in the following terms: " The solution of a technical problem distinguished by its essential novelty, in the field of national economy, culture, public health or national defence, which produces positive results."

By section 4 of the Law, an inventor is free to request

(*a*) Mere recognition of his authorship—in which case a certificate of authorship will be issued: or

(*b*) Recognition of his authorship and of his exclusive right to the invention—in which case a patent will be granted.

The three most important features of the certificate of authorship are:

(1) The right to use the invention belongs exclusively to the Government.

(2) The Government assumes responsibility for exploitation of the invention.

(3) The inventor is entitled to remuneration, dependent on the invention being exploited, which is determined in accordance with the provisions of the " Regulation on Compensation for Discoveries, Inventions and Innovation Proposals." The amount of remuneration cannot exceed 20,000 roubles and is dependent on the savings or other positive results effected by use of the invention.

The grant of a certificate entitles the inventor to be named as inventor and in the case of an important invention, the invention may be given the name of the inventor. The inventor is entitled also to consideration for privileges which include the following:

(1) The first 1,000 roubles of remuneration are exempt from income tax.

(2) Better living accommodation.

(3) Certain preferential rights in appointments to scientific staff in scientific research institutions and experimental enterprises.

Privileges are not extended to an inventor possessing certificates for some of his inventions and patents for others. He would, however, still qualify for remuneration. The holder of a certificate has the right of actively assisting in the development and use of his invention.

In the case of outstanding inventions, the inventor may be eligible for academic distinctions and for awards of the Academy of Sciences.

Neither certificates of authorship nor patents are granted for chemical substances, but only for new methods of preparing such substances.

Certificates, but not patents, are granted for medical, flavouring or food substances obtained by non-chemical processes; but only patents may be granted for methods of preparing such substances.

Further, only certificates may be issued in the following cases:

(1) If the invention has been made in connection with the work of the inventor in a state, co-operative or public enterprise or organisation;

(2) if the inventor has received pecuniary or other material aid from a state, co-operative or public enterprise or organisation for the purpose of developing his invention;

(3) if the invention relates to

(a) approved new methods of treating diseases; or

(b) new and improved breeds of agricultural animals and poultry, species of silkworms feeding either on mulberry or oak, or varieties of agricultural crops, any of which have been obtained through selection.

Both applications for certificates and for patents are examined for usefulness, not only the likelihood of immediate usefulness of the invention to the national economy, but also the possibility of its future usefulness. The possibility of the application of different standards of usefulness to applications for certificates and for patents may exist, since in the case of certificates the state assumes also the obligation to exploit. The law does not differentiate between the two forms of protection as to degree of examination for usefulness.

For both forms, the standard of novelty is absolute. In the case of certificates, however, prior disclosure is excused if the application is filed not later than four months from the date of the offending act. Prior local applications or patents are effective, from the point of view of destroying novelty, as of their date of application; but foreign applications are effective only as of their day of publication.

A patent may be converted at any time to a certificate of authorship provided that the patentee has not assigned the rights in the patent nor has granted any licence.

So far as application papers and the treatment of applications generally are concerned, there is no difference as between an application for certificate of authorship and one for a patent, but the following additional differences in result should be noted:

(1) Application for a patent may be made in the name of the inventor or assigns; for a certificate only the inventor, his heirs or an authorised enterprise or organisation may apply.

(2) Fees are payable for patent applications, and subsequently heavy renewal fees. No fees are payable in respect of applications for certificates, nor are any renewal fees payable.

(3) Patents are granted for 15 years from the date of application; certificates are unlimited in term.

(4) Action for nullity of a patent may be taken at any time during its life; action against a certificate can only be taken within one year from the date of publication.

(5) A patent may be assigned or licensed and recording of the deed is compulsory. A certificate cannot be assigned but may pass by inheritance.

(6) Use, or preparation for use, of an invention by an enterprise or organisation prior to the date of filing the application for patent gives the user the right to free continued use.

(7) Where an invention is of importance to the state, and in the absence of agreement with the patentee, a government agency may be allowed to use the invention, subject to royalty.

The International Convention was revised at Stockholm in 1967 to make certain that a right of priority within Article 4 can be claimed on the basis of an application for a certificate of authorship. For any country which has not yet ratified the Stockholm revision, the position would appear to be that it may agree to a claim to priority based on an application for a certificate of authorship, but is not bound to do so.

This form of protection is to be found also in the laws of Albania, Algeria, and Bulgaria, where the laws concerning certificates of authorship have been modelled on those of the U.S.S.R. Thus, also in these countries the right to use the invention is vested in the state which has a responsibility to exploit the invention and to remunerate the inventor. There are variations in details in the respective laws but there is really no major difference apart from Algeria where freedom of choice as between a certificate and a patent is even more limited by reason of the fact that Algerian nationals can obtain only a certificate. It is worth mentioning too that Albania, Bulgaria, and the U.S.S.R. restrict the form of protection to a certificate in the case of inventions in the fields of medical, flavouring and food substances, treatment of diseases and agriculture. This restriction does not appear in the laws of Algeria.

Poland also provides for the issue of certificates, but here there is the significant difference that for a patentable invention both a certificate and a patent are issued; in the case of foreign applicants the certificate is not issued automatically, but only on request. If an invention has been made as a result of work instigated by, or with the aid of, a sector of the national economy, or if it has been made by an employee of such a sector in the course of his employment or in connection with his work within the sector, it ranks as an "employee-invention." In such a case

(*a*) the invention is the property of the state;

(*b*) the right to a patent belongs to the state—the application being made by the appropriate Minister or the relevant state enterprise;

(*c*) if a patent is obtained by the state, the inventor has the right to a certificate;

(*d*) if an application is not filed on behalf of the state, the inventor may himself apply for a patent.

In the case of " non-employee inventions " the inventor may come to an arrangement with a state enterprise so that the patent may be granted to the enterprise. In both cases, the inventor will qualify for remuneration depending on the use made of the invention.

Although the laws of East Germany do not provide for certificates of authorship as such, they do provide for so-called " industrial " patents as well as for the normal type which in East Germany are called " exclusive " patents. The provisions affecting " industrial " patents show certain similarities to certificates and therefore warrant inclusion here.

In the first place, there is freedom of choice between the two types, except in the case where the invention was made in connection with the inventor's work in a nationalised undertaking or other public body or with government subsidies, when only an industrial patent will be granted. The inventor must disclose the invention to the undertaking. If the inventor waives his right to apply for a patent, the undertaking is free to do so.

The right to use an invention protected by an " industrial " patent is vested in the patentee *and* in any person to whom the right has been given by the Patent Office. Remuneration is payable by such licensee and is envisaged " in principle " in the East German enactment as a single payment. This payment appears to deprive the patentee of all rights and obligations under the patent which then pass to the competent Ministry. Supplementary payments, when the original settlement has been in error, are provided for in the law.

The application and renewal fees for an " industrial " patent are on a much lower scale than that for an " exclusive " patent, which can be converted into an " industrial " patent on request.

In Czechoslovakia a form of certificate is issued for new methods of curing or preventing disease, for new varieties of seeds or of plants, and for the results of new methods of breeding. However, it has been made clear that this certificate merely acknowledges authorship and does not in any way afford the protection accorded to a patentable invention and so cannot be regarded as bearing any relation to the certificate of authorship issued in the U.S.S.R. and other countries.

Earlier provisions in Hungary, Roumania and Yugoslavia for the issue of certificates of authorship have been repealed.

In the People's Republic of China there is also found a form of protection which can be assimilated to the certificate of authorship, but it should be emphasised that there is no provision whatsoever for protection by patent grant, the earlier provisions of 1950 having been repealed.

The "Regulations Governing the Encouragement of Inventions," promulgated by the State Council in 1963, state explicitly that they are enacted for the purpose of encouraging invention and promoting the utilisation of things invented, so as to expedite the development of sciences and techniques and of the national economy.

"Invention" is defined as a new scientific or technical achievement, which must also meet the following conditions:

(1) it must never before have been made by anyone or, if made in a foreign country, must not have been publicly announced;
(2) it must, after experiments, be proved applicable; and
(3) it must be more advanced than what is in existence.

The Regulations set out the competent organisations having responsibility for directing the declaration of invention, for examination, for identification of inventions, and for supervising the extensive utilisation of inventions.

The inventor is required to declare his invention and to submit a report thereon, including the date of invention, the reasons for making the invention and details of the invention itself. When an invention has been examined and found to be satisfactory by the competent organisation, the inventor will be encouraged by the award of a combined honorary and material reward, comprising for all grades of invention an "invention certificate" and cash, and in the higher grades a greater cash reward and a medal. The cash awards range from JMP 500 to JMP 10,000. Inventions of special importance may result in special rewards.

Inventions are owned by the state and may be utilised by any unit in the country.

These provisions are open to residents of China and to Chinese nationals residing in foreign countries as well as to foreign individuals and companies.

Reference may be made to the following published articles which discuss, *inter alia*, certificates of authorship:

(1) " Protection of Invention in the U.S.S.R.: Basic Principles " by J. I. Swjadosz of the Central Scientific Research Institute of Patent Information and Technical-Economic Studies—1966.

(2) " Soviet Patent and Trade Mark Law "—Report by a United Kingdom delegation to the Soviet Union—1960.

(3) " Russian Patents "—Derwent Information Service—1961.

(4) *Journal of the Patent Office Society* (U.S.A.)

(*a*) " The new Structure of the Protection of Industrial Property in Eastern Europe "—Professor Konst Katzarov—September 1960.

(*b*) " Soviet Law on Inventions and Patents "—P. J. Federico—January 1961.

(*c*) " The Significance of Soviet Accession to the Paris Convention for the Protection of Industrial Property "—Peter B. Maggs and James W. Jerz—April 1966.

(*d*) " Commentary on Roumanian Industrial Property Laws "—Arthur O. Klein—December 1965.

(5) " Industrial Property "—April 1964—Study Group on Certificates of Authorship.

(6) " Industrial Property "—April 1965—Committee of Experts on Inventors' Certificates.

Precautional Patents

This form of patent (if patent it can be called) is for a short term only and in effect is in the nature of a caveat, as indeed it is so called in some countries.

The term varies in different countries and the effect of the patent is that while it is in force no patent relating to its subject-matter will be granted without previous notice to the holder of the precautional patent who is given the opportunity to lodge objections within a stipulated term.

Country	*Type*	*Period*
Argentina	Precautional	1 year; renewable for 1 year
Bolivia	Precautional	1 year; renewable for 1 year
Canada	Caveat	1 year
Chile [1]	Caveat	1 year; renewable for 1 year
Guatemala	Caveat	6 months; renewable further 6 months

[1] Granted only to residents of Chile and Peru, respectively.

Country	*Type*	*Period*
Honduras	Provisional	unlimited
Peru [1]	Limited	1 year
Salvador	Caveat	1 year; renewable for 1 year

Secret Patents

In most countries the government has the right to make secret any patent application covering an invention which is of importance, *e.g.*, for the defence of the state. Governments may also generally use such inventions, subject to payment. Once directions for secrecy are given, the application proceeds through the normal examination stages up to acceptance, but acceptance is not advertised, nor is the specification published, nor is a patent granted, until secrecy is removed. If and when secrecy is removed, the application proceeds normally to grant.

In the following exceptional countries, however, the patent laws, or special laws, contain provisions for the grant of patents on applications which have been made secret:

Bangladesh	Section 21A of the Patent Act
Belgium	Law of January 10, 1955
Brazil	Article 45 of Patent Law
Canada	Section 20 of the Patent Act
Denmark	Secret Patents Act 1960
Finland	Section 55 of the Patents Act 1943
E. Germany	Order on Secret Patents and section 4 Amending Law, both of July 31, 1963
W. Germany	Sections 24 (3), 30A–30G of the Patent Act
Greece	Law 4325/1963
Ireland	Section 90 of the Patent Act
Netherlands	Section 29A–F of the Patent Act
Norway	Secret Patents Act 1953
Pakistan	Section 21A of the Patent Act
Poland	Articles 58–60 of the Patent Act
South Africa	Sections 59–61 of the Patent Act
Sweden	Secret Patents Act 1946–1967
U.S.S.R.	Sections 42, 58 of the Patent Act
Yugoslavia	Sections 70–78 of the Patent Act

Reissue Patents

Although this form of patent is, in effect, equivalent to amendment after grant, it is dealt with in the present chapter because a new patent is issued for the remainder of the term of the original patent which is cancelled.

Broadly, when a patent is vulnerable by reason of a defective specification or drawing or by improper claiming (whether more or less) a reissue patent may be obtained in

Canada	Philippines
Jamaica	U.S.A.

These patents originated in the U.S.A. in 1832 and the provisions of U.S. law prior to the 1952 Act have been very substantially incorporated in the laws of the other countries.

Reissue provisions have always been held by the U.S. courts as being remedial in nature, being based on fundamental principles of equity and fairness and should be so applied to facts in any given case that justice will be done both to patentees and public (see, for example, *Re Willingham*, 127 USPQ 211).

This is also illustrated, for example, by the case of *Brenner* v. *State of Israel*, 158 USPQ 584, where it was held, by the Court of Appeals, District of Columbia, that a patentee who had neglected, due to a clerical error, to file a certified copy of the original foreign specification was entitled to correct the error by a reissue patent with the priority rights included.

The case *Ex p. Scudder*, 169 USPQ 814 illustrates the possibility of obtaining correction of a misjoinder of inventors by means of reissue patents under section 251, where action under section 256 (Correction of misjoinder or non-joinder of inventors) is inadequate. Here the Board of Appeals ruled that section 256 was not intended by Congress to be the only avenue for correcting misjoinder of inventors, and that section 251 must be interpreted to cover a situation where it is discovered that one of several joint inventors is the sole inventor of some of the claimed subject-matter in a patent issued to the joint inventors. Such a sole inventor may obtain a reissue of the patent so that he will obtain a patent naming him as the sole inventor of the subject-matter of which he is sole inventor. It had been discovered at an early stage in interference proceedings that the applicant for reissue was the sole inventor of the subject-matter forming the counts of the interference, but that he was a joint inventor, with two others, of the subject-matter of other claims of the patent. Action under section 256 would have necessitated giving up all the claims which were the joint invention of the three inventors. (A separate application for reissue was also filed, listing the three inventors, in respect of the claims invented jointly.) This decision overrules *Ex p. Johnson*, 117 USPQ 412.

If an error has been made without deceptive intention, the court will adopt a liberal attitude. On the other hand, the deliberate cancellation of a claim during prosecution of the original application in order to secure a patent has been held not to be the type of " error " contemplated in U.S. law as justifying a reissue with such claim reinstated (*Re Byers*, 109 USPQ 53).

The changes made in the U.S. Act of 1952 were, in the main, changes in language but not in substance. There is no reason to believe, therefore, that the difference in language between the present U.S. provisions and those of Canada, Jamaica and the Philippines, will result in any real difference in practice.

35 USC 251 provides for reissue whenever a patent is, through error without any deceptive intention, deemed wholly or partly inoperative or invalid, by reason of a defective specification or drawing, or by reason of the patentee claiming more or less than he had a right to claim in the patent.

The provisions of the other countries require that the error arose from inadvertence, accident or mistake, and without fraudulent or deceptive intention. The words " wholly or partly " do not appear in the Canadian and Jamaican versions. Also, the words " or less " do not appear in the Jamaican and Philippines versions.

No new matter may be introduced into an application for reissue in any of the four countries.

In Canada, the Philippines and U.S.A., several reissue patents for distinct and separate parts of the patented invention may be granted, subject to payment of a separate fee for each reissue. This provision does not appear in the Jamaican law.

The normal regulations for patent applications apply to reissue applications, but in U.S.A. the application must be made by the inventor(s) except that it may be made by the assignee of the entire interest if the reissue does not seek to enlarge the scope of the claims of the original patent. In all cases the application must be supported by evidence setting forth all the relevant facts.

In the U.S.A., application for reissue should be lodged without unreasonable delay, but within two years of the date of the original patent if the effect of the reissue is to enlarge the scope of the claims. In Canada there is a time limit of four years from the date of issue in all cases. There are no time limits in Jamaica and the Philippines, but in the latter if the broadening of any claim is desired the applicant must explain (a) when and under what circumstances the lack of breadth became known, and (b) any delay thereafter in filing the reissue application.

The surrender of the original patent takes effect on the issue of the reissued patent, and the reissued patent has the same effect, in any subsequent action, as if originally granted in the amended form. Where the original and reissued claims are identical, the surrender does not affect any pending action nor abate any existing cause of action.

In the U.S.A. a reissued patent cannot affect the right of a third party who made, purchased or used prior to the grant of a reissue anything patented thereby, to continue his operations unless they infringe a valid claim of the reissued patent which was in the original patent. The court may provide for protection of such intervening rights, and also in the case where the third party has made substantial preparation for his operations before grant of the reissue. Although there are no such specific provisions in the patent laws of Canada, Jamaica or the Philippines, it would appear likely that their courts would adopt the same interpretation.

U.S.A.	35 USC 251, 252
	rr. 171–179
	See also *Commentary on the New Patent Act* by P. J. Federico
Canada	s. 50
	rr. 81, 82
Jamaica	s. 33
Philippines	s. 27A
	rr. 162–172

Plant Patents

Only the following countries have made special provision in their laws for the grant of plant patents as such:

Cuba South Korea U.S.A.

It should be noted that in each case protection is given for new varieties of plants asexually produced and not tuber-propagated.

The U.S. Patent Law Amendment of 1930 introduced specific provision for plant patents, and in fact this is believed to be the first legal provision in any country for such patents. The present provisions are contained in U.S. Code, Title 35, Chap. 15, ss. 161–164, and set out that a patent may be granted to whoever invents or discovers and asexually reproduces any distinct and new variety of plant, other than a tuber-propagated plant. The claim in the specification must be in formal terms to the plant shown and described, and the patent grants the right to exclude others from asexually reproducing the plant or selling or using the plant so reproduced. The term is 17 years from the date of issue. The appropriate Rules are 161–167.

The Plant Variety Protection Act 1970, provides protection for certain novel varieties of plants which reproduce through seeds (sexually).

The Cuban Law of 1936, Art. 41 (3), provides for the grant of patents for new varieties of plants asexually reproduced, excepting plants propagated by means of bulbs. Patents are granted for a term of 17 years from the date of issue.

The South Korean Law of 1961 provides for the grant of plant patents for any asexually reproduced distinct and new variety of plant, for a term of 12 years from the date of publication of the application, but with a maximum of 15 years from the date of application.

For these three countries the requirements for renewal and working are the same as for patents of invention.

In Belgium, W. Germany, Hungary, Italy and Luxembourg (and in Roumania to State Enterprises) it is possible to obtain patents for new plant varieties under the ordinary patent laws, without the necessity for special provisions.

Patents are not granted in Scandinavia for new varieties of plants as such, although methods of plant propagation would appear to be patentable, if the method is not essentially biological.

In France the Law on the Protection of New Plant Varieties (No. 70489 of June 11, 1970) which came into force on September 18, 1971, makes provision for the protection, by "New Plant Variety Certificates" of the following species, namely: wheat, barley, oats, rice, maize, potatoes, peas, beans, lettuce, rose trees and carnations, all of which are included in the Annex to the Convention for the Protection of New Varieties of Plants. In addition, this form of protection may be obtained for the following species, namely: flax, tomatoes, strawberry plants, plum trees, peach trees, pear trees, quince trees, cherry trees, apricot trees, vines and poplars, but by foreigners only if French nationals can receive reciprocal protection for those species in the state of which the foreigner is a national or in which he has his domicile or establishment. It is probable that the Law will be progressively extended to cover genera and species additional to those enumerated above. The new Law also amends the Patent Law by excluding from patent protection any new plant variety of a genus or species protected under the new Law. Thus it appears that protection for all other genera and species may still be obtained under the Patent Law.

Reference may also be made to the International Convention for the Protection of New Varieties of Plants (1961), which recognises the right of the breeder of a new plant variety to protection either by a special title or by a patent.

Registrations

The patent laws of most countries having colonies or responsible for the administration of other territories provide that a patent granted in the mother country covers also the other territories. Thus, a Spanish patent covers all Spanish colonies and a Portuguese patent all Portuguese colonies. The picture is also the same in the Netherlands and France except that in the case of the Netherlands the former colony of Indonesia is now completely independent, and so far as France is concerned, at the present time there are separate patent laws in Algeria, Tunis, Vietnam, Cambodia, Laos, French Morocco and others which have gained independence in recent years. However, the former French colonies of Guinea and Mali have not joined the African and Malagasy Union nor have they promulgated separate patent legislation. It appears that French patent law is still applicable as the national law in these territories and it is possible to file applications therein. In the absence of any implementing regulations, it is not possible at this time to determine the value of such patents, if granted.

A U.S. patent automatically extends to Puerto Rica, Guam, Virgin Islands, American Samoan Islands and the Panama Canal Zone. In respect of the three first-named territories, however, it is believed desirable to register locally a certified copy of the U.S. letters patent or at least a certified printed copy of the U.S. patent specification, to obtain positive protection.

The following is a list of " mother countries " with the additional territories covered by their patents:

Australia	Territories of New Guinea, Norfolk Island, Papua. Protection in Nauru is obtained by

	registering the Australian patent within three years from the date of sealing.	
France	Corsica Comores Archipelago French Guiana French Somaliland Guadeloupe and dependencies Martinique New Caledonia and dependencies New Hebrides Polynesia Reunion St. Pierre and Miquelon	
Germany	Saar. In 1959 the Saar territory, then under the control of France, became reunited with the Federal Republic of Germany. Provision was made for the maintenance in the Saar of French patent rights then in force but it was necessary for the owners to file special petitions to ensure continuance of their rights. It was further provided that to maintain the original French rights in force annual taxes had to be paid to the German Patent Office on each French patent maintained in force in the Saar. The law also provides for the automatic extension to the Saar of any German patent rights then in force and further for the extension to the remainder of the Federal Republic of French rights of inhabitants in the Saar.	
India	Burma	
Italy	San Marino Vatican City	
Netherlands	Dutch Antilles Surinam	
	West Irian	But only in respect of Dutch patents granted and applications filed before May 1, 1963.

New Zealand	Western Samoa
	Cook Islands
	Tokelau Islands
Portugal	Angola
	Azores
	Cape Verde Islands
	Macao
	Madeira
	Mozambique
	Portuguese Guinea
	Sao Tome & Principe Islands
	Timor
Spain	Alhucemas
	Balearic Islands
	Canary Islands
	Ceuta
	Chaffarinas
	Ifni
	Melilla
	Penon de Velez
	Spanish Guinea
	Spanish Sahara
Switzerland	Liechtenstein
U.K.	Lesotho
	Botswana
	Swaziland
	The laws of these protectorates provide also for registration of a South African patent at any time during the life of that patent.
U.S.A.	Puerto Rica
	Guam
	Virgin Islands
	American Samoan Islands
	Panama Canal Zone

The attitude of the various states to their colonies has been reflected in their patent laws, but today it is only in the British Commonwealth that separate protection must positively be sought in the various constituent parts and colonies, if protection is desired.

In the British Commonwealth the patents laws of Australia, Bangladesh, Canada, India, Malawi, Mauritius, New Zealand, Nigeria, Pakistan, Rhodesia, Sri Lanka, U.K. and Zambia provide for independent patenting in these territories, but in most of the Crown colonies, or former Crown colonies, the only means of obtaining patent protection is by registering the British patent in the territory. Newly independent states may eventually promulgate their own patent laws. Generally, protection can be obtained only by the U.K. patentee or his assignee registering a printed copy of the British patent specification having attached thereto a certificate of the Comptroller giving full particulars of the issue of the patent in the United Kingdom. In some territories, a certified copy of the U.K. letters patent is called for.

Registration confers on the applicant privileges and rights, subject to all conditions established by the law of the territory, as though the patent had been issued in the United Kingdom with an extension to the territory. The privileges and rights date from the date of the patent in the United Kingdom and continue in force only so long as the patent remains in force in the United Kingdom. Renewal fees are not payable except in Barbados, Bahrain and Sri Lanka. No action for infringement will be entertained in respect of any manufacture, use or sale prior to the date of issue of the certificates of registration in the territory. If the term of the U.K. patent is extended, the patentee should register a certified copy of the order of extension.

The local court generally has the power to revoke the rights conferred by the certificate of registration on any of the grounds *mutatis mutandis* upon which the U.K. patent might be revoked. Such grounds include the manufacture, publication, use or sale of the invention in the territory prior to the date of the patent in the United Kingdom but *do not* include the manufacture, publication, use or sale of the invention in the territory *after the date of the patent* in the United Kingdom *and* prior to the date of issue of the certificates of registration in the territory.

The parts, or former parts, of the Commonwealth in which there is provision for registration of a British patent are as follows:

Aden	Bermuda [1]	Br. Virgin Islands [1]
Antigua [1]	Br. Honduras [1]	Brunei
Bahrain	Br. Solomon Islands	Cyprus
Barbados [1]		

[1] The laws of these territories also provide for independent patents.

Dominica [1]
Falkland Islands
Fiji [1]
Gambia
Ghana
Gibraltar
Gilbert & Ellice Islands
Grenada [1]
Guernsey
Guyana [1]
Hong Kong
Jamaica [1]
Jersey
Kenya
Malaya
Montserrat [1]
Sabah
St. Christopher—Nevis & Anguilla [1]
St. Helena
St. Lucia [1]
St. Vincent [1]
Sarawak
Seychelles [1]
Sierra Leone
Singapore
Somalia (Northern Region)
Sri Lanka [1]
Tanganyika
Trinidad [1]
Uganda
Zanzibar

Registration may be effected not later than three years from the date of sealing the British patent, with the exception of Hong Kong, where the period is five years, and Barbados, Guernsey, Jamaica, Jersey and Sri Lanka, where registration may be effected at any time during the life of the British Patent. With regard to Jersey, however, it should be noted that an application for registration may be opposed on the ground that three years having elapsed since the date of sealing of the British Patent, the patented invention is being used in Jersey on a commercial scale. The same ground is available in revocation proceedings.

In Barbados and Jamaica, registration of any foreign patent may be effected at any time during the life of that patent and these territories, which also provide for independent patents, are dealt with in the chapter on patents of importation.

Petty Patents (Utility Model: Gebrauchsmuster)

This form of protection is available in a relatively small number of countries. It covers generally only the shape or configuration of an object as far as it serves some useful purpose. Processes, therefore, cannot be the subject of such protection. The scope of protection is narrower that that of a patent but broader than that of a purely decorative design, so that petty patents may be regarded as bridging the gap between patents and designs.

The best known types of petty patents are the West German Gebrauchsmuster and the Japanese utility model, but this form of protection is also available in Brazil, Italy, Poland, Portugal, Spain, South Korea, Tangier and the Philippines.

The term of protection varies as with patents from country to country. In some countries petty patents are treated for practical purposes in the same manner as patents and in some there is an examination for novelty. Thus, in Japan, a utility model application is examined as to novelty and is open to opposition.

Except in Portugal where only photographs are called for, a specification with claims is required as for a patent application.

Brazil

Utility Model protection may be obtained for any new arrangement or form introduced or obtained in known objects, provided they serve a practical work or use. The expression "object" comprises tools, instruments of work or implements. Protection is granted only to the new form or arrangement which results in improved utilisation of the function to be performed by the object, and will not be granted to anything patentable as an invention, nor to works of sculpture, architecture, painting, engraving, enamelling, embroidery, photographs or any other models or designs of a purely artistic character.

The criterion for patentability of an invention applies also to a utility model, namely that it must be new and capable of industrial application.

The term is 10 years from the date of application, subject to payment of annual renewal fees beginning with that for the third year. In the absence of working within three years from grant, or if working is interrupted for more than one year, compulsory licences may be granted. Forfeiture may occur if working has not begun within four years (or five if a licence has been granted) from grant, or if working has been discontinued for more than two consecutive years.

West Germany

Utility Model (Gebrauchsmuster) protection under the Utility Model Law of 1961 is available in respect of implements or articles of everyday use in so far as they are intended to serve their purpose by means of a new configuration, arrangement or design.

Gebrauchsmuster registration is thus available for the protection of practically all articles of manufacture which form a unit. Excluded from protection are, for example, processes, chemical products, electrical circuitry, anything immovably fixed to the ground such as buildings and bridges, and arrangements consisting of separate parts of independent character.

There is no examination for novelty, technical progress or inventive step. The examination is simply to determine whether the subject-matter is suitable for Gebrauchsmuster registration. The Patent Office has power of refusal.

Although to be valid a Gebrauchsmuster must have a certain degree of technical progress and a certain degree of inventive step, these are required to a much lower degree than in the case of patents. It is therefore possible to obtain Gebrauchsmuster registration for an invention not patentable on these grounds. It is also more difficult to invalidate a Gebrauchsmuster registration than a patent, on the grounds mentioned.

An important feature of this form of protection is that it is possible, and indeed common practice, to file simultaneously a patent application and a Gebrauchsmuster application but to leave the Gebrauchsmuster pending until the scope of protection to be given by the patent is ascertained. This type of Gebrauchsmuster is termed " Hilfsgebrauchsmuster " which in English is generally given the name " eventual Gebrauchsmuster." If the patent is of sufficient scope, the Gebrauchsmuster application can be abandoned. Alternatively, if the patent is refused the Gebrauchsmuster can be completed. Yet again it is possible for the Gebrauchsmuster registration and the patent to exist side by side. Thus, the patent might cover only a certain arrangement while the Gebrauchsmuster covered the details. In case of infringement during pendency of the patent application, the Gebrauchsmuster may be completed and then an infringement action started without detriment to the patent application.

It is not possible to convert a German patent application into a Gebrauchsmuster or vice versa.

The term is six years from the day following the application date, subject to payment of a renewal fee at the end of the third year.

There are no opposition proceedings, nor are there legal provisions for working, nor for marking.

Italy

There may be protected by utility model registration new designs capable of conferring upon machines or machine parts, instruments, utensils or useful objects in general, an efficiency or a special facility of application or use, such as new models consisting in a particular conformation, disposition, configuration or combination of parts.

As in Germany, Italian law provides for the simultaneous filing of a patent application and a utility model application and for the latter to be held in suspense pending the outcome of the patent application.

The term is four years from the application date, subject to payment of a granting fee. This may be paid in full on grant or in two instalments—one on grant, the other at the end of two years from application. There is no novelty examination, nor opposition provisions, nor marking requirements. In the absence of working within one year from grant, the registration may be revoked.

Japan

Prior to 1960, Japanese Utility Model Law was such that protection was afforded to minor inventions. The Law introduced in 1960, however, radically changed the position so that today the rights given by a utility model registration are only slightly inferior in strength to those given by a patent. The novelty requirements and examination are the same in both cases, but the degree of technical advance required for a utility model is less than that required for a patent.

Utility model registration is available for any new device capable of industrial use and relating to the shape, structure or assembly of an article.

The term is 10 years from publication, but with a maximum of 15 years from the date of application, subject to payment of annual renewal fees from the end of the third year. In the absence of working within three years from grant compulsory licences may be granted. Opposition is possible within two months from publication. The owner of a registration is required to mark articles, or packaging containing them, with an indication of the registration number. It is possible to convert a patent application into one for a utility model, or vice versa.

Philippines

Any new model of implements or tools or of any industrial product, or a part of the same, which does not possess the quality of invention, but which is of practical utility by reason of its form, configuration, construction or composition may be protected by the author thereof in the same manner and subject to the same provisions and requirements as relate to patents and inventions in so far as they are applicable.

The term is 15 years from date of issue, subject to payment of renewal fees at the end of the fifth and tenth years. In the absence of working within three years from issue, compulsory licences may be granted. There is an examination as to novelty and the application in general is treated in the same manner as a patent application.

There are no provisions for opposition, nor are there any marking requirements.

Poland

Utility model protection is obtained for any new form of a known article which is distinguished by the shape, construction or material of the article and in which the object of the novel feature is to enhance the utility of the article.

The term is 10 years from registration, subject to payment of renewal fees at the end of the third and sixth years. In the absence of working within three years from registration compulsory licences may be granted; if there has been no working within four years from registration, revocation may occur. There is a novelty examination and the application in general is treated in the same manner as a patent application.

There are no provisions for opposition, nor are there any marking requirements. It is possible to convert an application for a patent into one for a utility model, or vice versa.

Portugal

There are considered as utility models and protected as such, models of machines, utensils, crockery and other articles or parts of articles intended for practical use and which increase or improve the usefulness of such article, owing to a novel shape, arrangement or mechanism.

There is no set term and the registration may be renewed every five years. Compulsory licences may be granted in the absence of working. There is an examination as to novelty and provision for opposition within three months from publication. There are no marking requirements.

South Korea

A utility patent may be granted for any industrial device which is new and useful in regard to its shape or structure or assemblage.

The term is 10 years from the date of registration, but with a maximum of 12 years from the date of application, subject to payment of annual renewal fees. In the absence of working within three years from grant compulsory licences may be granted or the registration revoked. There is a novelty examination and the application in general is treated in the same manner as a patent application. Opposition may be entered within two months from publication. It is possible to convert an application for a patent into one for a utility model, and vice versa. The owner of a registration is required to mark articles with an indication of the registration number.

Spain

There are registrable as utility models, instruments, tools, devices and objects, or parts thereof which bring about, in the function they fulfil, an advantage or a novel effect, or a saving in time, energy or labour, or an improvement in hygienic or psycho-physiological conditions of labour.

The term is 20 years subject to payment of annual renewal fees. In the absence of working within three years from grant the registration should be entered in the Compulsory Licensing Register. There is no novelty examination and the application is in general treated in the same manner as a patent application.

Opposition may be entered within two months from publication. It is possible to convert an application for a patent into one for a utility model, or vice versa.

There are no marking requirements.

Taiwan

A utility model may be granted to anyone who first creates a practical design relating to the shape, structure or construction of any article.

The term is 10 years from application date, subject to payment of annual renewal fees. There are no working requirements. The examination for registrability and novelty is the same as for patents. Opposition may be entered within six months from publication. It is possible to convert a patent application into one for utility model registration. The marking requirements are the same as for patents, that is, articles must be marked with the patent mark and registration number, otherwise there can be no claim for damages in case of infringement.

Tangier

The Tangerine law stipulates that the protection of a utility model cannot have any object other than the utility claimed by virtue of the new form. The definition of a utility model is: " Any plastic shape or any industrial article, whose novel form is designed to increase its utility or to impart an efficiency, facility of application or special use."

The term is 10 years from application; there are no renewal fees. In the absence of working within three years from grant the registration may be revoked. There is no examination for novelty and the application is in general treated in the same manner as a patent application.

There are no provisions for opposition nor are there any marking requirements.

It is possible to convert an application for a patent into one for a utility model, or vice versa.

Miscellaneous

Limited Terms

In respect of patents for special processes or methods for making foodstuffs, medicines or pharmaceutical products the term is limited to 10 years in Kuwait, Libya and the United Arab Republic. For India, see page 314.

Cautionary Notices

In the following countries there are no patent laws:

Afghanistan	Qatar
Andorra	Saudi Arabia
Ascencion	Sudan
Ethiopia	Thailand
Maldive Islands	Tongan Islands
Muscat and Oman	Tristan da Cunha
People's Democratic Republic of Yemen (except Aden)	Trucial States
	Yemen Arab Republic

In some at least of such countries a fairly common practice is to insert so-called " cautionary notices " in the local gazette and/or press. The notice generally comprises a statement to the effect that the advertiser is the owner of the invention, with a short description thereof, and with a reference to the domestic patent. Alternatively, there may be deposited in the Consulate of the national concerned a certified copy of the domestic patent. There does not appear to be any sound basis in law for either practice and in any event reliance would need to be placed on such common law as might exist in the country concerned.

Other countries in which there is no patent law as such at this time are the People's Republic of China and Indonesia. As to the former, it may be said that the earlier legislation of 1950 on patents was rescinded and that there were promulgated in 1963 "Regulations Governing the Encouragement of Inventions." These Regulations are discussed in the section dealing with certificates of authorship.

So far as concerns Indonesia, there have been in existence since 1953 provisions for the filing of patent applications, including the right to claim Convention priority. Unless and until a patent law is promulgated, there can be no official action, beyond recordal, on any applications.

CHAPTER 2

APPLICATION FOR PATENT

The Applicant for Letters Patent

GENERALLY speaking, the applicant for letters patent may be the actual inventor, or his heirs, or assigns, the latter term including bodies corporate. Co-applicants who are not co-inventors may generally be joined to the application. Declaration or proof of inventorship, however, is not requested in many countries.

In the following countries, however, the application must be filed in the name of the inventor alone (or his personal representative if, for example, the inventor has died);

Albania	Cuba	Jamaica
Bermuda	Grenada	St. Vincent
Br. Honduras	Iraq	U.S.A.

In Iraq, if a foreign patent exists in the name of a company or the like, the application may be in the name of the company. But the inventor may be a " communicatee " in some of these territories (see below).

In Malta (in a non-Convention application) and in Jordan, the inventor must be a party to the application, that is to say there may be a co-applicant or co-applicants with the inventor.

In the case of patents of importation and the like, and also for registrations, the applicant should be the patentee in the basic country, or his assignee, with the notable exceptions of Spain (patents of importation) and Cuba and Venezuela (patents of introduction) already referred to.

Communications

United Kingdom law permits a patent application to be made in the name of a person or corporate body within the United Kingdom to whom the invention has been communicated from someone abroad, and the applicant in such a case is entitled to declare himself (or itself) to be the true and first inventor.

This feature of patent law is also found in the following countries:

Australia (but the communicator must be the actual inventor or assign or legal representative)

Bangladesh

Barbados (but only with the authority of the actual inventor, his legal representatives or assigns)

Bermuda
Eire
Jamaica
New Zealand
Pakistan
Sri Lanka
Trinidad & Tobago

It is believed that this form of application is permissible in Jordan and in the following parts of the British Commonwealth having independent patent systems, namely:

Antigua
Br. Honduras
Br. Virgin Islands
Dominica
Fiji
Grenada
Guyana
Malta
Montserrat
St. Christopher
St. Lucia
St. Vincent
Seychelles

Documents Required

For the filing of applications for patents, or for confirmation or registration of existing patents, there are certain documents which will be required, and for convenience these are discussed under three separate headings:

(1) Applications for patents generally.

(2) Applications for patents of importation, revalidation, confirmation and introduction.

(3) Registrations.

Group 1—General

The basic documents required for Group 1 are:

(a) Specification (and drawings).

(b) Application form.

(c) Authority to enable local patent agent to act on behalf of applicant.

(d) Assignment from inventor when application is to be made in the name of someone other than the inventor.

(e) Certified copy of basic application when claiming priority under the International Convention.

(f) Attested translation of (e).

(g) Assignment of priority rights when application is to be made in the name of someone other than the basic applicant.
(h) Additional requirements in specific countries.

(a) Specification and drawings

Except in English-speaking countries, it is sufficient to send one copy of the specification to the local agent, because he will prepare the appropriate number of copies in the appropriate language required by the local Patent Office.

For English-speaking countries it is customary to send to the local agent the number of copies required by the local Patent Office together with at least one copy for his file.

For all countries it is customary to send the agent the drawings (when the nature of the invention requires drawings) in the form required by the local Patent Office, together with copies for his file.

The following table sets out the drawing requirements.

PATENT DRAWINGS

Sizes in Centimetres unless otherwise Indicated

Country	*Card*[1]	*Paper*[2]	*Cloth*[3]	*Print*	*Size*	*Remarks*
African & Malagasy Union		2			27–31 × 21 or 42	Marginal line all round at least 2 cm. from edges
Albania			3		34 × 29	May be on tracing or transparent paper
Algeria	1	1			27–31 × 21 or 42	Clear margin of 2 cm. all round
Antigua		2			13″ × 8″	
Argentina	1	1	1		29·7 × 21	Clear margin of 1 cm. all round
Australia		2			13″ × 8″	International Paper Size A4 acceptable ½″ margin all round
Austria		2	1		33 × 21	International Paper Size A4 acceptable. Marginal line drawn all round 2 cm. from edges
Bahamas		2			13″ × 8″	Clear ½″ margin all round

Country	*Card*[1]	*Paper*[2]	*Cloth*[3]	*Print*	*Size*	*Remarks*
Bangladesh		1	1		13″ × 8–8¼″ or 13″ × 16–16½″	Clear margin of at least ½″ all round. International Paper Size A4 acceptable
Barbados		2			13″ × 8″	Clear ½″ margin all round
Belgium		2			33 × 21	Clear margin 3 cm. all round
Bermuda		3			13″ × 8″	Clear ½″ margin all round
Bolivia	2				33 × 22	Marginal line all round 1·5 cm. from edges
Brazil		3			29·7 × 21	Drawing area must not exceed 25·7 × 17. Upper margin 2·5; lower margin 1·5; left margin 2·5; right margin 1·5 cm.
Br. Honduras		2			13″ × 8″	Clear ½″ margin all round
Br. Virgin Islands		2			13″ × 8″	Clear ½″ margin all round
Bulgaria	2		1		33 × 21 or 33 × 42	Clear margin of 2 cm. all round
Burundi		1	3			Actual size not prescribed
Cambodia			2		29–34 × 21	Marginal line all round 2 cm. from edges
Canada	1	1			13″ × 8″	Clear margin of at least 1″ on all sides. 1 copy may be on tracing cloth in lieu of paper.
Chile			2		33 × 22	Clear margin of 1·5 cm. all round
Colombia		2			33 × 22	Marginal line all round 2 cm. from edges

Country	*Card*[1]	*Paper*[2]	*Cloth*[3]	*Print*	*Size*	*Remarks*
Costa Rica			2			Actual size not prescribed
Cuba		2	1		33–38 × 20–25	
Czecho-slovakia	1	3			29·7 × 21	The figures should be numbered consecutively Obr. 1, Obr. 2, etc.
Denmark		3			29·7 × 21	Clear margin of at least 2·5 cm. on left-hand side
Dominica			2			Actual size not prescribed
Dominican Republic			2			Actual size not prescribed
Ecuador			2			Actual size not prescribed
Fiji		2			13″ × 8″	
Finland		3			29·7 × 21	Clear margin of at least 2·5 cm. on left-hand side
France		4			29–34 × 21 or exceptionally × 42	Drawing area must not exceed 25·7 × 17 or 25·7 × 35·5 cm. At least one of the copies must be on sheets of size 29·7 × 21 cm.
E. Germany	2		1		29·7 × 21	Margin 2·5 cm. on left-hand side. Drawing area must not exceed 28 × 18 cm.
W. Germany		2	1		29–34 × 21	Drawing area must not exceed 25·7 × 17 cm.
Greece	1		1		30 × 20 or 30 × 40	Clear margin of 2 cm. on all sides
Grenada		2			13″ × 8″	

Country	*Card*[1]	*Paper*	*Cloth*[3]	*Print*	*Size*	*Remarks*
Guatemala			2			Actual size not prescribed
Guinea			2		29–34 × 21	Marginal line all round 2 cm. from edges
Guyana	2				13″ × 8″	
Haiti		2	1			Actual size not prescribed
Honduras Republic			3			Actual size not prescribed
Hungary	1	2			33 × 21 or 33 × 42	Clear margin 2 cm. all round. Clear space of 3 cm. at top of sheet within the margin
Iceland	1		1		33 × 21 or 33 × 42	
India		1	1		33 × 20·5 or 41	Clear margin of at least 1·5 cm. all round
Indonesia	1		1		29–34 × 20–22 or 40–44	
Iran	1	1	1		34 × 22	Clear margin of 3 cm. on left hand side
Iraq		6			33 × 20·5	
Ireland		1	1		13″ × 8″–8¼″ or 13″ × 16–16½″; or 33 × 21 or 42	A clear margin of ½″ or 2 cm. must be left at each side of the sheet
Israel		2			29–34 × 21 or 42	Drawing area must not exceed 25·7 × 17 or 25·7 × 34 cm.
Italy		2			33 × 21	Clear margin 2 cm. all round. The drawings may in fact be on Bristol board, drawing paper, tracing cloth or tracing paper.
Jamaica		2			13″ × 8″	

Country	*Card*[1]	*Paper*[2]	*Cloth*[3]	*Print*	*Size*	*Remarks*
Japan			1		25·7 × 18·2 or 25·7 × 36·4	Clear margin of 2 cm. all round
Jordan		2			33 × 21–22 or 33 × 42–45	Clear margin of 1·5 cm. all round
Kuwait	2				33 × 20–21 or 33 × 40–42	Clear margin of 1·5 cm. all round
Laos			2		29–34 × 21	Marginal line all round 2 cm. from edges
Lebanon		2			33 × 20·5	
Liberia		2	2			Actual size not prescribed
Libya	2		1		33 × 20–22 or 33 × 40–42	References and leading lines in pencil. Clear margin 1·5 cm. all round
Luxembourg		3	1		33 × 21 or 29·7 × 21	Clear margin of at least 2·5 cm. on all sides
Malawi		2			13″ × 8″ or 16″	1½″ clear binding margin on left-hand side and ½″ clear margin on other sides. Larger size to be used only when required by size of a figure
Mali			2		29–34 × 21	Marginal line all round 2 cm. from edges
Malta		1	1		13″ × 8″	
Mauritius		2			13″ × 8–8¼″ or 13″ × 16–16½″	Clear ½″ margin to be left at edges of sheet. Larger size to be used only when required by size of any figure
Mexico	1	3			33 × 21·5	Marginal line 1·5 cm. from left hand edge

Country	*Card*[1]	*Paper*[2]	*Cloth*[3]	*Print*	*Size*	*Remarks*
Monaco	2		1		27 or 31 × 21 27 or 31 × 42	Marginal line all round 2 cm. from edges
Montserrat		2			13″ × 8″	
Morocco	1		1		33 × 21 or 33 × 42	Marginal line all round 2 cm. from edges
Nepal		1	1		13″ × 8″–8¼″ or 13″ × 16″–16½″	Clear margin of at least ½″ all round
Netherlands		2	1		29–34 × 21	Letter "1" should not be used as reference. Drawing area not to exceed 24 × 17 cm.
New Zealand		2			13″–13½″ × 8″–8½″	Clear ½″ margin all round. International Paper Size A4 acceptable, with left side margin at least ¾″ and other three sides at least ½″
Nicaragua			2			Actual size not prescribed
Nigeria		2			13″ × 8″	Left-hand margin not less than 1½″
Norway		3			29·7 × 21	Clear 2 cm. margin all round
Pakistan		1	1		13″ × 8–8¼″ or 13″ × 16–16½″	Clear margin of at least ½″ all round. International Paper Size A4 acceptable
Panama			2			Actual size not prescribed
Paraguay	1		1		33 × 22	Marginal line all round 1·5 cm. from edges
Peru		3				Quality and size optional

Country	*Card*[1]	*Paper*[2]	*Cloth*[3]	*Print*	*Size*	*Remarks*
Philippines	1				13″ × 8″	Single Marginal line 1″ from longer edges and 1½″ from shorter edges; space of not less than 1¼″ downwardly from upper marginal line to be left blank
Poland	1		1		29·7 × 21 or 29·7 × 42	
Portugal	1		1		33 × 21 or 33 × 42	Marginal line all round 2 cm. from edges
Rhodesia		2			13″ × 8″ or 16″	1½″ clear binding margin on left-hand side and ½″ clear margin on other sides. Larger size to be used only when required by size of a figure. International Paper Size A4 acceptable
Rwanda		1	3			Actual size not prescribed
Roumania	2	1	2		27 × 21 or 54 × 21	Marginal line all round 2 cm. from edges
St. Christopher		2			13″ × 8″	
St. Lucia		2			13″ × 8″	
St. Vincent		2			13″ × 8″	
Salvador			2			Actual size not prescribed
Seychelles		2			13″ × 8″	
Somali Republic	1	2			34 × 22	
South Africa		2			29·7 × 21	Clear margin of 1·3 cm. at edges of sheet

Country	*Card*[1]	*Paper*[2]	*Cloth*[3]	*Print*	*Size*	*Remarks*
South Korea		1	1		26 × 19	2 cm. margin both sides and bottom; 3·5 cm. margin at top
South West Africa		1			13″ × 8″	
Spain	1	1	1		31 × 21 or 42 × 63	Marginal line all round 2 cm. from edges
Sri Lanka		2			13″ × 8″ or 13″ × 16″	Clear margin of 1″ all round. All lines in absolutely black India ink
Sweden		3			29·7 × 21	Clear margin of 2 cm. all round
Switzerland	1		1		29–34 × 21 or 42	Drawing area not to exceed 25·7 × 17 or 25·7 × 38
Syria		2				Actual size not prescribed
Taiwan		4				Actual size not prescribed
Tangier	1	1	1		29–34 × 20–22 or 40–44	Marginal line all round 2 cm. from edges
Trinidad & Tobago		2			13″ × 8″	
Tunisia		2			33 × 21	Clear margin of 2 cm. all round
Turkey		2	1		34 × 20–21 or 34 × 42	Clear margin of 2 cm. all round
U.S.S.R.	4				29·7 × 21 or 42	Margin of 3 cm. on all sides. Reference characters in numerals, may be on tracing-paper or cloth

Country	*Card*[1]	*Paper*[2]	*Cloth*[3]	*Print*	*Size*	*Remarks*
U.A.R.	2	2	1		33 × 20 or 33 × 40–42	Only the paper copies should contain references and leading lines. Marginal line 1·5 cm. from edges
U.K.		2			13″ × 8–$8\frac{1}{4}$″ or 13″ × 16–$16\frac{1}{2}$″	Clear $\frac{1}{2}$″ margin to be left at edges of sheet. Larger size to be used only when required by size of any figure. International Paper Size A4 acceptable
U.S.A.	1				$8\frac{1}{2}$″ × 14″	Top margin of 2″ and bottom and side margins of $\frac{1}{4}$″, from the edges; but no marginal lines. Drawings must be in India ink
Uruguay	1	3	1			Actual size not prescribed
Venezuela			2			Actual size not prescribed
Vietnam		1	2		33 × 21 or 33 × 42	Marginal line all round 2 cm. from edges
Yugoslavia		2			29·7 × 21 or 29·7 × 42	Clear margin of 2 cm. all round
Zaïre		1	3			Actual size not prescribed
Zambia		2			13″ × 8″ or 16″	$1\frac{1}{2}$″ clear binding margin on left-hand side and $\frac{1}{2}$″ clear margin on other sides. Larger size to be used only when required by size of a figure

[1] Card = Bristol Board.
[2] Paper = Good/White unglazed drawing paper, *e.g.*, Kent.
[3] Cloth = Tracing cloth or tracing linen.

(b) Application form

Generally speaking, it is only in English-speaking countries that the applicant requires to sign a form of application. In other countries the application is prepared and signed by the local agent, except in Jordan.

Of the English-speaking countries it is only in Australia and Canada that an application as such is not required to be signed by the applicant.

The following is a list of those countries where the applicant must personally sign the application form as such:

Antigua[1]
Bahamas
Bahrain
Bangladesh
Barbados[1]
Bermuda[1]
British Honduras[1,3]
Br. Virgin Islands[1]
Dominica[1]
Fiji[3]
Grenada[1]
Guyana
India
Ireland
Israel
Jamaica[1,3]
Jordan[2]
Liberia
Malawi
Malta[1] (includes assignments, if applicable and declaration of inventorship and novelty)
Mauritius[1,3]
Montserrat[1]
Nepal
New Zealand
Nigeria
Pakistan
Philippines[6]
Rhodesia[7]
St. Christopher[1]
St. Lucia[1]
St. Vincent[1]
Seychelles[1]
South Africa
South Korea[5]
South West Africa
Sri Lanka[1]
Taiwan[5]
Trinidad & Tobago[1]
U.K.
U.S.A.[4]
Zambia

[1] In these territories the application must be sworn and signed before a notary public (with legalisation by a British Consul, if executed outside the British Commonwealth).

[2] The application must be sworn and signed before a Notary Public, with legalisation by a Jordanian Consul. If no Jordanian Consul is available legalisation may be effected by a British Consul.

[3] In British Honduras, Fiji, Jamaica and Mauritius the application is in the form of a petition which is accompanied by a separate declaration. Except in Fiji, the declaration must be sworn and signed before a notary public, with subsequent legalisation by a British Consul.

[4] The application may take the form of a combined declaration and power, or a combined oath and power, the requirement for a petition having been revoked. If the declaration form is used, the declarant must set forth in the body of the declaration that all statements made of his own knowledge are true and that all statements made on information and belief are believed to be true. Further, the declarant should declare that the statements are made with the knowledge that wilful false statements and the like so made are punishable by fine or imprisonment, or both, under Section 1001 of Title 18 of the United States Code and that such wilful false statements may jeopardise the validity of the application or any patent issuing thereon. If the oath form is used it may be made before any person within the United States authorised by law to administer oaths, or when made in a foreign country before any diplomatic or consular officer of the United States, or other person in the foreign country having an official seal and authorised to administer oaths, whose authority must thereafter be proved by a certificate of a diplomatic or consular officer of the United States. When the oath is taken outside the United States the application papers, except the drawings, must be attached together and a ribbon passed one or more times through all the sheets of the application, except the drawings,

and the ends of the ribbon brought together under the seal before the latter is affixed and impressed; alternatively each sheet must be impressed with the official seal of the officer before whom the oath is taken.

5 In South Korea and Taiwan the application takes the form of an oath.

6 In the Philippines the application comprises a petition (which may incorporate a power of attorney), a specification in English, Spanish or the Philippines national language, and an oath which requires consular legalisation. The petition, power and oath may be combined in a single document. All parts of the application, except the drawings should be fastened together and a ribbon passed one or more times through all the sheets and the ends of the ribbon brought together under the notarial or other official seal, before the latter is affixed and impressed by the notary or other officer before whom the oath is taken.

7 The Application form may be signed by an Agent, but proof of his authority may be called for.

(c) Authority

The applicant must authorise a local patent agent to act and this authority may take the form of a power of attorney or an authorisation, either of which documents may require notarial attestation and/or consular legalisation.

It can be taken that in foreign-language countries, generally, the document required is a power of attorney. Of these countries, consular legalisation is necessary in the following:

Albania	Haiti	Peru
Bolivia	Honduras	Rwanda
Burundi	Iran	Salvador
Chile	Iraq	Turkey
Colombia	Jordan	United Arab Republic
Costa Rica	Kuwait	U.S.S.R.
Cuba	Liberia	Venezuela
Dominican Republic	Libya	Vietnam
Ecuador	Mexico	Zaïre
Greece	Nicaragua	
Guatemala	Panama	
	Paraguay	

Powers are *not* required in Portugal: nor in Venezuela after the first application. In Canada it is not necessary to file a power unless the Commissioner specifically calls for one. In Colombia, if the applicant is a corporate body the power must contain a notarial certificate as to its legal existence and of the corporate powers of the signatories on its behalf.

Legalisation may be effected by direct attendance on the Consul, or alternatively by attendance on a notary whose seal and signature must thereafter be legalised by the Consul.

It is perhaps worth noting that a power of attorney is a more effective legal document than the authorisation and generally contains wider authority. It is, therefore, safe to assume that it can never be wrong to send to a local agent a power of attorney rather than the simpler form of authorisation.

(d) Assignment

When the rights in an invention are passed from the inventor to a third party, that party ought to have the inventor execute a formal deed of assignment covering all territories in respect of which the rights are passing. In some territories, when an application is being filed by an assignee, the local Patent Office requires positive proof of the assignee's rights and it is therefore essential that he should be able to lodge a deed of assignment. The general custom therefore is to have, in addition to any general assignment, specific assignments for individual countries. In some countries it is not essential to file an assignment with the application, but it may be called for by the Patent Office.

In the following countries it is necessary to file an assignment in the local Patent Office:

Argentina	Guatemala	Pakistan
Bangladesh	Haiti	Panama
Barbados	Honduras	Paraguay
Belgium	Hungary	Peru
Bolivia	Iceland	Philippines
Brazil	India	Rhodesia
Bulgaria	Iraq	Roumania
Canada + affidavit of execution	Jamaica + affidavit by assignee	St. Lucia
Chile	Kuwait	South Africa
Colombia	Liberia	South Korea
Costa Rica	Libya	S.W. Africa
Cuba	Malawi	Sri Lanka
Denmark	Malta	Sweden
Dominican Republic	Mauritius	Taiwan
Ecuador	Mexico	Turkey
Finland	Nepal	Uruguay
E. Germany	Norway	U.S.S.R.
		Venezuela
		Zambia

(For the Central and South American States in this list, the assignment is generally combined in a single document with the power of attorney.)

Consular legalisation is required for all these countries except in:

Argentina	India	South Africa
Bangladesh	Malawi	South Korea
Barbados	Nepal	S.W. Africa
Brazil	Pakistan	Sri Lanka
Bulgaria	Rhodesia	Zambia
Canada	St. Lucia	

where only a simple signature is required, and in

Denmark	Liberia	Norway
E. Germany	Libya	Roumania
Iceland	Malta	Taiwan
Jamaica	Mauritius	

where notarial attestation only is called for. In Sweden execution before two witnesses is sufficient. In Finland the deed should be signed and confirmed according to the law of the assignor's home country.

In Canada, to secure registration of an assignment, it must be accompanied by the affidavit of a subscribing witness or established by other proof to the satisfaction of the commissioner that such assignment has been signed and executed by the assignor. The form of assignment according to the Canadian rules provides for execution in the presence of one witness. If that witness in fact is, for example, a notary public or commissioner for oaths, then an affidavit is not required. The form of affidavit is set out in the rules and must be signed before a notary public or other official having authority to take affidavits in the place where the affidavit is sworn. Rule 2 (b) sets out that " affidavit " includes a statutory declaration so that the affidavit could be sworn before a commissioner for oaths.

If the assignment is executed in duplicate, the certificate of registration eventually issued will have the duplicate attached. If the assignment, in fact, is executed in duplicate, the affidavit should also be executed in duplicate.

For Jamaica there must also be filed a notarially attested affidavit by the assignee. The Maltese assignment generally forms part of the application.

In the Philippines the assignment must be in duplicate and the consular certificate must be ribboned to the assignment.

It is customary to have executed deeds of assignment, although they are normally not filed, in the following countries:

Australia	W. Germany [2]	Israel
Austria [1,3]	Ireland	Italy

Japan [1]	New Zealand	Tunis
Lebanon	Spain	United Kingdom
Luxembourg	Switzerland	Yugoslavia [1, 3]
Morocco	Syria	
Netherlands	Tangier	

1 In these countries the Patent Office may call for the production of the deed of assignment.
2 Consular legalisation required; but if executed in Austria, Finland, France, Japan, Liechtenstein, Malawi, Malta, Netherlands, Portugal, United Kingdom or Yugoslavia, notarial attestation followed by endorsement by the Foreign Office is sufficient.
3 Consular legalisation required.

(e & f) Certified copy of basic application and attested translation

Article 4D (3) of the International Convention provides that any country of the Union may require to be filed, without fee, in support of a Convention application a certified copy of the basic application, and further may require an attested translation of the certified copy. The period allowed by the Convention for filing such documents is a minimum of three months from the date of application. These documents are generally referred to as the priority documents. Attested translations are normally prepared by the local agent.

In the following countries of the Union, a certified copy is not required:

Belgium	Luxembourg	Tunisia

In West Germany, for applications filed after October 1, 1968, an uncertified copy of the basic foreign application is sufficient. For the filing of this document a period of two months is set by the Patent Office after receipt of the claim to priority.

In the following countries the certified copy need only be filed if called for by the examiner:

Austria	Finland	Portugal
Canada	E. Germany	Sweden
Denmark	Norway	Yugoslavia

Certified copies are required to be filed in all other countries, and the periods allowed for filing them, reckoned from the date of filing, are as shown:

African & Malagasy Union—6 months
Algeria—3 months
Argentina—90 days
Australia—3 months (extensible on payment of fees—up to acceptance)
Bahamas—3 months

Brazil—180 days
Bulgaria—2 months (extension allowable)
Cuba—6 months
Czechoslovakia—3 months
Dominican Republic—no delay allowed—must be filed with application
France—4 months
Greece—delay allowed subject to Director's discretion
Haiti—with application
Hungary—3 months
Iceland—no set term
Indonesia—no set term
Iran—before issue
Ireland 6 months (extensible by further 12 months on payment of fees)
Israel—one year
Italy—6 months
Japan—3 months
Laos—6 months
Lebanon—3 months
Libya—3 months
Malawi—6 months
Malta—3 months
Mexico—90 days
Monaco—6 months
Morocco — a reasonable term will be allowed
Netherlands—5 months
New Zealand—3 months
Nigeria—3 months
Philippines—6 months
Poland—3 months
Rhodesia—6 months
Roumania—3 months
South Africa—6 months
Spain—3 months
Sri Lanka—delay allowed subject to Registrar's discretion—2 certified copies must be filed.
Switzerland—(a) Application not subject to novelty examination—before grant
Switzerland—(b) Application subject to novelty examination—6 months from decision to publish
Syria—3 months
Tangier—3 months
Trinidad & Tobago — 3 months
Turkey—3 months
United Arab Republic — 3 months
United Kingdom—3 months
Uruguay—90 days
U.S.S.R.—3 months
U.S.A.—before issue but commissioner may require earlier filing
Vietnam—6 months
*Yugoslavia—3 months
Zambia—6 months

* It is possible to file a patent application with either a positive request for priority or a request for reservation of the priority right. In either case, a declaration must be made at the time of filing the application. If recognition of the priority right is required, then priority documents must be lodged; on the other hand, if mere reservation is requested, it is not necessary to file priority documents. If it were eventually necessary to obtain recognition of the priority right previously reserved, a period of three months would be given for filing the appropriate priority documents.

When priority documents are filed, attested translations are required in the following if the priority document is not in the language of the country where the application is being filed, or in one of the languages indicated:

Australia
Austria—English, French or Italian
Bahamas
Brazil
Canada
Cuba
Denmark—English, French, German, or a Scandinavian language
Finland—English, French, German, or a Scandinavian language
Greece
Indonesia—English
Ireland
Israel — English, Arabic, French or German. Where an attested translation is to be filed this translation is general in English.
Italy—French
Japan—English, French, German (but translation only of certificate)
Malawi—English
Malta—English
Mexico
Monaco
Netherlands
New Zealand
Nigeria—English
Norway—English, French, German or a Scandinavian language
Philippines—English
Poland—English, French, German, Russian
Rhodesia—English
Roumania — English, French, German
South Africa — Dutch, English
Sri Lanka—English
Sweden—English, French, German or a Scandinavian language
Switzerland — English, French, German, Italian
Tangier—Spanish, French
Turkey
United Arab Republic
United Kingdom
U.S.S.R.
Vietnam—English, French
Yugoslavia
Zambia—English

In the following countries, the Patent Office may call for an attested translation:

Argentina
Czechoslovakia
E. Germany
W. Germany
Hungary
Portugal
Uruguay
U.S.A.

(g) Assignment of priority rights

Article 4 A (1) of the Convention permits an assignee to claim priority (which belongs to the basic applicant) and in the following countries, when a Convention application is filed in the name of such an assignee, an assignment of priority rights must be filed within the periods indicated, reckoned from the date of filing:

African & Malagasy Union —6 months
Algeria—3 months
Argentina—90 days
Belgium—4 months; only 2 months if applicant resides in Europe
Brazil—60 days
[1] Bulgaria—3 months
[2] Cuba—6 months
[3] Czechoslovakia—3 months
[3] Denmark—term fixed by Patent Office
[2] Dominican Republic—with application
[5] Finland—term fixed by Patent Office
France—4 months
[3] E. Germany—term fixed by Patent Office
[1] Greece—2 months
[2] Haiti—with application
[1] Hungary—3 months
[1] Iceland—term fixed by Patent Office
Indonesia—no set term
[1] Iran—before issue
[1] Italy—6 months
Japan — term fixed by Patent Office
[1] Laos—6 months
[1] Lebanon—with application
[1] Libya—3 months
Luxembourg—4 months
Malawi — term fixed by Patent Office
Malta—3 months
[1] Mexico—90 days
Monaco—6 months
Morocco—30 days
Netherlands—5 months
[3] Norway—term fixed by Patent Office
[3] Poland—3 months
Rhodesia—6 months
[3] Roumania—3 months
South Africa—term fixed by Patent Office
[4] Sweden—term fixed by Patent Office
[1] Syria—with application
[1] Tangier—3 months
[1] Turkey—3 months
[1] United Arab Republic—3 months
[2] Uruguay—90 days
[1] U.S.S.R.—3 months
[3] Vietnam—6 months
Zambia — term fixed by Patent Office

[1] Consular legalisation required.
[2] May be combined with power: consular legalisation required.
[3] Notarial attestation required.
[4] Before notary or two witnesses.
[5] Sign and confirm according to law of assignor's home country.

In Canada and U.S.A. priority rights are regarded as belonging to the inventor(s). If, therefore, a Convention application is filed in Canada in the name of an assignee of the inventor(s), the application should be accompanied by an assignment covering also priority rights, but such assignment may be filed within 12 months of the Canadian filing date. In the U.S.A. the application must, of course, be filed in the name of the inventor(s), but here again in appropriate cases an assignment covering also priority rights should be filed. Since the claim to priority for a U.S. application is not made until the priority document is filed, the assignment may be filed at any time during pendency.

In the following countries, it is customary to have an assignment of priority rights signed but not filed in the local patent office unless it is called for:

Austria	Israel	Switzerland
W. Germany	Spain	Yugoslavia

The Austrian and Yugoslavian assignments require consular legalisation. The Swiss assignments require notarial attestation. For W. Germany consular legalisation is required unless the document is executed in Austria, Finland, France, Japan, Liechtenstein, Malawi, Malta, Netherlands, Portugal, United Kingdom or Yugoslavia, when notarial attestation followed by endorsement by the Foreign Office is sufficient.

(h) Additional requirements

1. *Proof of status*

(*a*) *Kuwait, Libya and United Arab Republic.* If the applicant is a corporate body, there should be lodged a legalised official copy of

(i) an extract from the Home Commercial Register; or
(ii) an extract from the Articles of Association; or
(iii) the certificate of incorporation.

(*b*) *South Korea and Taiwan.* Whether the applicant is an individual or a body corporate, there must be lodged in South Korea a certificate of nationality which is a notarial declaration.

A similar document, but legalised, is required for Taiwan. An applicant whose country has no diplomatic relations with the Republic of China (Taiwan), or where there is no diplomatic representative to execute the legalislation, may have the nationality certificate attested by his Foreign Ministry and a British Consul in his country. Legalisation of a certificate thus attested may then be effected through the British Consul in Tapei and the Foreign Affairs Department of the Taiwan Provincial Government.

2. *Corresponding application*

Peru. Where a foreign application has been filed, the Peruvian application must be filed within two years after the first filing date and must be accompanied by a legalised certified copy of the basic specification. A period of 30 days is allowed for filing this document.

Taiwan. Where a foreign application has been filed, the Taiwan application must be filed within one year after the first filing date and must be accompanied by a certified copy of the basic specification.

3. *Abstracts*

An abstract summarising the invention must be furnished in:

Algeria	France	Taiwan
Belgium	Hungary	United Arab Republic
Brazil	Iraq	U.S.A.
Canada	Kuwait	
Colombia	Libya	

These abstracts are not regarded as having any legal significance and certainly in Belgium, Canada, France and the U.S.A. they cannot be taken into account by the court in determining the actual scope of the patent.

For Algeria, Belgium, Iraq, Kuwait, Libya, Taiwan and the United Arab Republic, the abstract should comprise in about 100 words a description of the essential features of the invention and should be illustrated by a suitable figure of the drawings (if any).

In Brazil, with effect from March 15, 1971, patent applications will be accepted only if accompanied by a separate abstract of the disclosure of the invention. The abstract must:

(*a*) be a synthesis of what is disclosed in the specification, claims and drawings;

(*b*) specify the technical field covered by the invention;

(*c*) permit a clear understanding of the technical problem involved giving a gist of the solution of such problem and setting out the principal uses of the invention;

(*d*) indicate, where applicable, the chemical formula which best characterises the invention;

(*e*) be as concise as possible, preferably within the limits of 50 to 200 words, and (*f*) not contain any statement concerning the alleged merits or value of the invention.

In Canada, with effect from July 1, 1969, the Patent Rules have been amended to provide for the filing of an abstract consisting of a brief technical statement of the disclosure indicative of the utility of the invention and the manner in which the invention is distinguishable from other inventions. The abstract must be in such form and contain such information as the Commissioner may require. If the Commissioner considers that it is not in the prescribed form he may require the applicant to amend the abstract, under penalty of forfeiture of the application. The Commissioner has himself the right to alter any abstract that is not acceptable to him.

The Canadian Patent Office Record will hereafter publish abstracts of patents instead of the single drawing and two claims which have heretofore been published, but it is expected that the transition in the Record will take approximately six months to complete. If the abstract has been included in the specification, it will also appear in the issued printed patent.

The Commissioner has stated that the primary object of the change is to provide the public and, in particular, Canadian industry, with a short clear statement of the contents of the disclosure of each patent published so that the nature of the invention can be quickly assessed, not only by patent agents and attorneys but by laymen who are interested in the particular art involved.

The amended Rules make it clear that an abstract shall not form the basis for any legal interpretation of the invention and shall not be used to interpret the scope of the invention claimed.

As of July 1, 1969, the procedure for the filing of abstracts will be as follows:

(1) For *new applications* the abstract must be filed with the other application papers and the application fee. It may be furnished either in duplicate on a separate sheet, or may be incorporated at the beginning of the specification provided a duplicate abstract is also lodged. Failure to file an abstract at the proper time will result in loss of the filing date.

(2) For *applications pending* on July 1, 1969, but which have not been passed to allowance, the applicant must file an abstract in duplicate when paying the final fee. Failure to do so within a set period will result in cancellation of the notice of allowance, in which case the application will be deemed to have been abandoned. Thereafter it can be reinstated within one year from

the end of the set period but only on payment of the prescribed fee and with proof, in affidavit form, that the failure to supply the abstract was not reasonably avoidable.

(3) For *applications which have been allowed* but have not gone to issue, at least one claim of the patent will be published.

The Commissioner has issued the following guidelines to assist in the drafting of abstracts:

(1) The abstract should consist of a technical statement of the contents of the disclosure. It should not be a description of the disclosure, but a condensation of the technical content.

(2) It should be written to include the advancement in the art and the utility of the invention. It should include the organisation and operation of a machine or apparatus invention; the physical characteristics of a product invention; the identity and use of a chemical compound invention; the ingredients and use of a mixture invention; the various steps of a process invention.

(3) It should consist of a single paragraph of 50–250 words under a separate heading, "Abstract of the Disclosure." It should be clear and concise and should not be in single sentence, patent claim form or language.

(4) It should be written for the purpose of providing a searcher in a particular art, such as a scientist or engineer, with a means of quickly determining the nature of the technical disclosure or whether a study of the full specification would be warranted.

(5) It should not be confined to the invention of the application but should include all the subject-matter disclosed.

(6) It will not be used to limit the scope of the claims in any way.

In Colombia the abstract must comprise at least one claim characterising the invention.

In France the Rules require that each application be accompanied by an abstract of the technical content of the invention, but it is emphasised that the abstract is required only for documentary purposes, that it does not form part of the patent and that it cannot be taken into account for defining the rights attached to the patent.

The abstract should comprise the title of the invention, the name of the applicant, where appropriate the priority claimed, and three paragraphs having as their respective object:

(*a*) to place, as precisely as possible, the invention in the technical field to which it relates;

(*b*) to describe the principal technical characteristic of the invention in its preferred form with, if applicable, references to the drawings; and

(*c*) to list the principal applications of the invention disclosed in the specification.

When the application includes drawings there should be filed with the abstract a drawing, in duplicate, containing the most representative figure illustrating the invention.

The complete abstract must not exceed 18 lines if there is a drawing, or 50 lines if there is no drawing, each line containing not more than 50 letters or signs.

In Hungary there is required an abstract comprising 50–150 words, which may take the form required under U.S. practice. The abstract serves for technical information concerning the essence of the invention. In the case of applications directed to the preparation of pharmaceutically active new compounds, the general formula of the desired end-products, the definition of the substituents and the utility are to be disclosed.

In U.S.A. a brief abstract of the technical disclosure in the specification must be set forth immediately following the title and preceding the disclosure in a separate paragraph under the heading " Abstract of the Disclosure." The purpose of the abstract is to enable the Patent Office and the public generally to determine quickly from a cursory inspection the nature and gist of the technical disclosure. The following " Guidelines for the Preparation of Patent Abstracts " have been issued by the U.S. Commissioner of Patents and appear in MPEP—608.01(b):

" *Background.* The Rules of Practice in Patent Cases require that each application for patent include an Abstract of the Disclosure, Rule 72 (b).

The content of a patent abstract should be such as to enable the reader thereof, regardless of his degree of familiarity with patent documents, to ascertain quickly the character of the subject-matter covered by the technical disclosure and should include that which is new in the art to which the invention pertains.

The abstract is not intended nor designed for use in interpreting the scope or meaning of the claims, Rule 72 (b).

Content. A patent abstract is a concise statement of the technical disclosure of the patent and should include that which is *new* in the art to which the invention pertains.

If the patent is of a basic nature, the entire technical disclosure may be new in the art, and the abstract should be directed to the entire disclosure.

If the patent is in the nature of an improvement in an old apparatus, process, product, or composition, the abstract should include the technical disclosure of the improvement.

In certain patents, particularly those for compounds and compositions, wherein the process for making and/or the use thereof are not obvious, the abstract should set forth a process for making and/or a use thereof.

If the new technical disclosure involves modifications or alternatives, the abstract should mention by way of example the preferred modification or alternative.

The abstract should not refer to purported merits or speculative applications of the invention and should not compare the invention with the prior art.

Where applicable, the abstract should include the following: (1) if a machine or apparatus, its organisation and operation; (2) if an article, its method of making; (3) if a chemical compound, its identity and use; (4) if a mixture, its ingredients; (5) if a process, the steps. Extensive mechanical and design details of apparatus should not be given.

With regard particularly to chemical patents, for compounds or compositions, the general nature of the compound or composition should be given as well as the use thereof, *e.g.* 'The compounds are of the class of alkyl benzene sulfonyl ureas, useful as oral anti-diabetics.' Exemplification of a species could be illustrative of members of the class. For processes, the type reaction, reagents and process conditions should be stated, generally illustrated by a single example unless variations are necessary.

Language and format. The abstract should be in narrative form and generally limited to a single paragraph within the range of 50 to 250 words. The form and legal phraseology often used in patent claims, such as 'means' and 'said,' should be avoided. The abstract should sufficiently describe the disclosure to assist readers in deciding whether there is a need for consulting the full patent text for details.

The language should be clear and concise and should not repeat information given in the title. It should avoid using phrases which can be implied, such as, 'This disclosure concerns,' 'The disclosure defined by this invention,' 'This disclosure describes,' etc.

Responsibility. Preparation of the abstract is the responsibility of the applicant. Background knowledge of the art and an appreciation of the applicant's contribution to the art are most important in the preparation of the abstract. The review of the abstract, for compliance with these guidelines, with any necessary editing and revision on allowance of the application is the responsibility of the Examiner.

Sample abstracts. A heart valve with an annular valve body defining an orifice and having a plurality of struts forming a pair of cages on opposite sides of the orifice. A spherical closure member is captively held within the cages and is moved by blood flow between open and closed positions in check valve fashion. A slight leak or backflow is provided in the closed position by making the orifice slightly larger than the closure member. Blood flow is maximised in the open position of the valve by providing an inwardly convex contour on the orifice-defining surfaces of the body. An annular rib is formed in a channel around the periphery of the valve body to anchor a suture ring used to secure the valve within a heart.

A method for sealing, by application of heat, overlapping closure panels of a folding box made from paperboard having an extremely thin coating of moisture-proofing thermoplastic material on opposite surfaces. Heated air is directed at the surfaces to be bonded, the temperature of the air at the point of impact on the surfaces being above the char point of the board. The duration of application of heat is made so brief, by a corresponding high rate of advance of the boxes through the air stream, that the coating on the reverse side of the panels remains substantially non-tacky. The bond is formed immediately after heating within a period of time for any one surface point less than the total time of exposure to heated air of that point. Under such conditions the heat applied to soften the thermoplastic coating is dissipated after completion of the bond by absorption into the board acting as a heat sink without the need for cooling devices.

Amides are produced by reacting an ester of a carboxylic acid with an amine, using as catalyst an alkoxide of an alkali metal. The ester is first heated to at least 75°C.

under a pressure of no more than 500 mm. of mercury to remove moisture and acid gases which would prevent the reaction, and then converted to an amide without heating to initiate the reaction."

Where an application contains an abstract when sent to issue, the abstract will be published in the *Official Gazette* instead of a claim.

When an application is being passed to issue, the examiner is required to ensure that the abstract is an adequate and clear statement of the disclosure and generally in line with the guidelines. The abstract may be changed by the examiner's amendment where he deems it necessary.

4. *Evidence of novelty*

In Ireland, when filing a complete specification, there must be lodged a statement of the form of evidence of novelty the applicant proposes to furnish.

5. *Drawings*

In South Africa, in addition to the formal drawings, there must also be filed an additional original drawing of prescribed size containing a single view, adequately illustrating the invention, for advertisement purposes.

6. *Declaration—mention of inventor*

In Nigeria there must be filed, where appropriate, a Declaration signed by the true and first inventor requesting that he be mentioned as such in the patent, and giving his name and address.

Group 2—Importation, Revalidation, Confirmation and Introduction

No application forms need be executed by the applicant for any of the countries concerned but specifications (and drawings, if any), powers of attorney and assignments, as discussed under Group 1 ((a), (c) and (d)), are required. In addition certified copies of the basic patent, having a copy of its specification attached, are required in certain countries.

(1) Powers of attorney

Neither notarial attestation nor consular legalisation is required for Argentine, Barbados, Belgium, Spain and Tangier.

Notarial attestation is required in Jamaica.

Consular legalisation is required in all other countries, namely:

Bolivia	Guatemala	Rwanda
Burundi	Haiti	Turkey
Chile	Honduras	Uruguay
Costa Rica	Iran	Venezuela
Dominican Republic	Iraq	Zaïre
Ecuador	Panama	
	Paraguay	

(2) Assignment

Consular legalisation is required for all countries except Argentine, Barbados, Belgium, Burundi, Jamaica, Rwanda, Spain, Tangier and Zaïre.

For Jamaica the assignment requires notarial attestation and must be accompanied by an affidavit by the assignee also notarially attested.

(3) Certified copies

These are required in:

Argentine	Ecuador [1]	Jamaica
Barbados	Guatemala [1]	Panama [1]
Bolivia [1]	Haiti	Turkey
Chile	Honduras [1]	Uruguay [1]
Costa Rica [1]	Iran	Venezuela [1]
Dominican Republic	Iraq [1]	

For Barbados and Jamaica the certified copies take the form shown in the Table set out below in connection with Registrations.

[1] Consular legalisation required.

Group 3—Registrations

(a) Of United Kingdom patents

For this kind of patent, typewritten copies of the specification are generally not required by the local agent except as noted below, but he is sent a power of attorney or authorisation, an application form, and an assignment if the legal rights are to be obtained in the name of a party other than that of the U.K. patentee.

In Antigua, Bermuda, Dominica, Jamaica, Montserrat and St. Christopher it is necessary also to furnish two typewritten copies of the complete specification.

There is also required proof of the existence of the British patent, in one or other of the forms of certified copies discussed below.

(1) *Powers of Attorney Authorisation*

Powers of attorney are required in all countries except in:

Fiji	Jersey
Gibraltar	Nigeria
Gilbert & Ellice Islands	Somalia (Northern Region)
Guernsey	

where an authorisation is sufficient.

Notarial attestation of the power of attorney or authorisation is required in:

Falkland Islands	Seychelles
St. Lucia	Sri Lanka

(2) *Application*

In the following countries the application should be executed before a notary public:

Antigua	Jamaica	Seychelles
Bermuda	Montserrat	Sri Lanka
Br. Virgin Islands	St. Christopher	Trinidad
Dominica	St. Lucia	
Grenada	St. Vincent	

No application form is required in Barbados, Ghana, Guernsey, Jamaica and Jersey.

(3) *Certified copies*

The certified copies may take one or other of the following forms:

A A certificate of the Comptroller setting out details of the grant, and having attached thereto a copy of the letters patent, a printed copy of the patent specification, and a copy of the Patent Register;

B A certificate of the Comptroller setting out details of the grant, and having attached thereto a printed copy of the patent specification, and a copy of the Patent Register;

C A printed copy of the patent specification impressed with the Patent Office seal and bearing a rubber-stamp certification.

The form of proof required, and the numbers of certificates are set out in the following table:

	A	*B*	*C*
Aden	–	3	–
Antigua	–	1	1
Bahrain	1	–	–
Barbados	2	–	–
Bermuda	–	1	–
British Honduras	–	1	–
British Solomon Islands	–	1	–
British Virgin Islands	–	1	1
Brunei	–	1	–
Cyprus	–	2	–
Dominica	–	1	1
Falkland Islands	–	1	1
Fiji	–	1	–
Gambia	–	1	–
Ghana	–	1	–
Gibraltar	–	1	1
Gilbert and Ellice Islands	–	1	–
Grenada	–	1	–
Guernsey	1	–	1
Guyana	–	1	–
Hong Kong	–	1	–
Jamaica	–	1	–
Jersey	–	1	–
Kenya	–	1	1
Malaya	–	1	–
Montserrat	–	1	1
Sabah	–	1	–
St. Christopher—Nevis and Anguilla	–	1	1
St. Helena	–	1	1
St. Lucia	2	–	–
St. Vincent	–	1	–
Sarawak	–	1	–
Seychelles	–	1	–
Sierra Leone	–	1	–
Singapore	–	1	–
Somalia (Northern Region)	–	1	1
Sri Lanka	2	–	–
Tanganyika	–	1	1

	A	*B*	*C*
Trinidad	–	2	–
Uganda	–	1	1
Zanzibar	–	1	1

(b) Of Australian patents

For registration of an Australian patent in Nauru, it is believed that a certified copy of the Australian letters patent will suffice.

(c) Of South African patents

For registration of a South African patent in Botswana, Lesotho or Swaziland, all that is required is an unlegalised power and the South African letters patent (or a certified copy thereof).

Declarations of Inventorship

In the note on " Documents Required " for the filing of overseas patent applications reference was not made to declarations of inventorship because they are required only in a relatively small number of countries as specific documents, although of course many applications contain declarations of inventorship.

In the following countries specific declarations of inventorship are called for:

Czechoslovakia: The declaration recites that the inventor is the author of the invention and he is not bound to offer the invention to the Czech State.

E. Germany: The declaration comprises an affirmation by the inventor that no other person is concerned in the invention and whether or not the invention was made with state support. If the right to the patent has been transferred the assignee or the like must be named and the means by which transfer was effected must be stated. The Patent Office has the right to call for an attested copy of the transfer deed.

W. Germany: There must be filed a Declaration signed by the applicant, in which he states the name of the true inventor and affirms that according to the applicant's knowledge, no other person

	is entitled to a share in the invention. When the applicant is not the inventor, he must state how he obtained the invention from the inventor, for example, by assignment, service agreement or the like. Normally, the name of the inventor is mentioned on the printed specification but if the inventor does not wish his name to appear, and if he is not the applicant, he must also sign a Renunciation.
South Korea	The inventor declares that he considers himself the original and first inventor.
Switzerland	The declaration names the inventor and, if he is not the applicant, the means by which the right to the patent has been transferred; the declaration is signed by the applicant.
Taiwan	A declaration of inventorship in the form of an oath must be signed by the inventor(s).
U.S.S.R.	The inventor declares that the invention was not obtained from anyone and that he is the true author.

A British Patents Form No. 1 can be regarded as comprising (a) a declaration of inventorship and (b) a prayer or petition for the grant of a patent. The same is true of the ordinary application form in:

Bahamas	Malawi	Rhodesia
Bangladesh	New Zealand	South Africa
India	Nigeria	Sri Lanka
Ireland	Pakistan	Zambia

A declaration of inventorship is included in a U.S. oath or declaration and in a Canadian petition.

In the United Kingdom it is not required to lodge an assignment with an application in the name of an assignee, but the application form for a non-convention application contains a declaration of assent to the making of the application, and this must be signed by the inventor(s). A delay of three months is allowed for execution of the assent. Again, when there is filed a complete specification following a provisional one, it is required to lodge a declaration of inventorship (Patents Form No. 4) which also contains an assent to be executed by any inventor who is not named in the application form. In respect of Convention applications also Form 4 is required, but the assent does not require to be executed. In both these cases, Form 4 may be lodged at any time before the expiry of the period allowed for putting the application in order for acceptance.

The same practice prevails in Ireland, although there is no prescribed form of assent and the term for lodging the assent is limited in all cases to 6 months (extensible by a further 12 months on payment of fees).

The U.K. procedure has also been adopted in New Zealand, but in respect only of complete specifications. In Bahamas, the assent is a separate document which must be filed within three months of application.

The position in Australia is somewhat special in that the application is merely a request for a patent for the invention described in the provisional or complete specification and is signed by the agent. However, there must be filed in Australia, at any time up to acceptance, a declaration which includes a declaration of inventorship.

There are a few countries in which the forms required for filing may be likened to a British Form No. 1 but split into two separate documents, namely a petition and a declaration, the declaration including a statement of inventorship. These countries are:

British Honduras	Fiji	Mauritius

Provisional Specifications

United Kingdom patent law provides for the filing of a patent application accompanied by a provisional specification and for the subsequent filing of a complete specification within 12 months of the date of filing the application or, subject to payment of a fee, within an extended period of 15 months from the date of filing the application.

The following is a list of countries which also permit the filing of applications accompanied by provisional specifications, and there is shown the period within which the complete specification must be filed and any extension of that period.

Country	*Period (in months)*	*Extension (in months)*
Antigua	9	1
Australia	12	None

Bangladesh	9	1
Barbados	9	1
Bermuda	9	None
Br. Honduras	6	None
Br. Virgin Islands	9	1
Dominica	9	1
Grenada	9	None
Guyana	12	1
India	12	3
Ireland	12	3
Malawi	12	3
Malta	9	1
Montserrat	9	1
New Zealand	12	3
Pakistan	9	1
Rhodesia	12	3
St. Christopher, Nevis & Anguilla	9	1
St. Lucia	6	1
St. Vincent	9	None
Seychelles	9	1
South Africa	12	1
South West Africa	9	None
Sri Lanka	9	3
Trinidad & Tobago	9	None
Zambia	12	3

It will be noted that all these territories are members, or former members, of the British Commonwealth.

Such protection as is now afforded by the filing of a provisional specification should not be confused with the term " provisional protection " which was defined in section 4 of the U.K. Act of 1932.

The modern counterpart of this latter section is section 52 of the 1949 Act which contains also provisions in section 5 regarding priority dates for claims, and the term " provisional protection " is no longer categorically defined.

These provisional specifications should not be confused with what are sometimes loosely referred to as " provisional " applications, but which are really applications with informal papers. Thus, in Brazil, Chile, Czechoslovakia, Denmark, Hungary, Norway, Netherlands and Sweden, it is sometimes possible in an emergency to file a foreign text provisionally and a domestic text later. In Spain, an application may be lodged

with claims only and the full specification and claims lodged within one month.

In Portugal, an informal application may be lodged giving merely the name of the applicant, the title of the invention and the priority date.

CHAPTER 3

EXAMINATION OF APPLICATION

UNDER the earliest enactments, patents were granted provided formal requirements were met, it being understood that invalidity might subsequently be shown on various grounds, for example, if it were proved that there was lack of novelty or that the alleged inventor was not in fact the true and first inventor.

Examination for novelty was first provided for in patent legislation in the U.S. Law of 1836, and opposition first provided for in the U.K. Law of 1852. The German Law of 1876 included both these features. There are now many variations of procedure in different countries which may be classified for convenience as follows:

(1) Registration, subject only to a formal examination which may include suitability for patenting and unity of invention; *e.g.*, Belgium and Italy.

(2) Formal examination coupled to a rigorous examination for unity of invention as well as of the structure and succinctness of the specification and claims; *e.g.*, Switzerland (except for certain industries for which class 5 examination is conducted).

(3) Formal examination, with opposition proceedings; *e.g.*, Bahamas, Bolivia.

(4) Formal and novelty examinations, with opposition proceedings; *e.g.*, U.K. and Australia.

(5) Formal and novelty and subject-matter examinations without opposition proceedings; *e.g.*, Canada and U.S.A.

(6) Formal and novelty and subject-matter examinations with opposition proceedings; *e.g.*, Germany and Sweden.

In considering the various examination systems in vogue one frequently finds an apparent difference between law and practice, in that although, for example, the law may provide for examination of certain aspects of an invention in practice these aspects are not examined, or at best only perfunctorily. Here, the requirements of the law are set out.

The five main aspects forming the basis upon which the above types of examination are conducted are:

(*a*) formality;

(*b*) Suitability for patenting;

(*c*) unity of invention;
(*d*) novelty;
(*e*) subject-matter and patentability, which are considered under one or more of the headings:
  (i) utility;
  (ii) technical advance;
  (iii) inventive level;
  (iv) non-obviousness.

(*a*) A *formal examination* ensures that the documents lodged are complete and correctly drawn in accordance with existing regulations.

(*b*) The *suitability for patenting examination* is not concerned with quantum of invention but ensures that the subject-matter is not of a prohibited class. Thus, in many countries there are certain inventions which are not entitled by law to patent protection. Examples of inventions subject to such prohibition, but varying from country to country, are those relating to:

chemical compounds and other substances *per se*;
medicines, foodstuffs, curative devices and processes therefor;
agricultural processes and products;
inventions contrary to law, morality or public order;
inventions prejudicial to health or public safety;
credit or financial schemes.

(*c*) A single patent in all countries is intended to be granted in respect only of a single invention, and in almost all countries examination of the specification and claims is required by law to include consideration of the question of unity of invention. Normally, if two separate inventions are found to be present the applicant is entitled to divide his application. Inevitably, concepts as to unity or separateness of invention differ in different countries and claims to different aspects of the same invention allowed in a single application in some countries will be regarded as separate inventions in others.

(*d*) As will appear from a later section the requirements as to novelty of an invention vary as between countries; in almost half the countries which have patent laws there is an examination into the novelty of the invention.

(*e*) In only a few countries is there an examination as to the subject-matter of an invention.

Standards of examination, as to be expected, vary from country to country. Generally speaking, the more developed and industrialised the country the higher is the standard of examination into the various aspects as laid down by law. Also, in some countries lack of technically qualified staff precludes the examination of applications, particularly in regard to novelty, in the manner prescribed by law.

The following lists set out the nature of the examination prescribed in the various countries:

(a) Formal

All countries.

(b) Suitability for Patenting

African & Malagasy Union
Albania
Algeria
Argentina
Australia
Austria
Bahamas
Bangladesh
Bolivia
Brazil
Bulgaria
Cambodia
Canada
Costa Rica
Czechoslovakia
Denmark
Finland
France
E. Germany
W. Germany
Guatemala
Guinea
Hungary
India
Iraq
Ireland
Israel
Italy
Japan
Jordan
Kuwait
Laos
Libya
Malawi
Mali
Mexico
Monaco
Morocco
Nepal
Netherlands
New Zealand
Nicaragua
Norway
Pakistan
Panama
Peru
Philippines
Poland
Rhodesia
Roumania
South Africa
South Korea
Spain
Sri Lanka
Sweden
Switzerland
Tangier
United Kingdom
U.S.A.
U.S.S.R.
Vietnam
Yugoslavia
Zambia

(c) Unity of Invention

African & Malagasy Union
Albania
Algeria
Argentina
Australia
Austria
Brazil

Bulgaria
Cambodia
Canada
Colombia
Cuba
Czechoslovakia
Denmark
Finland
France
E. Germany
W. Germany
Greece
Guatemala
Guinea
Hungary
Iceland
India
Iran
Iraq
Ireland
Israel
Italy
Japan
Jordan
Kuwait
Laos
Lebanon
Libya
Malawi
Mali
Mexico
Monaco
Morocco
Netherlands
New Zealand
Nigeria
Norway
Pakistan
Peru
Philippines
Poland
Portugal
Rhodesia
Roumania
South Africa
South Korea
Spain
Sri Lanka
Sweden
Switzerland
Syria
Tunisia
Turkey
United Arab Republic
United Kingdom
U.S.A.
U.S.S.R.
Venezuela
Vietnam
Yugoslavia
Zambia

(d) Novelty

Albania
Argentina
Australia
Austria
Bangladesh
Brazil
Bulgaria
Canada
Colombia
Costa Rica
Cuba
Czechoslovakia
Denmark
Finland
France
W. Germany
Guatemala
Guyana
Honduras
Hungary
Iceland
India
Ireland
Israel
Japan
Jordan
Liberia
Malawi
Mexico
Nepal
Netherlands
New Zealand
Nicaragua
Norway
Pakistan
Philippines
Poland
Rhodesia
Roumania
South Korea
Sri Lanka
Sweden
Switzerland [1]
United Kingdom
Uruguay [2]
U.S.A.
U.S.S.R.
Yugoslavia
Zambia

[1] For certain technical fields only.
[2] For inventions of state interest only.

(e) Subject-Matter and Patentability

(*i*) *Utility*

Albania	W. Germany	Norway
Brazil	Hungary	South Korea
Colombia	Japan	Sweden
Denmark	Nepal	U.S.A.
Finland	Netherlands	U.S.S.R.

(*ii*) *Technical Advance*

Bulgaria	W. Germany	Norway
Czechoslovakia	Hungary	Roumania
Denmark	Israel	Sweden
Finland	Netherlands	Switzerland [1]

(*iii*) *Inventive Level*

Denmark	Hungary	Norway
Finland	Israel	Sweden
W. Germany	Netherlands	Switzerland [1]

[1] For certain technical fields only.

(*iv*) *Non-obviousness*

In general this aspect is not positively written into patent laws, but a specific example is to be found in section 103 of the U.S. Patent Law, and the requirement also appears in the Strasbourg Convention on the Unification of certain points of Substantive Law on Patents for Invention and in the new Acts in Denmark, Finland, France, Israel, Norway and Sweden.

Other Examination Features

Other features of some examination procedures include:

(1) *Dependency on Earlier Patent*

Albania	Bulgaria	Poland
Austria	Czechoslovakia	U.S.S.R.

in each of which countries patents of dependence may be issued.

Examination in Argentina should be mentioned in this connection since there may be offered during examination grant of a patent of addition to a dominating patent held by another party. The remaining countries listed along with Argentina on page 3 in connection with patents of addition of this nature are not likely to raise this question during examination.

In U.K., Eire and New Zealand, the examiner is empowered to check whether use of an invention would involve substantial risk of infringement of an earlier patent.

(2) *Structure of Specification and Claims*

In Switzerland there is a very rigorous examination into the structure and succinctness of the specification and claims.

(3) *Conflict (Canada): Interference (U.S.A. and Philippines)*

The examination in these countries especially will involve consideration of pending applications and patents as to possible conflict.

The term " conflict " is often used in Europe to refer to situations involving one or more unpublished prior applications capable of giving rise to a situation of prior patenting.

(4) *Deferred Examination*

This is a system of Patent Office examining procedure whereby patent applications are examined for (a) novelty, and (b) patentability only on the express request of the applicant (or a third party) within prescribed periods and on payment of prescribed fees.

There is evidence that this system was suggested in Hungary some 60 years ago, but it was first introduced into national patent law by the Netherlands in 1964, West Germany in 1968, Australia and Hungary in 1970, and Japan and Brazil in 1971.

It is sometimes suggested that the new French law includes a system of deferred examination, but this is not strictly correct because novelty reports are established automatically once the patent application has been filed (if the invention falls within one or other of specified classes) and the applicant merely has the right to request postponement of the establishment of the novelty report for a period of two years.

NETHERLANDS

For various reasons the Dutch Patent Office was faced with an increasing number of unexamined patent applications. With a view to lessening the volume of work involved in examination and the delay in granting patents, the amended law of May 1963 introduced a system of examination which may be summarised as follows:

1. Search for novelty conducted only at request of applicant, or of third party after application has been laid-open, on payment of fee.

2. Examination for patentability conducted, after issue of novelty report, only at request of applicant, or of third party after application has been laid-open, on payment of fee.

3. Fixed period of seven years (with possibility of short extension) after filing date for lodging request for examination for patentability.

4. Annual maintenance fees payable on applications.

5. Automatic laying-open to public inspection of application 18 months after filing date, or, if convention priority has been claimed, 18 months after convention date. Copies of specifications and drawings as laid-open available in a printed form.

6. Third party may submit prior art to Patent Office.

7. Protection against third parties infringing application in period between laying-open and publication for opposition. Reasonable compensation payable after grant of patent.

These seven essential features are also present substantially in the amended Patent Laws of Australia, Brazil, West Germany, Hungary and Japan, variations being as set out below.

1, 2 *and* 3.—*Examination*

Brazil: Only a single request for examination is laid down and the period is 2 years (not extensible) after the application has been laid-open.

Germany: It is not necessary to await issue of the novelty report before requesting examination for patentability; a combined request may be filed, although there is no saving in fees. The seven-year period is not extensible. If a request for the search or examination in respect of an application for a patent of addition is made the applicant will be required to make the same request in respect of the main application, otherwise the application for a patent of addition will be treated as one for an independent patent. (Details of the German system are set out on pages 258 to 260.)

Australia: Only a single request for complete examination is laid down, and that must be filed within five years (not extensible) of filing the complete specification. The Patent Office is empowered, however, to direct an applicant to request examination. An application for a patent of addition will not be examined before a request is made for examination of the main application. Further, the law provides for a so-called "Modified Examination" in respect only of applications claiming priority under the International Convention from a basic application filed in the United Kingdom or the United States. (Details of the Australian system are set out on pages 287 to 291.)

HUNGARY: Only a single request for examination is laid down, which is to be filed within four years (not extensible) after the application has been laid-open. Further, in respect of certain subject-matter, patent applications will be subjected automatically to complete examination. (Details of the Hungarian system are set out on pages 302 to 304.)

JAPAN: Only a single request for examination is laid down and the period is seven years (not extensible) for patent applications but only four years (not extensible) for utility model applications. (Details of the Japanese system are set out on pages 306 and 307.)

4.—*Maintenance Fees*

WEST GERMANY: Annual fees for applications and patents are now payable at the beginning of the third and each subsequent year following the day after application.

AUSTRALIA: Continuation fees are payable on the expiration of the second year from the date of lodgment of the complete specification and annually thereafter while the application is pending. For the fifth and subsequent years the fees are equal in amount to the renewal fees payable for the corresponding year of a patent. Thus these continuation fees merge into renewal fees.

BRAZIL: Annual renewal fees are payable from the beginning of the third year from filing.

HUNGARY: Annual renewal fees are payable, as before, from the application date.

JAPAN: No application maintenance fees have been prescribed, patent renewal fees being payable as before.

5.—*Early Publication*

AUSTRALIA: Laying-open to public inspection occurs 18 months after lodgment of the complete specification. An applicant may request laying-open after the expiry of three months from lodgment of his complete specification. Specifications are not available in a printed form, but a printed abstract, generally comprising the main claim, is available.

HUNGARY: The laying-open occurs after the initial formal examination, but there is no set period. If complete examination is requested on filing the laying-open takes place after acceptance. An applicant may request postponement of the laying-open for a period of one year. Specifications are not available in a printed form until after acceptance.

JAPAN: The laying-open in the case of patent applications takes the form of printed publication in the Patent Gazette of the full text of the specification, claims and drawings (with amendments, if any). In the case of utility model applications, only the claim, drawings and a brief explanation of the drawings will be printed in the Utility Model Gazette, but the full specification, claims and drawings will be available for public inspection in the Patent Office.

6.—*Common Informer*

In all countries except Brazil third parties may inform the Patent Office of prior art.

7.—*Protection against infringement*

BRAZIL: When the patent has issued the patentee may take action for infringement committed during pendency of the application.

GERMANY: An applicant may demand appropriate compensation, but does not have the right of a prohibitory action or for damages. The court may stay the trial of the action if the validity of the application is in dispute. Although the filing of a request for examination is not a prerequisite to institution of a suit, the absence of such a request may be raised as an objection. If compensation has been paid but no patent is granted, the third party may sue the applicant at least for recovery of the compensation paid.

AUSTRALIA: There can be no action for infringement until the patent is sealed and then only in respect of a valid claim in the patent.

HUNGARY: Proceedings may be instituted but must be suspended until the application procedure has been completed and protection becomes definitive.

JAPAN: An applicant has the right to claim compensation from any third party who is working the invention, but the claim cannot be made until publication of the application after full examination. Also, the applicant must give advance warning to the third party or be able to prove that working of the invention has taken place in the knowledge that it is the invention claimed in the application laid-open to public inspection. The amount of compensation will be equivalent to what would normally be received in royalties if the invention were patented and a licence granted. The period of unauthorised working which will rank for compensation will run from the date of receipt of the warning letter up to the date of publication of the application after examination. Where an applicant receives compensation and a patent is not granted on the application, or if the working by the third party is outside the scope of the claim of the patent, the applicant will be liable to pay damages to the third party.

Chapter 4

NOVELTY

[*Where a section of an Act is mentioned in parentheses following a country the section refers to the Patents Act of that country*]

Broadly speaking, an invention is novel if it was not known or available to others prior to the date of application for a patent. An invention is deemed to have become known and available to others if it was

(*a*) described in a printed publication in such a manner as to render possible its use by those skilled in the art; or

(*b*) openly used, exhibited or presented in such a manner as to render possible its use by those skilled in the art; or

(*c*) previously patented in the respective country;

prior to the date of the application for patent (or an earlier filing date under the International, or any similar, Convention), except under the circumstances referred to in pages 94 to 113.

In some countries, the standard of novelty is "absolute," that is to say an invention is not novel if it has been described in print or made known in any other way in any country prior to the date of the patent application. In other countries, the standard of novelty is "relative," that is to say there is some limitation as to the nature, place and/or time in respect of prior publication or prior user.

Relative novelty falls into two classes which are destructive of novelty:

(i) prior printed publication anywhere; or local prior user;

(ii) prior printed publication or prior user; both local.

So far as concerns prior patenting, since no state can make more than one valid grant for the same invention, the existence of a prior local patent will preclude the grant of a valid patent on a later application. It will be appreciated further that a prior foreign patent which has been published, in one form or another, will be destructive of novelty in those countries where the standard of novelty is absolute, but in countries providing for patents of importation or the like, this latter situation applies only in respect of parties other than the applicant for the patent of importation. Published prior foreign patents, even though not printed, rank as anticipations in some countries otherwise adhering to concepts of relative novelty—class (i).

The following lists set out the novelty requirements so far as concerns prior publication and prior user:

Absolute Novelty

Novelty destroyed by prior publication or by the invention being made known in any other way in any country prior to the date of application

African & Malagasy Union
Albania
Algeria
Argentina
Bahamas
Bolivia
Brazil
Bulgaria
Cambodia
Chile
Colombia
Costa Rica
Cuba
Czechoslovakia
Denmark
Dominican Republic
Finland
France
Guatemala
Guinea
Haiti
Honduras
Hungary
Indonesia
Iran
Iraq
Ireland
Israel
Italy
Laos
Lebanon
Luxembourg
Mali
Malta
Mexico
Monaco
Morocco
Netherlands
Nigeria
Norway
Portugal
Roumania
Salvador
Spain
Sweden
Syria
Tunisia
Turkey
U.S.S.R.
Uruguay
Venezuela
Vietnam
Yugoslavia

In all these countries, except Chile, the mere laying open to public inspection of a foreign application ranks as destructive of novelty.

Relative Novelty

(a) Novelty destroyed by printed publication anywhere or by local **prior public use**

Austria
Belgium [3]
Burundi [3]
Canada [1]
E. Germany [2]
W. Germany [1]
Iceland
India
Japan [1]
Malawi [2]
Peru [5]
Philippines [1]
Poland
Rhodesia [2]
Rwanda [3]

South Africa [2]	Taiwan [4]	Zaïre [3]
Switzerland	U.S.A.[1]	Zambia [2]

[1] In Japan and West Germany a prior unprinted specification laid open to public inspection in any country is also destructive of novelty. In U.S.A. and probably also in Canada and the Philippines an unprinted specification laid open to public inspection is not effective as a prior printed publication but may be effective as a prior patent grant.

[2] In East Germany, Malawi, Rhodesia, South Africa and Zambia, the laying open of an earlier local application is destructive of novelty.

[3] In Belgium, Burundi, Rwanda, and Zaïre a prior foreign patent of a third party effective as from a date earlier than that of a local patent application, will invalidate the local patent even though no publication of the foreign patent has occurred prior to the local application date. A patent grant is made in these countries provided the invention has not already been patented in any country.

[4] The application in Taiwan must be filed within one year of the date of filing the earliest corresponding application in any country.

[5] The application in Peru must be filed within two years after the date of filing the earliest corresponding application in any country.

(b) **Novelty destroyed by** local **printed publication or by** local **prior public use**

Antigua	Jamaica	St. Christopher
Australia	Jordan	St. Lucia
Bangladesh	Kuwait	St. Vincent
Barbados	Liberia	Seychelles
Bermuda	Libya	South Korea
Br. Honduras	Mauritius	S.W. Africa
Br. Virgin Islands	Montserrat	Sri Lanka
Dominica	Nepal	Trinidad & Tobago
Ecuador	New Zealand	United Arab Republic
Fiji	Nicaragua	United Kingdom
Greece	Pakistan	
Grenada	Panama	
Guyana	Paraguay	

Prior local patent specifications laid open to public inspection, even though not printed would be destructive of novelty, apart from Bermuda, Ecuador and Trinidad where only prior local use is destructive.

"Prior patenting" has been referred to on page 84 as a novelty objection or an objection capable of giving rise to "conflict" where co-pending applications of different priority dates are concerned.

Apart from U.S.A., Canada and the Philippines, where a patent is granted to the first inventor, the proper priority dates for the same or similar inventions determine the situation between co-pending patent applications although practice may vary in different countries from that in which the earlier application is regarded as part of the prior art effective against the later application to that in which only overlap between the claims of the applications must be avoided, for example, by means of a disclaimer of the earlier claim inserted in the later application.

Novelty Examination—Information on Prior Art Cited in Other Countries

In many countries the patent law provides for an examination, in greater or lesser degree, as to the novelty of an alleged invention, but in not a few of such countries the examining staffs are inadequate in numbers, technical knowledge and experience, properly to conduct the examinations required by the law. This problem has been recognised by all the countries concerned, but only in relatively few of them has anything been done to overcome it, as by requiring applicants to furnish particulars of prior art cited against corresponding applications in other countries, and thereby reducing the burden imposed on the examining staff.

In recent years there has been an increase in the number of countries calling for particulars of prior art cited in other countries, but for the purpose of reducing the burden on an effective but overloaded staff. In most Patent Offices where an effective novelty search is conducted, there is a very considerable backlog of work which is not diminishing. Therefore, in an endeavour to assist the process of examination and to shorten the period of examination, applicants are now requested to supply particulars of known prior art. Obviously, the supply of such material will not only provide a check on the official search but will save time in searching because if he is made aware of any pertinent prior art an examiner will not require to waste time considering less pertinent material which he might otherwise have to study.

The requirement to provide particulars obtained from other countries of prior art in whole or in part is statutory in:

Brazil	Finland	Netherlands
Bulgaria	W. Germany	New Zealand
Canada	India	Norway
Czechoslovakia	Ireland	Sweden
Denmark	Israel	

Applicants are requested to provide particulars of prior art obtained from other countries but there is no statutory force behind the request in the U.S.A.

In Mexico there is neither a statutory requirement to provide particulars of prior art nor are the applicants requested to provide details. However, if it can be proved that for an application pending in Mexico a patent has been issued in any foreign country in which strict novelty examinations are being carried out, then a patent will be allowed in Mexico. For this purpose, it is necessary to submit to the Mexican Patent Office a print of the granted patent together with a sworn Spanish translation thereof. It is understood that patents in the United Kingdom, U.S.A., Germany and Sweden rank for this purpose.

In Nepal, see p. 12, a patent will be granted without novelty examination if the invention has already been protected by the inventor or assignee by patents in the home country and in any three other countries.

Dealing with the countries listed above:

Brazil

If an application carries a claim to priority the applicant may be called on to supply information concerning any objections and the results of novelty searches or examinations, in respect of corresponding applications in other countries.

Bulgaria

There must be lodged within three months of the filing date of the Bulgarian application a list of the countries in which corresponding applications have been filed. Subsequently, up to grant of the Bulgarian patent, there should be lodged copies of official letters received on such applications.

Canada

Under Rule 39 an examiner may require an applicant of any Canadian application to furnish any of the following information in respect of any corresponding application that may have been filed, in any country specified by the examiner, on behalf of the applicant or on behalf of any other person claiming under the inventor named in the Canadian application:

(*a*) prior art cited against the applications;
(*b*) the application numbers, filing dates and, if granted, the patent numbers; and

(*c*) particulars of interference or similar proceedings.

An examiner may also require the applicant of the Canadian application to identify, to the extent known by the applicant, the first publication of or patent for the invention described in his application.

Where information required by the examiner is not available to the applicant, the reasons why the information is not available must be stated by the applicant.

The Commissioner has power to refuse an application if he has cause to believe that information required by the examiner, but not supplied to him, was available to the applicant. Before refusal the applicant is notified of the position and given the opportunity to satisfy the Commissioner.

Czechoslovakia

Decree No. 43/57, s. 1, para. 6, sets out that at the request of the Czech Patent Office an applicant must state in what countries he has filed an application for a patent for the same subject-matter and what " opposition " was raised in these countries. He must also state the result of any such application. (Opposition is here interpreted as the prior art cited by the other Offices.)

Denmark, Finland, Norway, Sweden

The Patent Offices are authorised under the new Acts to require an applicant to provide information regarding the results of examination as to patentability of the invention, of which he has been informed by the patent authorities in any country where he has filed a corresponding application.

In practice, in each country, the Patent Office issues an official letter, with an inextensible term of three months for reply, requiring the applicant to file copies of any official letter issued in the basic country and giving the result of the examination for patentability. If no official letter has been issued in the basic country, the applicant is required to file a declaration to that effect. If a reply is not filed within the set term the application will lapse and may be restored only if a reply is filed within four months of expiry of the set term and on payment of a special fee.

Each Office also requests the applicant to report any examination results received from countries other than the basic country, or from the International Patent Bureau, but a reply to this part of the official letter is not mandatory.

West Germany

An applicant is required to inform the Patent Office of the countries and numbers of any corresponding applications filed by him, and to furnish particulars of any printed citations made against any such application. It is not, at the present time, necessary to supply the information until the Patent Office calls for it.

India

An applicant will be required to furnish the following information in respect of any corresponding application (whether filed in his name alone or jointly with another person, or by anyone from whom he claims title):

(i) A statement on Form 4, to be filed with the application, setting out:

(*a*) names of countries where corresponding applications have been filed, with details of the application numbers and filing dates;

(*b*) whether any of the applications has been accepted, refused, abandoned or withdrawn;

(*c*) whether a patent has been granted on any of the applications;

(*d*) name and address of anyone to whom the rights in any of the applications have been assigned; and

(ii) An undertaking that, up to the date of acceptance of his Indian application he will keep the Controller informed in writing, from time to time, of similar information in respect of every other corresponding application filed outside India subsequent to filing the statement referred to, the information to be supplied within three months from the date of filing each such application.

The Controller is also empowered to call for details relating to any objections, made against any corresponding application, on the ground of lack of novelty or patentability, the amendments effected and the claims allowable.

Failure to disclose the information required or the furnishing of false information is a ground of opposition and of revocation.

Ireland

Section 8 (6) requires an applicant who has filed a complete specification to furnish such evidence as may be prescribed of:

(*a*) the result of any novelty examination made in respect of a corresponding application filed in any prescribed Patent Office outside Ireland; or

(*b*) the acceptance by any prescribed Office of a corresponding application.

The prescribed Offices are those of the United Kingdom and W. Germany.

The prescribed evidence is set out in Rule 27 (1) (2) and (3), from which it is apparent that the novelty examination under (*a*) above is not necessarily that of the U.K. or German Office. Under Rule 26 (1) (*h*) the applicant must state, within three months, extensible to nine months, of filing his complete specification which of the alternative forms of evidence he proposes to furnish.

The evidence may take any one of the alternative Forms numbered 1–5 set out below.

1. A declaration by an Irish or British patent agent.
2. A certificate from the British Patent Office.
3. A certificate from the International Institute of Patents in the Hague.

Any declaration or certificate made under 1, 2 or 3 above must testify as to the result of an investigation made for the purpose of ascertaining whether the invention has been published, in any specification of a British application made within 30 years next before the date of filing the Irish complete specification. In the case of 2 and 3 the evidence must be accompanied by a certified copy of the specification in respect of which the investigation was made.

4. A certified copy of the accepted complete specification of the corresponding British application, if any; or
5. A certified copy of the published specification of the corresponding German application, if any.

Evidence in accordance with 1, 2 or 3 should be furnished within two-and-a-half years, extensible to three years, from the date of filing the complete specification in Ireland; evidence in accordance with 4 or 5 should be furnished within the five-year period (extensible by three months) prescribed for acceptance of the Irish application. In all cases the periods may be extended without fee if the Irish Controller is satisfied that the delay is due to circumstances beyond the control of the applicant.

It should be noted further that under section 7 (6) every application for a patent shall give such information as may be prescribed, and Rule 27 (4) empowers the Controller to obtain from an applicant a statement of all foreign countries, if any, where corresponding applications have been made, together with the result of any search for novelty made on such applications.

Israel

Under section 18 an applicant may be called on to furnish details of the results of the examination of corresponding applications in other countries.

Netherlands

Section 22 A (2) requires a Dutch application to be accompanied by a declaration stating whether and if so in which countries and on what dates, an application in respect of the same invention has been filed earlier than that in the Netherlands, and, where such countries are indicated, by an authorisation empowering the Patent Office to make inquiries in those other countries. This declaration may be filed within five months from the Dutch filing date.

New Zealand

Section 15 empowers the Commissioner to obtain from an applicant information as to corresponding or substantially corresponding applications in the United Kingdom, Canada, Australia or U.S.A., or in any other country which has been declared by Order in Council to be a country to which the section applies. The Commissioner is further entitled to obtain from the applicant in respect of any such application the following information so far as it is reasonably available to the applicant:

(*a*) the number and filing date of the application;

(*b*) particulars sufficient to identify the prior art cited against the application;

(*c*) the number allotted to the patent when granted on the application and the form of the claim allowed;

(*d*) particulars of any other application or patent with which the corresponding application is or has been involved in opposition, conflict, interference or similar proceedings.

U.S.A.

In 1963 consideration was given to amendment of the Rules to provide a statutory requirement for the submission of prior art, but it was decided to leave matters on a voluntary basis. Accordingly, applicants and attorneys were advised by public notice that it was considered highly desirable, as well as proper, that the Office should be informed of any prior art which might be helpful in examination of an application. Any prior art so cited was to be listed in the patent as printed. It was not the intention to rely on such citations as a substitute for all or any part of the official search nor as an admission by the applicant that the cited art was anticipatory of any claim or that it should form a basis for rejection. The object in requesting citation of prior art was to provide a check on the official search and also to facilitate that search, in that an examiner who is advised of prior art of a given degree of pertinence before beginning his search does not need to spend time in considering art which is obviously less pertinent but which he would otherwise have been required to consider.

Notices published in 797 O.G. 733, 802 O.G. 601, 804 O.G. 1, 805 O.G. 294 and 812 O.G. 953 refer.

By the notice dated April 13, 1967 (837 O.G. 1032) the Commissioner announced adoption of the following policy in the hope of encouraging more frequent and meaningful citations of prior art on a voluntary basis:

> " Prior art cited by applicants or their attorneys within thirty days of the filing of a patent application, or prior to

the first Office action, whichever is later, will be fully considered by the examiner, will be part of the official record and will be included in the list of references cited in the patented file and in the printed patent provided the applicant:

(*a*) limits the number of references cited to not more than five separate items, unless a satisfactory explanation is given as to why more than five citations are necessary, and submits one copy of each of the references: and

(*b*) submits a detailed discussion of the references, which discussion points out, with the particularity required by Rule 111 (b) and (c), how the claimed subject-matter is distinguishable over the references.

References cited by applicants or attorneys under the ' special ' examining procedure announced on March 2, 1965, and published in 812 O.G. 953 will also be included in the list of references cited in the patented file and printed patent.

Prior art cited by the applicants and attorneys under the practice set forth in the notices published in 797 O.G. 733; 802 O.G. 601; 804 O.G. 1 and 805 O.G. 294 will no longer be listed in the printed patent."

It is noteworthy that the new policy seeks to limit the " assistance " which may be given to an examiner.

Savings as to Anticipation

Some countries specifically provide certain savings as to anticipation in respect of patent applications, and the nature of the differing savings provided may be stated briefly as follows:

(1) a time limit in antiquity for prior specifications and abridgments which can be cited;

(2) publication of an invention obtained from another party without their consent to publication, provided the patent application is made as soon as reasonably practicable by the legitimate party after becoming aware of the publication;

(3) filing of a prior patent application, with or without publication or use of the invention, in contravention of the legitimate applicant's rights;

(4) disclosure to a government department;

(5) disclosure at an exhibition certified by the state, if the patent application is made not more than six months after opening of the exhibition;
(6) disclosure in a paper read by the true and first inventor before a learned society, or published with his consent in the transactions of such a society, if the patent application is made not more than six months after the reading or publication of the paper;
(7) public working for reasonable trial, provided the patent application is filed within one year.

Dealing with these provisions in turn:

1. *Time Limit*

(*a*) Fifty years time limit on prior specifications or abridgments:

Australia	New Zealand	Zambia
Guyana	South Africa	
Malawi	United Kingdom	

(*b*) In the United Arab Republic, Iraq and Libya prior use, publication or patenting must not be more than 50 years prior to the application, and in Kuwait not more than 20 years.

(*c*) In West Germany, East Germany and Hungary, prior printed publication must not be more than 100 years old.

(*d*) In India, a prior Indian specification must not be dated before January 1, 1912.

2. *Publication of an Invention Obtained from Another Party*

Australia	Jamaica	South Africa
Bahamas	Jordan	United Kingdom
Guyana	Malawi	Zambia
India	New Zealand	
Israel	Rhodesia	

and the following countries, but with six months' limitation for filing the application:

Bangladesh	Ireland	South Korea
Colombia	Japan	Sweden
Denmark	Mauritius	Taiwan
Finland	Norway	
France	Pakistan	

3. *Prior Application in Contravention of Rights*

Bahamas	Netherlands	South Africa
W. Germany	New Zealand	United Kingdom
Ireland		

Although the above countries, except the Netherlands, provide for the possibility of allocation of the priority date of the earlier fraudulent application to that of the subsequent application, actual transfer of the fraudulent application or the making of a substitute grant to the true applicant in case of disputes as to inventorship is provided for in, for example:

Bulgaria	Israel	South Africa
Czechoslovakia	Netherlands	Sweden
Denmark	Nigeria	U.S.S.R.
Finland	Norway	Yugoslavia
France	Poland	
E. Germany	Roumania	

4. *Disclosure to Government Department*

Australia	Malawi	United Kingdom
India	New Zealand	Zambia
Ireland	Rhodesia	

5. *Disclosure at Certified Exhibition*

Algeria [1]	Hungary	Pakistan [1]
Australia [1]	Iceland	Peru
Austria [1]	India	Poland [1]
Bahamas	Iraq [1]	Portugal
Bangladesh [1]	Ireland [1]	Rhodesia [1]
Barbados [1]	Israel [1]	Roumania
Brazil	Italy [1]	South Africa [1]
Colombia (grace only for domestic exhibitions)	Japan [1]	South Korea
	Jordan [1]	Spain [1]
	Kuwait [1]	Sri Lanka [1]
	Lebanon [1]	Sweden
Czechoslovakia	Libya [1]	Switzerland
Denmark	Malta [1]	Taiwan
Finland	Mexico [1]	Tunisia [1]
France [1]	Netherlands	U.A.R.[1]
E. Germany [1]	New Zealand	United Kingdom
W. Germany	Nigeria	U.S.S.R.
Guyana [1]	Norway	Yugoslavia

[1] In these countries notice of disclosure must be given to the local Patent Office.

In Bahamas, Colombia, Denmark, Finland, France, Japan, Nigeria, Norway, Poland, Roumania, Sweden, Taiwan and the U.S.S.R., the six months' period counts from the date of publication at the exhibition.

In Brazil, if it is intended to communicate, publish or display an invention, for example to a learned society or at an exhibition, before filing the patent application, a guarantee of priority may be obtained from the Patent Office by lodging a detailed description, with drawings if any, of the invention, and a certificate will be issued which will give protection for a period of one year from its date. For utility models the grace period is six months. If the patent or utility model application is not lodged by the end of the appropriate grace period the guarantee of priority will lapse and the invention or utility model will be deemed to be in the public domain.

In Italy (for domestic exhibitions), Lebanon, Portugal, Spain and Tunisia, the period is 12 months from the date of publication at the exhibition, and in Italy the priority of the patent is antedated.

In Algeria the period is six months, in Mexico four months, and in Austria, Czechoslovakia and Yugoslavia three months, all reckoned from the closing of the exhibition.

In Peru there is no set period.

6. *Disclosure to a Learned Society*

Australia [2]	Italy [3]	Rhodesia [2]
Bangladesh	Japan [2]	South Africa [2]
Brazil [1]	Jordan [2]	Taiwan
Guyana [2]	New Zealand	United Kingdom
India	Pakistan [2]	
Israel [2]	Portugal [3]	

[1] In Brazil, if it is intended to communicate, publish or display an invention, for example to a learned society or at an exhibition, before filing the patent application, a guarantee of priority may be obtained from the Patent Office by lodging a detailed description, with drawings if any, of the invention, and a certificate will be issued which will give protection for a period of one year from its date. For utility models the grace period is six months. If the patent or utility model application is not lodged by the end of the appropriate grace period the guarantee of priority will lapse and the invention or utility model will be deemed to be in the public domain.

[2] In these countries notice of the disclosure must be given to the local Patent Office; in Israel the notice must be given before the lecture is delivered.

[3] In Italy and Portugal, the period is 12 months, rather than six months, from disclosure, and in Italy the priority of the patent is ante-dated.

7. *Public Working for Reasonable Trial*

Australia	Bangladesh	Guyana

India	Pakistan	Taiwan
Ireland	Rhodesia	United Kingdom
Japan	South Africa	Zambia
Malawi	South Korea	
New Zealand	Spain	

In Malawi, Rhodesia and Zambia there is apparently no time limitation; in South Korea the limitation is six months from completion or first discontinuance of the experiments; in Taiwan the period of grace is six months from the date of use.

In Japan and Taiwan notice of the experiments must be given to the Patent Office when filing the application.

Periods of Grace

Certain countries allow periods of grace prior to the date of filing in the respective country in respect of acts which would otherwise destroy novelty, and these are as follows:

Bolivia	The period between filing and earlier foreign filing up to 1 year.
Canada	2 years allowed for any prior patent of another or printed publication anywhere, or public use or sale in Canada, provided the applicant made the invention before such patenting, publication or use or sale.
E. Germany	Publication or public use if based on invention of applicant or legal predecessor, within 6 months prior to filing.
W. Germany	Any description or use which has taken place within a period of six months prior to the filing of the application will not be taken into consideration if it is based on the invention of the applicant or his predecessor in title. According to a Final Decision of the Federal Court (published in GRUR 1969, p. 271) it is not necessary that the publication is based on the invention. It is sufficient that the publication is based on the intellectual production of the inventor which need not be identical with the invention.

	Thus it is only necessary to prove the identity of the inventor and the author of the ideas expressed in the publication.
Haiti	1 year from date on which the invention was first published, or on sale or publicly used.
Japan	A period of grace of 6 months is allowed in cases where there has been publication of the invention at the instigation of the applicant. In claiming the period of grace at the time of filing the Japanese application, the applicant is required to file a copy of the publication within 30 days from the date of filing the Japanese application.
Mauritius	Public use by applicant within 1 year prior to date of application.
Peru	2 years from the date of filing the earliest corresponding application in any country.
Philippines	1 year for any prior patent or printed publication anywhere, or public use or sale in the Philippines, provided applicant made the invention before such patenting, publication, use or sale.
Poland	6 months' grace if invention has been notified to a government agency.
Roumania	6 months' grace for prior disclosure by inventor.
S.W. Africa	2 years' grace from sale elsewhere, provided still unknown in the territory.
U.S.A.	1 year for prior patent or printed publication anywhere, or public use or sale in U.S.A., provided applicant made the invention before such patenting, publication, use or sale.
U.S.S.R.	For certificates of authorship only—4 months' grace for publication or use, at the instigation of the inventor;

12 months' grace if publication or use has been effected without knowledge of the inventor.

These periods of grace are separate from, and not additional to, the period of priority allowed under the International and similar Conventions.

Novelty in Certain Countries (Recognising Date of Inventorship, or Otherwise Exceptional)

In most countries, including the United Kingdom, it is the date of filing a patent application in a Patent Office that is fundamental; no earlier date is legally recognised for the origin of the patent or the invention (except an earlier filing date under the International, or any similar, Convention). On the other hand, there are three countries, namely, U.S.A., Canada and the Philippines, where a different concept prevails in that recognition is given to the antecedent date of inventorship. Thus, while in say the United Kingdom it is the first applicant who is regarded as the person entitled to the patent, in these other countries it is the first inventor who is so entitled. This different concept has naturally given rise to somewhat special novelty requirements in these three countries.

Also there are at least three other countries, Belgium, Ireland and Switzerland, whose treatment of patent applications from the point of view of novelty and other aspects of patentability merits mention. In the notes that follow these six countries are considered seriatim.

U.S.A.

Section 102 of the Act

This section contains the conditions destructive of novelty. These may conveniently be divided into three groups, according to the occurrence of the anticipating circumstance:

(1) *Prior to date of invention in U.S.A.*

(*a*) Knowledge or use by others in U.S.A. (s. 102 (*a*)).

(*b*) Patenting anywhere or description in a printed publication anywhere (s. 102 (*a*)).

(*c*) An application which ultimately matures into a U.S. patent disclosing the invention (s. 102 (*e*)).

(*d*) Invention in the U.S.A. by another who has not abandoned, suppressed or concealed that invention (s. 102 (*g*)).

(2) *More than one year prior to date of application*

(*a*) Public use or sale in U.S.A. (s. 102 (*b*)).

(*b*) Patenting anywhere or description in a printed publication anywhere (s. 102 (*b*)).

(3) *Prior to U.S. filing date*

Patenting outside U.S.A. by U.S. applicant (his assigns or legal representatives) on an application filed more than one year before his U.S. application (s. 102 (*d*)).

Section 102 also mentions two other circumstances whereby patentability is destroyed. These are:

(*a*) If there has been abandonment of the invention by the applicant (s. 102 (*c*)).

(*b*) If the applicant is not the inventor (s. 102 (*f*)).

By section 119, a U.S. application which has a valid claim to a priority date under, for example, the International Convention, has the same effect as if it had been filed in U.S.A. on the priority date, except in relation to section 102 (*b*), the requirements of which are indicated under paragraph (2) above.

Notes on section 102

In considering those of the U.S. novelty requirements that relate to prior knowledge or use, it is essential to understand and to appreciate the basic motive underlying that part of the U.S. Constitution concerned with patent law and procedure. Article 1, s. 8, cl. 8, of the Constitution gives to Congress the power " To promote the progress of science and useful arts, by securing for limited times to authors and inventors the exclusive right to their respective writings and discoveries." The basic intention of U.S. patent law is to encourage the disclosure of useful information to the public in return for a limited monopoly. It is a natural concomitant thereof that an inventor who makes knowledge of his invention available to the public will be favoured as against the inventor who, in order to preserve it for his own purposes, suppresses publication of information of his invention: an inventor should by means of the patent statutes enjoy his discovery for a period of years (17) with a right to exclude others from practising his invention, but at the end of that limited period of monopoly, the invention should be available to the public and may be practised by anyone.

It may therefore be said that the inventor who is diligent in contributing his discovery to the store of public knowledge will be accorded whatever protection may be available under the laws, but an inventor who is unwilling so to do will receive little or no consideration.

Section 102 (*g*) provides that in determining priority of invention there is to be considered not only the respective dates of conception and reduction to practice, but also diligence between these dates.

Knowledge or use abroad

Novelty is not negatived by prior knowledge or prior use in a foreign country of the subject-matter of a U.S. patent, provided that such subject-matter had nowhere been patented by another and had nowhere been described in a printed publication at the moment when it was invented by the applicant for the U.S. patent. Mere knowledge possessed in the U.S.A. by someone other than the applicant that the subject-matter was known and used in some foreign country before its being invented in the U.S.A. is not such knowledge in the U.S.A. as will defeat the patent. This is the case even where someone who acquired the prior knowledge of the foreign invention or use came to the United States and disclosed his knowledge to others.

Prior user in U.S.A.: secret or non-secret

U.S. practice concerning " secret use " may be stated: All and any prior use will be deemed to be public use (so as to constitute priority of invention) unless actual secrecy is proved. The secrecy must have been deliberate and long continued and with the intent to maintain either a trade secret or a continuously secret business. A mere temporary secrecy (such as during the pendency of a patent application) is not in this category. Thus a man may keep his invention secret for a limited time (at his own peril as to intervening rights) and eventually get a valid patent. Conversely, a deliberate and permanent maintenance of secrecy will give an opposite result. Again, a prior use will be regarded as public even though some effort has been maintained to keep the knowledge from the general public. Therefore, an ordinary attempt to run a business plant, without letting the public in at any time, does not constitute a secret use. To achieve " secret use " an injunction to secrecy must be placed upon the workers by the management and must be carefully maintained.

Thus, prior use may be classified as either:

(*a*) a true trade secret maintained with jealous care; or

(*b*) a public use not maintained with a sufficiency of care.

The presumption in the U.S.A. is always that use is public use, and the burden of proof is on him who asserts the contrary.

Prior user in U.S.A.: quantum

A single instance of public use is sufficient to negative novelty, as has been stated by the Supreme Court:

> ". . . to constitute the public use of an invention it is not necessary that more than one of the patented articles should be publicly used. The use of a great number may tend to strengthen the proof, but one well-defined case of such use is just as effectual to annul the patent as many."

Prior user in U.S.A.: experimental user

Experimental user may negative novelty, but not when it is an unsuccessful abandoned experiment, and such an experiment, in a machine, manufacture, composition of matter or process, will not constitute prior use of a successful patented invention in the same art. On the other hand, where an experiment is completed and used sufficiently to demonstrate its practicability, the abandonment of its use for good and sufficient reasons will not help a later patentee to assert first inventorship.

Where an experimental use is not completed, or is shrouded in secrecy with the intent to deprive the public of any benefits which might come from the invention, then it will not be a reliable ground on which to attack a later patent.

In cases of experimental user, the proofs are most important because the courts tend to be sceptical of claims to prior inventorship, knowledge or use, based on mere experimental development of an invention as against the same invention later patented to another, especially if the patented invention has proved a commercial success.

Prior patenting—U.S.A.—effective date (s. 102) (e)

This subsection was introduced into the U.S. statutes in 1953 as a result of a decision of the U.S. Supreme Court under which a U.S. patent disclosing an invention dates from the filing of the application for the purpose of anticipating a later inventor, whether or not the invention is claimed in the patent.

Prior abandoned U.S. application (s. 102) (g)

In general novelty is not negatived by prior abandoned applications. They do not constitute evidence that the processes or developments described therein were ever made or used anywhere nor do they prove that the processes or developments which they disclosed were ever known in any country. Where there is evidence that an inventor filed and abandoned an application for a patent and also made efforts to put the invention into practice then the abandoned application might be used to assist in determining the date and nature of the invention which was sought to be embodied in a working form. However, if upon the whole of the evidence it appears that what the inventor did outside of his abandoned application was not sufficient to negative the novelty of the subsequent patent for a later invention then the existence of the abandoned application has no additional relevance.

Prior patenting—foreign—effective date

The statutory bar of prior patenting by anyone anywhere is contained in section 102 (*a*) and (*b*). Prior patenting is also a bar under section 102 (*d*) but in this case the bar operates only in respect of patenting outside the United States, before the filing date of the U.S. application, by the U.S. applicant (or his assigns or legal representatives) on an application filed more than one year before his U.S. application.

So far as concerns prior patenting it is well established that "patented" is limited to patents which are available to the public, that is to say there must have been some official publication of the specification and/or claims, and U.S. courts will not regard the grant of a prior secret patent abroad as a bar to patenting in the United States, provided the secrecy is imposed by operation of law and not merely at the option of the patentee.

The Manual of Patent Examining Procedure, section 901.5 (*a*) and (*b*) sets out for a number of countries the dates which are customarily used by the U.S. Patent Office in the identification of foreign patents cited as references.

There are a number of decisions and rulings which are significant in considering the effective dates of patents of specific foreign countries, and these are summarised in the following notes.

(a) Belgium

In the case *Re Ekenstam*, 118 USPQ 349, it was ruled by the

Court of Customs and Patent Appeals that " patented " in section 102 (*a*) and (*b*) is limited to patents which are available to the public and that since a Belgian patent is not so available prior to its " brevet publié " date, it does not become a patent, within the meaning of the statute, until that date; it is not available as a reference as of its " brevet octroyé " date. The Court also held that there is nothing in the nature of a patent which requires it to be printed. A Belgian patent is a patent on its " brevet publié " date, even though it is not printed at that time and is only open to inspection in typewritten form, a form which has been held not to be a printed publication; it is thus possible for a document to be a patent without also being a printed publication.

(b) France

The M.P.E.P. sets out that the date of French patents (going back only to number 1,148,401 and for patents of addition to number 67251) to be taken as the effective date *as a patent* (rather than as a printed publication) for reference purposes is the date of the Official Bulletin of the French Patent Office in which the granting of the patent was announced. This followed a change of practice in the French Patent Office whereby specifications of granted patents are now not available to the public until the date of the Official Bulletin, and thus making necessary application of the *Ekenstam* ruling.

No change of practice is indicated with respect to French patents prior to the numbers quoted, so that for such patents the effective date is the date on which the patent was granted, indicated on the printed copies of the specification by the word " delivré."

(c) West Germany

In the case *Ex p. Gruschwitz and Fritz*, 138 USPQ 505, the Board of Appeals held that with regard to German patents the effective date of a patent for the purposes of section 102 (*d*) is the date of publication of the specification (the " Auslegeschrift ") on allowance of the application. This on the ground that patent rights are legally in existence in Germany by virtue of sections 6 and 30 (1) of German Patent Law, and are vested to the fullest extent, when the said publication occurs. The Board stated that their decision indicated a change in Patent Office practice but emphasised that their consideration of German practice had been only of German patents having numbers higher than one million. This decision was followed in the case *Ex p. Beik and Thiele*, 161 USPQ 795, in which the Board also stated that the fact that the rights granted on allowance may be termed provisional and that a patent might not subsequently be granted was considered immaterial, since this did not indicate any difference in the nature of the rights, and that patent rights in connection with any granted German patent may also be wiped out by a proceeding which may be instituted by anyone.

According to Notice in the Official Gazette, Volume 820 Number 1, a German *Gebrauchsmuster* may be cited as a prior patent, effective as of its date of registration.

The position with regard to a German Industrial Design (*Geschmackmuster*) is set out in the case *Re Talbott*, 170 USPQ 281, wherein the C.C.P.A. held that such an Industrial Design may be considered for purposes of applying the statutory time bar of 35 USC 102 (d) and 172 against an application for a United States Design Patent on the same subject-matter. It was further held that an applicant may not avoid the bar by maintaining the subject-matter of the German grant in secrecy, *i.e.* not available for public inspection, until after his United States application has been filed. This decision upheld earlier decisions of the Board of Appeals, in one of which (*Ex p. Weiss*, 159 USPQ 122) the Board had distinguished from the *Ekenstam* decision, pointing out that that case involved secrecy imposed by law and not, as in the *Weiss* case, by option of the patentee.

(d) Italy

In a Memorandum to all Patent Office Examiners dated October 25, 1960, it is pointed out that Italian patents are automatically kept secret for a period of three months (which may be extended to six months) and that the *Ekenstam* decision is therefore applicable to Italian patents. Thus, the effective date, as a prior patent, of an Italian patent is three months and a day after the granting date or, if the period of secrecy has been extended to six months, the effective date is six months and a day after the granting date.

(e) Japan

In the case *Ex p. Iizuka*, 171 USPQ 50, the Board of Appeals held that because of the exclusive rights arising from publication of the specification and claims on allowance of an application, the effective date of a Japanese patent is the date of publication for opposition.

(f) Switzerland

There are two relevant cases, *Ex p. Reuge*, 115 USPQ 51, and *Ex p. Appeal No. 194–38*, 152 USPQ 70, as a result of which the position is:

(1) A Swiss patent issued under the *non-examining* system is effective under section 102 (*d*) not as of the date on which the patent was technically granted but as of the date on which the specification was published;

(2) A Swiss patent issued under the *examining* system is effective under section 102 (*d*) as of the date of publication on allowance.

(g) United Kingdom

In the *Iizuka* case referred to under Japan, the Board in fact considered also British practice and held that the effective date of a British patent under section 102 (*d*) is the date of publication following acceptance. This because on publication an applicant for a British patent receives like privileges and rights as if a patent had been sealed on the date of publication, although he is not entitled to institute any proceedings for infringement until the Patent has been sealed. The Board distinguished from earlier cases wherein it had been held that the British "patenting" date is the date of sealing.

In the cases referred to above it is reiterated that in order to determine whether a statutory bar under section 102 (*d*) applies, one must look to the substance of what is actually done in a foreign country rather than to the form or literal meaning of the language used in such country. While, says the Board of Appeals, a patent right impliedly includes a legal mode for excluding others from infringing upon the patent right, the Board has not been persuaded that the time for exercising such remedy must be coincidental with the date upon which said exclusive right is created.

There appears to be no ground for attributing to "patented" in section 102 (*a*) and (*b*) a meaning different from that attributed to "patented" in section 102 (*d*). Thus the position would seem to be that for any foreign country where exclusive patent rights come into being before the patent is technically granted, then for the purposes of section 102 the effective date of a patent in that country is the date when the rights come into being, or the date when the specification is available to the public, whichever is the later. The statutory bar remains even though a patent is not subsequently issued on the foreign application, or if secrecy is optionally assumed by the foreign patentee and not by operation of law.

Prior printed publication

Hitherto, to be effective a prior publication must be printed, and typewritten specifications laid open for public inspection were not effective. It must be recorded, however, that a typewritten college thesis placed on library shelves in U.S.A. has been held to be effective publication (45 USPQ 594) and a recent decision (148 USPQ 537) indicates that " printed publication " in section 102 might be said to include " a document printed, reproduced or duplicated by modern-day methods, including microfilming, upon a satisfactory showing that such document has been disseminated or otherwise made available to the extent that persons interested and ordinarily skilled in the subject-matter or art, exercising reasonable diligence, can locate it and recognize and comprehend therefrom the essentials of the claimed invention without need of further research or experimentation."

The cited case related to a microfilm available in U.S.A.

It is important to note that by section 119 the benefits of patent priority rights are not available to overcome statutory references cited either as a patent or as a printed publication under section 102 (*b*), nor to circumvent prior public use or sale, as specified in section 102 (*b*).

Obviousness

Section 103 provides that if the differences between the subject-matter sought to be patented and the prior art are such that the subject-matter as a whole would have been obvious at the time the invention was made to a person having ordinary skill in the art, a patent may not be obtained. The case *Re Papesch* (137 USPQ 43) is of significance.

When objection is made under section 103, there may be invoked the special provisions of Rule 131 to present an affidavit to establish that the claimed invention was made in the United States by the applicant before the effective date of the reference relied on by the examiner; by so doing the applicant may prove that at the time the invention was made the subject-matter as a whole would not have been obvious. A foreign applicant can rely only on his Convention date, and the foreign specification, then filed, unless the invention can have been shown to have been introduced into the United States at a sufficiently early date.

Inventions made abroad

It is section 104 that sets out that an applicant may not *establish a date of invention* by reference to knowledge or use or other activity in a foreign country except within the limits of section 119. When no suitable overseas priority can be invoked in respect of the citation of a U.S. or foreign patent, or printed publication, the procedure of Rule 131 may still be available whereby the applicant makes oath to facts showing a completion of the invention in the United States before the effective date of the citation. These facts must be such as to establish either reduction to practice or conception of the invention prior to the effective date of the reference coupled in the latter case with due diligence from said date to a subsequent reduction to practice or to the filing of the application.

It sometimes happens that the U.S. Office will make a citation of a document which was published less than 12 months prior to the date of the U.S. application, but which can be shown without question to be publication of the applicant's own invention so that the applicant is in effect the author of the citation. The applicant does not then require to proceed under Rule 131. He merely shows that the publication is, in fact, that of his own invention and that the authorship is, in effect, his (confirmed by the *Lemieux* decision—115 USPQ 148).

Canada

The novelty requirements for Canada are contained in section 28 and may be summarised as follows:

(1) no prior knowledge or use by others before the invention by the applicant;

(2) not patented or described anywhere in any printed publication more than two years prior to the Canadian application;

(3) not any public use or sale in Canada for more than two years prior to the Canadian application;

(4) if the inventor or his legal representative has earlier filed abroad, the Canadian application must be filed either (a) before issue of any patent to the inventor (or his legal representative) for the same invention in any

other country or (b) if a patent has issued, within 12 months of filing first application in any other country.

By section 29, a Canadian application which has a valid claim to a priority date, under, for example, the International Convention, has the same effect as if it had been filed in Canada on the priority date, except in relation to items (2) and (3) above (s. 28 (1) (*b*) and (*c*)).

Further features affecting novelty appear in sections 43 and 63.

Section 43 empowers the Commissioner to cite any patent against an application filed within two years after the date of grant of the said patent if the Commissioner has any doubt whether the patentee, as between himself and the applicant, is the first inventor. The applicant may overcome the citation by establishing, by affidavit, a date of invention anywhere in the world prior to the earliest date mentioned in the citation. Because of section 29 (2), it would appear that the filing date referred to in section 43 is the actual filing date of the application in Canada and not a priority date. However, the current Patent Office view is that it is the priority date, if any, which is the effective date.

By section 63 a patent or a claim in a patent cannot be invalidated on the ground that there had been prior knowledge or use of the invention by others before the invention was made by the applicant, unless it is established either that:

(*a*) before the date of the application the prior knowledge or use had become available to the public; or that

(*b*) the other person had, before issue of the patent, filed a Canadian application upon which conflict proceedings should have been directed; or that

(*c*) the other person had at any time filed a Canadian application with, under section 29, an effective date earlier than the date of issue of the patent and upon which conflict proceedings should have been directed.

Philippines

The Philippines Act is also based primarily on the U.S. Act and the novelty requirements for the Philippines may be summarised as follows:

(1) no prior knowledge or use by others in the Philippines before the invention by the applicant;

(2) not patented or described anywhere in a printed publication more than one year prior to the application in the Philippines;
(3) no prior public user or sale in the Philippines more than one year prior to the application in the Philippines;
(4) not the subject of a valid Philippines patent granted on an application made before the filing of a later application.

Belgium

According to Article 25 of the Belgian Patent Law, one factor which will invalidate a Belgian patent of invention is the previous patenting of the invention in Belgium or elsewhere. " Previous " here means prior to the application date or Convention priority date in Belgium. If, however, the prior foreign patent was granted to the same patentee as the later Belgian patent, it is possible for the latter to be upheld as a patent of importation. Similar conditions apply where the Belgian patent was granted to an assignee of the foreign patentee.

Commercial use or working in Belgium by third parties, or publication anywhere, prior to the date of a Belgian patent invalidates a patent of invention or a patent of importation, with the important difference, as set out above, that the noxious character of prior publication is restricted in the case of a patent of importation to publications other than those necessarily connected with the grant of the prior patent abroad.

So far as concerns the interpretation given in Belgium to the term " previously patented " in Article 25, these words should be interpreted according to the law of the country in which the earlier patent has been granted. Thus if the earlier patent is a French patent the pertinent date would be the date of application in France because a French patent is dated from the date of application. If the foreign patent is a United States patent, then the pertinent date is the date of grant.

Ireland

The Irish Act of 1964 is based primarily on the United Kingdom Act of 1949, but regard has been paid in drafting to recent and projected changes in international arrangements. One result is that whereas in matters affecting the grant of a patent the standard of novelty would appear to be relative in the sense that novelty can be destroyed only by some prior act in Ireland, after grant the standard appears to be absolute, since in revocation proceedings before the court, a patent may be revoked on proof of prior publication or use anywhere.

The unique requirements of the Irish Act and Rules concerning evidence of novelty to be furnished by an applicant are discussed earlier. So far as examination for novelty is concerned, the examiner must consider any information furnished under these requirements and in addition must make a search to ascertain if the invention claimed has been published in any Irish specification before the date of applicant's complete specification. (He may also be directed to search for publication in any other document.) Further, the examiner is required to ascertain if the invention claimed has been claimed or disclosed in any other Irish specification published on or after the date of applicant's complete specification, but dated prior to that date. In the first case the applicant may clear any citation by showing that he has a priority date not later than the date of publication of the citation; in the second case that he has a priority date not later than the priority date of the citation.

Switzerland

The 1954 Act makes provision for the gradual introduction of examination for novelty and the Act provides for examination initially in respect of:

(*a*) inventions of products made by processes of not purely mechanical nature for the finishing of raw or processed textile fibres of all kinds, as well as of such finishing processes insomuch as they are applicable in the textile industry; and

(*b*) inventions which according to their characteristics specifically belong to the domain of the art of time measurement.

At the present time the Swiss Patent Office has a considerable backlog of work and it has been decided that to simplify the technical examination of applications which do not undergo novelty and patentability examination it will no longer check that all examples described or illustrated are in fact in conformity with the main claim. Examples which are not in conformity with this claim will in particular not be protected by the patent. This is of considerable importance because interpretation in Switzerland is much more restrictive than in other countries.

In addition to the requirement for novelty, it must be borne in mind that to be patentable in Switzerland an invention must show technical progress and inventive merit. Prior to 1962 Swiss practice was such that apart from novelty, a patent could be valid if it involved an important technical advance in addition to small inventive merit. However, the Federal High Court decided in late 1962 that in fact a higher degree of inventive merit is required for Swiss patents than is the case in Germany.

Finally, in Switzerland there is a very rigorous examination into the structure and succinctness of the specification and claims as well as of unity of invention.

CHAPTER 5

POST-ACCEPTANCE

[*Where a section of an Act is mentioned in parentheses following a country the section refers to the Patent Act of that country.*]

Publication: Acceptance

IT sometimes happens that an applicant wishes to avoid premature publication of his invention before some particular date and if applications are to be filed it is important to consider the dates of official publication and acceptance in overseas countries. It may well happen that in certain countries the applicant may have to decide whether to forgo protection or to forgo any claim to priority under the International Convention, in order to secure a desired delay in publication.

In certain overseas countries, there are definite periods within which a patent application must be accepted or be in order for acceptance, and publication will then take place. These periods are:

Australia	12 months, extensible to 21 months, from the date of first report arising out of examination.
Bahamas	12 months from application.
Bangladesh	18 months from application—extensible by 3 months.
India	15 months from date of first statement of objections by Controller.
Ireland	5 years from date of filing complete specification—extensible.
Malawi	18 months from application—extensible by 3 months.
New Zealand	15 months from date of filing complete specification—extensible by 3 months.
Pakistan	18 months from application—extensible by 3 months.
Rhodesia	18 months from lodging complete specification—extensible by 3 months.

South Africa	18 months from application—extensible by 3 months.
U.K.	2½ years from date of filing complete specification—extensible by 3 months.
Zambia	30 months from application—extensible by 3 months.

With regard to New Zealand, it is important to note that on his first report the examiner extends the period of acceptance to end 15 months after the date of the report.

In the following countries it is possible formally to postpone acceptance for specific periods which are as follows:

Australia	12 months, extensible to 21 months, from date of first report arising out of examination.
Belgium	6 months postponement of grant and publication.
France	18 months from date of application or date of priority.
W. Germany	15 months from date of application or date of priority.
India	18 months from date of first statement of objections by Controller.
Ireland	15 months from filing complete specification.
New Zealand	18 months from filing complete specification.
Malawi	18 months from date of application.
Rhodesia	18 months from date of filing complete specification.
U.K.	15 months from filing complete specification.
Zambia	18 months from date of application.

There are moreover certain countries where applications are laid open to public inspection at the end of definite periods if the application has by then not been accepted. These are:

Australia	18 months from filing complete specification (and abstract printed)—whether Convention or not.
Bangladesh	18 months from earliest priority date.

Brazil Denmark Finland France W. Germany Ireland Japan Netherlands Norway Sweden	18 months from earliest priority date or from filing date if no priority claimed.
Pakistan	18 months from earliest priority date.
South Africa	18 months from earliest priority date.

Delay in publication may also be securable by the filing of applications without any priority claim and accompanied by provisional rather than complete specifications. In certain countries it may well be possible to delay filing until patents of importation can be obtained.

Finally, there are numerous countries where the procedure is such that early publication must readily or inevitably occur merely because there is little or no more than a formal examination of documents, for example Portugal and Jamaica, and where any effort to delay publication may well fail.

When aiming to secure delayed publication in overseas countries, it is desirable to have a definite date in mind and it is important that overseas agents should be instructed that there is to be maximum delay in publication (or some suitable period set) and that publication should not be allowed to occur without specific authority. Notwithstanding these precautions it is, of course, possible for acceptance and publication to take place by error despite formal requests to the contrary.

In some countries where there is a proper examination and an effective novelty search publication can be delayed by holding up replies to official actions and taking all extensions possible for replying thereto.

Amendment before Grant

A situation often arises when it is desirable for an applicant voluntarily to amend his specification or claims while the application is pending. However, two points should be noted. In the first place, in many countries there is a relatively short period between filing and grant, and the time factor is therefore of importance. Secondly, it must be borne in mind that any amendment having a broadening effect will probably necessitate post-dating of the application.

With the exceptions noted at the end of the list, it does *not* appear possible voluntarily to amend before grant in the following:

African & Malagasy Union
Algeria
Antigua
Barbados
Belgium
Bolivia
Br. Virgin Islands
Burundi
Cambodia
Chile
Colombia
Costa Rica
Dominica
Dominican Republic
Fiji
France
Greece
Grenada
Guatemala
Guinea
Haiti
Honduras
Indonesia
Iran
Iraq
Jamaica
Laos
Lebanon
Liberia
Luxembourg
Mali
Malta
Monaco
Montserrat
Morocco
Nigeria
Panama
Paraguay
Peru
Roumania
Rwanda
St. Christopher
St. Lucia
St. Vincent
Salvador
Seychelles
S.W. Africa
South Korea
Syria
Trinidad & Tobago
Tunis
Turkey
Uruguay
Venezuela
Vietnam
Zaïre

In Belgium, Burundi, Rwanda and Zaïre, no amendment may be made in an application, but the applicant (or patentee) may at any time file a so-called " letter of correction " setting out the corrections which he would wish embodied in the specification. This letter is attached to the patent and any person asking for a copy of the present specification receives also a copy of this letter. The courts alone are competent to decide whether the corrections desired by the applicant can be admitted.

In Brazil, an applicant is entitled voluntarily to amend his specification, claims, drawings and abstract only in the following instances:

(1) to correct typographical errors;

(2) to clarify, specify or restrict the application, if this is essential, but only up to the date of request for examination;

(3) in response to Official Actions.

In France, generally speaking, amendment of a specification is permissible only in respect of clerical errors. Amendment of the claims to overcome an objection that the specification is not in proper form is not covered either by the Law or the Decree. The latter merely stipulates that an applicant may present "observations" to the Patent Office within three months from the receipt of the objection. It is therefore not clear whether amendment of claims would be interpreted by the Patent Office as "observations" and accepted by them as such. If an application is divided, the applicant is allowed to make amendments to the main specification and claims, but within narrow limits. Thus, it is not permissible either to add new claims or to modify existing claims except by amendment consequential on the limitation or from the requirements of the wording. It is permissible to amend the claims of an application following documentary notification but consequential amendment of the specification is not permissible. In the case of applications not subject to novelty examination it is permissible to file new claims at any time before grant but, as stated above, amendment of the specification is permissible only for correcting clerical errors.

In the African and Malagasy Union, Algeria, Cambodia, Guinea, Laos, Mali, Monaco, Morocco, Tunis and Vietnam, no amendment of any kind may be made in an application after filing, but any obvious clerical error may be corrected at any time before grant. In Luxembourg, an obvious error may be corrected within four months of filing.

In West Germany, up to the decision to publish the provisional patent, amendments are permissible provided they do not broaden the scope of the subject-matter of the application. However, before the filing of the petition for examination the only allowable amendments are those for correction of obvious errors, the removal of defects to which the examiner has called attention, or the addition to or correction of the statement of claim.

In those countries where there is an examination for novelty of subject-matter, it will be possible for an applicant to make any amendments he may desire at the time when novelty or subject-matter amendments are being effected.

Special Points

A. Canada—supplementary disclosure

This procedure is peculiar to Canada, but may be regarded as akin to a patent of addition or a U.S. continuation-in-part.

Under Canadian practice, no amendment is permitted that describes matter not shown in the drawings or reasonably to be inferred from the specification as originally filed, and no amendment to the drawings that adds matter not described in the disclosure (Rule 52). Where an amendment is not permissible under Rule 52, but describes matter so intimately associated with the matter described in the disclosure that the patent to be issued on the application should have regard to the new matter, then the new matter may be made the subject of a separate supplementary disclosure which is attached to and forms part of the patent as issued and is taken as having been filed on the day upon which the amendment was applied for. An application containing a supplementary disclosure is not allowable if the application contains no claims supported by the principal disclosure.

A supplementary disclosure can claim priority from an earlier foreign application filed not more than 12 months prior to the supplementary disclosure.

Only one supplementary disclosure may be filed (Rule 56).

There must be complete identity of inventors as between the supplementary disclosure and the application.

A supplementary disclosure can be granted only up to allowance of the application (Rule 55), but a forfeited application under section 75 can be restored and is subject to re-examination.

The supplementary disclosure takes the form of a separate addition at the end of the principal disclosure and a separate set of claims headed "Claims supported by Supplementary Disclosure," at the end of the original claims. Allowance of a supplementary disclosure is requested in the form of a letter setting out the amendment desired, with duplicate copies of the amended pages and the fee of $50.00. The request should state that the amendment is for the purpose of inserting as supplementary disclosure new matter which is intimately associated with the matter described in the application as previously framed (Rules 53–57).

An alternative to a supplementary disclosure would be to abandon the application, rewrite the specification and claims and file a new application in the absence of a statutory bar, *e.g.*, before grant of any patent on the original case, in any country, if the original convention period has expired.

B. Final rejection

(i) *Canada*

A second action on an application, by an examiner on the same ground as the first action, may be made final. A notice to the applicant of any final action must bear the notation "Final Action" and must prescribe the time within which the applicant may amend the application as required by the examiner or lodge a request that the action by the examiner be reviewed by the Commissioner.

After receipt of a Final Action an applicant may not amend his application except:

(a) by cancellation of rejected claims;

(b) as required by the examiner in the disposition of the Final Action;

(c) by permission of the Commissioner; or

(d) by order of the Exchequer Court if an appeal was lodged.

Failure to meet the examiner's requirements in the Final Action, or to request review by the Commissioner, will result in the application being deemed to be abandoned.

(ii) *U.S.A.*

The subject is discussed on pages 239 and 240.

C. Amendment after allowance

(i) *Canada*

After allowance of a Canadian application, the applicant cannot amend his application as of right, but the Commissioner may exercise his discretion and allow an amendment presented before payment of the final fee, provided that the result of the amendment will not necessitate a further search by the examiner in respect of the application. This procedure does not operate to extend the time for payment of the final fee (Rule 76).

(ii) *U.S.A.*

Amendments after allowance of an application are not permitted as a matter of right. However, such amendments may be made if filed not later than the date the issue fee is paid, on the recommendation of the primary examiner, approved by the

Commissioner, without withdrawing the case from issue (Rule 312).

Printing of Specifications

In the following countries, the specification is printed, either on acceptance of the application or on issue of the patent:

African & Malagasy Union	France	Poland
Australia	E. Germany	Roumania
Austria	W. Germany[1]	South Korea
Bangladesh	Hungary	Sweden
Belgium	India	Switzerland
Bulgaria	Ireland	United Arab Republic
Canada	Italy	United Kingdom
Czechoslovakia	Japan	U.S.A.
Denmark	Morocco	U.S.S.R.
Finland	Netherlands[1]	Yugoslavia
	Norway	
	Pakistan	

[1] Also printed on laying-open to public inspection.

In the above countries photographic or manuscript copies are normally obtainable when there is delay in printing. Such copies are similarly obtainable in countries which do not print their specifications.

Opposition

In certain countries provision is made whereby any interested party may oppose the grant of a patent in respect of an application which has been passed by the examiner to acceptance. The normal practice is upon acceptance to advertise the fact in the official journal, gazette or the like and simultaneously to lay the specification and claims open to public inspection and the period allowed for opposition counts from the date of advertisement and laying open. Any variance with the normal procedure is marked in the following list of countries which provide for opposition proceedings:

Country	*Period*	*Country*	*Period*
Albania	3 months	Australia	3 months (with possibility 3 months extension)
Antigua	3 months		

Country	*Period*
Austria	4 months
Bahrain	2 months
Bangladesh	4 months
Barbados	2 months
Bermuda (U.K. Regns. only)	2 months
Bolivia	30 days
Brazil	90 days
Br. Honduras	21 days (6 months U.K. Registrations)
Br. Virgin Islands	3 months
Chile	30 days
Colombia	60 days
Cuba	2 months
Czechoslovakia	3 months
Denmark	3 months
Dominica	3 months
Ecuador	90 days
Fiji [1]	3 months (2 months if registration of U.K.)
Finland	3 months
W. Germany	3 months
Grenada	2 months
Guatemala	1 month
Guernsey	7 days
Guyana	2 months
Honduras	90 days
Hungary	3 months
Iceland	12 weeks
India	4 months
Iran	Probably 30 days
Ireland	3 months
Israel	3 months
Japan	2 months
Jersey	2 months
Jordan	2 months
Kuwait	2 months
Libya	2 months
Malawi	3 months
Malta	2 months
Mauritius	1 month
Montserrat	3 months
Netherlands	4 months
New Zealand	3 months (extensible by 1 month)
Nicaragua [1]	30 days
Norway	3 months
Pakistan	4 months

[1] As regards these territories:

Fiji: The applicant advertises the application twice in the official gazette and once in a local newspaper. The period for opposition counts from the date of the *first* advertisement.

Nicaragua: An abridgment is published three times within 30 days in the official journal and the period counts from the date of the *last* advertisement.

Panama: The application is published twice in the official gazette and the period counts from the date of the *first* advertisement.

Peru: The applicant advertises it in *El Peruano* during six consecutive days and the period counts from the date of the *last* advertisement.

Salvador: Applications are published three times and the period counts from the date of the *last* advertisement.

Uruguay: Applications are published for 10 consecutive days in the official journal and in a Montevideo newspaper and the period counts from the date of the *last* advertisement.

Venezuela: The application is advertised, at applicant's expense, in a Caracas newspaper three times at intervals of 10 days and thereafter once in the *Industrial Property Bulletin*. The period counts from the date of the *last* advertisement.

Country	*Period*	*Country*	*Period*
Panama [1]	90 days	Sri Lanka	3 months
Peru [1]	30 days	Sweden	3 months
Poland	3 months	Switzerland	3 months (only for applications examined for novelty)
Portugal	3 months	Taiwan	2 months
Rhodesia	3 months (extensible)	Tunis	2 months
Roumania [2]	3 months	United Arab Republic	2 months
St. Christopher	3 months	United Kingdom	3 months
St. Lucia	2 months	Uruguay [1]	20 days
St. Vincent	2 months	Venezuela [1]	60 days
Salvador [1]	90 days	Yugoslavia	3 months
Seychelles	2 months	Zambia	3 months
South Africa	3 months (extension possible)		
South Korea	2 months		

[2] If the examination shows that the requirements for the existence of a patentable invention are satisfied, a patent will be granted. The decision to grant the patent may be opposed within three months from announcement of the decision.

Amendment after Grant

Unlike amendments before grant there are relatively few countries which permit voluntary amendment of a specification after grant and these are as follows:

Argentine (certificate of correction)	Guyana	Nigeria
Australia	Haiti	Pakistan
Bahamas	India	Philippines
Bangladesh	Iraq	Poland
Barbados	Ireland	Rhodesia
Bermuda	Israel	South Africa
Br. Honduras	Jamaica	South Korea
Canada	Japan	Taiwan
Colombia	Jordan	Trinidad & Tobago
France	Kuwait	U.K.
E. Germany	Libya	U.S.A.
W. Germany	Malawi	Zambia
	Mauritius	
	New Zealand	

Under sections 29 and 31 of the United Kingdom Patents Act 1949 amendment of a complete specification after acceptance is permissible only if the amendment is by way of disclaimer, correction or explanation. Further, except for correcting an obvious mistake, the amended specification must not claim or describe matter not in substance disclosed in the unamended specification and each claim of the specification as amended must fall wholly within the scope of the specification before amendment. Any amendment may be the subject of opposition. Substantially similar provisions appear in the laws of the following countries:

Australia (ss. 77–89)
Bahamas (s. 16)
Bangladesh (s. 17)
Barbados (s. 21)
Guyana (s. 25)
India (s. 59)
Ireland (s. 37)
Israel (s. 65)
Jordan (s. 18)
Malawi (s. 41)
New Zealand (ss. 38–40)
Pakistan (s. 17)
Rhodesia (s. 37)
South Africa (s. 37)
Zambia (s. 41)

In Bermuda (s. 7), British Honduras (s. 33), Jamaica (s. 34) and Trinidad & Tobago (s. 7), the amendment is referred to as a disclaimer. Opposition may be entered in each of those countries with the exception of Bermuda.

In France, Colombia and Nigeria the permissible amendment is by way of renunciation of the entire patent or one or more of the claims.

In West Germany an amendment, including the addition of further embodiments of the invention, is permitted but must not go beyond the scope of the invention as defined in the original application. Also the patentee may restrict his patent to part of its original scope with a view to avoiding a possible nullity action or to take account of the state of the prior art. If any amendment submitted appears to amount to a broadening instead of a limitation the amendment may form a ground for a nullity action.

In East Germany the authorities appear to be lenient in permitting amendment of claims or amplification or modification of the specification.

In Japan a patentee is permitted to demand a trial hearing for amendment of the specification or drawings but only in the case of (a) reduction of the scope of the claim; (b) correction of a mistake; (c) explanation of an ambiguous statement.

There are certain similarities between the permissible amendments after grant in Canada, the Philippines and U.S.A., but they are substantially different from other countries. They may be set out as follows:

Disclaimer

Under section 51 of the Canadian Act, when a Canadian patentee has by mistake, accident or inadvertence and without any wilful intent to defraud or mislead the public, claimed more than he was entitled to, or claimed any material or substantial part of which he was not the inventor, he may, on payment of a fee of $5, disclaim such part or parts. By disclaimer, one merely limits the scope of the claims of a granted patent by reducing the generality of expressions which these claims contain, but without introducing new elements into the claims. Once a disclaimer is filed, its registration follows practically immediately without examination by the Patent Office. Disclaimers may be made at any time during the life of a patent, but once made cannot be withdrawn.

In January 1970 the Canadian Commissioner issued a statement in the following terms:

> "In view of the increased filings of disclaimers in which patentees are attempting to give up only some of the subject-matter covered by individual claims, practitioners are advised that the Office will record disclaimers only when directed to complete claims. Where section 51 (1) refers to disclaimer of 'parts' of the invention, it will be interpreted as relating only to complete claims.
>
> It may be noted that section 64 also refers to 'parts' of a patent. Since the only parts of a patent other than the whole which may be declared void under section 64 (when read in conjunction with section 62) are claims, I consider the same interpretation for 'parts' of the invention must be used in interpreting section 51. Furthermore, the introduction of new claims and the amendment of claims already issued is contrary to the meaning of the word 'disclaimer' and it is improper to renounce a claim to something by attempting to claim something else. It is also apparent from the nominal fee charged for disclaimer that it must be considered a simple clerical matter, and one which would not require an assessment of new claims."

Under section 253 of the U.S. Law whenever, without any deceptive intention, a claim of a patent is invalid, remaining claims are not thereby rendered invalid. A patentee, whether of the whole or any sectional interest therein may, on payment of the fee required by law, make disclaimer of any complete claim, stating therein the extent of his interest in such patent. The disclaimer is in writing and is recorded in the Patent Office; thereafter it is considered as part of the original patent to the extent of the interest possessed by the disclaimant and by those claiming under him.

Similarly, any patentee or applicant may disclaim or dedicate to the public the entire term or terminal part of the term of the patent granted or to be granted: Rule 321, fee $15.

Section 24 of the Philippines Act makes provision for the surrender of a patent or of any claim or claims of the patent and under the former Rule 90 of the 1948 Rules, the procedure for disclaiming was set out. However, there is no reference to this procedure in the 1953 Rules, but reissue is provided for.

Reissue patents

These are discussed in detail on pages 22 to 25.

Publication, Printing and Sealing Fees

In many countries the applicant is, on completion of examination, required to pay special fees before issue of the patent. These fees may be grouped as:

(1) publication and/or printing;

(2) sealing, final, issue.

A publication fee is one paid in respect of the cost of advertising acceptance of a patent application in the local gazette. In some cases it takes the form of a fixed government fee; in other cases (mainly within the British Commonwealth) it is a fee in the sense that the applicant is responsible for, and pays the cost of advertising acceptance.

A printing fee is one paid in respect of the cost of printing the specification so that the fee in any particular country will vary with the length of the specification and the number of sheets of drawings. In some countries a printing fee is payable only if the specification and/or drawings exceed certain prescribed limits.

There is no real difference, other than one of nomenclature, in the terms " sealing," " final " and " issue." In each case the fee is one payable for issue of the letters patent.

1. *Publication and Printing Fees*

Countries in which publication or printing fees are payable are as follows:

(a) Publication

African & Malagasy Union [1]	W. Germany	Montserrat
Algeria [1]	Iran [1]	Netherlands
Antigua	Israel	Rhodesia
Bermuda [1]	Jordan	St. Christopher
Bolivia	Kuwait	South Africa
Br. Virgin Islands	Laos [1]	Syria [1]
Bulgaria	Lebanon [1]	Trinidad & Tobago [1]
Cambodia [1]	Libya	United Arab Republic
Dominica	Luxembourg [1]	Yugoslavia [2]
France [1]	Malawi	Zambia
	Monaco [1]	
	Morocco [1]	

[1] In these countries the fee is normally paid on filing.
[2] In Yugoslavia the first annuity is also payable with the publication fee.

(b) Printing

Austria	France	Portugal
Bulgaria	Hungary	Sweden
Canada	Italy	Switzerland
Czechoslovakia	Morocco	United Arab Republic
Denmark	Norway	Yugoslavia
Finland	Poland	

In Italy and Portugal the printing fee is payable on filing.

In Austria, France, Italy, Morocco and Switzerland, printing fees are payable only if the specification exceeds a certain stipulated length or if the number of sheets of drawings exceeds a stipulated number.

In Czechoslovakia and Hungary the first annuity is payable with the printing fee; in Austria the period set for payment of the printing fee (if any) and for the first annuity is the same.

In United Arab Republic and Poland accrued annuities are also payable at this stage.

2. *Sealing, Final or Issue Fees*

Countries in which sealing, final or issue fees are payable are as follows:

Sealing	*Final*	*Issue*
Antigua	Argentina	Bahamas
Australia	Brazil	Bolivia
Bangladesh	Canada	Ecuador
Br. Honduras	Chile	E. Germany
Br. Virgin Islands	Cuba	Haiti
Costa Rica	Dominican Republic	South Korea
Denmark	Honduras	Sweden
Dominica	Mexico	U.S.A.
Fiji	Paraguay	U.S.S.R.
Finland	Spain	Venezuela
Grenada		
Guyana		
India		
Ireland		
Jamaica		
Jordan		
Malawi		
Mauritius		
Montserrat		
Nepal		
New Zealand		
Norway		
Pakistan		
Rhodesia		
St. Christopher		
St. Lucia		
St. Vincent		
South Africa (payable on filing)		
Sri Lanka		
Turkey		
U.K.		
Zambia		

When payment of the final fee is made in Mexico, it is necessary also to pay any accrued annuities; when paying the final fee in Brazil and Spain it is necessary also to pay the first annuity.

In the Argentine the fee is in fact the second half of a tax of which the first half is payable on application. The second half may be paid in one sum or in equal instalments over the period for which the patent is granted.

CHAPTER 6

TERMS OF PATENTS

WE are concerned here with two separate factors, one the term in years for which a patent is granted, the other the date from which that term starts.

Various reasons have been advanced as determining an equitable term, for example, the philosophical concept of civil rights, economic conditions and industrial conditions prevailing in the particular country, as a sufficient reward for the inventor's creative power. In fact, in any given state, a compromise will be made.

The Venetian Law of 1474 set a term of 10 years, whilst the British Statute of Monopolies of 1623 set one of 14 years or under. It has been said that the latter term was arrived at as being double the time, limited by law, of apprenticeship. The 14-year term was not unnaturally adopted as standard in the British Empire (with the exception of Bahamas and Canada). At the present time there is a variety of terms throughout the world. The former 14-year term of the United Kingdom still prevails in many parts of the Commonwealth but has been replaced in others by the present 16-year term. It will be seen from the following list that the most popular term is one of 15 years. The 17-year term is peculiar to Scandinavia and to the U.S.A., Canada, Cuba and the Philippines. The 20-year term may well set the pattern in the future.

At the present time there are five different dates from which the term may commence, namely: priority; application; complete specification; publication; grant.

One might endeavour to relate the term and date of commencement to the particular examination system (or lack of a system) prevailing in the country. Thus, it would not appear unreasonable in countries with strict examination systems to commence the term as from publication or even issue, and in countries with no examination as from application or registration (in the main there is no great length of time between these two). However, inspection of the attached list will show that there is no consistent pattern.

Term in years	*Commencement of Term*				
	Priority	*Application*	*Complete specification*	*Publication*	*Grant*
3–12					Ecuador[1]
5 or 10					Venezuela[6]
5, 10 or 15					Argentine[6] Dominican Rep.[6] Panama[6] Salvador[6]
5, 10, 15 or 20		Iran[6]			Chile[3, 6]
5, 10 or 20		Vietnam[6]			Haiti[6]
10					Nicaragua Peru
10, 15 or 20					Honduras[6]
12				SouthKorea[12]	Colombia[14]
14	Sri Lanka[2]	Barbados Br. Honduras Grenada India[17] Jamaica[9] Malta Mauritius St. Lucia St. Vincent Seychelles S. W. Africa			Antigua Br. Virgin Is. Dominica Fiji Montserrat St. Christopher Trinidad/ Tobago
15		Albania Brazil[11] Bulgaria Czecho-slovakia Greece Iraq Italy Kuwait[4] Lebanon Libya[4] Mexico[5] Paraguay Poland Roumania Syria		Japan[10] Yugoslavia	Bolivia Guatemala Iceland Nepal Portugal Uruguay

Term in years	*Commencement of Term*				
	Priority	*Application*	*Complete specification*	*Publication*	*Grant*
		Taiwan Turkey U.A.R.[4] U.S.S.R.			
16	Bangla-desh[2] Pakistan[2]	Bahamas Jordan	Australia Guyana Ireland[7] Malawi New Zealand S. Africa United Kingdom Zambia		Bermuda
17		Denmark Finland Norway Sweden			Canada Cuba Philippines U.S.A.
18		W. Ger-many* E. Ger-many* Switzerland *(day following appln. date)		Austria	
20		A. & M. Union Algeria Belgium Burundi Cambodia France Guinea Hungary Israel[13] Laos Luxem-bourg Mali Monaco Morocco Nether-lands[8] Nigeria Rwanda Tangier Tunisia Zaïre	Rhodesia [15]		Costa Rica Indonesia Liberia[16] Spain

[1] In Ecuador the term is determined by importance of the invention.

[2] In the three countries Bangladesh, Pakistan and Sri Lanka the term will, in the absence of a priority date, begin on the application date.

[3] The 20-year term in Chile is a term granted only for important inventions and when the inventor is resident in Chile.

[4] U.A.R., Kuwait and Libya. The term is limited to 10 years if the invention relates to processes for the manufacture of foodstuffs, medicines or pharmaceuticals.

[5] If a Mexican patent is not worked during the first 12 years, the term will be reduced to 12 years unless a licence has been granted or offers to license have been made in the *Gazette of Industrial Property* and in suitable local publications (amounting to some 32 advertisements), in which case it will continue for the full term of 15 years.

[6] In those countries with variable terms the applicant normally elects the term on filing. It is possible before grant to extend the elected term in Argentine, Honduras, Iran, Venezuela and Vietnam by payment of additional fees. The terms in Chile, Dominican Republic, Haiti, Panama and Salvador may be extended on application made prior to expiry of the original term.

[7] Ireland. For patents granted before July 13, 1957, on Convention applications, the term runs from the priority date.

[8] Netherlands. (a) Old patents and patents on application with application department at January 1, 1964—18 years from grant.

(b) Patents on old applications not with application department at January 1, 1964—as (c) but 18 years from end of month of O.P.I. if latter period is longer.

(c) Patents on new applications (filed on or after January 1, 1964)—20 years from the 1st of the month following application date—minimum 10 years from grant.

[9] Jamaica. Strictly the patent may bear date as of the day of application or as of the day of sealing or of any other date between the dates of application and sealing.

[10] Japan. This term applies to all patents granted on applications filed before promulgation of the 1959 Act (April 1, 1960). For patents granted on applications filed under 1959 Act the term is 15 years from publication but with a maximum of 20 years from the date of the application.

[11] Brazil. This term applies to patents granted under the 1971 Act. For patents granted under the 1967 Act the term is 20 years from the date of application or 15 years from the date of grant, in case grant takes place more than five years after the filing date. For patents granted under the 1969 Act the term is 15 years from grant.

[12] South Korea. The term can in no case exceed 15 years from the date of application.

[13] Israel. The term for patents granted under the former Act, that is prior to April 1, 1968, was 16 years from application.

[14] In Colombia Patents of Invention are granted for a maximum period of 12 years. There is an initial grant for eight years but the patentee has the right to an extension of four years if he can prove that the invention is being exploited in Colombia or that it has been exploited there during the eighth year of the original term.

[15] For patents granted on applications filed prior to April 1, 1958, the term is 14 years from the date of application.

[16] In Liberia the normal practice is to make the grant for a 15-year term. If the invention is regarded by the authorities as of importance a 20-year term could be granted, but in practice such grants are not made.

[17] This term applies to patents granted under the 1970 Act; but where such patents are for methods or processes of manufacture of substances intended for use, or capable of being used, as food, or medicine or drugs, the term will be five years from the date of sealing or seven years from the date of the patent, whichever period is shorter. Patents granted under the former Act have a term of 16 years from the earliest priority date.

Extension of Term

Relatively few countries, and these mainly in the British Commonwealth, provide for extension of the normal term of a patent. In such countries extension is generally dependent on the patentee not having received what the court regards as adequate remuneration, it being accepted that an inventor, or other person beneficially entitled to a patent, should receive reasonable remuneration having regard to the nature of the invention. In some countries specific provision is made for extension where the patentee has suffered loss or damage (including loss of opportunity of dealing in or developing the invention) by reason of hostilities. In other countries an extension is possible if the invention is regarded by the Government as of special importance, or for some other special reason.

1. *Inadequate Remuneration*

The following countries have provision for extension on this ground:

Antigua	Jamaica	Seychelles
Australia	Kuwait	South Africa
Bangladesh	Libya	S.W. Africa
Barbados	Malawi	Sri Lanka
Bermuda	Malta	Trinidad & Tobago
British Honduras	Mauritius	United Arab Republic
British Virgin Islands	Montserrat	United Kingdom
Dominica	New Zealand	Zambia
Grenada	Pakistan	
Guyana	St. Christopher	
Ireland	St. Lucia	
	St. Vincent	

In the United Kingdom, the term of a patent may be extended if the court is satisfied that the patentee has not been adequately remunerated by the patent. The court may by order extend the term, subject to any restrictions, conditions or provisions as it thinks fit, for a period not exceeding five years or, in an exceptional case, ten years. Such an order may be made even after the term of the patent has already expired.

In considering an application for extension on this ground the court will pay regard to the nature and merits of the invention in relation to the public, to the profits made by the patentee as such (that is to say the total remuneration received by all who were patentees during the life of the patent), and to all the circumstances of the case (including validity). The application for extension must be supported by fully documented evidence.

The application for extension is made by petition to the High Court, after advertisement of intention to apply, which must be presented not more than twelve nor less than six months before expiration of the term, or at such later time as the court may allow, but not later than expiration of the term of the patent. The advertising procedure is such that it should be started well in advance of presentation of the petition.

Only one order may be made under the provisions, but it may be made in addition to any extension granted on the ground of war loss.

Opposition to the making of an order, or a claim to the inclusion in the order of any restrictions, conditions or provisions, may be made by any person within a period which is set out in the advertisements.

The petition for extension may be made only by the patentee.

Renewal fees are not payable in respect of extended terms.

In the following countries the provisions for extension are, in substance, the same as those of the United Kingdom, on which in fact they are based:

Antigua [2]
Australia [1]
Bangladesh
Barbados [2]
British Honduras [2]
British Virgin Islands [2]
Dominica [2]
Grenada [2]
Guyana
Ireland
Malawi [1]
Malta [2]
Montserrat [2]
New Zealand
Pakistan
St. Christopher [2]
St. Lucia [2]
St. Vincent [2]
Seychelles [2]
South Africa [1]
S.W. Africa [1]
Sri Lanka [2]
Zambia [1]

[1] In those countries an exclusive licensee may apply.
[2] In those countries the period of extension will be one not exceeding seven years or, in an exceptional case, fourteen years.

In Jamaica, the Governor has power to insert in any Letters Patent a provision extending the operation thereof for a further term of seven years. An application for extension is made by petition, supported by a Statutory Declaration, at last six months before expiry of the normal term. Possible grounds are that the patentee was unable to exploit the invention in Jamaica because a market could not be developed within the normal term, or that in spite of repeated and sustained efforts the patentee had not obtained a benefit from the patent.

In Kuwait, Libya and the United Arab Republic, a patentee is entitled to apply for an extension for a period not exceeding five years. The extension should be sought during the last year of the normal term of the patent and the patentee must prove that the invention is of special importance and that he has not derived from it remuneration commensurate with his efforts and expenses. The provisions do not apply to 10-year patents, *i.e.* those relating to processes for the manufacture of foodstuffs, medical drugs or pharmaceutical preparations.

In Mauritius there is provision for the grant of patents for a term of fourteen years from the date of the patent, and for such further term, if any, not exceeding fourteen years from the expiration of the first fourteen years as the Governor in Executive Council may think fit to direct upon petition presented by the patentee at any time not more than one year and not less than six months before expiry of the term first granted. The grounds on which an application for extension may be made are not set out and in fact the matter is left entirely to the discretion of the Governor in Executive Council. It is believed that the patentee would be required to prove that he had not received sufficient remuneration during the normal term of the patent, and that because of the nature of the invention and its general utility an extension was warranted.

In Bermuda and in Trinidad and Tobago, there are provisions whereby the Registrar may, with the sanction of the Governor-in-Council extend the term of a patent for any period not exceeding seven years as the Governor-in-Council may direct and may in like manner extend any such further period for any period not exceeding seven years as often as such extension is sanctioned as aforesaid. There are no rules regarding the grounds on which a petition for extension may be filed, the matter being entirely within the Governor's discretion. The petition for extension should be made by the patentee before expiration of the term of the patent and it is believed that there would be required evidence similar to that required in the United Kingdom.

2. *War Loss*

The following countries have specific provisions for extension on this ground:

Australia	New Zealand	Taiwan
Guyana	South Africa	United Kingdom
Malawi	S.W. Africa	Zambia

In the United Kingdom the term of a patent may be extended if the court or the Comptroller is satisfied that the patentee as such, or an exclusive licensee as such, has suffered loss or damage, including loss of opportunity of dealing in or developing the invention, by reason of hostilities between the United Kingdom and any foreign state. An order for extension may be made subject to any restrictions, conditions or provisions, and may be made after expiry of the patent.

More than one order for extension of the same patent may be made on the ground of war loss, and an order may be made even though an order has been made in respect of inadequate remuneration. The aggregate term of extensions granted in respect of war loss, however, cannot exceed ten years.

The provisions are not available to subjects of the foreign state involved, nor to companies managed or controlled, or carried on mainly for the benefit of, such subjects.

The application for extension may be made by the patentee, or by an exclusive licensee, to the High Court (involving the same procedure as with inadequate remuneration) or to the Comptroller who may, if he thinks fit, refer the matter to the court. The application must be made not more than twelve nor less than six months before expiration of the term or at such later time as the court or Comptroller may allow, but not later than expiration of the term of the patent unless it is proved that the applicant has been prevented from making the application by being on active service or by other circumstances arising from the hostilities.

Opposition to the making of an order, or a claim to the inclusion in the order of any restrictions, conditions or provisions may be made by any person.

Renewal fees are not payable in respect of extended terms.

If there are grounds for seeking extension on the ground of inadequate remuneration and also on the ground of war loss it is preferable for the latter issue to be raised first.

The provisions for extension in Australia, Guyana, Malawi, New Zealand, South Africa and Zambia are in substance the same as those in the United Kingdom. In Malawi, South Africa and Zambia the application may be made before expiry of the patent or within two years after cessation of hostilities, whichever is later, and the maximum extension will not exceed the period of hostilities.

In S.W. Africa an extension will be granted if one has been granted on the corresponding South African patent.

Application may be made only by the patentee in Malawi, S.W. Africa and Zambia.

In Taiwan there is provision enabling a patentee who has suffered loss owing to the outbreak of war between the Republic of China and any foreign country to apply for his patent to be extended for a period of five or ten years. The provisions do not apply to patents held by nationals of a belligerent country. The request for extension must contain a statement of the facts regarding the loss suffered from war. Only one extension is permitted.

3. *Miscellaneous*

(*a*) *Canada*: Extension of the term is theoretically possible by promotion of a special parliamentary Bill; in practice it is virtually impossible.

(*b*) *Panama*: On lapse of a 15-year patent the patentee may obtain an extension of five years but only if the Government regards the invention as of sufficient importance.

(*c*) *Salvador*: The duration of a patent may be extended, in an exceptional case, by five years, at the option of the Patent Office. Renewal fees are payable during the extended period.

(*d*) *U.S.A.*: Extension of the term is theoretically possible by promotion of a special Bill of Congress; in practice it is virtually impossible.

(*e*) *Registrations*: If the term of an Australian, British or South African patent is extended, any registration based on that patent may also be extended by lodging a certified copy of the order for extension.

CHAPTER 7

RENEWAL FEES

THE laws of most countries provide for maintenance of patents by payment of so-called annuities or renewal fees. These may be justified on two counts. First the existence of a patent monopoly naturally restricts in some degree commercial and industrial freedom and in those cases where a patented invention is not being exploited successfully it is in the public interest that the dead wood should be cleared. The simplest way is by levying renewal fees, so that the patentee may allow his patent to lapse by non-payment of a renewal fee, if in fact his invention is not commercially successful. Secondly, particularly in examination countries, the cost to the state of granting a patent is considerably greater than the fees demanded from an applicant and it is not considered unreasonable that patentees benefiting from a patent system should help to subsidise it.

There is a great diversity in the amounts and scales of renewal fees in different countries, but generally the fees increase with each year of the patent's life.

Renewal fees are not payable on patents of addition or improvement except in:

Belgium (if in name of 3rd party)	Iran	Roumania
Bolivia	Iraq	Salvador
Guatemala	Lebanon	Syria
Honduras	Japan (if granted on or after April 1, 1960)	Uruguay
		Venezuela

Renewal fees are payable on patents of dependence in:

Albania	Bulgaria	Poland
Austria	Czechoslovakia	U.S.S.R.

Renewal fees are not payable on registration of British patents except in:

Barbados	Bahrain	Sri Lanka

They are also payable on registrations of South African patents in:

Lesotho	Botswana	Swaziland

Of the three countries which grant plant patents as such, no renewal fees are payable in any case in U.S.A. and Cuba, but in South Korea the normal renewal fees are payable in respect of plant patents.

Generally renewal fees are payable on the anniversaries of the date of the patent but are not payable unless and until the patent is granted, and in those states where the patent term commences prior to grant any outstanding fees may be paid up prior to actual grant. In the following states however, renewal fees are payable on the anniversary of the application date, whether or not the patent has been granted:

Belgium	Guinea	Monaco
Brazil	Iran	Morocco
Bulgaria	Laos	Togo
Cambodia	Lebanon	Tunisia
France	Luxembourg	
W. Germany [1]	Mali	

[1] The first fee is payable by the second anniversary of the application date.

The various systems of renewal fees may be grouped as follows:

(1) No fees payable.
(2) Several fees each covering a period of years.
(3) Initial period free, then fees payable annually.
(4) Fees payable annually.

Most countries allow a period of grace for payment of a renewal fee but a surcharge is exacted for belated payment. The International Convention provides for a period of grace of three months subject to payment of a surcharge, and also for the extension of the period to six months or for facilities for restoration of a lapsed patent. (As amended at Lisbon the provisions now call for a minimum period of grace of six months and for restoration facilities.)

In many countries provision is made for restoration of a patent which has lapsed unintentionally, provided application for restoration is made within a limited period after expiry. Even in those countries where no time limit is set for applying for restoration, undue delay in applying may prejudice the application for restoration.

Renewal Fees

1. *No Fees Payable*

Argentina [1]	Fiji	Trinidad & Tobago
Bermuda	Haiti	U.S.A.
Burundi	Jamaica	Zaïre
Canada	Liberia	
Chile	Mauritius	
Colombia	Nepal	
Costa Rica	Nicaragua	
Cuba	Panama	
Dominican Republic	Paraguay	
Ecuador	Peru	
	Rwanda	

[1] The annual fees payable in the Argentine are not in fact renewal fees. They are annuities which are a firm debt to the Argentine Government and are recoverable by law. The law fixes a sum which must be paid for the grant of a patent, and stipulates that one half must be paid on application and that the other half may be paid on grant or, at the option of the applicant, in annual instalments over the term of the patent. If the working requirements of the law are not met the patent will lapse but a patentee's decision to allow his patent to lapse does not relieve him from the obligation to pay for the grant.

2. *Several Fees Each Covering a Period of Years*

(a) Two fees

	1st before end of	2nd before end of		Grace	Restoration
Bahrain	5th yr.	10th yr.		None	None
Br. Honduras	3rd yr.	7th yr.		None	None

(b) Three fees

	1st before end of	2nd before end of	3rd before end of	Grace	Restoration
Botswana (S. African registrations)	3rd yr.	7th yr.	10th yr.	3 mths.	No limit
Iceland	On Issue	5th yr.	10th yr.	6 mths.	None
Jordan	4th yr.	8th yr.	12th yr.	3 mths.	No limit
South West Africa	3rd yr.	7th yr.	10th yr.	3 mths.	None

(c) Miscellaneous

Grenada St. Lucia St. Vincent	1st fee before end of 4th year, then before end of 5th, 6th, 7th, 8th and 11th years. 3 months' grace; no restoration.
Czechoslovakia	1st fee due within 6 months of issue; 2nd fee before end of 5th year, 3rd fee before end of 8th year; thereafter annually. 6 months' grace; restoration 12 months.
Israel	For patents granted on applications accepted on or after April 1, 1968, a renewal fee, in respect of the first 6 years, is payable within 3 months from the date of acceptance; subsequent renewal fees are payable biennially on the anniversary date of the patent. For patents granted on applications accepted before April 1, 1968, renewal fees are payable biennially as from the next renewal date; thus if a renewal fee on an old patent has been paid before that date the next renewal fee will not be due until expiry of the current four-year period.
New Zealand	1st fee due before end of 4th year; 2nd fee before end of 7th year; 3rd fee before end of 10th year; 4th fee before end of 13th year. 3 months' grace; restoration—no limit.
Poland	For patents granted from October 1, 1970, the 1st to 5th years' fees are due on grant. The 6th to 8th years' fees are due at the end of the 5th year from the date of application and thereafter fees are payable annually. For patents granted prior to October 1, 1970, when paying a renewal fee falling in the first or second period of protection, the fees for the unpaid years of the relevant period must also be paid. 6 months' grace; no restoration.

3. *Initial Period Free, then Fees Payable Annually*

(a) First fee due before end of fourth year

	Grace	*Restoration*
Antigua	6 months	None
Australia	6 months	No limit
Bahamas	6 months	None
Bangladesh	3 months	No limit
Barbados	None	6 months
Br. Virgin Islands	6 months	None
Dominica	6 months	None
Guyana	3 months	No limit
Ireland	3 months	3 years
Malta	3 months	No limit
Montserrat	6 months	None
Pakistan	3 months	No limit
Philippines	6 months	2 years
St. Christopher	6 months	None
Seychelles	6 months	None
Sri Lanka	6 months	No limit
United Kingdom	6 months	3 years

(b) First fee due before end of third year

	Grace	*Restoration*
India	6 months	12 months
Japan [1]	6 months	None
Lesotho (South African registrations)	6 months	No limit
Malawi	3 months	No limit
Mexico [2]	12 months	None
Rhodesia	6 months	3 years
South Africa	6 months	No limit
South Korea [1]	6 months	None
Swaziland	6 months	No limit

[1] Japan, South Korea, Taiwan: Strictly there are separate renewal fees for each of the first three years, but they must be paid within 30 days from issue of the official decision of grant in the case of Japan and Taiwan and within six months from allowance in the case of South Korea.

[2] Mexico: The period of grace in fact runs until June 30 of the year following the year in which payment should have been made, regardless of the date of the patent.

	Grace	*Restoration*
Switzerland [3]	3 months	3 months
Taiwan [1]	6 months	No limit
Zambia	3 months	None

[3] Switzerland: Applies only to patents which have undergone a novelty examination. For other patents the fees are due annually.

(c) First fee due before end of second year

	Grace	*Restoration*
Brazil	180 days	30 days
W. Germany *	2 months [4]	12 months
E. Germany *	2 months	12 months

* A period of grace of two months is allowed and if by then a renewal fee has not been paid, the Patent Office issues an official reminder that the patent will lapse if the fee, together with a fine, is not paid, and sets a period for payment. For East Germany the period is within one month from the date of receipt of the reminder. For West Germany, the period is six months from the due date or within one month after receipt of the notification, whichever period is last to expire. Also, restoration is possible if an incontrovertible case is lodged not later than two months after removal of the cause of delay, and in any case within 12 months from the due date. In West Germany the fees are payable although the application is pending.

[4] It should be noted that, in this special case, the due date is included in the two-month period. Thus for an application filed April 1 the renewal fees for the third and subsequent years are due on April 2, but the two-month period ends on June 1.

4. *Annual*

	Grace	*Restoration*
African & Malagasy Union	6 months	None
Albania	None	None
Algeria	6 months	None
Austria	3 months	12 months
Belgium	6 months	2 months
Bolivia [1]	6 months	None
Bulgaria	1 month	None
Cambodia	6 months	None
Denmark	6 months	6 months
Finland	6 months	6 months

	Grace	Restoration
France	6 months	6 months
Greece	6 months	6 months
Guatemala [1]	None	None
Guinea	6 months	None
Honduras [1]	None	None
Hungary	6 months	None
Indonesia	6 months	None
Iran	6 months	None
Iraq	2 months	None
Italy	6 months	None
Kuwait	6 months	None
Laos	6 months	None
Lebanon	6 months	None
Libya	6 months	None
Luxembourg	12 months	No limit
Mali	6 months	None
Monaco	6 months	None
Morocco	6 months	None
Netherlands [6]	6 months	None
Nigeria	6 months	None
Norway	6 months	6 months
Portugal	2 months	12 months
Roumania	6 months	None
Saar	6 months	None
Salvador	None	None
Spain [3]	6 months	No limit
Sweden	6 months	6 months
Switzerland [2]	3 months	3 months
Syria	6 months	None
Tangier [5]	12 months	None
Togo	6 months	None
Tunis	6 months	None
Turkey [4]	12 months	None
U.A.R.	6 months	None
U.S.S.R.	None	None
Uruguay	6 months	None
Venezuela	3 months	3 months
Vietnam	6 months	None
Yugoslavia	9 months	12 months

[1] In Bolivia, Guatemala and Honduras the renewal fees are due by January 31 next following the date or the anniversary date of the patent.

[2] In Switzerland in respect of a patent which has undergone a novelty examination the first renewal fee is due before the end of the third year and thereafter annually.

[3] Spain—the fourth year's fee will not be accepted by the Patent Office if, when the fee is tendered, the working or licence requirements already due have not been effected. Renewal fes are due on the last day of the anniversary month of the date of issue; working or licence formalities are due on the actual anniversary day of the date of issue.

[4] Under Turkish Law No. 492 renewal fees were not required for patents issued on applications filed after November 1, 1964. Payment of renewal fees, however, once more applies to all patents, such fees being due annually on the anniversary of the filing date, subject to the following:

(i) For patents applied for before November 1, 1964, the fees may be paid, with fines, within a period of grace of one year.

(ii) For patents applied for between November 1, 1964, and August 10, 1970, payment of back fees is not called for and it is necessary only to pay fees falling due after August 10, 1970. *No period of grace is allowed for payment of such fees.*

(iii) In respect of patents applied for after August 10, 1970, it has not been made clear whether payment of the second and subsequent fees will be due on acceptance or after grant. *For such fees also no period of grace is allowed for payment.*

[5] Tangier—the fees are payable annually in the month of the anniversary of grant. A further six months' extension is obtainable on a showing of *force majeure.*

[6] Netherlands—the fees are payable annually by the end of the month of the anniversary of grant. Maintenance fees are also payable on applications.

CHAPTER 8

WORKING

SINCE patents are granted to encourage industrial progress, a patent grant may be likened to a contract between a state and an individual; the state gives to the patentee the right to prevent others from making use of his invention under the implied condition that the patentee undertakes to exploit his invention in the state and so permit the community to obtain the benefits thereof, the community ultimately, of course, having the right to exploit the invention freely.

It is, therefore, not surprising that in most countries the patentee who fails to put his invention into practice in the state within a prescribed period may have his patent rights reduced or revoked. Failure to exploit the invention is regarded as an abuse of the monopoly rights, in most countries, and may lay the patent open to compulsory licensing, or to revocation or indeed may result in automatic lapsing of the patent.

It will be recalled that Article 5 of the International Convention sets out that no patent should be revoked for abuse of monopoly rights unless a compulsory licence has proved insufficient to prevent abuses and then only after the expiry of two years from the date of granting the first compulsory licence. An application for a compulsory licence cannot, under the International Convention, be made less than three years from the date of grant of the patent. (Under the Lisbon Amendments that period has been altered to four years from the date of application for the patent or three years from the date of grant, whichever is the longer.) The same article also provides that a compulsory licence should be granted *only* if the patentee fails to justify himself by legitimate reason, *i.e.*, *force majeure*.

In some countries, but only a few, importation of the patented product by the patentee may be regarded in fact as exploitation of the invention in that country.

Over the years there has grown up a practice known as nominal working which is adopted when the patentee in fact is not exploiting the patent in any particular country. Nominal working consists in the insertion of advertisements in suitable trade or official journals offering to sell the patent or to grant licences. Direct offers to parties likely to be interested are often made simultaneously with the advertisement. It is only in a few countries that the practice of nominal working is regarded as having any force in law and basically nominal working is no more than an endeavour to put the patentee into a position, should his patent be attacked for abuse of monopoly rights, to plead *force majeure.*

In a limited number of states it is necessary to produce to the local patent office proof of the actual working of the patent in that country.

1. *No Working*

There is no penalty for non-working in the following countries:

Albania	Fiji	South West Africa
Bahamas	Haiti	U.S.A.
Bahrain	Jamaica	U.S.S.R.
Br. Honduras	Mauritius	Vietnam
Chile	Salvador	Zaïre
Czechoslovakia	Somalia	

Also there are no specific working provisions in those British Colonies or Commonwealth countries (except Guernsey and Jersey) where the only means of obtaining patent protection is by registration of a British patent.

2. *Term*

The normal term for working is three years from the date of grant, except in the following countries:

No period	W. Germany [1]
1 year from grant	Guatemala
	Honduras
	Nicaragua
2 years from grant	Argentina
	Bolivia
	Costa Rica
	Ecuador
	Peru

[1] If it is in the public interest a compulsory licence may be granted to a third party willing to pay adequate remuneration, where the patentee or applicant refuses to grant a licence. This feature operates from publication of the application. Non-working or insufficiency of working is only one reason for grant of a licence.

	Syria
	Venezuela
2 years from date of foreign working	Burundi
	Rwanda
3 years from date of application	Mexico
3 years from date of grant or 4 years from date of application whichever is longer	African & Malagasy Union, Algeria, Austria, Colombia,[1] Denmark, Finland, France, Hungary, Ireland, Israel, Italy, Nigeria, Norway, Rhodesia, Roumania, Sweden
4 years from date of grant	Guernsey
5 years from date of patent	Iran
5 years from grant	Dominican Republic
	Iceland
	Indonesia
1/3 of term	Panama

[1] Colombia. Where application is made for a patent for a process of manufacture of pharmaceutical preparations or active ingredients therefor, or of medicines, beverages or foodstuffs for human or animal consumption or for plant use, the applicant must prove, within one year from filing the application, that he is exploiting the process in Colombia and that he is able to supply the market under reasonable conditions of quality, quantity and price. Otherwise the application will be rejected.

In the following countries extensions of the basic term are available:

Belgium	1 year	Kuwait	2 years	if *force majeure* proved
Bolivia	2 years	Libya	2 years	if *force majeure* proved
Cuba	4 years	Peru	2 years	

3. *Compulsory Licences*

Of the countries where there are penalties for non-working, compulsory licences are not available in:

Argentina	Honduras	Nicaragua
Burundi	Iran	Panama
Costa Rica	Lebanon	Rwanda
Dominican Republic	Liberia	Syria
Ecuador	Libya (except to Govt. Depts.)	Tunis
E. Germany	Morocco	Venezuela

4. *Revocation*

In most countries where there are penalties for non-working there is provision for revocation (possibly only after the failure of compulsory licences) or for automatic lapsing of a patent in the absence of proper working. The following countries do not contain any such provisions:

African & Malagasy Union	Hungary	Norway
Algeria	Iceland	Peru
Barbados	Japan	Philippines
Bulgaria [3]	Kuwait	Portugal
Cambodia	Laos	South Africa
Colombia	Luxembourg	Spain [2]
Denmark	Malawi	Sweden
Finland	Mali	Taiwan
France	Mexico [1]	Tangier
Guatemala	Monaco	Togo
Guinea	Netherlands	Turkey
	Nigeria	Zambia

1 Nominal working is not recognised in Mexico and a Mexican patent cannot be cancelled owing to non-working by the patentee. If a patent is not worked by the patentee during the first three years, from the filing date, a third party may apply for a compulsory licence to the Patent Office. After investigation the Patent Office may grant such a licence. If the patent is not worked during the first 12 years and no licence has been granted the term of the patent will be reduced from 15 to 12 years. However, if a licence offer is inserted during the 12th year in the *Gazette of Industrial Property* and other local publications by the patentee, even if it is not accepted, then the original term of 15 years will be maintained.

2 Patentees are bound to prove the working of their inventions in one of two ways. Either they must prove actual working in Spain or the patent must be placed on the Compulsory Licences Register. In the case of patents of importation, however, actual working must be proved.

3 If a patentee fails to work his invention within three years from grant, an author's certificate may be substituted for the patent.

5. *Importation*

Importation of the patented product ranks as working in:

Cuba	Nicaragua
Hungary	Venezuela

6. *Working in another State*

Ecuador	Working may be effected in any state.
W. Germany	U.S. nationals do not require to work in W. Germany. Swiss and Greek nationals do not require to work in W. Germany if working is being effected in their own country.

Greece	W. German nationals do not require to work in Greece if working is being effected in W. Germany.
Honduras	Working may be effected in any state.
Libya	Under the Libyan law working may be effected in the country of origin of the patentee.
Switzerland	W. German nationals do not require to work in Switzerland if working is being carried out in W. Germany. U.S. nationals do not require to work in Switzerland if working is being effected in U.S.A.
Tangier	Working may be effected in any country of the International Convention.

7. *Repetition of Working*

There must be no interruption of working for specific periods in the following countries:

Africa & Malagasy Union	3 years	Kuwait	2 years
		Laos	3 years
Argentina	2 years	Mali	3 years
Belgium	1 year	Mexico	6 months
Bolivia	1 year	Monaco	3 years
Brazil	1 year	Morocco	3 years
Cambodia	3 years	Nicaragua	1 year
Colombia	1 year	Paraguay	3 years
Costa Rica	3 years	Portugal	3 years
Dominican Republic	3 years	Roumania	2 years
Egypt	2 years	Syria	2 years
France	3 years	Tangier	3 years
Greece	1 year	Togo	3 years
Guinea	3 years	Tunis	2 years
Honduras	1 year	Turkey	2 years
Iraq	2 years	Uruguay	3 years
Italy	3 years	Venezuela	2 years

8. *Nominal Working*

In the following countries nominal working is officially regarded as satisfactory in the absence of actual working:

Bolivia
Bulgaria
Ireland
Lebanon
Nicaragua (for re-working only)
Roumania
Syria
Turkey

In the following countries nominal working may be satisfactory:

Greece
Iran
Luxembourg
Morocco
Venezuela

9. *Force Majeure*

Force majeure may be pleaded in:

African & Malagasy Union
Algeria
Argentina
Australia
Austria
Belgium
Brazil
Colombia
Denmark
Dominican Republic
Finland
Honduras
Iraq
Ireland
Israel
Italy
Japan
Jordan
Kuwait
Libya
Luxembourg
Morocco
Norway
Peru
Roumania
South Africa
South Korea
Sweden
Switzerland
Tunis
Turkey
Uruguay
Venezuela
Yugoslavia

10. *Proof of Working*

Proof of working when done should be filed in in the local Patent Office in the following countries:

Bolivia
Brazil [1]
Colombia [2]
Costa Rica
Cuba
Dominican Republic
Ecuador
Honduras
Iraq [3]
Mexico
Nicaragua
Peru
Spain
Syria
Turkey
Uruguay
Venezuela

[1] This is required only when a compulsory licence or forfeiture of the patent is being sought.

[2] Where application is made for a patent for a process of manufacture of pharmaceutical preparations or active ingredients therefor, or of medicines, beverages or foodstuffs for human or animal consumption or for plant use, the applicant must prove, within one year from filing the application, that he is exploiting the process in Colombia and that he is able to supply the market under reasonable conditions of quality, quantity and price. Otherwise the application will be rejected.

[3] Notification must be given within thirty days from the beginning of working.

The proof generally takes the form of a declaration by the patentee, but in some countries it is merely a declaration by the patentee's agent.

As noted above, for Honduras, working may have taken place anywhere.

CHAPTER 9

LICENSING

Licences of Right—Voluntary Endorsement

[*Where a section of an Act is mentioned in parentheses following a country the section refers to the Patents Act of that country.*]

THE following countries provide for the voluntary endorsement of patents "licences of right," with the general result that thereafter (a) the patentee is bound to grant a licence, on reasonable terms, to anyone who applies for one, and (b) renewal fees payable after endorsement are reduced by one half:

Algeria	Malawi	South Africa
W. Germany	New Zealand	United Kingdom
Greece	Nigeria	Zambia
Ireland	Rhodesia	

Endorsement of the main patent covers also any patent of addition, and vice versa.

With the exception of West Germany and possibly Greece, an endorsement may be cancelled (but the patentee must then pay the balance of any renewal fees paid at the half-rate). In Germany the endorsement cannot be revoked; Greek law is silent on this point.

The specific provisions may be stated as follows:

Algeria—Articles 53 and 41–43

Any applicant or patentee may request endorsement, and when endorsement has been effected, any person may thereafter obtain at any time a licence on such terms as, failing agreement, may be fixed by the court.

Fees applying to patents will be reduced by one half for patents which have been endorsed licences of right.

The patentee may at any time request cancellation of the endorsement and this will be done subject to payment of the balance of any renewal fees paid at the half-rate.

Licences must be in writing, signed by the contracting parties, and must be recorded. Unless the licence provides otherwise the patentee is not precluded from granting other licences under the patent, nor is he precluded from exploiting the invention himself. Licences concluded with foreigners may require the approval of the Minister of Finance and Planning.

West Germany—section 14

Provided an exclusive licence has not been recorded or is not in process of recordal, the patentee can lodge with the Patent Office a written declaration that he is agreeable to allow anyone to use the patented invention in return for reasonable remuneration. Thereafter renewal fees payable are reduced by one half. The declaration covers any patent of addition carried by the main patent, it is irrevocable and it must be recorded. Anyone wishing to use the invention must inform the patentee and must indicate the proposed manner of use. The user is required to make quarterly returns of use and pay the royalties due thereon.

The Patent Office may, on request of an interested party, assess a reasonable remuneration; their assessment may be varied if circumstances warrant it.

Greece—Article 15 (Law 2527)

A patentee may declare his willingness to grant licences on terms fixed by the Ministry of National Economy. The patent is endorsed and thereafter renewal fees are reduced by one half.

Nigeria—section 10

A patentee may request endorsement provided he is not precluded by the terms of any previously registered licence from granting a further licence. On endorsement (a) any person has the right to obtain a licence to exploit the patent; failing agreement between the parties, terms will be settled by the court; and (b) annual fees payable thereafter are reduced by half.

A licensee is not entitled to assign the licence or grant further licences under it.

An endorsement may be cancelled on the request of the patentee provided there is agreement by the holders of any licences granted under this section and subject to payment of the balance of all fees paid at the half-rate.

Other Countries

The provisions in the United Kingdom (ss. 35, 36); Ireland (ss. 37, 38); Malawi (ss. 33, 34); New Zealand (ss. 44, 45);

Rhodesia (ss. 29, 30); South Africa (ss. 46, 47); and Zambia (ss. 33, 34) are substantially identical and are as follows:

(1) At any time after sealing, a patentee may apply for endorsement of his patent " licences of right," and in so doing must state that he is not precluded by contract from granting licences. The Comptroller may call for evidence to establish this fact. The Comptroller will inform any recorded licensee that application to endorse has been made.

(2) Application for endorsement of a patent of addition covers also the main patent; and application for endorsement of a main patent covers any addition thereto. Where a patent of addition is subsequently granted to an endorsed patent, the addition will also be endorsed.

(3) Endorsements are entered in the Register and published in the official journal and in any other manner considered desirable by the Comptroller for bringing the endorsement to the notice of manufacturers.

(4) After endorsement anyone is entitled to a licence on such terms as may be agreed, or as settled by the Comptroller.

(5) Existing licences my be exchanged for new licences on terms as may be agreed, or as settled by the Comptroller.

(6) If the defendant to an action for infringement (other than by importation) agrees to take a licence on terms to be settled by the Comptroller, no injunction will be granted against him and any damages awarded will be not more than twice the amount which would have been payable by him as a licensee.

(7) Renewal fees payable after endorsement are reduced by one half.

(8) Unless the licence provides otherwise, a licensee may call on the patentee to take proceedings to prevent infringement; if the patentee refuses, or neglects to do so within two months, the licensee may institute proceedings in his own name, making the patentee a defendant. The patentee will not be liable for costs unless he enters an appearance and takes part in the proceedings.

(9) An endorsement may be cancelled on application by the patentee and on payment of the balance of the renewal fees, provided the Comptroller is satisfied that there is no existing licence, or if there are that all licensees consent to cancellation of the endorsement.

(10) Cancellation of an endorsement may be applied for by anyone who claims that the patentee is, and was at the time of

endorsement, precluded by a contract in which the claimant is interested, from granting licences under the patent. Such an application may be filed within two months after endorsement in the United Kingdom, Ireland and New Zealand. The period is six months in Malawi, Rhodesia, South Africa and Zambia.

(11) If the Comptroller is satisfied that the patentee was precluded, he will cancel the endorsement and the patentee will be liable to pay a sum equal to the balance of renewal fees which would have been payable had the patent not been endorsed. If that sum is not paid within one month, the patent will cease.

(12) When an endorsement is cancelled, the rights and liabilities of the patentee are thereafter the same as if the endorsement had not been made.

(13) An application for cancellation is advertised and is open to opposition for one month from the date of advertisement.

(14) An application for cancellation of an endorsement of a patent of addition covers also the main patent; and an application for cancellation of an endorsement of a main patent covers also any patent of addition thereto.

Compulsory Licences for Foods and Medicines

In the following countries, namely: Canada (s. 41); Ireland (s. 42); Malawi (s. 36); New Zealand (s. 51); Rhodesia (s. 32); South Africa (s. 48); United Kingdom (s. 41); Zambia (s. 36) any interested party may apply to the Comptroller for a licence, at any time after a patent has been sealed, if the patent is in respect of

(*a*) a substance capable of being used as food or medicine or in the production of food; or

(*b*) a process for producing such a substance; or

(c) any invention capable of being used as or as part of a surgical or curative device.

The terms of any licence granted are settled by the Comptroller who must endeavour to secure that food, medicines and surgical and curative devices shall be available to the public at the lowest possible prices consistent with the patentee deriving a reasonable advantage from his patent rights.

If, in the opinion of the Comptroller, there are no good reasons for refusing an application for the grant of a compulsory licence, the application must be granted. A patentee may appeal against a decision granting a licence.

Any licence granted entitles the licensee to exploit the invention as a food or medicine, or for the purposes of the production of food or medicine or as, or as part of, a surgical or curative device but for no other purposes.

The Canadian provisions, which do not apply to patents for surgical or curative devices, permit the Commissioner to grant also licences to *import medicines* in any form, and to grant an interim licence where he has not finally disposed of an application for a licence, under a patent relating to a medicine, within six months. In settling the terms of licences and fixing royalties or other considerations payable, the Commissioner must have regard to the desirability of making the medicine available to the public at the lowest possible price consistent with giving to the patentee due reward for the research leading to the invention and for such other factors as may be prescribed.

In New Zealand the provisions specifically include the granting of a licence which will permit the licensee to import the patented article. Such a licence is not precluded by section 41 in the U.K., where licences to import have been granted—see, for example, *Hoffmann-La Roche's Patent* reported in 1969 RPC 504.

France

Sections 37 and 38 provide that where required in the interests of public health (for instance, where a patented medicine is not available to the public in sufficient quantities, or if it is of an insufficient quality, or is sold at an excessively high price), a patent for a medicinal product or for a process of manufacture of a medicinal product may be subjected at the instigation of the Minister of Health to a special licence of right system. Such a licence may be granted irrespective of the date of the patent and is available to qualified parties immediately following publication of an order of the Minister for Industrial Property subjecting the patent to the system. Licences may be granted under specific conditions, especially as to duration and scope. Royalty terms must be approved by the Ministers for Industrial Property and Health, and in the absence of agreement between the parties the royalties will be settled by the court.

A licensee may institute action for infringement if the patentee fails, on request, to take action.

The rights under a licence of right cannot be assigned or transferred.

Israel

Section 120 of the new Act provides for the grant of compulsory licences at any time after a patent has been sealed, in respect of:

(*a*) a product capable of being used as, or for the manufacture of, a medicament;

(*b*) a process for the production of a product of the kind set out in (*a*);

(*c*) a device usable for medical purposes, or as part of such a device.

Colombia

At any time the Ministry of Public Health, or other appropriate ministry, may apply to the court for an order subjecting a patent to licensing on any of the following grounds:

(*a*) the patent is of interest for public health;

(*b*) the patent is of importance in the economic development of the country;

(*c*) the patented product has not been made available to the public in sufficient quality and quantity for normal consumption, or the price is excessive;

(*d*) the patent hinders working of another patent.

Once an order has been made any person who can show ability to work the invention, or any public entity, may apply to the Patent Office for grant of a licence.

This form of licence, which is referred to as a routine licence, is non-exclusive and the licensee cannot assign it nor grant sub-licences.

The licence will contain provisions as to the conditions under which it is granted, and the duration and field of application, but will not include royalty terms. These will be determined by agreement between the parties, with the approval of the Patent Office. In the absence of agreement the terms will be settled by the court.

Nigeria

Orders may be made by the Federal Commissioner for Trade providing for the grant of compulsory licences before expiry of the normal working period in respect of patented products and processes declared to be of vital importance for the defence or the economy of Nigeria or for public health.

Any Federal or State Commissioner who is satisfied that it is in the public interest to do so may authorise any person to purchase, make, exercise or vend any patented article or invention for the service of a Government agency. A Commissioner's authority may be exercised before or after the relevant patent is granted, before or after the doing of the acts for which authority is given, and may be given to any person whether or not he is authorised directly or indirectly by the patentee in respect of the article or invention. Further, the Government, authorised persons, suppliers of the Government or authorised persons and agents of the suppliers are exempt from liability for infringement of any relevant patent and from liability to make any payment, whether by royalty or otherwise, to the patentee.

Patentees may be furnished with such information as they require as to the extent of any acts done under a Commissioner's authority.

There are also rendered nugatory the provisions of any licence, assignment or agreement, of whatever date, between a patentee and any person other than the Government or a Ministry in so far as the provisions restrict or regulate the use of a patented article or invention or provide for the making of payments in respect of any such use or are calculated by reference thereto.

During any period of emergency, the powers are available for any purpose which appears to a Commissioner necessary or expedient.

Specific " articles " coming within the scope of these measures include:

(*a*) any drugs or pharmaceutical preparations, substances or materials, and

(*b*) any plant, machinery or apparatus, whether fixed to the land or not after importation.

India

Every patent in force at the commencement of the Patents Act 1970, that is to say on April 20, 1972, in respect of inventions relating to foods, medicines, drugs and chemical substances shall be deemed to be endorsed " Licences of Right " from that date or from the expiration of three years from the date of sealing the patent, whichever is later. Similarly, every patent granted after April 20, 1972, in respect of any invention within the fields mentioned will be deemed to be endorsed from the expiration of three years from the date of sealing. The licence royalty or other remuneration under any endorsed patent relating to foods, medicines or drugs will in no case exceed 4 per cent. of the net ex-factory sale price in bulk of the patented article.

The Controller may, before settlement of licence terms, permit an applicant for a licence under an endorsed patent to work the patent on such terms as the Controller thinks fit.

Chapter 10

CONVENTIONS

[Where a section of an Act is mentioned in parentheses following a country the section refers to the Patents Act of that country.]

International (Paris) Convention for the Protection of Industrial Property

Prior to 1883, the rights of a foreigner to protection in the field of industrial property were dependent mainly on reciprocity between the laws of his own country and those of the country in which he desired to obtain protection. This was generally not a satisfactory position because of the many fundamental differences between the laws of different countries. A Union between various countries was therefore created to provide, as far as possible, for more uniform protection. The basis of this Union has always been that a national of, or a person who has established himself in, any country of the Union, receives the same protection in all other countries of the Union where he may apply for protection as is granted to the nationals of those countries.

The main instrument of the Union is the International Convention for the Protection of Industrial Property. It is concerned with patents, utility models, industrial designs or models, trade marks, trade names and indications of source or appellations of origin and the repression of unfair competition.

The International Convention was signed in Paris in 1883, and has since been revised at Brussels in 1900, Washington in 1911, The Hague in 1925, London in 1934, Lisbon in 1958 and Stockholm in 1967.

The founder members of the Convention were:

Belgium	Netherlands	Switzerland
Brazil	Portugal	Tunisia
France	Spain	United Kingdom
Italy		

There are now 79 members of the Convention, as set out in the table below. Of these, three (Brazil, Dominican Republic and Poland) are bound only by the Convention as revised at The Hague, 17 countries are bound by the Convention as revised at London, 35 by the Lisbon provisions, and 21 by the Stockholm provisions. In addition, Canada and Finland are bound by Articles 1–12 of London and Articles 13–30 of Stockholm; U.S.A. is bound by Articles 1–12 of Lisbon and Articles 13–30 of Stockholm.

Probably the most important feature of the Convention is that contained in Article 4 whereby a person who has duly filed a patent application in a member country is given a right of priority of 12 months for filing corresponding applications in other convention countries. Consequently, a subsequent application filed in one of those countries before expiry of the 12-month period cannot be invalidated by any act whatever accomplished in the interval, nor can such acts give rise to rights of third parties or any rights of personal possession.

International Convention—List of Member Countries

1. *Hague Text* 1925

Brazil
Dominican Republic
Poland

2. *London Text* 1934

Australia
  Territory of Papua and territory under mandate of New Guinea
  Territory of Norfolk Island
  Territory under mandate of Nauru
Canada [1]
Finland [1]
Greece
Holy See
Iceland
Indonesia
Lebanon
Luxembourg
Netherlands
  Dutch Antilles
  Surinam
New Zealand
  Western Samoa
Portugal with Azores and Madeira
San Marino
Sri Lanka
Syria
Tunisia
Turkey
United Arab Republic
Vietnam

[1] Articles 1–12 only.

3. *Lisbon Text* 1958

Algeria
Argentina
Austria
Belgium
Cameroon
Central African Republic
Cuba
Cyprus
Dahomey
France (including Departments of Guadeloupe, Guyane, Martinique, Reunion and Overseas Territories)
Gabon
Haiti
Iran
Italy
Ivory Coast
Japan
Malta
Mauritania
Mexico
Monaco
Nigeria
Niger Republic
Norway
People's Republic of the Congo
Philippines
Rhodesia
South Africa
Tanzania (except Zanzibar)
Togo
Trinidad & Tobago
Uganda
Upper Volta
Uruguay
U.S.A.
  Territories of Puerto Rico, Virgin Islands, Eastern Samoa and Guam (Articles 1–12 only)
Yugoslavia
Zambia

4. *Stockholm Text* 1967

Bulgaria
Canada
  (Articles 13–30 only)
Chad
Czechoslovakia
Denmark
  Faroe Islands
Finland
  (Articles 13–30 only)
Germany (Federal Republic of)
Hungary
Ireland
Israel
Jordan
Kenya
Liechtenstein
Madagascar
Malawi
Morocco
Roumania
Senegal
Spain
Sweden
Switzerland
U.K.
  Bahamas (Lisbon Act)
U.S.A.
  Territories of Puerto Rico, Virgin Islands, Eastern Samoa and Guam (Articles 13–30 only)
U.S.S.R.

East Germany

East Germany is not included in the foregoing list because the position with regard to its membership is confused and there is disagreement among member-states on the question.

The Federal Republic of Germany ratified the Convention as revised at Lisbon in 1958, this being a continuance of the original adhesion of Germany in 1903.

In 1956, the German Democratic Republic (East Germany) declared that it regarded the Paris Convention, as revised at London in 1934, as applicable to its territory. Again in 1964, the German Democratic Republic declared its accession to the Convention as revised at Lisbon, and in 1968 its accession to the Stockholm Text.

The Swiss Government communicated the 1964 declaration to all member-states of the Convention, with the comment that, in its opinion, the fact of notification or reception of such a declaration did not imply recognition of the author of the declaration. Replies received from member-states are summarised in *Industrial Property*, April 1967, in the following terms:

(1) The governments of the following states have indicated that they did not recognise the " German Democratic Republic " as a state, or that they considered the Government of the Federal Republic of Germany as the only freely and legally constituted government to make declarations in the name of Germany and the German people, and most of them have added that therefore they were unable to take cognisance of the declaration or that the declaration was of no (legal) effect or could not be received by them:

Australia	Haiti	Norway
Belgium	Iceland	Portugal
Brazil	Ireland	South Africa
Canada	Ivory Coast	Spain
Denmark	Japan	Turkey
Federal Republic of Germany	Luxembourg	United Kingdom
France	Madagascar	U.S.A.
Greece	New Zealand	Vietnam

(2) The governments of the following states have indicated that the receipt or taking cognisance of the declaration did not imply recognition of the author of the declaration or the " German Democratic Republic ":

Austria	Iran	San Marino
Central African Republic	Netherlands	Sweden
Holy See	Niger	Switzerland

(3) The governments of the following states have indicated that, by virtue of the declaration, they considered the German Democratic Republic as a party to the treaties referred to in the declaration:

Hungary	Roumania

So far as can be ascertained at present the position with regard to the practical issue of filing patent applications with claims to convention priority is:

(*a*) The German Democratic Republic will accept a claim to priority based on the first regularly filed application in any member-state.

(*b*) The only member-states who will accept a claim to priority based on an application filed in the German Democratic Republic are:

Austria	Iran	Switzerland
Bulgaria	Nigeria	U.S.S.R.
Czechoslovakia	Poland	Yugoslavia
Hungary	Roumania	

Location of Member Countries

Before considering the main points of the International Convention, it is worthwhile noting the location of the various member countries:

Europe	31, *viz.*	all independent European states except Albania
Africa	25, *viz.*	Algeria; Cameroon; Central African Republic; Chad; Dahomey; Gabon; Ivory Coast; Kenya; Madagascar; Malawi; Mauritania; Morocco; Nigeria; Niger Republic; People's Republic of the Congo; Rhodesia; Senegal; South Africa; Tanzania (except Zanzibar); Togo; Tunisia; Uganda; United Arab Republic; Upper Volta; Zambia

Asia	12, *viz.*	Indonesia; Iran; Israel; Japan; Jordan; Lebanon; Philippines; Sri Lanka; Syrian Arab Republic; Turkey; U.S.S.R.; Vietnam
America	10, *viz.*	Argentina; Brazil; Canada; Cuba; Dominican Republic; Haiti; Mexico; Trinidad & Tobago; Uruguay; U.S.A.
Australasia	2, *viz.*	Australia; New Zealand

It will be noted that this geographical split up ignores certain colonial territories which are members by virtue of action taken by the mother-country. The colonies or protectorates involved are:

Australia	Territories of Papua, New Guinea, Norfolk Island and Nauru
Denmark	Faroe Islands
France	Departments of Guadeloupe, Guyane, Martinique, Reunion and Overseas Territories
Netherlands	Dutch Antilles, Surinam
New Zealand	Western Samoa
Portugal	The Azores and Madeira
United Kingdom	Bahamas

Principal Provisions regarding Patents

The principal provisions of the International Convention, so far as concerns patents, may be summarised as follows:

(1) Persons within the jurisdiction of a convention country enjoy in other convention countries the same protection in regard to industrial property as nationals of those countries.

(2) For nationals of contracting countries, no conditions are imposed as to domicile or establishment in the country where the Convention is being invoked; but for non-nationals a domicile or establishment is required in some country of the Union.

(3) A maximum period of priority of 12 months is allowed for patents inventors' certificates, and utility models based on the earliest application filed in any convention country.

(4) A subsequent application for the same subject as a previous application filed in the same country of the Union shall be considered as a first application, the filing date of which shall

be the starting point of the period of priority, provided that, at the time of filing the subsequent application, the previous application has been withdrawn, abandoned or refused, without being open to public inspection and without leaving any rights outstanding, and has not served as a basis for claiming a right of priority. The previous application may not thereafter serve as a basis for claiming a right of priority.

(5) An applicant claiming priority shall be required to specify the number of the basic application.

(6) Multiple and partial priorities for aggregated subject-matter are allowable: neither the claim to priority nor the application itself may be refused if there is unity of invention in the subject-matter of the application; added subject-matter giving rise to a right of priority under the usual conditions.

(7) No reservation of third-party rights accrues during the priority period.

(8) Proof of basic applications may be called for.

(9) Convention patents enjoy the same duration as if they had been applied for without benefit of priority.

(10) Importation of patented articles from a Union country by the patentee shall not entail revocation of the patent.

(11) No revocation of a patent for abuse of monopoly rights shall be effected unless grant of a compulsory licence is insufficient to prevent the abuse. No compulsory licence shall be applied for earlier than four years from the date of filing the patent application, or three years from the date of grant of the patent, whichever period last expires, and no revocation proceedings on the score of abuse are permissible before the expiry or two years from the date of the first compulsory licence. A compulsory licence so granted shall be non-exclusive and shall be non-transferable even in the form of a sub-licence, except with that part of the enterprise or goodwill using such licence.

(12) Use of patented inventions on board vessels temporarily in territorial waters. or on aircraft or land vehicles temporarily in a country shall not be considered as an infringement.

(13) Temporary protection shall be accorded for goods exhibited at officially recognised international exhibitions.

The following table sets out the Articles of the Convention, including the Lisbon amendments, and gives notes on the contents of such Articles.

The table is an amended extract from the printed report of the "Second William Henry Ballantyne" lecture given by Mr.

G. W. Tookey, Q.C., in 1955 to the International Association for the Protection of Industrial Property (British Group). The amendments are such as to take account of the changes in the Convention effected at Lisbon in 1958.

Article of Convention	Subject-Matter
1 (1)	Formation of Industrial Property Union.
1 (2)	Field of protection of industrial property.
1 (3)	Definition of industrial property.
1 (4)	Definition of patents.
2 (1)	Enjoyment in any convention country by persons within the jurisdiction of other convention countries of the same rights as nationals.
2 (2)	Domicile not necessary in country where protection is sought.
2 (3)	Reservation of provisions of local laws relative to judicial and administrative procedure, authorisation of agents, etc.
3	Persons within jurisdiction of a country outside the Union but domiciled or established in a convention country to be assimilated to persons within the jurisdiction of convention countries.
4A (1)	Convention priority right.
4A (2)	Every regular application to give rise to priority right.
4A (3)	Definition of regular application.
4B	Subsequent deposit in a convention country, publication or exploitation or use during period of priority right, not to give rise to third party rights.
4C (1)	Periods of priority rights—12 months for patents, 6 months for designs.
4C (2)	Period to run from date of first application, excluding day of deposit.
4C (3)	Extension of period to cover non-working day.
4C (4)	Exclusion of earlier dead application.
4D (1)	Declaration to be made in respect of convention application within a period to be determined by each country.
4D (2)	Particulars of convention applications to be published officially, including number, date and country of previous application.
4D (3)	If a certified copy of previous application is required, three months to be allowed without payment of fee.
4D (4)	Consequence of omission of formalities to be no more serious than loss of right of priority.
4D (5)	Further proof in support of declaration; number of previous application to be specified.
4E (1)	In cases of convention application for registration of a design based on an application for registration of a utility model, period of priority to be that fixed for designs.
4E (2)	Convention application for registration of utility model may be based on prior patent application and vice versa.
4F	Multiple priority patent claims allowed, provided that application relates to a single invention.

Article of Convention	Subject-Matter
4G (1)	Applicant to be allowed to divide without loss of date or rights of priority, where examination reveals more than one invention.
4G (2)	Applicant to be allowed voluntarily to divide without loss of date or rights of priority.
4H	Priority may be claimed in respect of matter disclosed in convention document even though not in the claims.
4 bis (1)	Patent granted in a convention country to be independent of patents granted in other countries whether members of the Union or not.
4 bis (2)	Above provision applies to convention applications.
4 bis (3) (4)	(Transitional provisions only regarding above matters.)
4 bis (5)	Convention patents to enjoy same duration as if they had been applied for without benefit of priority.
4 ter	Right of inventor to be mentioned as such in the patent.
4 quater	Grant not to be refused, nor patent invalidated, on ground that sale of patented product or of a product obtained by means of patented process is subject to restriction or limitations resulting from the domestic law.
5A (1)	Importation of patented articles not to entail revocation of patent.
5A (2)	Countries may take measures providing for the granting of compulsory licences to prevent abuses of patent monopoly.
5A (3)	Revocation not to be ordered unless grant of compulsory licence is insufficient to prevent abuse. No proceedings for revocation to be instituted before expiration of two years from granting of first compulsory licence.
5A (4)	No application for compulsory licence to be made before expiration of four years from date of filing patent application or three years from date of grant of patent, whichever period last expires, and then only if patentee fails to justify himself. Compulsory licence to be non-exclusive and not transferable, even in form of sub-licence, except with that part of the enterprise or goodwill using such licence.
5A (5)	Foregoing provisions apply to utility models.
5B	Design registrations not to be liable to revocation for non-working or importation of protected articles.
5D	No mention of patent or design required as a condition of recognition of right to protection.
5 bis (1)	Extension of time of not less than 6 months to be allowed for payment of renewal fees.
5 bis (2)	In case of patents countries have the right to provide for restoration.
5 ter	Use of inventions on board vessels temporarily in territorial waters, or on aircraft or land vehicles temporarily in a country, not to be considered as infringement.
5 quater	Protection accorded by convention country to patentee of process or manufacture of product against product manufactured in that country to be available also against imported product.
5 quinquies	All convention countries to provide for protection of industrial designs.

Article of Convention	Subject-Matter
10 bis (1)	Protection to be afforded against unfair competition.
10 bis (2)	Every act of competition contrary to honest practices in industrial or commercial matters to constitute an act of unfair competition.
10 bis (3)	All acts creating confusion with establishment, goods or activities of a competitor to be prohibited.
10 bis (3) 2	False allegations in the course of trade of such nature as to discredit the establishment goods or activities of a competitor to be prohibited.
10 bis (3) 3	Indications or allegations in the course of trade liable to mislead public as to nature, manufacturing process, characteristics, suitability for their purpose or the quality of goods, to be prohibited.
10 ter (1)	Remedies in respect of acts referred to in Arts. 9, 10 and 10 bis to be available to persons within jurisdiction of other convention countries.
10 ter (2)	Syndicates and associations representing industrialists, etc., to be entitled to take proceedings to repress acts referred to in Arts. 9, 10 and 10 bis, so far as local law permits such action.
11 (1)	Temporary protection to be provided in respect of exhibitions.
11 (2)	Temporary protection not to prolong periods of priority under Art. 4. If at a later date a right of priority is invoked, period may be dated from date of introduction of goods into exhibition.
11 (3)	Each country may require evidence of identity of object exhibited.
12 (1)	Industrial property department to be established.
12 (2)	Official Journal to be published.
13	International Office at Berne.
14	Revision of Convention.
15	Reservation of right for countries to make special agreements between themselves.
16	Accession to Convention.
16 bis	Notification of application of Convention to colonies, protectorates, etc.
17	Undertaking by each contracting country to adopt, in accordance with its constitution, measures necessary to ensure application of articles of Convention. Act of ratification or accession to be understood as meaning that particular country will be in a position under its domestic laws to give effect to terms of Convention.
17 bis	Duration of Convention.
18	Ratification.
19	Signature.

Amendments to International Convention

The main amendments of The Hague (1925), London (1934), Lisbon (1958) and Stockholm (1967) are indicated in the following notes:

1. The Hague

(*a*) Three months allowed for filing certified copy.

(*b*) Multiple priorities allowable.

(*c*) Plurality of inventions—must at least be allowed division.

(*d*) No revocation for non-working unless compulsory licence insufficient to prevent abuse of monopoly rights.

(*e*) Minimum three months' extension for payment of renewal fees, and either increase to six months or provide for restoration.

(*f*) No infringement by use on vessels of the Union temporarily or accidentally in territorial waters, or by use in construction or working of Union aircraft or land vessels, or of accessories, when such penetrate temporarily or accidentally into the country.

2. London

(*a*) Abolition of third party rights accruing in priority period.

(*b*) Any application equivalent to a regular national application to be recognised as giving rise to a right of priority.

(*c*) Excluded days extended to cover days when Patent Office is not open.

(*d*) Free filing of certified copy within three months.

(*e*) Priority allowable for matter disclosed but not claimed.

(*f*) Convention patents to have same terms as ordinary patents.

(*g*) No application for compulsory licence less than three years from grant; no revocation instituted before two years from first compulsory licence.

(*h*) Inventor has the right to be mentioned as such in the patent.

3. Lisbon

(*a*) By " regular national filing " is meant any filing that is adequate to establish the date on which the application was filed in the country concerned, whatever may be the outcome of the application.

(*b*) A subsequent application for the same subject as a previous application filed in the same country of the Union shall be considered as a first application, the filing date of which shall be the starting point of the period of priority, provided that, at the time of filing the subsequent application, the previous application has been withdrawn, abandoned or refused, without being open to public inspection and without leaving any rights outstanding, and has not served as a basis for claiming a right of priority. The previous application may not thereafter serve as a basis for claiming a right of priority.

(*c*) An applicant claiming priority shall be required to specify the number of the basic application.

(*d*) Multiple and partial priorities. Neither the claim to priority nor the application itself may be refused if there is unity of invention; added matter gives rise to a right of priority under the usual conditions.

(*e*) Division of an application is allowable on the initiative of the applicant.

(*f*) The grant of a patent shall not be refused and a patent shall not be invalidated on the ground that the sale of the patented product or of a product obtained by means of the patented process is subject to restrictions or limitations resulting from the domestic law.

(*g*) The provisions relating to the grant of compulsory licences and revocation have been rewritten; the differences are:

(i) that a compulsory licence cannot be applied for before the expiration of a period of four years from the date of filing of the patent application or three years from the date of the grant of the patent, whichever period last expires, and

(ii) the amended clause sets out that a compulsory licence shall be non-exclusive and shall not be transferable, even in the form of the grant of a sub-licence, except with that part of the enterprise or goodwill using such licence.

(*h*) The period of grace for payment of a renewal fee is increased to six months and the contracting parties have the right to provide for the restoration of patents which have lapsed by reason of non-payment of fees.

(*i*) When a product is imported in a country of the Union where there exists a patent protecting a process of manufacture of the said product, the patentee shall have all the rights, with regard to the imported product, as are accorded to him by the domestic law of the country of importation, on the basis of the process patent, with respect to products manufactured in that country.

(*j*) Industrial designs shall be protected in all the countries of the Union.

(*k*) Each contracting party undertakes to adopt in accordance with its constitution the measures necessary to ensure the application of this Convention, and it is to be understood that at the time an instrument of ratification or accession is deposited on behalf of a country, such country will be in a position under its domestic law to give effect to the terms of this Convention.

(*l*) Patent publications of convention countries to identify convention applications by reference to date of filing, country and application number of previous application.

4. Stockholm

In a country in which applicants have the right to apply at their own option either for a patent or for an inventor's certificate,

(*a*) an application for an inventor's certificate gives rise to a right of priority under the same conditions and with the same effects as an application for patent; and

(*b*) an applicant for an inventor's certificate has a right to priority based on an application for a patent, a utility model, or an inventor's certificate.

The remaining amendments relate to the administrative provisions of the Convention.

Who may invoke International Convention

Article 2 provides that nationals of each of the countries of the Union shall enjoy in all other countries of the Union the advantages that their respective laws grant to their own nationals, without prejudice to the rights specially provided by the present Convention; no condition as to the possession of a domicile or establishment in the country where protection is claimed may be required of persons entitled to the benefits of the Union.

Article 3, however, provides that nationals of countries not forming part of the Union must have a domicile or a real and effective industrial or commercial establishment in the territory of one of the countries of the Union before they can be treated in the same manner as nationals of countries of the Union.

Despite the wording of Article 3, it is believed that the following countries do not require of non-nationals a domicile or establishment in one of the countries of the Union:

Australia	Ireland	Sri Lanka
Bahamas	Israel	United Kingdom
Brazil	Netherlands	U.S.A.
Bulgaria	New Zealand	
Canada	Philippines	
Denmark	Rhodesia	
Greece	South Africa	

In all countries of the Union other than those listed above Article 3 is strictly applied for non-nationals, but it is believed that for these countries if a British national files an application as a communication and if that application is the first to be filed in a convention country then subsequent convention applications could be based on the British application in the name of the British applicant.

Periods allowed for Claiming Priority

In most member-states the claim to priority must be lodged with the application. The following states allow periods of grace for making the claim, reckoned from the date of filing the convention application in the country concerned:

African and Malagasy Union	6 months
Austria	2 months
Belgium	3 months (6 months if publication and grant delayed)
Canada	Prior to payment of Final Fee
Denmark	3 months
Finland	3 months
France	2 months
E. Germany	2 months
W. Germany	2 months
Iran	Before issue
Israel	2 months
Italy	2 months (but within International Convention period)
Lebanon	2 months
Luxembourg	2 months

Monaco	2 months
Netherlands	3 months
Norway	3 months
Poland	2 months
Sweden	3 months
Switzerland	(*a*) No novelty examination. Before registration
	(*b*) Novelty examination. Within 6 months of preliminary decision to publish
Syria	2 months
Turkey	2 months
U.S.A.	Before payment of issue fee

Strictly no period of grace is allowed in the U.K., but if an application is lodged before expiry of a convention period, the priority claim can be added by conversion or amendment of Application Form 1 up to the end of the basic convention period. Similar conditions are believed to obtain in Australia, Bahamas, Ireland, Israel, Malawi, New Zealand, Nigeria, Rhodesia, South Africa, Sri Lanka, Trinidad & Tobago and Zambia.

Multiple Priorities

In certain countries there may be included in one convention application matter which has been the subject of more than one application for patent in a suitable country of origin, and there may be claimed for each portion separately the priority of the respective application in that country, provided that the convention application is filed not more than 12 months after the earliest application of which priority is claimed. Further, the various originating applications need not have been filed in the same convention country. The provisions for multiple priorities first appeared in the Convention by the Hague Amendments (Art. 4 (f)), so that any country which has ratified the Hague Amendments, or the later amendments made at London, Lisbon, or Stockholm, should in theory allow multiple priorities. (In this connection it should be borne in mind that some countries do not regard adhesion to an international agreement as having any effect locally unless and until the agreement has been written into domestic legislation.) There must, of course, be unity of invention, but if in any particular case multiple priorities are refused, the applicant is entitled to divide and to preserve as the date of each divisional application the date of the initial application, and if necessary the benefit of the right of priority.

Partial Priorities

In certain countries there may be included in one application matter for which protection has not previously been sought in the country of origin or elsewhere and for which, therefore, no priority is claimed. In this case, a patent can issue having convention priority for part of the invention claimed, the remainder taking the date of filing in the particular country. In some countries it may be possible to include unpublished matter from an application (for which no priority can be claimed) earlier in date than that on which the claim to priority is based, but this is not possible in the U.K.

In the majority of convention countries, both multiple and partial priorities are allowed, these countries being as follows:

African & Malagasy Union	Haiti	Portugal
Algeria	Hungary	Rhodesia
Argentina	Iceland	Roumania
Australia	Indonesia	South Africa
Austria	Iran	Sweden
Bahamas	Ireland	Switzerland
Belgium	Israel	Syria
Brazil	Italy	Trinidad & Tobago
Bulgaria	Japan	Tunisia
Canada	Lebanon	United Arab Republic
Czechoslovakia	Luxembourg	United Kingdom
Denmark	Malawi	Uruguay
Dominican Republic	Malta	U.S.A.
Finland	Monaco	U.S.S.R.
France	Morocco	Vietnam
E. Germany	Netherlands	Zambia
W. Germany	New Zealand	
Greece	Norway	
	Philippines	
	Poland	

Mexico, Spain, Turkey and Yugoslavia allow multiple but not partial priorities.

The *Mexican* Patent Office requires that the application filed in Mexico be identical with the priority document if only one priority is claimed. If the application covers less or more than what is protected by the priority document, the applicant will eventually be required to choose between amendment to remove the disconformity or abandonment of the claim to priority.

Since the *Spanish* Office does not check the Spanish text against the certified copy, a claim to partial priority could be allowed by the Patent Office, leaving it to the court to adjudicate.

Neither multiple nor partial priorities are allowable in Sri Lanka (multiples are allowed if all are filed on the same day, by the same applicant, in the same country); nor in Cuba.

Post-dates

Section 6 (3) of the British Patents Acts 1949–61 provides for the voluntary post-dating of an application by a maximum term of six months and provided action is taken before acceptance of the complete specification. (In the case of a convention application post-dating cannot be effected beyond the last date on which the application could have been made unless the claim to priority is abandoned.) Voluntary post-dating can also be effected by abandonment of a provisional specification, under section 3 (5). Compulsory post-dating is covered by the terms of section 6 (4).

Voluntary post-dating provisions similar to those of sections 6 (3) and 3 (5) appear in the Patents Acts of Bahamas (s. 10 (6)); Ireland (s. 11 (3) and s. 8 (5)); Malawi (s. 17 (1) and s. 13 (7)); New Zealand (s. 12 (3) and s. 9 (5)); Rhodesia (s. 12 (1) and s. 8 (7)); South Africa (s. 16 (3) and s. 16 (2)); Zambia (s. 17 (1) and s. 13 (7)).

These provisions especially give rise to the questions:

(*a*) Can a valid patent be obtained in other countries under the Convention based on a voluntarily post-dated application and claiming the post-date as priority? and

(*b*) Can the Convention date so obtained be upheld?

Definite answers to these two questions cannot be given for all convention countries primarily because of the lack of decided cases so that many " answers " are in fact opinions only. However, so far as the Patent Offices are concerned, priority claims to post-dates will be allowed in the following convention countries:

Australia	Hungary	Poland
Austria	Iceland	Rhodesia
Bahamas	Japan	South Africa
Brazil	Malawi	Spain
Czechoslovakia	Netherlands	United Kingdom
Denmark	New Zealand	Zambia
W. Germany	Norway	

In Argentina a post-date is believed to be allowable provided that the country of origin allows claims to post-dates. The original filing date of the post-dated application should not have formed the basis for claiming priority rights in any other Convention country.

It should be appreciated that it by no means follows that the courts in the respective countries would uphold the claim to priority.

Post-dating is not recognised by the Patent Offices in:

Belgium [1]	France [1]	U.S.A. [2]
Canada	Italy	
Finland [1]	Switzerland	

[1] In these countries, although there is no guarantee that the Patent Office will allow a claim to a post-date, nor that the court would uphold such a claim, it is believed that no harm can accrue from a claim to priority based on a post-date. If it were passed by the Patent Office, but eventually rejected by a court, the validity of the patent would not be affected, the maximum penalty being loss of priority.

[2] A decision by the U.S. Commissioner of Patents (*Re Clamp*, 151 U.S.P.Q. 243) is to the effect that a claim to priority cannot be based on a post-date, but only on the earliest date on which the particular foreign application was filed.

Inter-Imperial Arrangements

Section 68 (1) of the United Kingdom Patents Acts 1949–61 permits, *inter alia*, of any part of the Commonwealth being declared a convention country, either for all or some only of the provisions of the Acts. This particular provision was first introduced in the Act of 1883 (s. 104). Somewhat similar provisions appear in the following patent laws: Australia (s. 140 (1)); Bahamas (s. 60); Canada (ss. 12 (1) (*b*) and 29); India (s. 78A (4)); Ireland (s. 93); New Zealand (s. 77 (1)); Pakistan (s. 78A (4)); South Africa (ss. 1 (iii) and 95); Sri Lanka (s. 48 (1)).

With the exception of India and Pakistan, these countries are members of the International Convention and therefore separate arrangements outside that Convention are not called for. Their non-membership of the Convention has however caused India and Pakistan to enter into separate bilateral arrangements with a view to obtaining convention benefits.

The United Kingdom Patents, etc. (Convention Countries) (No. 1) Order 1938 declared British India to be a convention country for all purposes except those of section 48 of the British Patents Act then in force (s. 70 of the current Act). The effect of this was that section 91 of the former Act (ss. 68 and 69 of the current Act) became applicable to British India, as the result of which reciprocal arrangements existed between the United Kingdom and British India. After the partition of India, Pakistan automatically became a party to the reciprocal arrangements by virtue of section 18 (1) of the Indian Independence Act 1947. These reciprocal arrangements cover patents and designs.

Both India and Pakistan have made reciprocal arrangements with other parts of the British Commonwealth, but the arrangements are limited to rights of priority.

India has made arrangements with:

Australia	(patents and designs)
Canada	(patents only)
Ireland	(patents and designs)
New Zealand	(patents and designs)
Pakistan	(patents and designs)
Sri Lanka	(patents only)
U.K.	(patents and designs)

Thus, an applicant in India may claim priority under the usual conditions from an earlier application filed in the United Kingdom, Australia, Canada, Ireland, New Zealand, Pakistan or Sri Lanka. Consequent on South Africa's withdrawal from the Commonwealth, India rescinded the reciprocal arrangements with South Africa, so that an applicant in India can no longer claim priority from a South African application no matter in whose name the South African application was filed. Citizens of the Republic of South Africa can continue to claim priority dates in India if based on the earliest corresponding application filed in any one of the countries with whom India still has reciprocal arrangements. It should also be noted that the reciprocal priority arrangements between India and Canada are now restricted to citizens or corporations of Indian and Canadian nationality.

Pakistan has made arrangements with:

Australia	India	Sri Lanka
Canada	New Zealand	United Kingdom

And thus an applicant in Pakistan may claim priority of an earlier application filed in the United Kingdom, Australia, India, New Zealand or Sri Lanka. The reciprocal arrangements which existed between Pakistan and South Africa have been rescinded by the Pakistan Government with effect from May 31, 1961 (the date when South Africa left the Commonwealth). As in the case of India, the benefits of the reciprocal arrangements between Pakistan and Canada are restricted to citizens or corporations of Pakistani and Canadian nationality.

Everything claimed in an Indian or Pakistani priority application must be specifically disclosed in the single application from which priority is claimed, the principle of legitimate development of an invention not being applicable, and a complete specification filed after a provisional is not recognised. Multiple or partial priorities are not allowable, except in the single instance in India when multiple priority is claimed from two or more applications filed by the same applicants on the same day in the same country. Claims which are the subject of a valid objection of disconformity with the priority documents must be cancelled or amended, or the priority date must be abandoned. Cancelled matter may form the subject of a divisional application(s) filed before acceptance of the parent application.

If an Indian complete specification includes matter first introduced into the U.K. complete following a provisional, the Indian Patent Office would normally object on this ground of disconformity. To secure the priority date of the U.K. complete specification in India in respect of the disconforming matter, the latter could form the subject of a divisional application in the United Kingdom and there could then be filed a fresh Indian application claiming priority from the divisional application. Normally the Indian application would itself be divided, but the foregoing procedure could on occasion be advantageous even if it were unnecessary to prosecute further the U.K. divisional.

For both India and Pakistan, priority must be claimed when filing the application and there should be furnished within three months a certified copy of the basic application.

If the applicant in India is the assignee of the basic applicant, there must also be furnished an assignment of the right to apply in

India or the application form may be endorsed as to assignment.

In both countries, the Patent Office allows claims to post-dates.

Bangladesh: Despite the Bangladesh "Laws Continuation and Enforcement Order 1972" it is believed that references in this section to Pakistan do not apply to Bangladesh.

Pan-American Conventions

Three Conventions have been made between countries on the Continent of America and these are chiefly concerned with priority rights. The principal Convention is the Buenos Aires Convention of 1910 of which the main provision is a period of priority of one year for patents of invention within which applicants in one of the convention countries may file applications in any of the other convention countries. This provision, of course, is similar to the International Convention.

The other two Conventions are Montevideo 1889 and Caracas 1911. They are substantially identical with one another but instead of giving a period of priority for filing applications they give periods of priority for registering patents obtained in one or other of the member countries. In the case of Montevideo the period is one year and in the case of Caracas two years.

(1) *Buenos Aires, 1910*

This Convention, for the protection of patents of invention, designs and industrial models, has been ratified by the following countries:

Bolivia	Ecuador	Paraguay
Brazil	Guatemala	U.S.A.
Costa Rica	Haiti	Uruguay
Cuba	Honduras	
Dominican Republic	Nicaragua	
	Panama	

The Convention provides:

(*a*) Enjoyment by patentee in any member-state of the legal advantages afforded by other member-states, with the consequent right to protection and legal remedies against attack on their rights, subject to compliance with the provisions of local laws.

(*b*) Convention priority rights. For patents of invention the period is 12 months from filing the first application in the convention country and four months for designs or industrial models. Consequently, a second filing in a member-state within the priority period is not affected by acts performed in the interval; particularly it is not affected by other applications, by the publication of the invention or by its working, or by the sale of copies of the design or model, nor do these give rise to third party rights.

(*c*) Patents resulting from applications filed under the Convention to be independent of each other and of corresponding patents obtained in countries not parties to the Convention.

(*d*) Questions concerning priority of patents to be decided with regard to the date of application in the respective countries.

(*e*) Patentable inventions are defined as (subject to local laws):

- (i) a new manner of manufacturing industrial products;
- (ii) a new machine or mechanical or manual apparatus serving for the manufacture of industrial products;
- (iii) a new industrial product;
- (iv) the application of known methods for the purposes of obtaining better results;
- (v) every new, original or ornamental design or model for an article of manufacture.

(*f*) Grounds for non-patentability:

- (i) publication anywhere prior to the date of invention;
- (ii) registration, publication or description anywhere more than one year prior to the date of application;
- (iii) public use or local sale one year prior to the date of application;
- (iv) contrary to morals or laws.

(*g*) Patentee to have positive rights, including right to assign or transfer in accordance with local laws.

(*h*) Legal remedies for infringement of patentee's rights to be taken under local laws.

(*i*) Certified copy of patent granted in basic country to be evidence of right of priority.

(2) *Montevideo*, 1889

This Convention, in respect of patents of invention, has been ratified by:

Argentina	Paraguay	Uruguay
Bolivia	Peru	

The Convention provides:

(*a*) Anyone obtaining a patent for invention in any of the signatory countries enjoys inventor's rights in the others, if within the maximum term of one year (from date of grant of patent) he registers his patent in the manner laid down by the laws of the country in which he applies for its recognition.

(*b*) The term of the privilege will be determined by the local laws. This period may be limited to that indicated by the laws of the country in which the patent was originally granted, should it be shorter.

(*c*) Any disputes arising as to the priority of the invention shall be settled taking into account the date of the application for the relevant patents in the countries in which they were granted.

(*d*) Patentable inventions or discoveries are defined as:
- (i) a new method of manufacturing industrial products;
- (ii) a new mechanical or manual apparatus for the manufacture of industrial products;
- (iii) a new industrial product;
- (iv) the application of improved means for achieving results superior to those already known.

A patent may not be obtained for:
- (i) inventions and discoveries which have had publicity in any of the signatory countries, or in others not bound by this agreement;
- (ii) those inventions or discoveries contrary to morals or the laws of the country in which the patents for invention are to be issued or recognised.

(*e*) The inventor's rights are positive and cover the power to enjoy his invention and to transfer it to others.

(*f*) Legal remedies for infringement of patentee's rights to be taken under local laws.

(3) *Caracas*, 1911

This Convention, in respect of patents of invention, has been ratified by:

Bolivia	Ecuador	Venezuela
Colombia	Peru	

The Convention provides:

(*a*) Anyone obtaining a patent or privilege of invention for the first time in any of the signatory countries will enjoy the rights of inventor in the others, if in the maximum period of two years he should register his patent in the manner laid down by the laws of the country in which its recognition is applied for.

(*b*) The term of the privilege will be determined by the local laws.

(*c*) Patentable inventions or discoveries are defined as:

(i) a new method of manufacturing industrial products;

(ii) a new mechanical or manual apparatus for the manufacture of industrial products;

(iii) a new industrial product;

(iv) the application of improved means for achieving results superior to those already known.

Patents may not be obtained or those already obtained be registered:

(i) if the inventions or discoveries to which they refer have already been published in any of the signatory countries, or in others which are not bound by this agreement;

(ii) if in accordance with the laws of the country where the patents of invention are to be issued or recognised, the inventions or discoveries relate to public health.

(*d*) The inventor's rights are positive and cover the power to enjoy his invention or to transfer it to others.

(*e*) Legal remedies for infringement of patentee's rights to be taken under local laws. The signatory countries undertake to maintain in their legislation a penalty against infringers of this right.

European Convention Relating to the Formalities Required for Patent Applications (December 11, 1953)

The governments of the following countries, all members of the Council of Europe, namely:

Austria	Denmark	Germany (Federal Republic—including Saar)
Belgium	France	

Iceland	Luxembourg	Sweden
Ireland	Netherlands	Turkey
Italy	Norway	United Kingdom

have signed and ratified this Convention which came into force on June 1, 1955, and which has for its objects the simplification and unification of formalities prescribed by the various national legislations in respect of applications for patents. Instruments of accession have also been deposited by

Greece	Spain
Israel	Switzerland
South Africa	

The Convention is now open to accession by any member of the International Convention. Renunciation of membership requires one year's notice.

Article 1

Article 1 provides that a patent application may be required to comply with specific requirements as to documents to be lodged, preserves the filing date of the application subject to compliance with specific requirements and protects the application from refusal on formal grounds, again subject to compliance with specific requirements. The formal requirements of the Convention should not be exceeded by member-states, who may, however, dispense with any of the requirements.

Article 2—Application Documents

States may require any or all of the following:

(*a*) Application form; states may require this in duplicate.
(*b*) Specification in duplicate; search countries may require this in triplicate.
(*c*) Drawings, where necessary, in duplicate; if required by local laws, in triplicate.
(*d*) Samples, if required by local laws.
(*e*) Authorisation to local agent if one employed—no legalisation or certification. If required by local laws, acceptance of authorisation by the local agent.
(*f*) Proof of status, or assent, of the inventor if non-inventor applicant, if required by local laws.
(*g*) Fees, or proof of payment thereof.

The application form and accompanying documents should be in the language of the state in which application is being made, or in a language recognised by that state; and may be sent by post, subject to local requirements.

In addition, for convention applications there may be required a certified copy of the basic specification and drawings and such other documents as may be required by local laws. If the certified copy is in English, French or German, or is accompanied by an officially certified translation in one of these languages, there should be no call for any other translation unless required by the competent authority.

Application form

This should be on strong white paper, size 29 to 34 cm. by 20 to 22 cm., and should contain

(*a*) full names, nationality and address of applicant;
(*b*) full name and address of agent, if any;
(*c*) short, precise title;
(*d*) declaration of inventorship, if required by local laws;
(*e*) statement as to kind of patent required and whether application is a divisional. Where applicable, *e.g.*, improvement, addition or divisional, the number of the earlier patent or application;
(*f*) name and address of person to whom official communications should be addressed, where there are several applicants and no common agent;
(*g*) signature of applicant; or of agent if permitted under local laws. If Form is required in duplicate, only one need be signed;
(*h*) where required by local laws, a list of the documents accompanying the application;
(*i*) an address for service where necessary.

Standard application forms are annexed to the Convention.

Specification

This should be on one side only of strong white paper, size 29 to 34 cm. long and 20 to 22 cm. wide; with the sheets connected to be readily separated and re-united; pages are to be numbered. Any means for inscribing a specification may be employed, provided the ink is dark and indelible, and the document is easily legible.

There should be a 3-4 cm. left-hand margin on each sheet, and spaces of about 8 cm. at the head of the first, and foot of the last, page; the spacing should permit interlineation. Any erasures, alterations or over-writings in the specification as filed should be mentioned in the margin or detailed at the end of the description, and initialled on all copies.

Specifications should not contain drawings other than graphic chemical and mathematical formulae. The metric system should be used for units of weight and measure, whilst temperatures should be in degrees centigrade and density expressed as specific gravity. For electrical units international practice should be observed and for chemical formulae local practice should be followed.

The heading should give the full names of the applicant and the title of the invention.

The specification should be signed by the applicant or his agent.

Drawings

There should be filed one copy on strong, non-shiny, flexible transparent material; and two at most, exact copies on strong, white, smooth, non-shiny paper; one may be required to bear no references.

Sheets should be 29 to 34 cm. long by 21 cm. wide, or exceptionally 42 cm. wide. With 21 cm. wide sheets, the drawing area should not exceed 25·7 cm. by 17 cm.

The drawings should be in durable, dark markings without colour or colour washes, capable of reproduction by photographic means or direct on a stereotype.

Sections should be indicated by oblique hatching.

The scale should be such as will allow of clarity of detail after reduction in size to two-thirds.

Figures should be clearly separated, arranged on as few sheets as possible and numbered continuously and independently of the number of sheets.

Numbers, letters and reference lines should be at least 0·32 cm. high; the same reference letter or number should denote the same part and in agreement with the specification.

Apart from exceptional cases, drawings should not contain explanatory matter.

Each sheet should carry in the margin the name of the applicant, the total number of sheets with the number of each sheet, and the signature of the applicant or his agent.

Informal applications

When the documents filed are drawn in accordance with paragraphs 4, 5 and 6, they are to be regarded as formally in order. However, an application should not be denied its date of filing if the application form, though not in accordance with paragraph 4, is accompanied by the relevant fees (or proof of payment) and by (*a*) one copy of a specification in the language of, or a language recognised by, the country where the application is being filed; and (*b*) one copy of drawings necessary for the understanding of the specification.

Time limits may be set for removal of the informalities.

International convention

A period of at least two months from the date of a subsequent application should be allowed for entering a claim to priority of an earlier application; but states may require that the claim to priority be entered within the priority period laid down in the International Convention.

International Classification of Patents

(*a*) European Convention (December 19, 1954)

This Convention came into force on August 1, 1955, and has as its object the adoption of a uniform classification system for patents of invention. The Convention, which derives from the Council of Europe, is a contribution to the harmonisation of national legislation and will provide for a common basis for searching. An amended form of Annex (setting out the system of classification) came into force on December 16, 1961.

The Convention has been ratified by:

Belgium	Ireland	Sweden
Denmark	Italy	Switzerland
France	Netherlands	Turkey
Germany (Federal Republic)	Norway	United Kingdom

Australia, Israel and Spain have adhered to the Convention.

Of the original signatories, only Greece, Iceland and Luxembourg have not yet ratified the Convention.

Under the Convention, each contracting party undertakes to adopt the system of classification, together with any elaborations or modifications which may come into force later; and each party is at liberty to apply the classification either as the principal or as a subsidiary system.

The Committee of Experts on patents of the Council of Europe is responsible for further elaboration of the classification and will give its opinion to the contracting parties on any modification which may be proposed by any one party. Any elaboration or modification approved by the Committee comes into force six months after all contracting parties have been notified, unless two at least of the parties have officially intimated objection to the proposed elaboration or modification not less than one month before expiry of the set period. The complete classification came into force on September 1, 1968.

Printed patent specifications issued by the contracting parties, or if printed specifications are not issued, any extract or similar document, are to be marked by the appropriate national authority with the complete symbols of the International Classification. Any party which does not classify patents for the purpose of novelty examination is permitted to declare that it will not undertake to mark patent specifications, extracts or similar documents. The symbols of the International Classification, preceded by the words " International Classification " or an abbreviation thereof, are to be printed in heavy type in the heading of the document. Any contracting party may also mark their specifications or other documents with other symbols. France and Belgium have declared that they do not undertake to mark printed specifications.

The main basis of the system of classification is as follows:

Sections and Subsections

(*a*) *Human necessities*
Subsections: Agriculture, Foodstuffs, Apparel, Medicine and hygiene.

(*b*) *Performing operations*
Subsections: Separating and mixing, Shaping, Printing, Transporting.

(*c*) *Chemistry and metallurgy*
Subsections: Chemistry, Metallurgy.

(*d*) *Textiles and paper*
Subsections: Textiles, Paper.

(*e*) *Fixed constructions*
Subsections: Building, Mining.

(*f*) *Mechanics, lighting and heating*
Subsections: Engines, Lighting and heating.

(*g*) *Physics*
Subsections: Instruments, Nucleonics.

(*h*) *Electricity*
Subsection: Electricity.

These subsections are divided into approximately one hundred classes which are themselves further divided.

(*b*) Strasbourg Agreement (March 24, 1971)

As a result of the Strasbourg Diplomatic Conference on the International Patent Classification, which took place in March 1971, there has now been prepared a new Agreement entitled "Strasbourg Agreement Concerning the International Patent Classification." This new Agreement was opened for signature on March 24, 1971, and has been signed by the following States (although it is not yet in force):

Austria	Holy See	Netherlands
Belgium	Iran	Norway
Brazil	Ireland	Spain
Denmark	Italy	Sweden
Finland	Japan	Switzerland
France	Liechtenstein	United Kingdom
W. Germany	Luxembourg	U.S.A.
Greece	Monaco	Yugoslavia

A limitation of the 1954 Convention was that although it was open to all member countries of the Paris Union, the power of decision in matters affecting the International Classification was retained by member countries of the Council of Europe. The 1971 Agreement removes this limitation by establishing a special Union open to any country party to the Paris Union and by transferring administration from the Council of Europe to the World Intellectual Property Organization (WIPO).

The member countries adopt a common classification, for patents for invention, inventors' certificates, utility models and utility certificates, to be known as the International Patent Classification. The Classification comprises the text established under the 1954 Convention, as subsequently amended, with any amendments which may hereafter be made under the 1971 Agreement. Member countries are required to include in specifications the complete symbols of the Classification applied to the invention to which the specification relates.

The Classification will be used on specifications of applications filed under the Patent Co-operation Treaty (PCT) and the proposed European Patent Convention.

The Agreement will enter into force one year after instruments of ratification or accession have been deposited by:

(i) two-thirds of the countries party to the 1954 Convention as at March 24, 1971 (Austria, Belgium, Denmark, France, W. Germany, Ireland, Israel, Italy, Netherlands, Norway, Spain, Sweden, Switzerland, Turkey, United Kingdom);

(ii) three countries party to the Paris Union which were not previously party to the 1954 Convention and of which at least one is a country where more than 40,000 applications for patents or inventors' certificates are filed annually.

Countries party to the 1954 Convention which ratify or accede to the 1971 Agreement are obliged to denounce the former at the latest by the time the latter comes into force with respect to those countries.

The following survey, reprinted from the text published by the World Intellectual Property Organization (WIPO), indicates the present and anticipated future use of the International Patent Classification (IPC) by countries and intergovernmental organisations:

A. Countries and Intergovernmental Organisations Using the IPC

African and Malagasy Industrial Property Office (OAMPI)

IPC to class level in all sections on domestic patents from 1966. Search files arranged accordingly.

Progressive extension to subclass, group and subgroup level envisaged.

Algeria

Using IPC from early 1969.

Australia

IPC to subclass level in all sections printed on abridgments of accepted complete specifications and on printed specifications. Years from May 1958 on covered.

One public search file arranged according to IPC to subclass level containing all specifications since May 1958.

Investigations in progress regarding the printing of IPC symbols to subgroup level on all abstracts, abridgments and printed specifications, and as to how the IPC symbols on foreign patent documents may be stored for easy access.

Austria

IPC on domestic patent specifications in all sections to subclass level from January 1, 1966, to subgroup level from September 1, 1969.

Investigations in progress to reclassify the search files according to IPC to subgroup level.

Belgium

From January 1955 IPC to subclass level in all sections on domestic patent specifications.

Chile

Using IPC from June 1969 in all sections to subclass level; extension to group and subgroup level envisaged.

Cuba

IPC from January 1968 in all sections to subclass level on domestic patent documents. Extension to subgroup level planned from January 1971. Search files to be arranged accordingly.

Patent documents of the Soviet Union, the German Democratic Republic, Roumania and other countries bearing IPC symbols from January 1, 1965, arranged in the search files according to IPC to subclass level. Extension to subgroup level under study; no final decision yet.

Cyprus

Registers granted United Kingdom patents; classification therefore same as applied by United Kingdom.

Czechoslovakia

Domestic patent applications:

All sections to subgroup level from July 1, 1969.

Domestic patents:

All sections to subgroup level from January 1, 1970. Reclassification of earlier granted domestic patents as soon as possible.

Use of IPC for foreign patent documents as far as classified according to it by country of origin.

Denmark

IPC on domestic patent documents in all sections to sub-class level from May 1958.

To subgroup level:

Section A from July 1964,
Section B from July 1967,
Section C from October 1966,
Section D from September 1967,
Section E from March 1965,
Section F from September 1967,
Section G from July 1967,
Section H from April 1966.

IPC to subgroup level in all sections on printed accepted applications from April 1968.

Finland

Printed domestic abridgments of patents from 1899 to 1944, complete domestic patent publications from 1944, and published domestic patent applications from 1968 classified according to IPC to subgroup level in all classes in which the German Classification System uses the IPC. Reclassification of older patents in 1971.

Search files containing patent documents of Denmark, France, Germany, Norway, Sweden, Switzerland, United Kingdom and United States of America arranged according to IPC as far as the documents have been classified this way by the originating country. Reclassification of backlog according to reclassification lists received.

France

From January 1955 to December 1968, IPC in all sections to subclass level, in selected subclasses to group level, from

January 1969 in all sections to group level on domestic patent documents.

Classification to subgroup level in certain sections latest at entry into force of Strasbourg Agreement.

Germany (Federal Republic)

IPC printed on first (OS) and second publications (DAS) and on patent specifications to subclass level in all sections since 1956, to subgroup level in 233 selected subclasses from August 1, 1968. Search files in these 233 subclasses arranged accordingly.

IPC in all sections to subgroup level on patent documents planned from autumn 1971, on utility model specifications from 1972. Reclassification of search files to be completed in 1975.

Search files of the 233 selected subclasses containing patent documents of Austria, Belgium, France, German Democratic Republic, Switzerland, United Kingdom and the United States of America arranged according to IPC to subgroup level; search files in all sections to be reclassified accordingly by 1975.

Ghana

Registers granted United Kingdom patents; classification therefore same as applied by United Kingdom.

Hungary

IPC in all sections to subgroup level on domestic patents published in and after 1970. Search files arranged accordingly. Reclassification into IPC to subgroup level of domestic patents published between 1916 and 1969 in 1971.

Search files containing French (from 1955) and USSR (from 1962) patent documents arranged according to IPC to subclass level, Swiss (from 1969) and United Kingdom (from 1968) patent documents to subgroup level.

International Patent Institute (IIB)

Whilst the International Patent Institute does not use the IPC in the sense of applying classification marks in printed specifications and like documents, since it does not publish any specifications or like documents, nevertheless it is a most important user of the IPC in that a large proportion of its searches are at present made, and a much greater proportion thereof will in future be made, in search files classified according to the IPC.

The IIB therefore has a very great interest in the development of the IPC.

Iran

IPC used (on a provisional basis).

Ireland

IPC in all sections to subclass level on domestic patent documents issued since November 1955, to subgroup level on domestic patent documents issued since June 1969. Search files arranged accordingly.

Israel

IPC in all sections to subclass level on domestic patents published in and after 1963, to subgroup level on domestic patents published in and after January 1969.

Domestic patents published in and after 1920 to be classified according to IPC to subgroup level by January 1972. Search files arranged accordingly.

Search files of patent documents issued by France from 1964 on, and by Germany from 1960 on, arranged according to IPC in all sections to subclass level.

Italy

IPC to subclass level on domestic patents since January 1, 1957, and utility models since January 1, 1970.

Japan

IPC in all sections to subclass level on domestic patents and in Utility Model Gazettes from October 1, 1970. Classification down to subgroup level as well as reclassification planned to begin in 1972.

Search files containing patent documents issued by France, Germany, Soviet Union, Switzerland, United Kingdom and the United States of America planned to be arranged according to IPC to subgroup level.

Kenya

Registers granted United Kingdom patents; classification therefore same as applied by United Kingdom.

Malawi

All sections, selected classes to subclass level from 1964. Domestic patent documents only.

Monaco

IPC is used.

Netherlands

IPC on domestic patent documents.

To subclass level:

Sections A to H

non-examined applications from January 1, 1964,
examined applications from November 15, 1955,
patents from March 15, 1956;

to subgroup level:

Section A

non-examined applications from August 1, 1966,
examined applications from March 1, 1965,
patents from July 1, 1965;

Section E

non-examined applications from September 1, 1966,
examined applications from April 1, 1965,
patents from August 1, 1965;

Section H

non-examined applications from July 1, 1967,
examined applications from March 1, 1966,
patents from July 1, 1966;

Sections B, C, D, F, G from July 1, 1969.

Search files containing domestic patent documents and patent documents issued by Belgium, France, Germany, Luxembourg, Switzerland, United Kingdom and the United States of America in certain subclasses and classes arranged according to IPC to subgroup level.

Investigations in progress to extend the arrangement of search files according to the IPC.

Nigeria

Registers granted United Kingdom patents; classification therefore same as applied by United Kingdom.

Norway

IPC on domestic patents to subclass level:

Sections A to H from 1956,

to subgroup level:

Sections A, C and E from January 1966,

Sections B, D, F, G and H from September 1968.

IPC to subgroup level in sections A to H on examined applications published in and after 1968.

Domestic patent documents from 1893 in certain subclasses reclassified according to IPC to subgroup level. Reclassification to be continued.

Search files containing patent documents issued by Denmark, Finland, France, Germany, Sweden and the United Kingdom in certain classes and subclasses arranged according to IPC to subgroup level; to be extended in the future depending on the receiving of reclassification lists.

Philippines

IPC as secondary classification to class level in mechanical fields. Extension to chemical and electrical fields in 1972.

Poland

IPC on domestic patent documents in all sections to subgroup level from January 1, 1970. Search files arranged accordingly.

Roumania

IPC in all sections to subclass level as secondary classification on domestic patents published from 1962, as primary classification to subgroup level on domestic patents and inventors' certificates from January 1970. Search files arranged accordingly.

Search files of domestic patent documents from 1957 to 1970 planned to be reclassified to IPC to subgroup level by 1973.

Singapore

Registers granted United Kingdom patents; classification therefore same as applied by United Kingdom.

South Africa

Not issuing patent documents. IPC reflected on patent application forms and in the advertisements of acceptances in the Patent Journal.

Soviet Union

IPC in all sections on domestic patent documents to subclass level from July 1962, to subgroup level from December 1969. Search files arranged according to IPC from 1924 on.

Search files containing German (Federal Republic), French, Swiss, United Kingdom and United States patent documents arranged according to IPC in all sections to subgroup level, before 1967 (GB), 1968 (FR) or 1969 (DT, CH) to subclass level. Reclassification to be continued as soon as reclassification lists available.

Spain

IPC in all sections to subclass level from January 1967 on domestic patent documents.

Sweden

IPC in all sections to subclass level on domestic patent documents from January 1958 to 1967.

To subgroup level:
Sections A and E from December 1965,
Section H from May 1966,
Section C from October 1966,
Sections B, D, F and G from 1967.

Search files containing French, Swiss and United Kingdom patent specifications published in 1970 arranged according to IPC to subgroup level.

Switzerland

IPC to subgroup level on domestic patents in
Sections B, D and H from March 1968,
Section C from August 1968,
Sections A, E, F and G from December 1968.

Turkey

All sections to subclass level from June 1956.

United Kingdom

IPC on newly issued patent documents (accepted complete specifications) in all sections to subclass level from January 1957; to subgroup level:
Section A from April 1965,
Section B from August 1967,

Section C from May 1966,
Section D from November 1967,
Section E from August 1965,
Section F from November 1967,
Section G from May 1967,
Section H from November 1965.

It is planned to arrange United States patent specifications issued on and after January 1, 1970, in the search files according to IPC to subgroup level by mid-1971.

United States of America

IPC in all sections to subgroup level printed on United States patents issued from January 1969. Wherever considered appropriate, as reclassification of national files is done, it will be structured to be compatible with IPC schedules.

Yugoslavia

IPC in all sections to subclass level on domestic patent documents from 1965.

Zambia

IPC is used.

B. Countries Intending to Use the IPC

Brazil	India	Luxembourg

C. Countries Not Planning to Use the IPC

Argentina *	Korea (Rep. of)	Tanzania
Burundi	Libya	Trinidad & Tobago
Canada *	Malta	United Arab Republic
Costa Rica	Mexico	Uruguay *
Guatemala	Morocco	Venezuela
Iraq	New Zealand	
Jamaica	Sudan	
Jordan	Syria	

* Argentina noted that it was studying the feasibility of converting its domestic classification to the IPC.

Canada indicated that no decision as to the use of the IPC for domestic patent documents has been made. A list of concordance between the IPC and the domestic classification is kept up to date.

Uruguay stated that it is intended to adopt the classification system used by Argentina.

European Convention on the Unification of Certain Points of Substantive Law on Patents for Invention (November 27, 1963)

This Convention, which was signed by the following members of the Council of Europe:

Belgium	Germany (Federal Republic)	Netherlands
Denmark	Ireland	Sweden
France	Italy	Switzerland
	Luxembourg	United Kingdom

will come into force if and when it has been ratified by eight of the signatories—an event which has not yet occurred. The Convention is open for signature by member-states of the Council of Europe and on ratification will be open to accession (by invitation) by any member of the International Union for the Protection of Industrial Property which is not a member of the Council of Europe.

The object of the Convention is to secure unification of certain points of the patent laws of the signatory countries concerning patentability, novelty, inventive step, contents of application and scope of protection.

The main provisions are as follows:

Patentability, Novelty and Inventive Step

There shall be patentable any invention which is:

(*a*) susceptible of industrial application, *i.e.*, if it can be made or used in any kind of industry, including agriculture;

(*b*) new, *i.e.*, if it does not form part of the state of the art;

(*c*) involves an inventive step, *i.e.*, if it is not obvious having regard to the state of the art.

The " state of the art " comprises everything made available to the public by means of a written or oral description, by use, or in any other way, before the date of the patent application or any earlier date validly claimed.

Contracting states are free to consider as comprised in the state of the art the contents of local pending applications or granted patents which have been officially published on or after the date of application (or its priority date) but which have an earlier priority date. States which do not apply this provision must provide that no invention shall be validly protected in so far as it includes matter which is or has been validly protected by a local patent which, though not comprised in the state of the art, has an earlier priority date in respect of that matter.

Contracting states are free to exclude from consideration in relation to the question of inventive step, either generally or in relation to particular classes of patents or applications, *e.g.*, patents of addition, all or any local patents or applications of earlier priority date which have been officially published on or after the priority date of the application.

Any invention not complying with the three foregoing conditions cannot be the subject of a valid patent, and a patent declared invalid for non-compliance therewith is to be considered as invalid *ab initio.*

Novelty Preservation

Novelty is not destroyed by prior disclosure of an invention (*a*) in evident abuse of the rights of an applicant, or his legal predecessor; or (*b*) by the applicant, or legal predecessor, at an official or officially recognised international exhibition; provided the application is filed within six months after the disclosure.

States may, however, for a period of five years, reserve the right to grant valid patents for inventions disclosed within the six months period either by the inventor himself or by a third party as a result of information derived from the inventor.

Non-Patentability

States are not obliged to grant patents for inventions whose publication or exploitation would be contrary to public order or morality. This provision does not include inventions whose exploitation is so contrary merely because it is prohibited by a law or regulation.

Also, states are not obliged to grant patents in respect of plant or animal varieties or essentially biological processes for the production of plants or animals. This provision does not apply to micro-biological processes and the products thereof.

However, states may, for a period of 10 years reserve the right not to grant patents in respect of food and pharmaceutical products, as such, and agricultural or horticultural processes other than those to which the preceding paragraph applies.

Contents of Application and Scope of Protection

Applications should contain:

(*a*) A description which discloses the invention in a manner sufficient for it to be carried out by a person skilled in the art; and (*b*) drawings where necessary; and

(*c*) one or more claims defining the protection sought.

Although the description and drawings may be used to interpret the claims, the scope of protection will be determined by the terms of the claims.

Agreements Concerning the Establishment of an International Patent Bureau (June 6, 1947 and February 16, 1961)

Following an agreement made in 1947 between Belgium, France, Luxembourg and the Netherlands, there was established, in The Hague, the Institut International des Brevets, whose purpose was to provide the governments of the four states with opinions regarding the novelty of inventions in respect of which applications for patents had been filed with the respective national Industrial Property Services. The Institute was also entitled to provide these Services with opinions regarding the novelty of inventions in respect to which applications for patents had not been filed.

The Agreement entered into force on June 10, 1949, and thereafter any non-signatory state which was a member of the International Union for the Protection of Industrial Property could accede to it. In fact, it was ratified by the signatory countries, Belgium, France, Luxembourg and the Netherlands, and was subsequently acceded to by Monaco, Switzerland, Turkey and the United Kingdom.

The 1947 Agreement was revised in 1961 resulting in a broadening of the scope of the Institute. The 1961 Agreement was signed by Belgium, France, Luxembourg, Monaco, Morocco, the Netherlands, Switzerland, Yugoslavia and Turkey. Membership is open to any state which is a party to the International Convention.

The 1961 Agreement provides that it shall come into force one month after ratification by the signatory states, and at the present time has been ratified by Belgium, France, Luxembourg, Monaco, the Netherlands, Switzerland and Turkey.

According to the Agreement the functions of the Institute are:

(1) To provide expert opinions on the novelty of inventions forming the subject of patent applications received or patents granted by the national government of each member-state or by any international inter-governmental organisation responsible for granting patents which is a member of the Institute.

(2) To provide opinions of a different kind from those set out in (1) (*e.g.*, on patentability) on the inventions referred to in that paragraph.

(3) To undertake, on behalf of any applicant any documentary search on the state of the art.

The member-states undertake to make provision for all or some of the applications for patents, or the patents, effective in their territory to be obligatorily the subject of an expert opinion as referred to in paragraph (1) above. To permit it to carry out this task, the Institute is entitled to receive from member-states or organisations copies of patent specifications and published patent applications as issued by the governments of these states or by the organisations.

A protocol to the Agreement sets out the following documents as comprising the minimum documentation to be consulted by the Institute:

Patents

(1) German patents from 1877
(2) U.S. patents from 1921
(3) Belgian patents from 1926
(4) British patents from 1909
(5) French patents from 1902
(6) Luxembourg patents from 1947
(7) Dutch patents from 1912
(8) Swiss patents from 1940

Published patent applications

(1) German patent applications from the year 1957
(2) Netherlands patent applications from the year 1912
(3) Swiss patent applications from the year 1961

Periodical Publications and Technical Books

Periodical publications and technical books written in the German, English, French or Dutch language, selected from among the most prominent.

All the above documentation is to be kept up to date.

In addition to the patent documents indicated above, the Institute also has at its disposal copies of patent specifications of Australia, Austria, Canada, Denmark, Ireland, Italy, Japan, Norway, Russia and Sweden, as well as earlier patent specifications of some of the eight countries numbered above. With regard to periodicals, the Institute has available such items as " Chemical Abstracts," " Nuclear Science Abstracts," " Science

Abstracts," "Engineering Index," "Technisches Zentral Blatt" and "Abstract Journal of the Academy of Science of the U.S.S.R."

The search material presently available to the Institute thus comprises some six million patent specifications, together with about thirty thousand technical books as well as a large number of technical and scientific reports and periodicals.

The Institute has published details of the procedure to be followed concerning its work in relation to "private" requests, that is, requests received under function (3) above. These may be summarised as follows:

Documentary research is divided into two classes, namely, that for (1) novelty reports and (2) special reports. In both cases documents are cited for their technical content without regard to legal considerations, and no opinion is expressed as to novelty or validity over the citations.

(1) Novelty reports

Requests for this form of report are receivable only from (*a*) nationals of member countries and (*b*) nationals or bodies corporate from other countries provided they are domiciled, or have their offices or operate industrial or commercial undertakings in a member country. Reports are furnished in respect of (i) unpublished applications and (ii) granted patents (to which are equated published applications), filed in member countries.

(*i*) *On unpublished patent applications*

Requests may be made only by the inventor, his assignee or an authorised agent, and requests concerning applications filed in Belgium, France, Luxembourg, Monaco, Netherlands or Turkey, must be transmitted through the local Patent Office. Those concerning applications filed in Morocco, Switzerland or the United Kingdom may be made direct to the Institute. The requests must disclose:

(*a*) the name and address of the applicant;
(*b*) the number and filing date of the application;
(*c*) the date and country of priority if it has been claimed;
(*d*) if the request is from a national or body corporate of a non-member country, a qualifying address in a member country;
(*e*) a copy of the description which accompanied the application;

(*f*) if the request is made direct to the Institute the copy referred to at (*e*) must be certified by the local Patent Office as being a true copy of the description filed therein.

A request may be based on a provisional specification, but because of the form of such a specification, it is recommended that there be included a draft claim or some other indication of the main features of the invention.

(*ii*) *On granted patents*

Requests may be made by letter direct to the Institute or through the national Patent Office, with the exception of requests from Turkey which can only be received through the Turkish Patent Office. In all cases, the request should be accompanied by a copy of the specification (not necessarily printed).

The novelty report issued by the Institute gives details of relevant documents located, with a summary of the contents and with indications of the points in common with the invention under scrutiny. With the exception mentioned below, the report is a provisional one and a period of six months is allowed for making observations or criticisms thereon, or to lodge a restricted statement of invention. Further consideration is then given to the case and a final report issued. (If no observations, criticisms or amended statement are received within the six-month period, the provisional report is regarded as a final one.)

The exception is that where the request concerning a granted patent is made by anyone other than the patentee or an authorised person, the first report is in fact the final one.

(2) Special reports

Documentary searches of a nature different from a novelty search are treated as special and requests for such special reports are receivable from (*a*) nationals of member countries; and (*b*) nationals or bodies corporate from any country provided they are domiciled, or have offices or undertakings in any country which is a member of the International Convention.

In addition, persons within (*b*), who are precluded from the ordinary form of novelty report, may nevertheless request searches for novelty (but relating only to published applications or granted patents in member countries) to be carried out as special reports.

The cost will be determined by the nature of the search required and the work involved, but the Institute will furnish estimates of the cost, if desired.

Examples of searches undertaken are:

(*a*) Novelty of applications or patents of any country other than unpublished applications in Belgium, France, Luxembourg, Monaco, Netherlands and Turkey.

(*b*) For anticipating literature in a given technical field and within given dates.

(*c*) For possible infringement in one or more countries.

(*d*) For all literature in a given technical field.

(*e*) For corresponding patents; effected by use of the classification systems and name indexes. With no restrictions in the following countries:

Australia	France	Poland
Canada	Hungary	Sweden
Czecho-slovakia	Ireland	Switzerland
	Netherlands	United Kingdom
Denmark	Norway	U.S.A.

With the noted restrictions in the following countries:

Austria	Except period 1941 to 1947.
Belgium	Except 1965; for chemical patents no restriction.
Colombia	Patents granted from March 1, 1958, onwards.
Finland	Class lists from January 1, 1944, onwards, alphabetical indexes only from January 1, 1964, onwards.
E. Germany	From January 1, 1951, onwards.
W. Germany	Except period September 30, 1943, to December 31, 1949.
India	Search according to filing date possible from January 1, 1965, onwards.
Israel	No alphabetical indexes and no patents available. Official patent journals available from January 1, 1951, onwards.
Italy	Alphabetical indexes up to December 31, 1958.
Japan	Only chemical patents from January 1, 1962, onwards.
Luxembourg	No alphabetical indexes; search according to filing date.
Mexico	From January 1, 1957, onwards.
New Zealand	Up to December 31, 1939, and from January 1, 1955, onwards.

South Africa	No alphabetical indexes and no patents available; search in the official patent journals possible according to filing date.
Spain	From January 1, 1960, to December 31, 1963.
Yugoslavia	From January 1, 1951, onwards.

(*f*) For patents granted in a specific name and for a specific purpose; effected by use of the alphabetical registers. With no restrictions in the following countries:

Australia	France	Poland
Austria	Hungary	Sweden
Canada	Ireland	Switzerland
Czecho-slovakia	Netherlands	United Kingdom
Denmark	Norway	U.S.A.

With the noted restrictions in the following countries:

Belgium	All chemical patents, non-chemical patents up to November 30, 1964, and again from January 1, 1966.
Colombia	From March 1, 1958.
Finland	From January 1, 1964.
E. Germany	From January 1, 1951.
W. Germany	All patents excepting the period from December 30, 1943, to December 31, 1949.
Italy	Up to December 31, 1958.
Japan	From January 1, 1962, *chemical patents only*.
Mexico	From January 1, 1957.
New Zealand	Up to December 31, 1939, and from January 1, 1955.
Spain	From January 1, 1960, to December 31, 1963, only.
Yugoslavia	From January 1, 1951.

(*g*) For literature disclosing solutions of a given technical problem.

Requests for special reports may be made direct to the Institute.

For accuracy in searching, speed and economy, requests should as far as possible precisely define the subject-matter involved, the object and purpose of the request, and should be accompanied where possible by a list of relevant literature known to the party making the request.

The Institute can supply photocopies of any document at its disposal.

The technical staff of the Institute comprises highly qualified engineers and science graduates who are governed by strict rules of secrecy; documents received by the Institute from those desiring search reports are treated as confidential.

When it is desired to obtain a report from the Institute, consideration must first be given to any secrecy provisions prevailing in applicants' own country. Thus, U.K. applicants requesting a report less than six weeks after the filing of the U.K. application, should first obtain a clearance from the U.K. Comptroller who may on request issue a statement as to whether a direction under section 18 of the Patents Act or section 12 of the Atomic Energy Act is contemplated.

Patent Co-operation Treaty

The Treaty was adopted on June 19, 1970, by the Washington Diplomatic Conference attended by delegations from 78 states and representatives of 22 international organisations, and has been signed by the following 35 states:

Algeria	Hungary	Roumania
Argentina	Iran	Senegal
Austria	Ireland	Sweden
Belgium	Israel	Switzerland
Brazil	Italy	Syria
Canada	Ivory Coast	Togo
Denmark	Japan	United Arab Republic
Finland	Luxembourg	United Kingdom
France	Madagascar	U.S.A.
Germany (Federal Republic)	Monaco	U.S.S.R.
Holy See	Netherlands	Yugoslavia
	Norway	
	Philippines	

The Central African Republic has declared its accession.

The states party to the Treaty constitute a Union, known as the International Patent Co-operation Union, for co-operation in the filing, searching, and examination of applications for the protection of inventions, and for rendering special technical services.

The Treaty will enter into force three months after eight states have ratified it, provided that each of at least four of those states is a major nation with regard to patent activity (defined by the number of applications filed in the state and by nationals of the state in other countries).

Its aims are to contribute to the progress of science and technology, to perfect the legal protection of inventions, to simplify and render more economical the obtaining of protection for inventions where protection is sought in several countries, to facilitate and accelerate access by the public to the technical information contained in documents describing new inventions, and to foster and accelerate the economic development of developing countries through the adoption of measures designed to increase the efficiency of their legal systems instituted for the protection of inventions.

At the present time protection of an invention in several countries necessitates the filing of individual national applications in the languages of each country, usually in different form and with a different approach as to the description of the invention and claims in each.

Chapter I of the Treaty will partially replace this system by a procedure based on the filing of a single " international " patent application filed in one country which is to have the same effect as if it had been filed in all the countries designated by the applicant. The formalities of the international application are regulated in detail. An international patent application will be filed at a national office, if necessary claiming priority under the Paris Convention in a similar way to a national application now; it will be checked for form and sent to an international searching authority (which may be either a national office or an inter-governmental organisation such as the International Patent Institute) which will establish a search report indicating the relevant prior art. After an applicant has had the opportunity to amend his claims, the international application and search report will be published by WIPO 18 months after its priority date if the applicant has not requested earlier publication. Up to 20 months after the priority date, the applicant will then send copies of the application and translations as required to the national office of each country in which he wishes to proceed, and to pay the national fees. The national processing of his applications will then start and each application will proceed as a national one.

Under the optional Chapter II, an applicant may seek an international preliminary examination and report on whether the invention appears to be new, non-obvious and industrially applicable. The report of the International Preliminary Examining Authority performing this examination will be sent to the countries where the applicant wishes to use it. In such countries examination and processing of the application will only start at the end of the 25th month after the priority date and the national fees and translations will become due only at that time.

The principal benefits of the system are that an applicant will be able to file one application in one language in his own country obtaining at the same time the effect of a national application in all other designated countries. He will also be able to postpone his decision on whether to proceed in the designated countries and incur the costs of translation and legal and official fees until he has seen the search report, and if he makes use of Chapter II need not pay official fees or file translations until he has seen the preliminary examination report. On the basis of the search and examination reports the national offices will have their work greatly facilitated and in countries which at present do not examine patent applications but merely register them the value of these registrations will be clearer in view of the corresponding reports issued with them.

The Regulations establish uniform requirements for sufficient, clear and complete description of an invention to enable an appropriately skilled person to carry it out, and lay down that the patent claims define the matter for which protection is sought, and that they shall be clear and precise and fully supported by the description. There are detailed formal requirements for making an application, claiming priority, and the contents and form of the description, claims and an abstract. Criteria for unity of invention and allowable types of patent claims are also laid down. The language in which the international application will be published is to be English unless the original application was in French, German, Japanese or Russian when that language will be used.

Novelty will be tested in relation to prior art published anywhere in the world, and an invention will be considered to involve an inventive step if the invention is not obvious having regard to the prior art to a person skilled in the art. An invention will be considered industrially applicable if according to its nature it can be made or used (in the technological sense) in any kind of industry.

The possibility exists under the Treaty of obtaining regional patents, where provisions for such exist, utilising an international application, provided such patents are available to all persons entitled to file international applications. Member states of regional patent treaties may require applicants to seek regional rather than national patents.

In view of the desirability of preparing the application of the Treaty, pending its entry into force, the Conference adopted a resolution as a result of which WIPO will adopt, direct and supervise the measures necessary for the preparation of the entry into force of the Treaty.

World Intellectual Property Organization

The Organisation was instituted by a Convention signed at Stockholm on July 14, 1967, which came into force on April 26, 1970, and established a new international organisation at the intergovernmental level.

The new Organisation (WIPO) is a continuation of the United International Bureaux for the Protection of Intellectual Property (BIRPI). WIPO will gradually be substituted for BIRPI until all the states at present members of BIRPI have become members of WIPO.

The objectives of the Organisation are; (i) to promote the protection of intellectual property throughout the world through co-operation among states; (ii) to ensure co-operation in the administration of international conventions and agreements for the protection of industrial property (patents, trade marks, industrial designs, appellations of origin) and literary and artistic property (copyright).

The following states are party to the Convention:

Bulgaria
Byelorussia
Canada
Chad
Czechoslovakia
Denmark
Finland
Fiji
Germany (Federal Republic of)
Hungary
Ireland
Israel
Jordan
Kenya
Liechtenstein
Malawi
Morocco
Roumania
Senegal
Spain
Sweden
Switzerland
Ukraine
U.S.S.R.
U.K.
U.S.A.

The German Democratic Republic (East Germany) has also declared its accession to the Convention, but the position with regard to its membership is confused and there is disagreement among member states on the question.

CHAPTER 11

MARKING

[*Where a section of an Act is mentioned in parentheses following a country the section refers to the Patents Act of that country.*]

IN most countries anyone falsely representing that any article manufactured or sold by him is a patented article is liable to a fine.

In some countries, for example, the U.K., U.S.A., Australia, Bangladesh, India, Philippines, South Africa, New Zealand, Pakistan and Ireland, damages may not be recoverable in infringement actions if the patented article has not been properly marked with the word " patent " accompanied by the number or other identifying data of the patent.

In Switzerland, a patentee may impose on a licensee an obligation to mark the patented article as such, and may recover damages from the licensee if the obligation is not complied with.

Marking is not compulsory under French law, but where articles are marked " Breveté," this word must be followed by the words " Sans garantie du Gouvernement," failing which a fine may be inflicted. In practice, there is normally used the abbreviated marking " Breveté S.G.D.G."

This form of marking also applies in the African and Malagasy Union.

Also, for French special medicament patents, there is no compulsion to mark, but a suitable marking would be " Brevet Spécial de Médicament " (or the abbreviation " B.S.M.") followed by the patent number.

There are certain countries where patent marking is obligatory, namely, Canada, Chile, Netherlands, Japan, Mexico, Salvador, Taiwan and Venezuela. Only in Canada and the Netherlands, however, is there any apparent monetary penalty. The marking requirements for these eight countries are as follows:

Canada—Patented 19—

The penalty for failure to mark is a fine not exceeding $100 or two months' imprisonment (ss. 24 and 80).

Chile—Patent No. .... dated ....

In order to enjoy legal protection, the number and date of the patent must be marked on the product, article, apparatus or wrapper. There is no monetary penalty for non-compliance, but no legal protection can be claimed if patented articles are not duly marked.

Exception is made in connection with patents for processes where no marking can be effected.

Netherlands—Ned. Octrooi No. ....

The penalty for failure to mark is a fine not exceeding Fl.300 (s. 36).

Japan

Article 187 stipulates that a patentee should endeavour to mark but does not indicate a particular marking nor is any penalty indicated; failure to mark may affect amount of damages in infringement suit. Suggested marking: article—Tokkyo then number; process—Hoho Tokkyo then number. Also, a patentee may impose on a licensee an obligation to mark the patented article as such and may recover damages from the licensee if the obligation is not complied with.

Mexico—Patent Number and/or Date

Strictly speaking, marking is not compulsory, but failure to mark entails loss of the right to institute infringement proceedings. Article 70 of the Mexican Patent Law reads:

> " All products covered by a patent must bear an indication to the effect that the object has been patented, the number and/or date of the patent. Should the nature of the object not lend itself to this, the number and date of the patent should appear on the box or container in which it is sold to the public.
>
> Failure to comply with this requisite shall not affect the validity of the patent, but it will deprive the owner from exercising the civil and penal actions granted by Title VIII of this Law."

Salvador—Pat. No. .... dated ....

Article 32 of the patent law stipulates that all products covered by a patent must bear a marking showing such fact, and the date and number of the patent in question.

No specific penalty is provided for failure to mark, but it seems probable that no legal protection can be claimed if patented articles are not duly marked.

Taiwan

Article 73 provides that a patentee shall affix the patent mark and the number of his patent certificate to a patented article or the container thereof and may require the holder of the right of exploitation to do so. The patent mark comprises four Chinese characters meaning patented; and this is followed by 13 Chinese characters meaning Patent Certificate—Taiwan Patent No.—.

If, in consequence of the patent mark not having been affixed, others are unaware that the article is patented and infringe the patent right, no claims for damages may be made.

Venezuela

Article 13 states merely that any party who may have obtained a patent should mention the circumstances on the products patented. Here again no penalty is indicated. A recommended marking is "Patentado," followed by the number of the patent.

Chapter 12

AFRICA

At the present time, patenting in Africa is an especially complicated subject. The territory comprises independent states, colonies, protectorates and mandated territories, ranging from the fully developed to the under-developed. This is not surprising bearing in mind the many political changes that have taken place in the past 25 years; for example, some 30 former colonies have achieved independence in that time.

This variation in territorial organisation is accompanied by a similar variety of patent systems. Thus, the territory includes states having independent patent systems; colonies covered by patent protection in the mother country; colonies or former colonies where protection is possible only by registration of a domestic patent in the mother country; colonies where independent and registration systems exist side by side; former colonies where no patent legislation has been promulgated and where the position is doubtful; states where separate forms of protection are necessary for different parts of the state; and states where the only form of protection (if any) flows from cautionary notices.

Apart from Algeria, the African and Malagasy Union and Nigeria, there has been a conspicuous lack of consolidation or promulgation of patent laws following political changes.

The following points may be noted:

(1) The most significant patent development in Africa is the formation of the African and Malagasy Union which has led to the setting-up, by members of the Union, of a joint Industrial Property Office. The Union, which is open to membership to any African state, at present comprises the following members, all former members of the French community:

Cameroon	Gabon	People's Republic of the Congo
Chad	Ivory Coast	Senegal
Central African Republic	Madagascar	Togo
Dahomey	Mauritania	Upper Volta
	Niger	

The Union patent law is patterned on French law and as well as providing for the grant of new patents covering the entire Union, permitted also certain belated claims to convention priority and the validation throughout the Union of rights accruing from French patents in force on the dates when the various members achieved autonomy (during the fourth quarter of 1958).

All member-states have adhered to the International Convention as revised at Lisbon.

It is interesting to note that the Union is the first example anywhere in the world where a group of separate independent states has promulgated a patent law providing for the grant of a single patent covering all member countries.

Togo has adhered to the Union as from June 28, 1967. Applications for patents, and patents granted in the Union since its creation, automatically extend to Togo from that date. Applications for patents filed in Togo and patents granted there, prior to June 28, 1967, continue to be effective in Togo only. Togo has also adhered to the International Convention as revised at Lisbon.

(2) So far as concerns former British colonies, apart from the former Central African Federation and Nigeria, no new patent legislation has been promulgated so that the *status quo* persists, *i.e.*, patent protection is obtainable as in the past by registration of British patents.

(3) On formation of the Central African Federation, the Federal Patents Act 1957, based on the British Patents Act 1949, was promulgated and patents were granted thereunder. With the break-up of the Federation into its constituent parts—Rhodesia (formerly Southern Rhodesia), Zambia (formerly Northern Rhodesia) and Malawi (formerly Nyasaland)—the Act became effective separately in these territories, so that if federal patents were to be maintained in all three, it was necessary to pay separate renewal fees for each territory. A patentee could, of course, renew in any or all of the three as he wished. To obtain patents for new inventions, it is likewise necessary to file separate applications in whichever territory or territories protection is desired.

So far as concerns Rhodesia, the 1957 Act has been amended by Acts of 1959, 1960, 1962, 1966 and 1971, and it is now known as the Patents Act 1971.

A Patent Office has been set up in Zambia and operates under the control of the Registrar of Patents, Trade Marks and Designs.

Patent applications for Malawi are received by the Registrar-General and a Patent Office has been established.

(4) In Nigeria the former provisions whereby patent protection was obtainable only by registration of a United Kingdom patent have been repealed and replaced by the Patents and Designs Decree 1970 which provides, *inter alia*, for an independent patent system. Nigeria acceded to the International Convention, as revised at Lisbon, on September 2, 1963.

(5) The Mauritius Act No. 29 of 1971 repeals the United Kingdom Patents Registration Ordinance so that protection is now available only by independent patenting under the Patents Ordinance (Title XXVIII—Chapter 406).

(6) The former French colonies of Guinea and Mali have not joined the African and Malagasy Union, nor have they promulgated patent legislation. In principle, French patent law is still applicable as the national law, and it is possible to file applications in each of these countries, although in the absence of any implementing regulations it is not possible at this time to determine the value of such patents.

(7) In Algeria, a patent law was promulgated in 1966. This law, as well as providing for the grant of patents and certificates of authorship on new inventions, provides also for the validation of French patents in force on July 3, 1962, and for the confirmation of foreign patents granted prior to March 1, 1966. In the latter case, confirmation is possible only if the importance of the invention, the industrial or agricultural advantages and usefulness for the public of its exploitation, justify it. Algeria has joined the International Convention with effect from March 1, 1966.

(8) The former Belgian Congo is split into three separate independent states, namely, Burundi, Rwanda and Zaïre, and separate applications are necessary if all three states are to be covered. The former Belgian Congo patent law remains in force in Zaïre and practice thereunder is exactly as it was prior to independence.

Rwanda has its own patent law dated February 25, 1963, and Burundi issued on August 20, 1964, a patent law identical to that in Rwanda. The provisions of Rwanda and Burundi laws are very similar to those of Zaïre. Since the laws do not provide for payment of renewal fees, there is no problem so far as concerns maintenance of patents granted by the former administration in the Belgian Congo, and such patents remain in force in all three states for the remainder of their terms.

(9) The Republic of Tanzania comprises the former independent States of Tanganyika and Zanzibar. To cover the Republic separate registration of a British patent is required in both parts within three years of sealing.

(10) Morocco comprises the former French Morocco, Spanish Morocco and Tangier. The patent laws have not been consolidated nor has a new patent law been promulgated, so that the former patent provisions apply in the constituent parts. Thus:

French Morocco	— independent system.
Spanish Morocco	— old rights based on Spanish patents continue to exist in theory, but they would require to be validated. There is as yet no procedure for validation.
Tangier	— independent system.

(11) Somalia comprises the Southern Region (formerly Italian Trust Territory) and the Northern Region (formerly British Somaliland). The patent laws have not been consolidated nor has a new law been promulgated so that the former patent provisions apply in the constituent parts. Thus:

Southern Region	— independent system.
Northern Region	— registration of British patents.

(12) The South West African Affairs Act No. 25 of 1969 provides that the future administration of the South West African Patents, Trade Marks and Designs Law (Proclamation No. 17 of 1923) will be effected through the Patent Office in Pretoria, South Africa, instead of through the Registrar of Deeds in Windhoek. The South West African Patent Law itself is unaltered but the Act contains provisions whereby the Law may be brought into conformity with South African Patent Law.

(13) The Republic of Equatorial Guinea, comprising the former Spanish territories of Fernando Poo and Rio Muni (Spanish Guinea) became an independent state on October 12, 1968. Spanish patent rights acquired up to December 31, 1969, will be recognised in Equatorial Guinea. It is to be expected that both Spain and Equatorial Guinea will promulgate legislation concerning the patent position.

(14) International (Paris) Convention: The following states have ratified the Convention as amended at Lisbon (1958):

Algeria	Central African Republic	Dahomey
Cameroon		Gabon

Ivory Coast	People's Republic of the Congo	Togo
Madagascar	Rhodesia	Uganda
Mauritania	South Africa	Upper Volta
Niger Republic	Tanzania (only for Tanganyika)	Zambia
Nigeria		

The following have ratified the Convention as amended at Stockholm (1967):

Chad	Malawi	Senegal
Kenya	Morocco	

The following have ratified the Convention as amended at London (1934):

Tunisia	United Arab Republic

(15) In the attached table there is set out the position in groups determined by the type of protection available, and this table includes some territories not specifically mentioned above in which there has been no recent change in the nature of protection granted.

(16) For the sake of completeness, there are included in the term "Africa," the many off-shore islands.

TABLE

1. *Independent patent systems*
   - African & Malagasy Union (Cameroon, Chad, Central African Republic, Dahomey, Gabon, Ivory Coast, Madagascar, Mauritania, Niger, People's Republic of the Congo, Senegal, Togo, Upper Volta)
   - Algeria
   - Burundi
   - Liberia
   - Malawi
   - Mauritius
   - Nigeria
   - Rhodesia
   - Rwanda
   - Seychelles (also has system of registration of British patents)
   - South Africa
   - South West Africa
   - Tunisia
   - United Arab Republic
   - Zaïre
   - Zambia
2. *Separate systems applying to constituent parts of states*
   - (*a*) Morocco
     - French Morocco — independent system
     - Spanish Morocco — rights from earlier Spanish patents

Tangier — independent system

(*b*) Somalia

Northern Region — registration of British patent

Southern Region — independent system

(*c*) Tanzania

Tanganyika — separate registration of British patent

Zanzibar — separate registration of British patent

3. *Registration of British patent* (within 3 years of sealing)

Gambia
Ghana
Kenya
St. Helena
Seychelles (also has an independent system)
Sierra Leone
Somalia (N.R.)
Tanganyika
Uganda
Zanzibar

4. *Covered by British patent*

Botswana
Lesotho
Swaziland

(It is also possible to register, at any time, during its life a South African patent in any of these territories)

5. *Covered by French patent*

Comore Islands
French Somaliland
Reunion

6. *Covered by Spanish patent*

Alhucemas
Canary Islands
Ceuta
Chaffarinas
Equitorial Guinea
Melilla
Penon de Velez
Spanish Sahara

7. *Covered by Portuguese patent*

Angola
Cape Verde Islands
Mozambique
Portuguese Guinea
Sao Tome & Principe Islands

8. *Protection doubtful*

Guinea
Mali

9. *Cautionary notices*

Ascension
Ethiopia
Sudan
Tristan da Cunha

CHAPTER 13

INTERFERENCE AND CONFLICT

U.S.A.—Interference Procedure

UNDER most patent systems, the first applicant is regarded basically as the person entitled to a patent, but in the United States an entirely different concept prevails, in that it is the first inventor who is entitled to the patent. This fundamental difference led to the interference provisions in the United States patent law for determining questions of priority of invention. The earliest provisions for interferences were those in the Act of 1793, but at that time decisions were reached by arbitration. The present interference provisions appear in sections 135, 146 and 291 of the U.S. Code Title 35, and the procedure is governed by Rules 201–286 and 301–304, and by section 5 (3) (*b*) of Title 37 of the Code of Federal Regulations.

In his book *Patent Law*, Biesterfeld says: " . . . it will perhaps not be amiss to say that we have before us the most technical and complicated part of Patent Office procedure," and " that an interference may be compared to a suit between two litigants who have as their bone of contention the problem of determining which one of them is the prior inventor and entitled to get the patent. Like other suits, the interference case begins with the filing of pleadings and motions which are eventually followed by the taking of testimony of witnesses and submission of documentary evidence. When this is completed, the litigants present their briefs and arguments before the tribunal whose duty is then to judge who is the victor. The victor in an interference is the party who has proved the earliest date of invention."

Section 135 provides that:

> (*a*) whenever an application is made for a patent which, in the opinion of the Commissioner, would interfere with any pending application, or with any unexpired patent, he shall give notice thereof to the applicants, or applicant and patentee, as the case may be. The question of priority of invention shall be determined by a board of patent interferences (consisting of three examiners of interferences) whose decision, if adverse to the claim of an applicant,

shall constitute the final refusal by the Patent Office of the claims involved and the Commissioner may issue a patent to the applicant who is adjudged the prior inventor. A final judgment adverse to a patentee from which no appeal or other review has been or can be taken or had shall constitute cancellation of the claim involved from the patent, and notice thereof shall be endorsed on copies of the patent thereafter distributed by the Patent Office.

(*b*) a claim which is the same as, or for the same or substantially the same subject-matter as, a claim of an issued patent may not be made in any application unless such a claim is made prior to one year from the date on which the patent was granted.

(*c*) any agreement or understanding between parties to an interference, including any collateral agreements referred to therein, made in connection with or in contemplation of the termination of the interference, shall be in writing and a true copy thereof filed in the Patent Office before the termination of the interference as between the said parties to the agreement or understanding. If any party filing the same so requests, the copy shall be kept separate from the file of the interference, and made available only to government agencies on written request, or to any person on a showing of good cause. Failure to file the copy of such agreement or understanding shall render permanently unenforceable such agreement or understanding and any patent of such parties involved in the interference or any patent subsequently issued on any application of such parties so involved. The Commissioner may, however, on a showing of good cause for failure to file within the time prescribed, permit the filing of the agreement or understanding during the six-month period subsequent to the termination of the interference as between the parties to the agreement or undertaking.

The Commissioner shall give notice to the parties or their attorneys of record, a reasonable time prior to said termination of the filing requirement of this section. If the Commissioner gives such notice at a later time, irrespective of the right to file such agreement or understanding within the six-month period on a showing of good cause, the parties may file such agreement or understanding within sixty days of the receipt of such notice.

Any discretionary action of the Commissioner under this subsection shall be reviewable under section 10 of the Administrative Procedure Act.

An interference is formally defined in Rule 201 (a) as:

"a proceeding instituted for the purpose of determining the question of priority of invention between two or more parties claiming substantially the same patentable invention and may be instituted as soon as it is determined that common patentable subject matter is claimed in a plurality of applications or in an application and a patent."

Interferences arise on the basis of at least one claim which is considered patentable and which is apparently capable of being awarded to two or more parties. This claim or claims may be taken directly from one of the interfering cases or may be intentionally drafted by the examiner for the purpose of bringing together conflicting applications for priority determination. Interferences may be declared between:

(*a*) two or more applications for original patents;

(*b*) one or more application(s) for original patent(s) and one or more application(s) for reissue patent(s);

(*c*) one or more application(s) for original patent(s) and an original patent;

(*d*) one or more application(s) for original patent(s) and a reissue patent;

(*e*) two or more applications for reissue patents;

(*f*) one or more application(s) for reissue patent(s) and an original patent; or

(*g*) one or more application(s) for reissue patent(s) and a reissue patent.

Interferences will not be declared, nor continued, between cases of the same inventor, nor between cases owned by the same party, unless good cause is shown. It is therefore important that changes in title should be recorded.

Under section 5 (3) (*b*) of Title 37 of the Code of Federal Regulations, interferences might be declared involving an application under secrecy order but unless otherwise specifically ordered or permitted such interferences are suspended after the approval of the preliminary statements. In practice, however, no interference will be declared involving an application which has a security status, unless and until the security status is removed. Claims will be suggested to all parties and when all applications contain these claims suggested the parties will be informed that action on the applications is suspended.

Although Rule 201 (b) permits the declaration of interference between two or more applications containing common patentable subject-matter, when none of the applications is in condition for allowance, in practice no interference will be declared when there is not involved either a patent or an application which, apart from the interference, is in condition for allowance, unless there are unusual circumstances which justify such action and then only after submission to and approval by a supervisory examiner. Also, no interference will be declared between pending applications if there is more than six months' difference between their filing dates, without the approval of the Commissioner based upon an exceptional situation. Under Rule 204 (b), when the effective filing date of an applicant is three months or less, subsequent to the effective filing date of a patentee, the applicant, before an interference will be declared, is required to file an affidavit that he made the invention in the U.S.A. before the effective filing date of the patentee, or that his acts in the U.S.A. with respect to the invention were sufficient to establish priority of invention relative to the effective filing date of the patentee.

Under Rule 204 (c), if the applicant's effective filing date is more than three months subsequent to the effective filing date of the patentee, then before an interference will be declared, the applicant is required to file affidavits by himself and by one or more corroborating witnesses, with any available supporting documentary evidence, setting out a factual description of acts and circumstances which would prima facie entitle him to an award of priority over the effective filing date of the patentee, and accompanied by an explanation of the basis on which he believes that the facts set forth would overcome the patentee's effective filing date.

In cases where interfering patents are issued, either patentee may institute a civil action in which the court may adjudge, *inter alia*, on validity of any of the patents involved either in whole or in part (ss. 291 and 146).

Normally, interference proceedings are initiated by the Patent Office, but an interference may be initiated by an applicant, who may copy the claim(s) of a patent within one year of its date of issue, and at the time of presenting the claim must identify the patent and the claim(s) by number and specifically apply the terms of the copied claim(s) to his own disclosure. He may insert the copied claim(s) in his pending application or he may file a continuation application containing the claim(s).

When a patent is involved in interference proceedings its validity cannot be attacked in such proceedings, since by copying a claim from a patent for interference purposes the validity of the claim is conceded.

In interference proceedings the applicant having the earliest U.S. filing date is referred to as the " senior party," the other party being referred to as the " junior party."

The following dates are of primary importance in deciding the issue of an interference:

(*a*) date of conception of the invention;
(*b*) date of actual or constructive reduction to practice of the invention; and
(*c*) date of filing a patent application in the U.S.A., while another important factor is
(*d*) diligence.

The above terms have the following significance:

Conception

The formation in the mind of the inventor of a definite and permanent idea of the complete and operative invention as it is to be applied in practice. (It is generally not difficult to ascertain this date in the case of sole inventors, but may become very complicated where joint inventors are concerned.)

Actual reduction to practice

The date of actual reduction to practice is the date when the invention was successfully carried out or embodied in physical form. (An abandoned non-copending application constitutes proof of conception, but not proof of reduction to practice.)

Constructive reduction to practice

An invention is constructively reduced to practice as of the filing date of a patent application with an adequate specification.

Diligence

Diligence consists in a reasonable effort directed towards a reduction to practice, and when required to be proved due diligence must be shown from a date prior to the date of conception relied upon by the other party continuously up to the date of actual or constructive reduction to practice.

It is difficult to prognosticate results in interference proceedings, but if there has been no concealment, abandonment or suppression of the invention by either party, the following statements are generally applicable:

(1) The first to conceive and the first to reduce to practice will always prevail;

(2) The first to conceive but the last to reduce to practice will prevail if he can prove due diligence;

(3) The last to conceive but the first to reduce to practice will prevail if the other party cannot prove due diligence.

Acts committed outside the U.S. cannot be relied on, so that anyone domiciled outside the U.S., who has not introduced his invention into the U.S. prior to his U.S. application, must normally rely on his earliest filed foreign application but he can do so only if the U.S. application is entitled to the priority of that foreign application. Of interest in this connection is the case *Lassmann* v. *Brossi, Gerecke and Kyburz*, reported in 159 USPQ 182. Both parties had identical effective filing dates (February 12, 1960), Lassmann in Great Britain and Brossi in Switzerland. Lassmann's evidence showed that in November 1959 his assignees' British Patent Agents had sent to their United States Patent Attorney a letter enclosing a confidential memorandum of his assignees. The memorandum disclosed a process (of preparing an alcohol) meeting the terms of Count 2 of the Interference. The covering letter emphasised that the contents of the memorandum, although to be studied by the United States Attorney, were strictly confidential and must not form the subject of any patent application without the Agents' express instructions. The Board of Interferences held that this evidence proved a date of conception in the U.S.A. which entitled Lassmann to priority on Count 2, and that the confidential nature of the memorandum did not amount to suppression or concealment of the invention. On Count 1 (drawn to an acetic acid ester of the alcohol) it was held that neither party had proved priority and there was not judgment of priority as to this Count. Reference may also be made to the Disclosure Document Programme discussed on pages 246 and 247.

A U.S. domestic inventor can go back to the actual date of conception of his invention (for example by production of laboratory notes), and provided he can show due diligence in reduction to practice and in the filing of his U.S. application, may well be given priority on the basis of his date of conception. Generally speaking, there is nothing a foreign national can do by way of upsetting a date of conception or a date of reduction to practice in interference proceedings but it is sometimes possible for a foreigner to succeed by producing either a printed publication or a granted patent for his own case which may defeat the other party in so far as the date of that other party's U.S. application is concerned.

Thus, it is fatal to a U.S. application if a patent for the same invention has actually been granted, or if the invention has been described in any printed publication, in any country more than one year prior to the date of the U.S. application. (See *Re Bo Thuresson AF Ekenstam,*" 1958 CD, where it was held that the word " patented " as used in 35 USC 102 (a) and (b) is limited to patents which are available to the public, and that it is not necessary that the patent specification should have been printed—it is sufficient that it has been laid open to inspection.)

Prima facie, the foreign national is at a disadvantage when involved in interference with a domestic inventor. However, it is generally easy for the former to prove his U.S. application to be fairly based on his basic application; on the other hand it may not be so simple for a U.S. inventor to prove his date of invention—because of the very strict standards followed in evaluating evidence directed at proving a date of invention.

Interference procedures are carried out in the following stages:

1. *Declaration of Interference*

When an interference exists the primary examiner forwards to the Board of Patent Interferences the files of the cases, and notices of interferences for the parties are prepared in which the issue is stated in the form of claims common to the several applicants. These claims are called the *Counts of the interference.* Thereafter, the examiner of interference institutes and declares the interference by forwarding the notices to the several parties and such notices contain a schedule of time for taking various actions, including the filing of preliminary statements. After the mailing of the notices of interference each party is permitted to see or to obtain copies of each other's applications which are set out in the notices (except for copies of certain affidavits relating to the date of conception of the invention in the U.S.A.).

The preliminary statements are open to the inspection of the senior party and of any junior party who has filed a statement, after the date set for the serving of preliminary statements.

2. *Preliminary Statement*

Each party to the interference is required to file a concise preliminary statement, signed and sworn, giving certain facts, on or before the date fixed by the Office. A party filing a preliminary statement is required at the same time to notify all opposing parties of that fact and within a later period he must serve a copy of his preliminary statement on every opposing party from whom he has received notification of the filing of the statement. A party who fails to serve a copy of his preliminary statement will be restricted to his effective filing date.

The preliminary statement must state that the party made the invention set forth by each count of the interference and whether the invention was made in the U.S. or abroad.

When the invention was made in the U.S. the statement must disclose:

(*a*) the date upon which the first drawing of the invention was made;

(*b*) the date upon which the first written description of the invention was made;

(*c*) the date upon which the invention was first disclosed to another person;

(*d*) the date of the first act or acts susceptible of proof (other than acts as specified in the three preceding sub-paragraphs) which could establish conception of the invention; and a brief description of such acts;

(*e*) the date of actual reduction to practice of the invention; and

(*f*) the date after conception of the invention when active exercise of reasonable diligence toward reducing the invention to practice began.

If any of the acts set out in sub-paragraphs (*a*)–(*f*) has not taken place prior to the filing date of the application, this must be so stated; and copies of the relevant drawing and/or written description must be attached to the statement.

If it is intended to rely solely on a prior application, whether U.S. or foreign, and on no other evidence, the statement may so state and need not be signed or sworn to by the inventor.

When the invention was made abroad the facts set out in sub-paragraphs (*a*)–(*f*) above are not required but in lieu thereof it should be stated:

(*a*) When the invention was introduced into the U.S. by or on behalf of the party, giving the circumstances, with the dates, relied on to establish the fact, and when appropriate, allegations of activity of the nature of that set out in sub-paragraphs (*a*)–(*f*) above;

(*b*) If a party is entitled to priority rights because he made the invention while domiciled in the U.S. but serving in a foreign country in connection with operation by or on behalf of the U.S., he must so state and his statement must include allegations of activity abroad corresponding to those required by sub-paragraphs (*a*)–(*f*) above.

The preliminary statement is a most important document because it is the foundation of the subsequent testimony and proof, and the applicant is held to the date set up in the preliminary statement even though the proof later on should disclose earlier dates. However, in case of inadvertence or mistake the preliminary statements may be amended if the Patent Office consents.

3. *Motions Period*

Within the period set in the notice of interference various motions may be brought by any of the parties. The main motions are as follows:

(*a*) to dissolve as to one or more counts;

(*b*) to amend the issue by addition or substitution of new counts;

(*c*) to substitute or include another application;

(*d*) to shift the burden of proof; and

(*e*) to amend an involved application by adding or removing one or more inventors.

Consideration of any motion is given by a primary examiner at a hearing appointed for the purpose. This period is best regarded as one of manoeuvre to obtain tactical advantages, and many complicated motions are possible within the main headings.

4. *Testimony*

After the conclusion of any motion proceedings, times are set by the Patent Office for the taking of testimony in support of the preliminary statements.

Testimony is normally taken in the form of answers to questions, under oath, before an officer authorised to administer oaths, and both parties are entitled to the usual right of cross-examination of the witnesses. After testimony is taken, the typewritten depositions are sent by the officer, duly certified, to the Patent Office. The costs involved in the taking of testimony are borne by the respective parties to the interference proceedings.

Instead of testimony, the parties may make an agreed statement of facts and the Patent Office will decide the case on the basis of that statement.

5. *Hearing*

Following the filing of testimony, briefs are submitted and the case is argued orally before the interference tribunal. The hearing is called a final hearing and is before the Board of Interference Examiners.

6. *Appeal*

A request or petition for rehearing or reconsideration or modification of the decision must be filled within 30 days from the date of the original decision.

An appeal from the decision of the Board of Interference Examiners may be taken to the Court of Customs and Patents Appeals within a period of not more than 60 days from the date of the decision, or within 30 days from the date of the decision on a petition for rehearing or reconsideration. The appeal will, however, be dismissed if any adverse party to the interference, within 20 days after notice of appeal has been filed, notifies the Commissioner that he elects to proceed under section 146, *i.e.*, by civil action in a district court. Thereupon the appellant has 30 days within which to file a civil action under section 146 and if he does not do so, the decision of the Board of Interference Examiners will govern any further proceedings.

Any party to an interference, instead of appealing to the Court of Customs and Patents Appeals may have remedy by civil action under section 146 if commenced within not more than 60 days from the date of the decision unless he has already appealed to the Court of Customs and Patents Appeals and such appeal is pending or has been decided.

There is no appeal from a decision of the CCPA but a decision of a District Court may be appealed to the Court of Appeals for that district. The Supreme Court may review any decision of the CCPA or of a Court of Appeals but such a review lies by way of writ of certiorari.

7. *Informal Settlement*

It frequently happens that, to save time and expense, an informal settlement is reached by the parties. In such cases the interference may be taken through all stages up to testimony to establish the real issues at stake. Instead of testimony, however, the parties confer to decide the issues between themselves and if unable to reach complete agreement, outstanding issues will be determined by the Patent Office. It is not, however, necessary to take the interference as far as testimony, because the proceedings may be terminated at any time by an applicant or patentee filing a written disclaimer or concession of priority or abandonment of the invention.

One difficulty to be considered in informal settlements is that due care must be exercised to avoid conflict with anti-trust laws.

Any agreement or understanding between parties in an interference, made in connection with or in contemplation of the termination of the interference must be in writing and a true copy thereof must be filed in the Patent Office before the termination of the interference. As provided in section 135 (*c*) any such agreement may, on request by the party filing it, be kept separate from the interference file and made available only to government agencies on written request or to any person on a showing of good cause.

Failure to file a copy of the agreement renders it permanently unenforceable, as well as any patent, or patent subsequently issued, of the parties and involved in the interference. The Commissioner is, however, empowered, on a showing of good cause for failure to file within the prescribed time, to permit filing of the agreement within a period of six months subsequent to termination of the interference.

The Commissioner is bound to give notice to the parties, a reasonable time before termination of the interference, of the requirement to file a copy of any settlement agreement. If notice is given after termination then, irrespective of the right to file within the six-months' grace period, the parties may file the agreement within 60 days of receipt of the notice.

The Court of Appeals, District of Columbia, has held that the Commissioner has no authority to accept a settlement agreement after expiration of the six-months' grace period following termination of the interference. The court pointed out that section 135 (*c*) does not distinguish between deliberate disregard and mere neglect in tendering the agreement. The requirement of the statute that the Commissioner should give notice of the filing requirement " a reasonable time prior " to termination of the interference is not to be construed to mean that notice must be given shortly before termination; notice given a few days after enactment of the statute was sufficient although the interference was not settled and terminated until 16 months later.

8. *Costs*

There is no provision under the patent laws or rules for costs—each party normally pays his own costs. However, testimony proceedings are conducted under the Federal Rules of Civil Procedure and a case might arise where some costs could be granted, but such a case would be exceedingly rare.

The foregoing comments are intended to apply to interferences declared after July 1, 1965.

Canada—Conflict Proceedings

Conflict proceedings in Canada are, in principle, akin to interference proceedings in the U.S., but in Canada they relate only to pending applications and there is really no comparison between the two sets of procedure, that in Canada being simple in the extreme as compared with that in the U.S. A fundamental difference between U.S. interference practice and Canadian conflict practice is that, in the latter, acts committed *in any country* may be relied on to establish date of invention. Conflict procedure is governed by section 45 and Rules 66–74.

In Canada, conflict between two or more pending applications (of different inventorship and ownership) exists:

(*a*) when each of them contains one or more claims defining substantially the same invention, or

(*b*) when one or more claims of one application describe the invention disclosed in the other application.

Procedure before Conflict is Declared

When two or more applications appear to be in conflict, the Commissioner notifies each of the applicants of the apparent conflict and transmits to each of them a copy of the conflicting claims and gives to each applicant the opportunity of inserting the same or similar claims in his application within a specified time. The alleged conflicting claims may be taken from either or both applications, or may be drafted by the Patent Office itself.

Preliminary Notice of Conflict

When two or more applications are regarded as in conflict, the Commissioner notifies each of the applicants and sets a time wherein each applicant wishing to pursue the conflict may adopt the claims in conflict or offer other claims. An applicant may avoid the conflict by amendment or cancellation of the conflicting claims or may submit prior art alleged to anticipate the claims. In the latter event each application is re-examined with reference to the prior art and the Commissioner decides whether or not the subject-matter of each claim is patentable. An applicant is not entitled to amend an application further except for the purpose of defining the conflict, and he may not subsequently reassert any claim which has been amended or cancelled to avoid a conflict, nor can he assert any claim not patentably different from that defined in the claim so amended or cancelled. As in the United States, a party having a much earlier filing date may be able to refer to an early publication, *e.g.*, of his Belgian patent as a statutory bar under section 28 (1) (*b*) to the later application.

Formal Declaration of Conflict

Where the subject-matter is found to be patentable and the conflicting claims are retained in the application, each applicant must file in the Patent Office, in a sealed envelope and within a period set by the Commissioner, an affidavit of the record of the invention. This affidavit must declare:

(*a*) the date at which the idea of the invention described in the conflicting claims was conceived anywhere;

(*b*) the date upon which the first drawing of the invention was made;

(*c*) the date when and the mode in which the first written or verbal disclosure of the invention was made; and (*d*) the dates and nature of the successive steps subsequently taken by the inventor to develop and perfect the said invention from time to time up to the date of the filing of the application for patent.

If the earliest date to be relied on is a priority date, then a certified copy of the basic application should be attached to the affidavit. If laboratory notebooks can be relied on, they likewise should form exhibits to the evidence. Weight will be given them even though there is no corroborative evidence of the experiments.

Withdrawal of the affidavit and substitution of a new affidavit is permissible but only if made before the opening of the affidavits by the Commissioner.

The envelope containing the affidavits cannot be opened nor can the affidavits be inspected unless there continues to be conflict, in which event all the envelopes are opened at the same time by the Commissioner in the presence of the Assistant Commissioner or the examiner and the date of such opening is endorsed upon the affidavits.

Decision

By examining the facts stated in the affidavits, the Commissioner determines which of the applicants is the prior inventor to whom he will allow the claims in conflict and forwards to each applicant a copy of his decision as well as copies of each affidavit by the other party or parties.

Appeal to Exchequer Court

The decision of the Commissioner becomes effective unless, before the expiry of a period set by him, one of the applicants appeals to the Exchequer Court, whereupon the Commissioner suspends further action pending the decision of that court.

Philippines—Interference Procedure

Interference procedure in the Philippines is covered by section 10 and by Rules 190–238. For all practical purposes the Act, rules and procedure are identical with those of the U.S. prior to July 1, 1965. The proceedings are taken by the Director of the Patent Office from whose decision an appeal may be made to the Supreme Court. It is difficult to believe, however, that the Philippines Patent Office is suitably staffed to cope with such complex procedure.

CHAPTER 14

UNITED STATES OF AMERICA

Patents in U.S.A.—Further Notes

[*Where a section of an Act is mentioned in parentheses following a country the section refers to the Patents Act of that country.*]

PATENT applications in the U.S.A. may be filed under a variety of circumstances.

Original or parent application

Either term may be applied to the first application of a series filed by the same inventor accompanied by a specification which first discloses an invention in respect of which the series of applications is being prosecuted. Such an invention may or may not be claimed in the original or parent application.

The term " original " may also be applied to any application which has not stemmed from an earlier filed application.

Divisional application

A later application is a division of a prior application of the same inventor when it is co-pending and when the entire subject-matter of the later application is found in the earlier application and there is also disclosed in the earlier application matter not claimed in the later application. Like most other applications the divisional application must be complete in itself, that is, it must include a separate petition, oath or declaration, etc.

When a new process is being separated from a new apparatus, for example, it is possible for the divisional application to be filed with a specification and drawings which are the same as those of the original or parent application, but in general the divisional application will have a specification which is restricted to the invention of the divisional case.

When justified by the circumstances of inventorship, one or more inventors of a parent application may be omitted from the divisional application.

Abandoned

An abandoned application to which the rights of further prosecution have been surrendered may be the subject of

A refile for abandoned application

(Sometimes called " substitute application ") which is an application not formally connected with the abandoned application disclosing common, but no new, patentable subject-matter.

Continuation application

When a second application is filed in respect of the same invention claimed in a prior application, and while the prior application is pending, the second application is known as a continuation application. The applicant must, except in the special circumstances provided by Rule 45, be the same as in the prior application. The continuation application must contain a specific reference to the prior application, and the disclosure must be the same as that of the prior application, that is to say, the continuation must not include anything which would constitute new matter if inserted in the prior application.

Where an application has been prosecuted to final rejection, an applicant may have recourse to filing a continuation in order to introduce into the case a new set of claims and to establish a right to further examination by the primary examiner. If the new claims, however, are in the opinion of the examiner met in the art of record in the original application, the examiner may make his rejection final on the first action on the continuation.

The filing of a " continuation " may therefore be useful where, after an application has been filed, the prosecution becomes " snarled," as by claiming the wrong subject-matter. The original application may be continued as to prosecution or abandoned, depending upon whether it could have any possible further value.

Streamlined continuation application

In a continuation case where specification and drawings are unchanged, a simple procedure is available whereby the original documents are adopted for the new case. Where this procedure is used the new application is known as a streamlined continuation. It should be emphasised that the procedure is limited to true continuation applications and is not available for use when filing any other type of continuing (*e.g.* a divisional) application.

As set out in MPEP—201.07, if the drawings and specification of a new application are to be identical with those of a pending application of the same applicant and if the claims are to be directed to the same invention as that prosecuted in the pending application, the application papers of the earlier case, excepting the claims but including the drawing, may be used in the new case. A request for the use of such papers must be made and such request will be considered a waiver of the right to further prosecution of the earlier application and will terminate proceedings therein as of the filing date accorded the new application. The streamlined continuation application will be considered as having been filed before the abandonment of the earlier application. A new set of claims directed to the same invention as that prosecuted in the pending application is required. The filing fee will be that appropriate to all the claims to be included in the new case. The entire file wrapper contents of the earlier application will be included in the file of the new one but the Office actions in the former will not be regarded as actions in the latter and the prosecution of the new application will be conducted in the same manner as if new application papers had been filed. A new serial number and filing date will be accorded but the effective filing date will be that of the earlier application.

The streamlined continuation application procedure may not be used when at the time of filing the continuation application:

(1) the parent application has been allowed and the issue fee has been paid;

(2) the parent application is, or has been, involved in court action;

(3) the parent application has been abandoned;

(4) the parent application is, or has been, involved in an interference declared prior to the date of filing the streamlined continuation application.

If there is a defect in the format of a streamlined application which can be corrected, such as failure to include claims drawn to the same invention prosecuted in the parent application, failure to grant a power of attorney in either application to the person filing the continuation application, or some other minor defect, the applicant will be given one month to correct the defect. Failure to do so will result in the cancellation of the continuation application.

While the conditions of the streamlined practice require that the claims are to be directed to the same invention as that prosecuted in the pending application, the inclusion of one such claim will be acceptable to preserve the serial number and filing date. Claims to the same invention in continuation cases are claims which cannot be properly restricted from the claims prosecuted in the parent application and are fully supported by that disclosure.

Although the filing of a defective streamlined continuation will not operate to abandon the parent case, neither will it prevent the parent case from becoming abandoned by operation of law. On the other hand, in situations where the parent case is awaiting action by the Office, no action will be taken while the streamlined continuation application is being reviewed for acceptability of its filing date.

Continuation-in-part application

A continuation-in-part application is similar to a continuation application except that it discloses added new patentable subject-matter.

A continuation-in-part application is entitled to the benefit of the parent application filing date only as to subject-matter common to the two applications.

A continuation-in-part application necessarily requires that additional subject-matter be included as where the disclosure is inadequate, or where additional inventive subject-matter has come forth since the filing of the parent case. Here, the continued prosecution of the parent case may be desirable to cover some particular phase, while the broad claims can be prosecuted in the continuation-in-part application.

As to whether or not the parent case should be continued will depend upon the individual circumstances of the case, but an application should not be abandoned if it can possibly be of further service, either from the standpoint of an interference problem, or to take care of some phase of the invention which cannot properly be claimed in connection with the continuation-in-part application.

In continuation-in-part applications it is not necessary to have absolute identity of applicants with the parent application. Thus, there can be a sole applicant (A) in a continuation-in-part of a joint (A+B) parent, or the converse. But, it is not possible to have a continuation-in-part where there is no common applicant.

Forfeited application

A forfeited application is one upon which a patent has been withheld for failure to pay the issue fee within the prescribed time.

Such an application is not considered as pending while forfeited and, if the issue fee is not subsequently paid and accepted, the application is abandoned as of the date it became forfeited, *i.e.*, the date of expiry of the three months' period allowed for payment of the issue fee.

If the issue fee is belatedly accepted, as it may be, within a further three months and on filing evidence showing cause of late payment, the patent is issued and there is no possibility of the forfeited application being restored to pendency.

Reissue application

This kind of application is discussed in detail on pages 22 to 25 hereof.

Final Rejection

On the second or any subsequent examination or consideration, the rejection or other action may be made final, whereupon the applicant's response is limited to appeal in the case of rejection of any claim, or to amendment by cancellation of rejected claims, or by complying with any requirement of form which has been made. Amendments presenting rejected claims in better form for consideration on appeal may be admitted; but the admission of any such amendment, or its refusal, and any proceedings relative thereto, do not operate to relieve the application from its condition as subject to appeal or to save it from abandonment under Rule 135.

Petition may be taken to the Commissioner in the case of rejections or requirements not involved in the rejection of any claim. Response to a final rejection or action must include cancellation of, or appeal from the rejection of, each claim so rejected and, if any claim stands allowed, compliance with any requirement or rejection as to form.

In making a final rejection, the examiner states specifically at the end of the official action " The above rejection is made final " or " This is a final rejection," and in the final action he must repeat or state all grounds of rejection then considered applicable to the claims in the case, clearly stating the reasons for rejection.

In certain instances the claims in a new application may be finally rejected in the first action. This may be done if (*a*) the new application is a continuing application of, or a substitute for, an earlier application, and (*b*) all the claims of the new application are drawn to the same invention claimed in the earlier application, and would have been properly finally rejected on the art of record in the next Office action if they had been entered in the earlier application.

A first action final rejection in a new application which is a continuation-in-part of an earlier application is usually not proper because ordinarily subject-matter included in the claims was not present in the parent application.

Under current practice, a second action on the merits will be made final unless (*a*) it introduces a new ground of rejection not necessitated by amendment of the application or (*b*) it includes a rejection of an unamended claim on the basis of newly cited art.

A final rejection may be withdrawn by the examiner if, for example, the applicant, who is normally permitted one interview after final rejection, can present convincing new facts or reasons to show that rejected claims are allowable or that specific amendments will overcome the objections. Unless the application can be amended so as to place it in condition for allowance before the period for final response expires, a notice of appeal must be filed if the application is to be maintained.

Supplemental Oath or Declaration

When an applicant presents a claim for matter originally shown or described but not substantially embraced in the statement of invention or claim originally presented, he must file a supplemental oath or declaration to the effect that the subject-matter of the proposed amendment was part of his invention.

In addition to the statements made in the original oath or declaration the applicant must also swear that the invention has not been abandoned.

A supplemental oath or declaration may be filed after allowance.

U.S.A.—Claims

The scope of a U.S. patent is determined by the claim or claims which are, however, construed in the light of the specification (Kotler 901 CD 62).

The basic provisions concerning claims are contained in sections 112, 253, 282 and 288, and in Rule 75, and may be summarised as follows:

(1) The specification must conclude with one or more claims particularly pointing out and distinctly claiming the subject-matter which the applicant regards as his invention or discovery.

(2) If more than one claim is presented, all must differ substantially from each other, and must not be unduly multiplied.

(3) Claims must conform to the invention set forth in the description, and terms and phrases used in the claims must find clear support in the description. Although a term may be given a special meaning in the description, the special meaning must not be repugnant to the usual meaning of the term.

(4) Claims may be written in independent or dependent form.

(5) Where the nature of the case admits, an independent claim should comprise, in the following order:

(*a*) a preamble reciting all the known elements or steps of the claimed combination;

(*b*) a phrase such as " wherein the invention comprises "; and

(*c*) a recital of those elements, steps and/or relationships which constitute that portion of the claimed combination which the applicant considers as the new or improved portion.

(6) An element in a claim for a combination may be expressed as a means or step for performing a specified function without the recital of structure, material, or acts in support thereof.

(7) A combination claim will be construed to cover the corresponding structure, material or acts described in the specification, and equivalents thereof.

(8) A dependent claim will be construed to include all the limitations of the claim incorporated by reference into the dependent claim.

(9) A dependent claim must refer back to and further restrict a single preceding claim which can itself be a dependent claim referring to a single preceding claim.

(10) Each claim is presumed valid, whether in independent or dependent form, and a dependent claim is presumed valid even though dependent on an invalid claim.

(11) An invalid claim may be disclaimed if there has been no deceptive intention.

(12) Where any claim is invalid (without deceptive intent) an infringement action may be maintained in respect of any valid claims; but costs will not be awarded the patentee unless a disclaimer of the invalid claim(s) has been entered before commencement of the suit.

Although the form of independent claim referred to above under (5) is a recent innovation in the Rules, its origin is to be found in the decided case, *Ex p. Jepson*, 1917 CD 62, in which this (European) type of claim was approved. Since the decision, the claim has been known in the U.S. as a " Jepson " type claim.

Approval for the dependent claim is found in *Ex p. Brown*, 1917 CD 22 wherein it was said " There are doubtless many cases where claims could not be successfully written in dependent clauses; but it seems to be perfectly logical to allow an applicant who wishes to do so to write his claim in that form in a proper case, as this is. A too strict adherence to form may be responsible for the obscurity and superfluity of claims in many patents."

From a consideration of the above requirements, the following principles are generally applicable in drafting U.S. claims:

(1) Elements should be positively claimed with appropriate antecedent basis.
(2) Alternative expressions are not proper, except where they are used to refer to the same element.
(3) An aggregation of elements cannot be claimed, an aggregation being a group of elements which are not dependent upon each other, to give the desired result. This is to be distinguished from a true combination where elements co-operate to give the result which is sought.
(4) Elements should be described sufficiently to give an operative device, process or composition.
(5) The use of exclusively functional terminology should be avoided. However, functional terminology is acceptable in defining means broadly or in amplifying upon the function of a specifically recited element.
(6) Single means claims are improper but a plurality of means clauses may be used to define a new combination.

(7) Negative expressions should be avoided if positive terminology is possible. Parenthetical expressions should also be avoided.

(8) Claims should not be drawn to " old " combination. For example, where two elements have previously been used in combination, an improvement in one element, as a general rule, should not be claimed as a combination but in the improved element *per se*.

(9) Claim terminology should be correlated with the description and should be consistent.

(10) Claims may depend upon only one preceding claim and reference to the specification is improper.

A type of claim frequently adopted in chemical cases is known as a " Markush " claim, the name deriving from the decided case, *Ex p. Markush*, 1925 CD 126, in which it was said ". . . where the validity of the claim is not involved, the paucity of the language may necessitate a waiver of technical rules of this Office, to the end that the applicant may protect his real invention." In the result the applicant was allowed to recite " material selected from the group consisting of aniline, homologues of aniline and halogen substitutes of aniline," there being unknown any term which would include the named substances but which would exclude inoperative materials.

This type of claim may also be used in the fields of metallurgy, refractories, ceramics, pharmacy, pharmacology and biology. It may not be used in claiming purely mechanical features or process steps.

Ex p. Burke, 1934 CD 5, provides authority for Markush claims of varying scope in the same case but only when there is some property in common to the members in the more restricted claim not shared by other members in the broader claim.

The use of Markush claims of diminishing scope is not in itself considered a sufficient basis for objection to or rejection of claims unless such a practice renders the claims indefinite or if it results in undue multiplicity.

In drafting " Markush " claims the following points are of importance:

(*a*) The proper form is " material selected from the group consisting of A, B, . . . N."

(*b*) It is improper to use the term " comprising " instead of " consisting of."

(*c*) When a proper Markush group exists it may be recited in the conventional manner, or alternatively for example, if " . . . wherein R is a material selected from the group consisting of A, B, C and D " is a proper limitation then ". . . wherein R is A, B, C or D " shall also be considered proper.

(*d*) The materials set forth in the Markush group ordinarily must belong to a recognised physical or chemical class or to an art-recognised class.

(*e*) A Markush expression in the negative—" a substance selected from the group consisting of nitrates other than silver nitrate "—was approved—53 USPQ 391.

U.S.A.—Generic and Species Claims

U.S. law does not allow two or more independent and distinct inventions to be claimed in one application, but up to five species of an invention may be specifically claimed in different claims in one application, provided (a) that the application also includes an allowable claim generic to all the claimed species and (b) all the claims to each species in excess of one are written in dependent form or otherwise include all the limitations of the generic claim (r. 141).

Election of Species

In the first action on an application containing a generic claim and claims restricted separately to each of more than one species embraced thereby, the examiner, if of the opinion after a complete search on the generic claims that no generic claim presented is allowable, shall require the applicant in his response to that action to elect that species of his invention to which his claims shall be restricted if no generic claim is finally held allowable. If the application contains claims directed to more than five species, the examiner may require restriction of the claims to not more than five species before taking any further action in the case (r. 146).

The non-elected inventions may be made the subject of separate applications, which must of course conform to the rules applicable to original applications (r. 147).

The following official notice dated March 11, 1965, concerning practice under Rule 147 (which applies to any application where there has been a call for division, *i.e.*, for election between separate inventions or species) is of interest:

" In view of the frequent misunderstandings which have arisen as to the filing of applications under Rule 147 it is considered advisable to issue the following statement as to the practice under that rule.

" The rule is clearly restricted by its terms to divisional applications directed to ' non-elected inventions, those not elected after a requirement for restriction.' It is thus more limited than 35 USC 121, on which it is based and applies only to divisional applications which are necessitated by a requirement for restriction in the parent case.

" It is further to be noted that a Rule 147 application comprises (a) a copy of the original application as filed, prepared and certified by the Patent Office and (b) a proposed amendment cancelling the irrelevant claims or other matter. The sole justification for the use of unexecuted copies in the divisional application is that their subject-matter has already been executed in the parent case. Accordingly, an application under Rule 147 should not, either as filed or by a preliminary amendment prior to the time when it is accorded a filing date, contain anything whatever that was not present in the parent application as filed. The Patent Office cannot undertake, prior to giving a filing date, to decide whether differences between the parent and divisional case involve matters of substance or of form only. It follows that any proposed amendments to the divisional application should be withheld until it has received a filing date.

" Since a Rule 147 application must be based on the parent case as filed and must be directed to non-elected inventions, the claims which it is sought to include in such an application must be original claims of the parent case and must have been present in that case in their original form when the restriction requirement was made; but if that condition is satisfied, it is not material that other claims were amended or new claims were added prior to the requirement so long as no such amended or added claim is to be included in the Rule 147 application.

" An amendment stating that the Rule 147 application is a division of the parent case may accompany the application but no other amendments to the specification or drawing should be requested until the application has received its serial number and filing date.

"Since Rule 147 is limited by its terms to cases in which the parent application is still pending when the divisional case is filed, it is necessary that all requirements of the rule be satisfied prior to abandonment or patenting of the parent application."

Disclosure Document Programme

Under this programme the U.S. Patent Office accepts and preserves for a limited time, under conditions of confidence, "Disclosure Documents" as evidence of the dates of conception of inventions. The programme thus provides a vehicle for Patent Office recordal of disclosures for conception or introduction into the United States, and the possibility of obtaining for interference purposes a date prior to that of a basic foreign filing.

As set out in MPEP 1706, a paper disclosing an invention and signed by the inventor(s) may be forwarded to the Patent Office by the inventor, or by any one of joint inventors, or by the owner of the invention, or by the attorney or agent of the inventor(s) or owner. The Disclosure Document will be preserved in the Patent Office for two years and then will be destroyed unless it is referred to in a separate letter in a related patent application filed within the two-year period. The Disclosure Document must be referred to in the separate letter by title, number and date of receipt. Acknowledgment of receipt of such letters will be made by the Patent Office. Unless it is desired to have the Patent Office retain the Document beyond the two-year period, it is not required that it be referred to in a patent application.

The Document is *not* a patent application, and the date of its receipt in the Patent Office will *not* become the effective filing date of any patent application subsequently filed. Like patent applications, however, the documents will be kept in confidence by the Patent Office. If patent protection is desired a patent application should be filed as soon as possible. It should be emphasised that the two-year retention period is not a "grace period" during which the inventor may defer the filing of his U.S. patent application without possible loss of benefits. It must be recognised that in establishing priority of invention, an affidavit or testimony referring to a Disclosure Document must usually also establish diligence in completing the invention or in filing the patent application subsequent to the filing of the Disclosure Document. Further, any public use or sale in the United States, or patenting or publication of the invention anywhere in the world more than one year prior to the filing of a United States patent application on that invention will prohibit the granting of a valid patent on it.

So far as concerns preparation of the Document, there are no restrictions as to content, and claims are not necessary. Since, however, the benefits afforded by the procedure will depend directly on the adequacy of the disclosure, the Document should contain a clear and complete explanation of the manner and process of making and using the invention in sufficient detail to enable a person having ordinary knowledge in the field of the invention to make and use the invention. When the nature of the invention permits, a drawing or sketch should be included. The use or utility of the invention should be described, especially in chemical inventions.

The Disclosure Document must be limited to written matter or drawing on paper or other thin, flexible material, such as linen or plastic drafting material, having dimensions, or being folded to dimensions, not exceeding $8\frac{1}{2}$ by 13 inches. Photographs also are acceptable. Each page should be numbered. Text and drawings should be sufficiently dark to permit reproduction with commonly used office copying machines.

In addition to the fee of $10.00, a Disclosure Document must be accompanied by a stamped, self-addressed envelope and a separate paper in duplicate, signed by the inventor, stating that he is the inventor and requesting that the material be received for processing under the Disclosure Document Programme. The papers will be stamped by the Patent Office with an identifying number and date of receipt, and the duplicate request will be returned in the self-addressed envelope together with a notice indicating that the Disclosure Document may be relied upon only as evidence and that a patent application should be diligently filed if patent protection is desired. The inventor's request may take the following form:

> "The undersigned, being the inventor of the disclosed invention, requests that the enclosed papers be accepted under the Disclosure Document Programme, and that they be preserved for a period of two years."

Defensive Publications

Under Rule 139, an applicant may waive his rights to an enforceable patent based on a pending patent application by filing in the Patent Office a written waiver of patent rights, a consent to the publication of an abstract, an authorisation to open the complete application to inspection by the general public, and a declaration of abandonment signed by the applicant and the assignee of record or by the attorney or agent of record.

This Rule was adopted in order to institute a new Defensive Publication Programme intended to provide better service to the public by making available the technical disclosure of certain applications in which the owner might prefer to publish an abstract in lieu of obtaining an examination by the Patent Office.

The procedure is set out in detail in MPEP 711–06.

A request to have an abstract of the technical disclosure of his application published as a defensive abstract may be filed, by an applicant, only (1) while a pending application is awaiting the first Office action or (2) within eight months of the earliest effective U.S. filing date if a first Office action has been issued and responded to within the said eight-month period. The application is laid open for public inspection and the applicant provisionally abandons the application but retains his rights to an interference for a limited period of five years from the earliest effective U.S. filing date.

No fee is required under the procedure.

The defensive publication of an application precludes of any continuing application filed under section 120 from being entitled to the benefit of the defensively published application unless the continuing application is filed within thirty months after the earliest effective U.S. filing date.

A request for defensive publication cannot be withdrawn after it has been accepted by the office.

The approved Defensive Publication Abstract and a selected figure of the drawing, if any, are published in the Official Gazette. Copies of the application are obtainable on payment of fee.

An application may be considered for defensive publication provided the applicant files a request under Rule 139 agreeing to the conditions for defensive publication. The statement requesting publication should be signed by the assignee of record, or by the attorney or agent of record, or by the applicant and the assignee of record, if any, and should:

(1) Request the Commissioner to publish an abstract of the disclosure in the Official Gazette;

(2) Authorise the Commissioner to lay open to public inspection the complete application upon publication of the abstract in the Official Gazette;

(3) Expressly abandon the application to take effect five years from the earliest U.S. effective filing date of the application unless interference proceedings have been initiated within that period, and

(4) Waive all rights to an enforceable patent based on said application as well as on any continuing application filed more than 30 months after the earliest effective U.S. filing date of said application.

The abstract should be entitled " Defensive Publication Abstract " and may contain up to 200 words and be an expanded version of the abstract required under rule 72 (b).

The application will be scrutinised by the examiner to determine whether it is suitable for publication, and he will also ascertain that the abstract and selected figure of the drawing, if any, adequately reflect the technical disclosure.

If there are defects in the request, the applicant will be given a period of one month within which to remove the defects. Failure to remove any defect will result in refusal of the request for defensive publication and in resumption of the prosecution of the application by the Office. Petition may be taken to the Commissioner from the disapproval of a request for defensive publication.

During the five-year period from its earliest U.S. effective filing date, interferences may be declared between defensive publication applications and other applications and/or patents, in accordance with existing interference rules and procedures. Abandonment of a defensive publication application will be stayed during the period beginning with the suggestion of claims or the filing of claims copied from a patent and ending with the termination of the interference proceedings or the mailing of a decision refusing the interference.

Termination of an interference in favour of a defensive publication application would render the express abandonment ineffective but would not result in the issuance of an enforceable patent. The Examiner will cancel all the claims in the case except those awarded to the applicant, and the notice of allowance will require the applicant, when remitting the issue fee, to include a disclaimer of the entire term of the patent to be granted.

CHAPTER 15

NEW LEGISLATION

ON January 1, 1968, new Patents Acts came into force in Denmark, Finland, Norway and Sweden; also part of the German amending Act came into force on that date, the remainder coming into force on October 1, 1968. The new Israeli Act came into force on April 1, 1968, whilst a new French Act was passed on January 2, 1968, and came into force on January 1, 1969.

These new Acts are indicative of the current activity, both nationally and internationally, in patent legislation.

Scandinavia

The new Patents Acts which came into force in Denmark, Finland, Norway and Sweden on January 1, 1968, are substantially identical and represent an almost complete harmonisation of patent law in the four countries. The main differences arise from the differing national Penal and Civil Codes, so that there are different legal procedures.

It should be emphasised that the new Acts represent harmonisation but not integration. Thus, at present, patent protection must be sought separately in the four countries. Although each of the Acts contains provisions whereby an applicant by filing and prosecuting an application in one of the countries may obtain separate national patents in three or all of the countries, these provisions will not come into force until the conclusion of a special agreement between the four countries.

The more important aspects of the new Acts are set out below.

Patentability

A patent may be granted in respect of any invention which (*a*) is susceptible of industrial exploitation; (*b*) is new; and (*c*) involves an inventive step.

There has thus been a widening of the field of patentable subject-matter so that, for example, new chemical compounds may now be protected *per se*. Also there was the possibility of introducing product claims into existing unaccepted applications which provided sufficient support therefor. Such claims, however, in all four countries, required limitation to specified intended uses of the product.

As before, processes are patentable and the patent covers the direct products of the patented process.

For a period as yet undetermined, it will not be possible to obtain patent protection for medicines and foodstuffs as products. Additionally in Denmark, protection is not obtainable for processes for producing foodstuffs.

Patents will not be granted for inventions the use of which would be contrary to morality or public order, nor for plant or animal varieties or essentially biological processes for the production of plants or animals. Patents may, however, be granted for microbiological processes and products resulting from such processes.

Novelty

The standard of novelty is now absolute, so that an invention will not be considered to be new if it has been made available to the public anywhere; by means of written or oral description, by use, or in any other way, before the date of application or of any earlier date validly claimed.

The prior art includes the contents of a local patent application of earlier date if it is made available to the public. But a main application will not prejudice an application for a patent of addition thereto which must be filed before the main application has been made available to the public.

Novelty is not destroyed through prior disclosure by (*a*) the legitimate applicant at an officially recognised international exhibition; or (*b*) by a third party in obvious abuse of the rights of the legitimate applicant; provided that a patent application is filed within six months after such disclosure.

It may also be noted that if a third party satisfies the Patent Office that legal title in an invention belongs to him, the Office may transfer the patent application to him. If there is doubt, the Office may direct that the matter will be taken to court. Pending the outcome of either form of action, the patent application is kept in abeyance.

Publication

The documents of an application will be made available to the public 18 months after the date of application, or if convention priority is claimed after the priority date.

The documents may be made available at an earlier date if the applicant so requests.

Dismissed or rejected applications will not be made available unless the applicant requests resumption of prosecution or enters an appeal.

Applications filed prior to January 1, 1968, were not made available before July 1, 1968, unless prior to that date the application was laid open to public inspection following acceptance, or the applicant requested that the documents be made available to the public.

A document containing, for example, trade secrets which do not concern the invention for which protection is sought, may be withheld from publication on a special request being made.

In the Norwegian text it is made clear that documents prepared by the Patent Office for its own use in the prosecution of an application will not be laid open unless the Patent Office itself decides.

Third Party Rights

Anyone who, on the date of an application, was legitimately using an invention commercially or had made substantial preparations to do so, may continue such use. Transfer of such rights may only be effected with the goodwill of the business concerned in the use or intended use. Similar rights extend to parties who had used, or prepared to use, a previously unpatentable invention if the invention is subsequently patented under the new Acts.

If the use or preparation for use occurred after the application date, but before the application documents were made available to the public, and if a patent is granted, the third party may be granted a compulsory licence provided

(*a*) there exist very special reasons in favour of the grant of a compulsory licence; and

(*b*) he had no knowledge of the application and had not reasonably been able to obtain such knowledge.

Compulsory Licences

After three years from grant (but not less than four years from the application date) compulsory licences are available if a patented invention is not being worked to a reasonable extent and there is no good reason for the lack of working.

The owner of a patented invention of which working is prevented by another patent may obtain a compulsory licence to exploit that other invention, when the importance of his invention justifies it. The owner of the dominating patent may obtain a cross-licence in the absence of good reasons against.

Compulsory licences may also be granted in the case of patented inventions of importance to public interest.

A compulsory licence will be granted only to a party having resources adequate to exploit the invention; they are granted by the court which determines all the terms and they may be varied or revoked should circumstances change.

The grant of a compulsory licence does not prevent a patentee from exploiting his invention nor from licensing other parties.

Effect of Patent

Grant of a patent confers on the patentee the exclusive right to use the invention commercially by using the patented process, by making, importing, using or offering for sale, leasing or lending a product protected by the patent, or in any other way. Rights in respect of a patented process extend to products made according to the process.

The exclusive rights do not extend to the use of products which have been sold retail if at the time of purchase the buyer did not know, or could not reasonably be expected to know, that an exclusive right was being infringed.

The rights commence with final acceptance of an application (*i.e.*, the granting decision), and an infringer may be required to pay compensation for use of the patented invention and also compensation for damage caused by the infringement over the last five years before commencement of the infringement action. However, where there is commercial use by a third party of an invention the subject of an application made available to the public under the Patent Act, compensation may be awarded in respect of infringement subsequent to the publication; if the action is brought within one year after grant, the five-year limitation does not apply.

Prior Art Cited in Other Countries

The Acts provide for decrees whereby examination of applications may be effected by an authority in another country or by an international institution, and for an applicant to inform the Patent Office of earlier corresponding applications and of the results of the official examination thereof.

Agreements may be made with other countries for the exchange of information concerning examination results, and the Scandinavian Offices may postpone their own examinations pending reports from other countries. The Patent Offices could also supply other agreement countries, under conditions of secrecy, with documents and information on unpublished and non-secret applications.

Transitional Provisions

The new Acts repeal the earlier ones and apply to all patents granted and applications filed before January 1, 1968, with the following reservations:

(1) The former Acts apply to patents granted thereunder in so far as concerns

(*a*) grounds for invalidation; and
(*b*) damages for infringement.

(2) For a period as yet undetermined, but likely to be less than 10 years, protection will not be obtainable for medicines and foodstuffs as products. Additionally in Denmark protection will not be obtainable for processes for producing foodstuffs.

(3) Applications pending on January 1, 1968, will be dealt with under the new Acts, except where notice of acceptance for publication has been issued.

(4) If an invention has been publicly disclosed by action of the applicant or his predecessor in title, and if the patent application has been filed before July 1, 1968, the former Acts will apply in determining novelty.

(5) The early publication provisions would not take effect until July 1, 1968.

(6) Rights of prior use which have been set up under the former Acts will continue to be valid.

(7) Use prior to January 1, 1968, of an invention which was not patentable under the former Acts may continue.

Germany

The amending Act of September 4, 1967, introduced fundamental changes in German patent law of which the following are the most important:

(1) Repeal of the prohibition on chemical substance protection, foodstuffs, luxury goods (in force from January 1, 1968).

(2) The laying open to public inspection of all patent applications 18 months at the earliest after the priority date or, if no priority is claimed, after the filing of the German application.

(3) Introduction of a limited provisional protection of applications laid open to public inspection.

(4) Deferred examination.

(5) Payment of renewal fees on patent applications from the beginning of the third year.

Items (2)–(5) came into force on October 1, 1968.

Details of these and other changes follow.

In these notes, applications pending and unpublished at October 1, 1968, are referred to as " old applications."

Chemical Products

There is no longer a ban on claims to chemical substances, and it is now possible to have claims to foodstuffs, luxury goods (*e.g.*, tea, coffee and other beverages, tobacco products, sweets, etc.), pharmaceuticals and chemically prepared products. As before, processes are patentable and the patent covers the direct products of the patented process.

Old applications which described new substances but had claims directed to a process for producing them, could be amended by adding claims to the new substances within six months from the date on which the applicant was informed by the Patent Office concerning laying open to public inspection under section 24 (3) or from the date of the *Patentblatt* containing notification of publication.

Third Party Rights

Previously, certain third party rights existed in favour of anyone who at the date of filing a German application (or if priority had been claimed, at the date of filing the basic application) had already made use of the invention in Germany, or who had made the necessary arrangements to that end. These rights are extended to cover the case of an invention relating to a new substance if a German application existed at January 1, 1968, and if use, or preparations for use, of that invention took place before that date.

Renewal Fees

Previously, renewal fees were not payable until after grant of a patent. Now, annual fees for applications and patents are payable at the beginning of the third and each subsequent year following the day after application. The fees are payable within a period not exceeding two months after the due date. It should be noted that, in this special case, the due date is included in the two-month period. Thus for an application filed April 1 the renewal fees for the third and subsequent years are due on April 2, but the two-month period ends on June 1. If not paid within this period, they may still be paid but with a fine, according to the following procedure: after the period for payment has expired the Patent Office notifies the applicant (or patentee) that the application (or patent) will be considered as withdrawn (or expired) if the overdue fee, with fine, is not paid within six months after the due date or within one month after receipt of the notification, whichever period is last to expire.

These annual fees become due irrespective of the stage the examination procedure has reached.

For old applications and those already accepted and published at October 1, 1968, annual fees must be paid only for those years beginning after that date. For earlier years, the former legislation applies, *i.e.*, fees for those years will not become due until grant.

The fees are not payable in respect of patents of addition or applications therefor, but if such a patent or application is converted to independent it will be treated as if it had always been independent and the overdue fees will have to be paid up.

It is not possible to obtain repayment of fees after withdrawal or refusal of an application.

Publication of Applications before Acceptance

From October 1, 1968, new applications will be laid open to public inspection 18 months after the date of application or of priority, but only after the publication of a notice in the *Patentblatt.*

The Patent Office is authorised to print the specifications and drawings of applications laid O.P.I.

Applications laid O.P.I. obtain a limited provisional protection. Wilful or negligent use of the invention by a third party gives rise to a claim for appropriate compensation but not for an injunction nor for damages.

Old applications were to be published not earlier than six months after the applicant had been notified of impending publication or publication of a notification in the *Patentblatt*, but in any event not before expiry of the 18-month period referred to above. If, during the six-month period, the applicant filed fresh application papers, they alone would be published. (This could be done, for example, to meet an examiner's objections or to keep certain parts of the file secret.)

Files of applications not laid open to public inspection, not published after acceptance and still in the course of examination, can be inspected only by persons showing a legitimate interest.

Information on Corresponding Applications

An applicant is required to inform the Patent Office of the countries and application numbers of any corresponding applications filed by him, and to furnish particulars of any printed citations made against any such application.

Voluntary Amendments

Non-broadening voluntary amendments are permitted up to acceptance. However, amendments requested prior to the filing of the petition for examination will be allowed only for the correction of obvious errors, for removal of defects pointed out by the examiner, or for adding to or correcting the statement of claim. Additions or corrections purporting to widen the scope of the subject-matter of the application cannot establish any rights; nor is it possible subsequently to divide out the new matter to form a new application for which the priority of the date of addition could be claimed.

Declaration of Inventorship

The declaration of inventorship must now be filed within three months after filing the application. Exceptional circumstances may justify a reasonable extension of this period up to the decision to grant a patent. If then the circumstances still persist, the period may be further extended. Failure to file the declaration entails lapsing of the application or the patent.

International Convention

Convention priority may still be claimed within two months following the filing date of the German application, but now the declaration of priority should contain also the application number(s) of the basic application(s) and be accompanied by a copy of the basic specification(s). If these have not been supplied with the declaration, the applicant will be allowed two months to furnish them. Within these periods, information given can be amended.

Formal Examination

Initially, the examiner will make only a formal examination for obvious defects in the application documents required by section 26 of the Act and by Rules, and will set a period for removal of the defects. If the period is for or includes the filing of priority documents, it shall not expire earlier than three months after filing the application. If the application does not comply with the Rules, the examiner may defer his objections until a petition for initiation of examination procedure has been filed.

If the examiner believes that the subject-matter of the application clearly conflicts with section 1, or section 10 (1), that is to say it

(*a*) is not in substance an invention; or
(*b*) is not capable of being exploited commercially; or
(*c*) is exempted from protection because its exploitation would be contrary to morals or law; or
(*d*) is the direct product of a process when the subject-matter of the invention is the process; or
(*e*) does not constitute an improvement in or further development of the main invention, if the application is one for a patent of addition;

the applicant must be informed and given a period for reply. If the defects are not removed, the examiner may reject the application and this can take place before the application is laid open to public inspection.

After filing of the petition (s. 28 (*b*)) for examination, a more exacting examination is made for defects under sections 26 and 1, and also under section 2 (prior publication or user) and section 4 (prior patenting).

Novelty Search

A novelty search will not be made unless the applicant, or a third party, makes written request accompanied by a fee (DM 100). If the request is in respect of an application for a patent of addition, the applicant must lodge a similar request in respect of the main application, otherwise the later application will be treated as one for an independent patent. Notification of receipt of the request will be advertised in the *Patentblatt* *after* the application has been laid open to public inspection. When the request is made by a third party, the applicant is informed, and he is also informed of the result of the search, but is not made a party to the procedure.

Any person may inform the Patent Office of printed publications affecting the application.

Only one request for novelty search will be accepted by the Patent Office. Also a request will not be considered if there has already been filed a petition for full examination of the application.

The applicant will be notified by the Patent Office of any printed publications located; if the search has been requested by a third party, that party will also be informed. Dispatch of the report will be published in the *Patentblatt*.

The Minister of Justice is empowered, with a view to accelerating the granting procedure, to decree

(*a*) the novelty search may be effected within the Patent Office, but by a branch other than the examination office; or

(*b*) by another national or international organisation, either in whole or in part.

It is open to the applicant (or an interested third party) either to request a novelty search and subsequently to file a petition for examination (under section 28 (*b*)) or to file a petition for full examination. In either case, the same total official fees are payable.

For old applications, no request for a novelty search can be made.

Full Examination

Examination of an application as to form and substance will not take place unless the applicant files a petition for examination to be made. The petition, which may also be made by a third party, must be lodged within seven years after the filing of the application, but only after the applicant has been informed of intended laying open to public inspection or the notice of such intent has been published in the *Patentblatt*.

The fee for examination is DM 200 if a request for novelty search has previously been filed, or DM 300 if it has not. In the case of unpublished applications pending at October 1, 1968 (in respect of which a request for novelty search cannot be made), the fee is DM 250 for the applicant, and DM 300 for a third party.

Examination is continued even if the petition is withdrawn.

Failure to file a petition results in the application being regarded as withdrawn and the provisional protection as never having existed.

When the petition is filed by a third party, he does not become a party to the examination proceedings. It does not appear that he is even informed of the result of the examination.

If a third party's petition is found to be ineffective, the applicant will be informed and may, within three months after receipt of the information, himself file a petition if this period expires later than the seven-year period. If the applicant himself does not file a petition, notice will be given in the *Patentblatt* of the inefficacy of the petition made by the third party.

Acceptance/Publication

On acceptance of an application, it is published and with publication the applicant receives provisional rights equal to those given on grant. Thus, he can ultimately obtain compensation or damages, and injunction if infringement is taking place.

Publication can be delayed at the request of the applicant for a maximum period of 15 months from the filing or priority date, whichever is the earlier.

France

The new Law of January 2, 1968, Law No. 68–1, came into force on January 1, 1969, the Rules for application of the law having been issued in December 1968. The new law contains radical changes of which possibly the most interesting are the introduction of a new form of protection, namely certificates of utility, repeal of the old law on Special Medicament Patents and the bringing of patents for medicines within the ambit of the new law, provisions for early publication, the requirement for claims, and examination for novelty and inventive merit.

Forms of Protection

There are two forms of protection of inventions, namely:

(1) patents of invention, granted for a period of 20 years from the date of filing; and
(2) certificates of utility, granted for a period of 6 years from the date of filing.

Both forms are subject to the payment of annual renewal fees.

As well as the two forms of protection, certificates of addition, *i.e.* patents of addition, may be obtained to either form, the duration and terms of grant being determined by the main title.

Certificates of utility

The certificate of utility is obtainable for any invention (except one relating to a medicine), and all the provisions of the law are applicable to these certificates except as follows:

(*a*) the term is limited to six years;
(*b*) there is no examination for novelty;
(*c*) medicines cannot be protected;
(*d*) action for infringement may be instituted without the need to obtain a novelty report;
(*e*) an application for a certificate cannot be converted to one for a patent, although a patent application can be converted to one for a certificate.

These certificates of utility cannot be assimilated to the German form of utility model since, for example, they can be used to protect a chemical product or a manufacturing process. Further, the certificate is not included in the forms of industrial property covered by the International Convention and it may well be that the certificate will not be generally recognised in other countries as a proper basis for a priority right.

Within the period between publication of the application for a certificate and publication of grant, third parties may submit to the Patent Office comments concerning the patentability of the alleged invention. The comments are transmitted to the applicant, who is not required to file comments in rebuttal but who may amend his claims in view of the comments. An applicant may also amend his claims of his own volition up to grant of the certificate.

Certificates of addition

An application for a certificate of addition may be filed only by the owner of the main patent or certificate of utility and it may be converted, at any time before grant, into an application for an independent patent or certificate of utility, depending on the form of protection covering the main case. It should be noted, however, that if the applicant has requested postponement of examination of his application for certificate of addition and does not withdraw the request within the prescribed two-year period, conversion into an independent patent application will not be possible and the certificate of addition will have a term of six years.

An invention forming the subject of an application for a certificate of addition is not required to show inventive activity over the invention of the main case.

Patentability

The new provisions are based on the Strasbourg Convention on Substantive Law. Thus, an application for a patent or certificate of utility may be made in respect of any invention in respect of a product, a process, an application or a combination of means, provided that the invention

(*a*) is susceptible of industrial application;

(*b*) is new; and

(*c*) involves an inventive step.

An invention is regarded as industrial if its object, application and result aid in the production of goods or technical results, whether by manual or mechanical means.

The inventive step is present when the invention is not obvious from the prior art. Inventive step is not required as between a patent of addition and the main patent or utility certificate.

The following are specifically excluded from protection:

(1) principles, discoveries and theoretical or purely scientific ideas;

(2) exclusively ornamental creations;

(3) financial or accountancy methods, rules of games and all other abstract systems, especially programmes or series of instructions for computer operation;

(4) inventions whose publication or use would be contrary to public order or morality (except where a prohibition on use arises from a legislative provision or administrative rule).

(5) New plant varieties of a genus or species under Law No. 70489 of June 11, 1970, on the Protection of New Plant Varieties.

Medicines (whether for man or animal) can be the subject of a patent or a patent of addition (but not of a certificate of utility) and then only if the product, substance or composition is newly proposed as a medicine. The former provisions governing Special Medicaments Patents (B.S.M.) have been repealed.

Novelty

The novelty provisions also are based on Strasbourg, so that an invention is to be regarded as novel if it does not form part of the prior art, which is defined as anything made known to the public by written or oral description, use or any other means prior to the filing date in France or any earlier date validly claimed.

Since the former provisions required absolute novelty, there is no substantial change.

Novelty is destroyed if the invention has been claimed in a French patent which though not published at the filing date of another application has an earlier filing or priority date.

Novelty is not destroyed through publication by

(*a*) the legitimate applicant at an officially recognised exhibition; or

(*b*) a third party in obvious abuse of the rights of the legitimate applicant;

provided that the French patent application is filed within six months after such disclosure, and in the case of an exhibitor he must claim and prove his right at the moment of filing.

It may be noted that where a patent application has been filed for an invention which was illegally procured from the legitimate owner, or in violation of a legal or treaty obligation, ownership of the application or patent can be claimed by the legitimate owner.

Early Publication

All the documents of an application will be made available to the public 18 months after the date of application or, if convention priority is claimed, after the priority date.

The documents may be made available at an earlier date if the applicant so requests.

A third party may, within a period of three months from the date of publication of the application documents by the Patent Office, and where the applicant has not withdrawn an earlier request for postponement, lodge with the Patent Office written comments regarding patentability of the alleged invention. Any such comments are transmitted to the applicant, who is not, however, required to make any reply thereto.

Applications filed prior to the coming into force of the Act will not come within the provision for early publication.

Postponement of Grant

If a request is made at the time of filing an application, grant may be postponed so that the application documents will not become available to public inspection during the period of 18 months from the filing date of the application or from the priority date if it is a convention application. The request for postponement may be withdrawn at any time during the said period.

Examination

An application will first be examined to ensure that the prescribed documents have been lodged and that they are in proper form, that there is unity of invention, and that the invention is industrial and does not come within any of the prohibited classes. Also if the application is divisional, it will be examined to ensure that it is not wider in scope than the parent application.

When the Patent Office is satisfied that the foregoing requirements are met, the application will be subjected to examination for novelty and inventive merit (for which a special tax is payable) and a documentation report issued. However, an applicant (except where the application relates to medicines) may, when filing his application, request postponement of issue of the documentation report for two years. Such a request may be withdrawn by the applicant at any time during the two-year period. If it is not withdrawn the patent application will automatically be converted to one for a certificate of utility. During the two-year period the applicant may also request conversion of his application into one for a certificate of utility, and this will be allowed if the applicant has not requested a documentation report.

The documentation reports are of an advisory nature only and are not binding on an applicant. It is only in a court of law that the validity of a patent may be tested.

The procedure for issuance of documentation reports is as follows:

(1) A provisional report comprising a list of prior art thought to affect patentability will be sent to the applicant, who may thereafter, if he wishes, make observations in support of his application and/or file new claims within a period of two, extensible to four, months.

(2) At the end of the period, a second report will be sent upholding or limiting the first report and setting a fresh period of two, extensible to four, months within which the applicant may, if he wishes, make observations and/or file new claims.

(3) Thereafter, intimation will be made in the *Official Bulletin* that the second report is available to the public.

(4) A third party may, within three months after publication of the second report, submit comments regarding the second report and the applicant may reply thereto, if he wishes, within a period of two, extensible to four, months.

(5) The final documentation report is then issued and the patent granted. The letters patent will include the documentation report in its final form.

The documentation report procedure will be introduced progressively in different technical fields and in accordance with the International Patent Classification. The novelty searches will be conducted by the International Patent Institute. The Decree of December 5, 1968, set out the technical fields to be examined for novelty as from January 1, 1969, and the Decrees of September 8, 1969, September 25, 1970, and September 3, 1971, set out additional fields to be examined as from January 1, 1970, January 1, 1971, and January 1, 1972, respectively.

Until such time as the procedure is applied to all technical fields, it is not compulsory to pay the examination fee or to request postponement of examination when filing the patent application, *except where the application relates to medicines.* The Patent Office will notify each applicant

(*a*) that the application is subject to examination, in which case the applicant is given an inextensible period of one month to pay the examination fee or request postponement of examination; or (*b*) that the application is not subject to examination, in which case if the examination fee has been paid it will be returned.

Approximately one-half of all technical fields are now covered and in the following list the subclass groupings affected are shown in chronological order of their introduction:

A.—(1969)—A 01 b, A 23 c, A 23 d, A 23 f, A 61 k 9/00 to 27/00, A 61 l,
(1970)—A 01 n, A 47 l, A 61 k 5/00 and 7/00,
(1971)—A 41 g, A 41 h, A 44 b, A 61 n,
(1972)—A 01 g, A 01 j, A 01 k, A 01 m, A 22 c, A 23 b, A 23 g, A 23 j, A 23 k, A 23 l, A 23 n, A 23 p, A 41 b, A 41 c, A 41 d, A 41 f, A 42 b, A 42 c, A 44 c, A 47 g, A 47 h, A 47 j, A 61 h, A 61 m, A 62 d, A 63 c,

B.—(1969)—B 22 d 11/00, B 29 d 9/00, B 32 b, B 60 v, B 64 b, B 64 c, B 64 d, B 64 f, B 64 g, B 65 g,
(1970)—B 03 b, B 03 c, B 03 d, B 21 d, B 21 j, B 21 k, B 22 c, B 22 d 1/00 to 9/00 and 13/00 to 47/00, B 25 j, B 29 d 27/00, B 60 b, B 60 f, B 60 j, B 60 t, B 65 d 1/00, 17/00 and 39/00 to 55/00, B 66 c, B 66 d, B 66 f,
(1971)—B 01 k, B 21 b, B 21 f, B 23 q, B 29 c, B 29 d 1/00 to 7/00 and 11/00 to 31/00, B 60 c, B 60 g, B 65 b 29/00 to 33/00, B 65 d 3/00 to 15/00 and 19/00 to 25/00,
(1972)—B 01 b, B 01 d, B 01 f, B 01 j, B 01 l, B 04 b, B 04 c, B 07 b, B 21 c, B 21 g, B 21 h, B 21 l, B 22 f, B 23 k, B 27 k, B 29 b, B 29 f, B 29 g, B 29 h, B 43 k, B 43 l, B 43 m, B 60 l, B 60 p, B 65 d 27/00 to 37/00, B 65 f, B 65 j, B 66 b, B 67 d,

C.—(1969)—C 01 f, C 01 g, C 03 b 37/00, C 03 c 13/00, C 03 c 21/00, C 03 c 25/00, C 05 b, C 05 c, C 05 d, C 05 f, C 08 g 1/00, C 08 g 3/00, C 09 b 1/00 to 5/00, C 09 b 27/00 to 45/00, C 10 g, C 10 m, C 21 c,
(1970)—C 03 b 1/00 to 35/00 and 39/00, C 05 g, C 07 c 17/00 to 25/00, C 08 f 3/00, C 08 g 17/00 and 39/00, C 21 b, C 22 d, C 23 b,
(1971)—C 01 b 15/00, C 03 c 1/00 to 11/00, 15/00 to 19/00, 23/00, 27/00 and 29/00, C 07 d 33/00 to 41/00, C 08 g 5/00 to 15/00, 20/00 to 37/00 and 41/00 to 53/00, C 22 b, C 23 c, C 23 f,

(1972)—C 01 b 1/00 to 13/00, 17/00 to 35/00, C 01 c, C 01 d, C 02 b, C 02 c, C 02 d, C 03 c 12/00, C 04 b 33/00 to 43/00, C 06 b, C 06 c, C 06 d, C 06 f, C 07 b, C 07 c 1/00 to 15/00, 27/00 to 75/00, C 07 d 1/00 to 31/00, C 07 f, C 07 g, C 08 b, C 08 f 1/00, 5/00, 7/00, 29/00 to 33/00, C 09 b 7/00 to 25/00, 47/00 to 67/00, C 09 c, C 09 d, C 09 f, C 09 g, C 09 h, C 09 j, C 09 k, C 10 b, C 10 c, C 10 f, C 10 h, C 10 j, C 10 k, C 10 l, C 11 d, C 12 b, C 12 c, C 12 d, C 12 f, C 12 g, C 12 h, C 12 j, C 12 k, C 12 l, C 13 c, C 13 d, C 13 f, C 13 g, C 13 h, C 13 j, C 13 k, C 13 l, C 21 d, C 23 d, C 23 g,

D.—(1969)—D 06 l, D 06 m, D 06 p, D 06 q,
(1970)—D 01 h, D 04 h, D 06 n,
(1971)—D 03 d,
(1972)—D 01 b, D 01 c, D 01 d, D 01 f, D 01 g, D 02 h, D 03 c, D 03 j, D 06 f,

E.—(1969)—E 04 c,
(1970)—E 01 c, E 04 b 1/00, E 21 b,
(1971)—E 04 b 2/00, 5/00 and 7/00,
(1972)—E 01 g, E 01 h, E 02 f, E 06 b, E 21 c, E 21 d, E 21 f,

F.—(1969)—F 15 c, F 25 j, F 28 d, F 28 f,
(1970)—F 02 k, F 25 d,
(1971)—F 02 c, F 15 b, F 15 d,
(1972)—F 17 b, F 17 c, F 17 d, F 21 h, F 21 k, F 21 l, F 21 m, F 21 p, F 21 q, F 21 s, F 21 v, F 23 g, F 23 q, F 24 b, F 24 c, F 24 f, F 25 b, F 28 b, F 28 c, F 28 g,

G.—(1969)—G 01 t, G 04 b, G 04 c, G 04 d, G 04 f, G 06 g, G 21 c,
(1970)—G 01 f, G 01 p, G 01 s, G 02 b, G 05 b, G 06 c, G 06 d, G 06 m, G 11 c, G 21 b, G 21 d, G 21 f, G 21 g, G 21 h, G 21 j, G 21 k,
(1971)—G 01 g, G 01 j, G 01 r, G 05 f, G 05 g, G 08 b, G 08 g,
(1972)—G 01 c, G 01 h, G 01 k, G 01 v, G 02 c, G 02 f, G 03 c, G 07 d, G 07 f, G 07 g, G 11 b 1/00 to 5/00,

H.—(1969)—H 01 f 15/00 to 41/00, H 01 l 3/00 to 11/00, H 01 m 27/00, H 01 q, H 04 n,
(1970)—H 01 b, H 01 h 7/00, 43/00 and 69/00 to 87/00, H 01 l 19/00, H 01 p, H 01 s, H 02 h, H 02 m, H 03 b, H 03 c, H 03 d, H 03 k 13/00, H 04 r,

(1971)—H 01 h 45/00 to 67/00, H 01 l 1/00 and 13/00 to 17/00, H 01 m 29/00 to 47/00, H 02 b, H 02 g, H 04 b, H 04 l,

(1972)—H 01 c, H 01 f 1/00 to 13/00, H 01 g, H 01 h 1/00 to 5/00, 9/00 to 41/00, H 01 j, H 01 m 1/00 to 25/00, H 01 r 15/00 to 23/00, H 02 j, H 02 k, H 02 n, H 05 b, H 05 g, H 05 h, H 05 k.

Specification and Claims

The Law requires an application to be accompanied by a specification, with drawings if required, and by a claim or claims defining the scope of protection sought. The specification, and drawings if any, may serve to assist in interpretation of the claims, but the latter cannot extend beyond the subject-matter disclosed in the specification and drawings.

The Rules require the specification to contain:

(1) a title;

(2) at least one industrial field, as precisely as possible, to which the invention relates;

(3) the state of the art in the field;

(4) at least one result at which the invention aims;

(5) the means used for achieving this result, distinguishing as far as possible the new elements from the known elements; the said means being, if need be, made clear by examples;

(6) the possibilities of industrial application of the invention.

These items should appear in the specification in the above order, unless the object of the invention warrants a different order.

Items (1), (2), (4) and (5) are compulsory; items (3) and (6) are optional.

When the invention relates to a medicine the description should include:

(*a*) Information on the pharmacological properties and on at least one therapeutic, dietetic or diagnostic application of the medicine described.

(*b*) The formula of the medicine and, if necessary, that of its constituents, the physical, chemical or biological characteristics enabling it to be identified, and at least one process for preparing it from known elements. If it cannot be identified by any formula or any physical, chemical or biological characteristic the medicine may be defined by a preparation process. In the case of a new association of already known active principles the properties of the association will have to be compared with the accumulated activities of its constituents considered separately.

(c) As far as possible, one example of a therapeutic application.

The claims must be limited to a single invention, or to a group of inventions so inter-related as to be unitary in character. Thus, according to the Rules, there may be included in the same application claims for a product, a use of the product, a process for manufacture of the product, and means specially intended for working the process. Where an application does not satisfy the conditions of unity of invention, the applicant has the right to divide his application but any divisional application must be filed within a period of three months (extensible by three months) from receipt of the official action calling for division. Where the Patent Office does not request division an applicant may nevertheless voluntarily divide at any time up to grant. Divisional applications are accorded the priority of the parent application.

Claims must not include, so far as the technical characteristics are concerned, any general reference to the description and drawings, but may refer, if necessary, to one drawing or one formula.

Each claim should include:

(a) a preamble mentioning the field to which the invention relates and, if need be, its known characteristics; and

(b) the technical characteristic with its particular and new elements, which characteristic, in combination with the preamble, defines the scope of protection.

Any claim may refer in the preamble to one or more earlier claims, and then set out the additional characteristics. General formulae such as " in combination or separately " are prohibited.

Abstracts

The Rules require that each application be accompanied by an abstract of the technical content of the invention, but it is emphasised that the abstract is required only for documentary purposes, that it does not form part of the patent and that it cannot be taken into account for defining the rights attached to the patent.

The abstract should comprise the title of the invention, the name of the applicant, where appropriate the priority claimed, and three paragraphs having as their respective object:

(*a*) to place, as precisely as possible, the invention in the technical field to which it relates;
(*b*) to describe the principal technical characteristic of the invention in its preferred form with, if applicable, references to the drawings; and
(*c*) to list the principal applications of the invention disclosed in the specification.

When the application includes drawings there should be filed with the abstract a drawing, in duplicate, containing the most representative figure illustrating the invention.

The complete abstract must not exceed 18 lines if there is a drawing, or 50 lines if there is no drawing, each line containing not more than 50 letters or signs.

Amendment Before/After Grant

Generally speaking, amendment of a specification is permissible only in respect of clerical errors. Amendment of the claims to overcome an objection that the specification is not in proper form is not covered either by the Law or the Decree. The latter merely stipulates that an applicant may present " observations " to the Patent Office within three months from the receipt of the objection. It is therefore not clear whether amendment of claims would be interpreted by the Patent Office as " observations " and accepted by them as such.

If an application is divided, the applicant is allowed to make amendments to the main specification and claims, but within narrow limits. Thus, it is not permissible either to add new claims or to modify existing claims except by amendment consequential on the limitation or from the requirements of the wording.

It is permissible to amend the claims of an application following documentary notification but consequential amendment of the specification is not permissible.

In the case of applications not subject to novelty examination it is permissible to file new claims at any time before grant but, as stated above, amendment of the specification is permissible only for correcting clerical errors.

After grant, the only amendments permissible are those under section 47, *i.e.* a patentee may abandon one or more claims.

Third Party Rights

Anyone who, on the date of filing an application (or on the priority date, if any), was legitimately in possession of the invention in French territory retains rights of exploitation, despite the grant of a patent. These rights are personal and may be transferred only with the goodwill of the business concerned.

Compulsory Licences

Compulsory licences may be granted subject to the following provisions and conditions:

(1) If at the expiry of three years from grant, or four years from application, and at the time of applying for a licence, the patent has not, without legitimate excuse, been seriously and effectively worked, or if such working has been discontinued for more than three years.

(2) The petitioner must prove that he has been unable to obtain a licence from the patentee and that he is able to work the invention to an extent sufficient to meet market requirements.

(3) The licence will be non-exclusive and will contain specific provisions as regards duration, scope and royalties.

(4) The licence terms may be altered by the court at the request of the patentee or licensee.

(5) Any assignment of the licence rights must be approved by the court.

(6) Failure to comply with the conditions of grant of the licence may lead to cancellation of the licence.

(7) A licensee may institute action for infringement if the patentee fails, on request, to take such action.

Further, the owner of a patent covering an improvement in an earlier patented invention cannot work his patent without licence from the earlier patentee, nor can the latter work the patented improvement without licence from the later patentee. However, at the expiry of three years from grant, or four years from the date of application, of the earlier patent, the junior patentee may obtain a non-exclusive licence to the extent necessary to enable him to work his own patent provided he is able to show that his invention represents an important technical advance over the earlier invention. The senior patentee may in turn obtain a licence under the junior patent. The conditions of paragraphs (2)–(6) above apply also to this form of compulsory licence.

Licences of Right

(1) Medicinal patents

Where required in the interests of public health (for instance, where a patented medicine is not available to the public in sufficient quantities, or if it is of an insufficient quality, or is sold at an excessively high price), a patent for a medicinal product or for a process of manufacture of a medicinal product may be subjected at the instigation of the Minister of Health to a special licence of right system. Such a licence may be granted irrespective of the date of the patent and is available to qualified parties immediately following publication of an order of the Minister for Industrial Property subjecting the patent to the system. Licences may be granted under specific conditions, especially as to duration and scope. Royalty terms must be approved by the Ministers for Industrial Property and Health, and in the absence of agreement between the parties the royalties will be settled by the court.

A licensee may institute action for infringement if the patentee fails, on request, to take action.

The rights under a licence of right cannot be assigned or transferred.

(2) Other patents

There may also be subjected to the licence of right system any other patent which in the opinion of the Minister of Industrial Property is not being worked to an extent sufficient to satisfy the needs of the national economy. Here again, no regard will be paid to the date of the patent, but the patentee will be given one year from the date of the order within which to remedy the working deficiencies. If at the end of that period the deficiencies seriously affect economic development and public interest, the patent may by decree be subjected to the system. This one-year period may be extended on a showing by the patentee of justifiable grounds and provided the extension is not contrary to national economy.

Immediately following publication of the decree any qualified parties may obtain non-exclusive licences under specific conditions especially as to duration and scope. Royalties will be determined between the parties, or, failing agreement, by the court.

A licensee may institute action for infringement if the patentee fails, on request, to take action.

The rights under a licence of right cannot be assigned or transferred.

Licences to State

At any time the government itself may obtain from the Minister for Industrial Property a licence of right for the working of an invention, the subject of a patent or a patent application where necessary for national defence. Working may be effected by the government or on its behalf. The licence will be granted by order of the Minister of Industrial Property at the request of the Minister for National Defence. The order will contain the licence conditions other than royalty terms, which latter will be determined between the parties, or, failing agreement by the court.

Infringement

The exclusive right given by a patent includes the prohibition for any third party to exploit the patented invention, and in particular:

(1) to manufacture a product the object of the patented invention;

(2) to use, introduce into the territory in which the law is applicable, sell, offer for sale or put on the market the patented product in another form, as well as to be in possession of the product with the intention of using it or of putting it on the market;

(3) to use, put into practice, sell or offer for sale, the process or means forming the object of the invention;

(4) to perform the acts referred to in (2) above in respect of a product obtained directly by a patented process.

The exclusive right also includes the prohibition on any third party to deliver or to offer to deliver to a party who is not a licensee, the means for working a patented invention.

Acts done for personal or domestic purposes, or for the purpose of testing the object of the patented invention, are not regarded as infringing acts.

Where a product patent does not describe any therapeutic application of the product the exclusive rights do not extend to use of the product for the manufacture of medicines. This provision does not, however, affect the rights given by a patent relating to a process for manufacture of the product.

In respect of patents applied for under the new law, suits for infringement cannot be instituted before the documentation report has been requested. A suit may be instituted immediately the report has been applied for but the hearing of the case will be deferred until the final documentation report has been notified.

In respect also of patents applied for under the former law, a documentation report must be produced, but in this case it is not necessary to show that the report was applied for prior to the suit being lodged.

A suit for infringement of a certificate of utility may be pursued without the need to lodge a documentation report.

Action for infringement may be normally instituted only by the patentee. However, the beneficiary of an exclusive right of working and also the owner of a compulsory licence may institute action provided the licence deed does not contain any provisions to the contrary and provided also that the patentee has not instituted action after having been formally requested to do so by the licensee.

International Convention

The period within which a claim to priority may be made is now restricted to two months from the filing date of the application.

The period within which priority documents may be filed is now four months from the filing date.

Transitional Provisions

The new law will, as from its effective date, apply to all applications filed thereafter. Applications lodged under the former law will be dealt with under the new provisions, but the exercise of patent rights on such applications and on patents granted under the former law will be governed by the new law. Thus, for example, an action for infringement of a patent cannot now be instituted without first obtaining a documentary report (novelty search).

Israel

The new Israeli Patents Act 1967, which came into force on April 1, 1968, represents an almost complete revision of the former provisions. In certain instances it is reminiscent of the United Kingdom Act. The more important aspects of the new Act are set out below:

Applicant

The owner of a patentable invention is entitled to apply for protection. Where more than one application is filed for a patent for the same invention, a patent will be granted to the first legitimate applicant.

Applications must be accompanied by a complete specification and claims.

Patentability

A patent may be granted in respect of any invention, whether a product or a process, which is

(*a*) new; and
(*b*) useful and susceptible of industrial or agricultural application; and which
(*c*) involves an inventive step.

Patents will not be granted for

(*a*) methods of therapeutic treatment of the human body;
(*b*) new varieties of plants or animals, except microbiological organisms not derived from nature.

Novelty

The standard of novelty is absolute, so that an invention will not be considered to be new if it has been published anywhere prior to the date of application, or of any earlier date validly claimed, by means of written, visual, audible or any other description or by exploitation or exhibition.

It would appear that the prior art includes the contents of a local patent application of earlier date if and when the earlier application is published.

Novelty is not destroyed through prior disclosure of matter obtained from the owner of the invention and published without his consent if the application is filed within a reasonable time after the publication became known to the owner.

Also, novelty is not destroyed by any of the following acts:

(1) By the owner of the invention

(*a*) display at an industrial or agricultural exhibition in Israel or a recognised exhibition in a convention country, official notice of which had been given to the Israeli Registrar prior to the opening of the exhibition;
(*b*) publication of a description of the invention at the time of an exhibition as aforesaid;
(*c*) use of the invention for the purposes of an exhibition as aforesaid at the place of the exhibition.

(2) By a third party

(*a*) publication by use of the invention without the consent of its owner at the time of the exhibition, whether at the place of exhibition or outside it. In these cases, the patent application must be filed within six months after the opening of the exhibition;

(b) publication by way of a lecture by the inventor before a scientific society or by way of publication of such a lecture in the official transactions of the society, provided the Registrar is given notice of the lecture before it is delivered and that the patent application is filed within six months after the publication.

International Convention

An application under the International Convention must be filed within 12 months from the date of the basic application, but the claim to priority may be made within two months after the date of filing. Multiple and partial priorities are now allowable.

The Registrar is permitted to extend the time for filing a convention application if he is satisfied that the Israeli application was filed late because of circumstances over which the applicant and his representative had no control and which they could not have prevented from arising.

Examination

The applications will first be examined for general patentability and if accepted will then be subjected to a novelty examination.

For prescribed classes of subject-matter, the examiner may refer the application for a novelty search by the International Patent Institute. For all classes the applicant is required to submit a list of the material relied upon by the patent authority in a foreign country in examining a patent application for the same invention filed in that country by the applicant or his predecessor in the ownership of the invention. The Registrar will notify the applicant when the information is to be furnished.

If examination shows that the application conflicts with an earlier unpublished application, the later application may be suspended from further examination until the earlier application has been published after acceptance.

The applicant will be notified of any defects and given a period for clearing them.

Voluntary amendment of an application is possible.

Opposition—Revocation

On acceptance, the application is published and open to opposition for three months. Opposition may be entered by any person on any ground on which the Registrar could have refused the application.

If an opposition is successful on the ground that the opponent is the owner of the invention, the patent may be granted to the opponent.

At any time after grant revocation may be sought before the Registrar on any ground on which the grant could have been opposed.

Form and Effect of Patent

There are two forms of patent, namely independent patents and patents of addition, the former being granted for a term of 20 years from the application date and the latter being coterminous with the main patent, although in the case of revocation of a main patent a patent of addition may, in certain circumstances, be converted into an independent patent.

The patentee is entitled to prevent others from exploiting the patented invention:

(*a*) as defined in the claims; or
(*b*) in a manner similar thereto and involving the main features as defined in the claims.

A process patent covers also the direct product of the process.

Anyone who, on the date of an application, was legitimately using an invention commercially or had made actual preparations to do so may continue such use without payment of royalty. Transfer of such rights may only be effected with the goodwill of the business concerned in the use or intended use.

Service Inventions

An employee who makes an invention as a result of, or during the period of, his service, must notify his employer of the invention and of any patent application he has filed.

An invention made by an employee as a result of and during the period of his service is termed a " service invention " and belongs to the employer, unless there is a mutual agreement to the contrary, or unless the employer renounces his rights within six months from receipt of the notification of the invention. The employee, in giving notice of the invention, may state that the invention will become his property unless the employer makes a reply within six months. If the employer does not reply, the invention then becomes the property of the employee.

There are also provisions for the settlement of disputes by the Registrar, for the determination of remuneration by a state committee and for inventions made by state employees.

The state may, when necessary, freely exploit a patented invention if

(1) it is also a service invention made by a state employee; and

(2) no protection has been claimed for the service invention anywhere; and

(3) the service invention was recorded by the state prior to the effective date of the application for the patented invention.

Patents of Addition

A patentee may obtain a patent of addition for an invention which is an improvement in or modification of the patented invention; the patent of addition need not involve an inventive step over the main patent or any patent of addition thereto.

An application for a patent of addition must be filed not earlier than the date of application for the main patent.

A patent of addition remains in force so long as the main patent is in force and without payment of renewal fees. If the main patent is revoked, the patent of addition may be converted to an independent patent which will remain in force for the remainder of the term for which the main patent was granted, but subject to payment of the renewal fees which would have been payable on the main patent.

Compulsory Licences

1. General

Where there is abuse of monopoly rights, compulsory licences may be granted after the expiry of three years from grant (or four years from application, whichever is the longer period). After the same period, a patentee may be called on by the Registrar to say if the patented invention is being exploited in Israel and if so the extent and place of manufacture.

2. Medicaments or medical devices

At any time after grant, the Registrar may, if it is necessary to assure to the public a reasonable quantity of medical supplies, grant a licence for

(*a*) a patented product capable of being used as a medicament or for the manufacture of a medicament;
(*b*) a patented process for the manufacture of a product as referred to in (*a*);
(*c*) a patented device usable as a device for medical purposes or as part of such a device.

3. Dependent patents

The owner of a junior patent which cannot be worked without infringing an earlier patent, may obtain a licence to the extent necessary to enable him to work his own patent, provided it serves a different industrial purpose from, or marks a considerable technical advance over, the earlier invention. When both inventions serve the same industrial purpose, cross-licences must be granted.

4. Revocation for abuse of monopoly rights

A patent the subject of a compulsory licence may be revoked if the grant has not prevented the original ground of abuse, but only after the expiry of two years from the date of grant of the licence.

The Act sets out various circumstances which result in abuse of monopoly rights and the factors to be taken into account in considering the grant of compulsory licences.

Infringement

Only the patentee or an exclusive licensee may institute an action for infringement. In the case of joint-owners each joint-owner is so entitled.

The action cannot be instituted before grant of the patent, but relief may be given for infringement committed after publication of the accepted application.

A person who intends to exploit any process or product may petition the court for a declaration that such exploitation is not an infringement of a specified patent.

Transitional Provisions

The former ordinance applies to all patents granted before April 1, 1968, and to all patents granted on application which were accepted before that date, so far as concerns patentability and validity.

Italy

By Presidential Decree No. 849, which became operative on August 15, 1968, a compulsory licence system was introduced. This followed ratification by Italy of the Lisbon Text of the International Convention. The Decree repeals section 54 of the law, which provided for lapsing of patents in the event of failure to meet the working requirements, and replaces it by a new section 54 providing for the grant of compulsory licences and for lapsing only if failure to meet the working requirements persists after two years from the grant of the first compulsory licence.

Sections 52 and 53, which are unaffected by the amendments, lay down the principles applying to the working of patented inventions, and they may be stated as follows:

(*a*) a patented invention must be worked in Italy to an extent which is not disproportionate to the needs of the country;

(*b*) display of patented articles at official or officially-recognised exhibitions in Italy may be considered as working during the first term for working;

(*c*) importation or sale in Italy of patented articles manufactured abroad does not constitute working.

The new section 54 provides for the grant of non-exclusive compulsory licences in the following circumstances:

(1) if a patent is not being worked to an adequate extent after three years from the date of grant, or four years from the filing date of the application, whichever is the longer term;

(2) if adequate working is discontinued for more than three years;

(3) if a patented invention cannot be used without prejudice to rights deriving from a patent granted on an application of earlier date. In this case the licence granted to the owner of the later patent will include the right to work the earlier invention to the extent necessary for working his own invention, provided that that invention represents a notable technical improvement over the earlier invention. If the two inventions have the same industrial aim, a licence will only be granted on condition that the owner of the earlier patent may, if he so wishes, obtain a licence under the later patent.

The provisions of the section do not apply to patented inventions owned by the Military Administration or to inventions which are kept secret under section 41 of the law.

Licences will not be granted in the following cases:

(*a*) where the inadequacy in working is due to reasons beyond the patentee's control. Such reasons do not include lack of financial means nor, if the patented product is marketed abroad, lack of demand on the Italian market for the patented product or the product obtained by the patented process;

(*b*) to an infringer;

(*c*) if the applicant for licence cannot prove that he had previously applied to the patentee but had been unable to obtain a licence on reasonable terms.

Licences will be granted against payment to the patentee of adequate royalties and subject to an undertaking from the potential licensee that he is able adequately to work the invention under the licence terms. Further, they will be granted for a term not exceeding the remainder of the term of the patent, and may be assigned only with the licensee's business or that part of the business with which the patented invention is concerned.

Grant of a licence does not stop the licensee, or anyone else, from bringing suit against the validity of the patent or any rights arising therefrom. Neither does it relieve the patentee from his obligation to work the invention, and if there is not adequate working within two years from the date of grant of the first compulsory licence, the patent lapses.

Anyone who wishes to obtain a licence must petition the Patent Office, setting out the grounds on which he relies, and the amount of royalty and terms of payment he offers. The Patent Office notifies the patentee of the petition and he is entitled, within 60 days from receipt of the notification, to state his grounds of objection to allowance of the petition or to the amount of royalty and terms of payment. The petitioner is then notified of the patentee's objections and is entitled, within 60 days from receipt of that notification, to submit further comments in support of his case. Thereafter the Patent Office will decide whether or not a licence should be granted.

Official fees are payable when applying for a licence and when the licence is granted.

Licences will be granted by decree of the Ministry of Industry, Commerce and Craftsmanship and will set out the licence period, the terms for working, any safeguards or other conditions to which the licence may be subject, as well as the terms and conditions for payment of royalties. In the absence of agreement between the parties it would seem that the Ministry will settle the licence terms.

A licence may be amended by the Ministry at the request of either party, provided there exist valid grounds for amendment.

Revocation of a licence may be ordered when the terms for working the patented invention are not complied with, or if the licensee fails to pay the agreed royalty.

If a patentee, subsequent to grant of a compulsory licence, grants another licence to a third party on more favourable terms than those of the compulsory licence, the holder of the compulsory licence may request amendment of his licence by substitution of these more favourable terms.

The Decree contained no retroactive provisions, but by a Judgment, dated March 17, 1970, the Court of Appeals in Milan held that the new Compulsory Licence Law was not retroactive and that a patent which had not been sufficiently worked prior to enactment of the new law was still open to revocation under the provisions of the old law.

According to the judgment, ratification by Italy of the London text of the International Convention did not imply cancellation of the revocation provisions in Italian patent law, but merely that those countries which adhered to the revised text were called on to modify their domestic legalisation so as to preserve revocation of patents, as a last resort, in case of non-working, if other remedies such as compulsory licences were insufficient to remove the abuse. The Court also held that the fact that Italy had not, prior to 1968, introduced domestic legislation providing for compulsory licences did not imply abandonment of the principle of revocation of patents as a penalty in the event of non-working.

The first Compulsory Licence under the new system was granted by a Decree, dated November 18, 1971, issued by the Minister of Industry. A plea of *force majeure* entered by the patentee was rejected. The non-exclusive licence granted provides for a royalty of 5 per cent. of the net sale price; on the product manufactured and utilised directly the royalty of 5 per cent. is to be calculated on the utilised product valued at cost, with the addition of 10 per cent. for general costs. The patentee is required to make available to the licensees know-how useful for proper exploitation of the patented process and apparatus. Other terms of the licence are that (*a*) the licensees will exploit the patented product in a proper way, according to the specification of the patent and the additional information supplied by the patentee, (*b*) the licensees will produce and place on sale products of good quality, and (*c*) that articles produced by the patented process will carry an indication that they are covered by patent, and the number of the patent will be quoted.

Iraq

Iraqui Patents and Industrial Designs Law, No. 65 of 1970 which came into force on April 6, 1970, repeals the earlier law of 1935 and amendments thereof.

Form and Scope of Patent

There are three forms of protection of inventions, namely:

(1) Independent Patents granted for a term of 15 years from the date of the application (or from the date when the application documents were completed) subject to the payment of annual renewal fees. Where a corresponding foreign patent exists the term will be equal to that of the foreign patent, subject to a maximum of 15 years.

(2) Patents of Addition for modifications, improvements or additions to an invention for which a patent has already been granted, available only to the patentee of the main invention, and co-terminous with the main patent.

(3) Patents of amendment granted in respect of an amendment, correction or complement to an invention for which a patent has already been granted. The owner of such a patent may not use the original invention without the consent of the principal patentee; nor may the principal patentee use the amendment, correction or complement without the consent of the proprietor of the patent of amendment.

Renewal fees are now payable on the anniversary of the application date.

Patentability and Novelty

Patents are granted for inventions which are new and capable of industrial exploitation, whether relating to new industrial products or to novel methods and techniques, or to both.

An invention is not new if:

(*a*) within 50 years preceding the date of the Iraqui patent application the invention is relevant to a patent already publicly used in Iraq or elsewhere; or if the specification or drawing of the invention was published in Iraq or abroad in such a way that it could be carried out by experts; or

(*b*) within 50 years preceding the date of the application, a patent has already been issued in respect of the invention or in respect of a part thereof to a person other than the inventor or his successor in title; or if a third party has already applied for a patent for the invention itself, or for part thereof, within the 50-year term.

Novelty is not destroyed by display at a national or international exhibition in Iraq, or in a country according Iraq reciprocal treatment, provided the Registrar is notified within the seven days preceding the date of exhibition.

The following are specifically excluded from protection:

(*a*) Inventions whose exploitation is prejudicial to public morals or public order, or which are contrary to public interest;

(*b*) medical and pharmaceutical preparations;

(*c*) methods or techniques used in financial, banking or accounting matters; and

(*d*) layouts of buildings and solid drawings related thereto.

Right to Patent

The rights in an invention belong to the patentee or his successor in title; in the case of joint inventorship, the rights accrue to the several parties jointly in the absence of an agreement to the contrary.

The right to obtain a patent is vested in the person who is first to file an application.

The following are entitled to apply for a patent:

(i) Iraquis and Arab citizens;

(ii) foreigners resident, and having a real place of business, in Iraq;

(iii) nationals of countries according reciprocal treatment to Iraq;

(iv) public administrations;

(v) companies, societies or organisations established in Iraq, or in countries according reciprocal treatment to Iraq; industrialists, producers, merchants or

> labourers; provided that the invention is initially registered in the name of the inventor, except where a foreign patent exists when it may be registered in the name of the company or the like owning it.

The grant of a patent confers on the patentee the exclusive right to exploit the invention only from the date of issue of the patent.

The right to inventions arising from execution of a contract or from a work or employment relationship belongs to the employer, provided that the invention is the subject of specific remuneration and falls within the terms of the contract or the work or employment relationship. In such cases the invention may be patented in the name of the employer provided that the inventor is named in the patent. Where no remuneration arises in respect of the invention, the inventor is entitled to fair compensation from the employer. In cases other than those referred to, but where the invention comes within the scope of the inventor's work, the employer may exploit the invention, or may acquire it, subject to payment of fair compensation to the inventor and provided the employer informs the Registrar of Patents in writing, within three months of the issue of the patent, whether or not he desires to acquire the invention.

An application for patent filed by an inventor within one year from the date of leaving an employment will be deemed to have been filed during the execution of the contract or during the work or employment relationship. The respective rights mentioned in the foregoing paragraph will then apply, provided that the inventor's work with the employer had contributed to the making of the invention.

Specification and Claims

The law calls for a detailed specification of the invention and the method, capable of execution, of its exploitation, with a clear indication of the new elements for which protection is sought. Where necessary, drawings should be filed. In addition an abstract of the invention comprising not more than about 150 words must be filed.

Examination

Applications are examined only for:

(*a*) Formalities;
(*b*) Unity of Invention;

(*c*) Sufficiency of specification and drawings; and
(*d*) Clarity of claims.

Applicants may be required by the Registrar to amend the application and will be given a period of six months to do so.

Amendment after Grant

Specifications and drawings may be amended after grant for the purpose of correction or explanation, and provided the amendment does not affect the scope of the invention.

Secrecy and Expropriation

Where the Registrar considers that an invention relates to matters of defence or has military value, he must allow the Minister of Defence to examine the documents of the application, and the Minister may ask that the application and the decision to grant a patent be not published. Further, the Minister may object to the grant of a patent to the applicant if he undertakes to buy the invention or reaches agreement with the inventor as to its exploitation.

Inventions may, by decision of the Minister, be expropriated if the public interest so requires, or for reasons of national defence. Expropriation may be total or partial, and is subject to payment of fair compensation to the owner of the invention.

Working and Compulsory Licences

A patentee must notify the Registrar of the date of working of the invention within 30 days from the beginning of such working.

Where an invention is not being worked in Iraq within three years from the grant of the patent, or where working is not sufficient for the country's needs, or where working is discontinued for at least two years, compulsory licences may be granted. If an invention is not worked within the two years following the grant of a compulsory licence, the patent may be revoked.

If working of an invention is of great importance to industry and requires the use of another invention covered by an existing patent, a compulsory licence to exploit the earlier invention may be granted if the owner refuses to agree to such working on reasonable terms settled by the Registrar. On the other hand the owner of the earlier invention may be granted a compulsory licence under the later patent if his invention is of greater importance.

United Kingdom

Section 59 of the Health Services and Public Health Act 1968 extends the scope of section 46 of the Patents Act 1949 (which allows any government department to make, use and exercise patented inventions for the services of the Crown). The effect of section 59 is that the Minister of Health and the Secretary of State for Scotland, acting jointly, may make regulations enabling a government department or an authorised person to make, use, exercise and vend a patented invention for the production or supply of drugs and medicines prescribed in the regulations and required for the provision of pharmaceutical services, general medical services or general dental services.

Australia

The Australian Patents Act 1969, which is an amending Act, received the Royal Assent on June 14, 1969. Specified sections came into force on that date; the remaining sections came into force on January 1, 1970, as did the amending Regulations (Statutory Rules 1969, No. 151). These Regulations were subsequently amended by Statutory Rules 1969, No. 212.

The most important changes brought about by the amending Act relate to the introduction of a system of deferred examination along with an optional modified examination for certain convention applications. Other notable changes relate to substitution of applicants, voluntary division, restoration of lapsed patents, the International Convention, the period for acceptance, priority dates of claims, common informers and opposition.

Deferred Examination

The earlier provisions for examination contained in sections 47, 48, 48A 49 and 49A have been repealed and replaced by new sections 47, 47A, 47B, 47C, 47D, 47E, 48, 48A, 49 and 49A.

(1) Under the new provisions examination will not take place until the applicant requests it. He must request examination of his application and complete specification before the expiry of

(*a*) five years after the date of filing his complete specification; or

(*b*) two years after the date when the deferred examination provisions come into force;

whichever is the later. Failure to request examination within the relevant period will result in lapsing of the application.

(2) The Commissioner may, however, direct an applicant to request examination on any or all of the following grounds:

(*a*) expediency, having regard to the progress made in the examination of applications lodged prior to the date of the application concerned;

(*b*) in the public interest;

(*c*) expediency, having regard to examination of another application.

The applicant will be informed of the ground or grounds on which the direction is given, and must lodge the request within six months after the date of the direction, otherwise the application will lapse.

It is believed that in practice applications will be taken up in turn for examination but when an application reaches the examination stage, the Commissioner will direct the applicant to request examination, unless the applicant has already lodged a request.

(3) If an application has been laid open to public inspection, a third party may require the Commissioner to direct the applicant to request examination. If a request has not already been received, the Commissioner will issue the direction, and the application will lapse if the request is not lodged within six months after the date of the direction.

On receipt of a request for examination of the application and complete specification, examination will proceed in substantially the same manner as heretofore, that is to say the examiner will, as under the former Act,

(*a*) determine whether the application complies with the requirements of the Act, and that the alleged invention is not one of a class for which protection is prohibited by section 155; and

(*b*) investigate for (i) prior claiming; (ii) prior publication; (iii) prior grant.

However, the following exceptions from the previous procedure may be noted:

(*a*) the examiner is no longer required to consider whether priority dates of claims are correct ones;

(*b*) the examiner is now required to take account of any document of which notice has been given to the Commissioner under the new common informer section;

(*c*) in replying to an examiner's report, an amendment is permissible even though it is not for the purpose of removing a ground of objection; and

(*d*) the applicant is now entitled to broaden his claims on amendment, provided the amended claims come within the disclosure in the complete specification as filed.

Modified Examination

The amendments also provide for a new procedure, referred to as "modified examination," which relates only to applications claiming priority, under the International Convention, from a basic application, in a prescribed convention country.

(1) Where a patent has been granted, either on the basic application, or on a corresponding application which also claimed the basic priority, then, if the specification of the patent is in the English language, the applicant may request a modified examination in place of the normal examination and within the same time limits. The request must be accompanied by a certified copy of the specification of the patent and the applicant must bring the text and drawings (if any) of his Australian complete specification into conformity, apart from matters of form, with the patent specification.

A request for modified examination may be withdrawn before acceptance of the application and complete specification and replaced by a request for normal examination.

The prescribed convention countries are the United Kingdom and the United States.

(2) Where a patent has not been granted on the basic, or a corresponding, application, and the Commissioner has directed the applicant to request examination, the applicant may, instead of complying with the direction, request deferment of the examination, and will be allowed a period of nine months, from the date of his request within which to request examination. Failure to make the request within that period will result in lapsing of the application, although it may be restored under the circumstances and conditions for restoration of lapsed applications, set out below. This procedure will of

course give to an applicant a greater possibility of obtaining grant of a patent on his relevant overseas application and thus enable him to bring his Australian application within the provisions for modified examination.

On receipt of a request for modified examination the examiner will determine:

(*a*) whether the request is as prescribed;
(*b*) whether the application complies with the requirements of the Act, other than that for unity of invention;
(*c*) whether the text and drawings are, apart from matters of form, the same as the patent specification;
(*d*) whether any proposed amendments are properly allowable; and
(*e*) whether the alleged invention is one of a class for which protection is prohibited by section 155.

Where an examiner reports adversely, the applicant may

(*a*) if the request is not as prescribed, lodge an amended request for modified examination; and/or
(*b*) amend the application or complete specification so as (i) to remove the objection; (ii) to exclude a claim or claims; and make consequential amendment of any other claim; (iii) to bring the text or drawings into conformity with the patent specification.

The applicant cannot, however, make amendments which would not be permissible under the ordinary examination procedure.

Advertisement of acceptance of an application which has been the subject of modified examination will include a statement that acceptance results from a modified examination.

The provisions concerning modified examination do not affect operation of the provisions relating to opposition, or revocation.

Examination

Complete specifications will, as far as practicable, be examined in the order in which requests for their examination are lodged, apart from cases where the Commissioner considers it expedient, having regard to the examination of another application, to direct the applicant to request examination.

After a request has been filed, the Commissioner may expedite examination if he is satisfied:

(*a*) that it is in the public interest; or

(*b*) that there are special circumstances that make it desirable; or

(*c*) that, after the complete specification has been laid open to public inspection, a prima facie case of infringement exists in respect of the claim or claims contained in the specification.

In carrying out a modified examination, the examiner is empowered to disregard, for the purposes of prior claiming, prior publication and prior grant, specifications of applications filed more than three years before the filing of the application under examination.

Action under section 57 (common informer) must be accompanied by a declaration to the effect that to the declarant's own knowledge the published document was published in Australia, and specifying the date of publication and at least one place in Australia where it was published. A copy of the published document must accompany the declaration, unless the document is available in the Patent Office or in the Patent Office Library. If the document is not in the English language, there must also be lodged a verified English translation.

Where an examiner has given an adverse report on an application, a complete specification, or a request to amend a complete specification, the applicant or patentee may, if he does not desire to be heard in connection with the exercise of the Commissioner's discretionary powers in relation to the matter, request the Commissioner to exercise his powers. The request must be accompanied by submissions in writing.

Request for Examination—Fees

The fees exacted for requests for examination are higher in all cases for complete specifications lodged on or after January 1, 1970, than for those lodged earlier. Also, where the Commissioner has not directed a request, the fees are higher if made prior to the expiration of four years and nine months after lodgment of the complete specification than if made after that period.

The official fees, which vary from 80.00 to 28.00 Australian dollars, are set out in the following table:

	Complete specification lodged 1/1/70 onwards	before 1/1/70
	Australian dollars	
A. Request lodged *before* expiration of 4 years and 9 months from lodgment of complete specification:		
Ordinary examination before direction	80.00	68.00
Ordinary examination after direction	60.00	48.00
Modified examination before direction	60.00	48.00
Modified examination after direction	40.00	28.00
B. Request lodged *after* expiration of 4 years and 9 months from lodgment of complete specification:		
Ordinary examination before direction	60.00	48.00
Ordinary examination after direction	60.00	48.00
Modified examination before direction	40.00	28.00
Modified examination after direction	40.00	28.00
C. Request to Commissioner under section 47B to direct request for examination	40.00	40.40
D. Request following action by third party under section 47B	40.00	28.00

Restoration of Lapsed Applications

Failure to request examination or to pay a continuation fee will result in lapsing of the application and this will be advertised in the *Official Journal*. The application may, however, be restored if the failure to make the request or to pay the fee was unintentional and resulted from an error or omission on the part of the applicant or his agent, or from circumstances beyond the control of the applicant, and if there has been no undue delay in applying for restoration. The application for restoration will be advertised in the *Official Journal* and opposition may be entered within three months from the date of the first advertisement therein. Appeal to the Patents Appeal Tribunal lies from any decision of the Commissioner.

Where a lapsed application is restored the fact will be advertised in the *Official Journal.*

Any person who availed himself, or took definite steps by contract or otherwise to avail himself, of the subject-matter of a lapsed application *after* the lapsing was advertised in the *Official Journal* and *before* the date of the first advertisement of the application for restoration, may apply to the Commissioner for the grant of a licence to make, use, exercise and vend the subject-matter of the restored application to the extent that he so availed himself, or took definite steps by contract or otherwise to avail himself, of the subject-matter. The applicant for licence is required to serve a copy of the application on the person whose application was restored and on such other persons as the Commissioner directs. Any person on whom a copy of the application for licence has been served may, within one month after the day on which the copy was served on him, give notice of opposition to the application. This one-month period may be extended if the request for extension is lodged before expiry of the period. An opponent must serve a copy of the notice of opposition on the applicant for licence. Thereafter the Commissioner will hear the application and, if he is satisfied that the application should be granted, may grant a licence on such terms as he thinks reasonable. Otherwise, the application will be dismissed.

On restoration, provision will be made for the protection of third parties who may have availed themselves of the invention in the period between the date of advertisement of lapsing and the date of the first advertisement of the application for restoration.

Infringement proceedings cannot be taken in respect of anything done during the period between lapsing of the application and the date of restoration.

Restoration of an application which has lapsed due to a formal defect in a complete specification is discussed under the heading " Documents, Specifications and Drawings."

Priority Dates of Claims

Section 44 has been amended so that it will no longer be necessary to indicate against each claim the date considered by the applicant to be the priority date of that claim. Consequential amendments have been made in other parts of the Act, and the Commissioner is empowered to allow amendment of complete specifications by omission of priority dates.

Assignment—Pending Applications

The provisions concerning applicants for patents (s. 34) have been amended to provide for the substitution of applicants. Thus, where an assignment takes place before grant, the assignment may be recorded and the application will proceed in the name of the assignee or in the names of the assignee and the applicant, or other joint applicants as the case requires.

Acceptance of Application

The period within which an application and complete specification should be accepted is now 12 months after the date on which the first report of the examiner, arising out of examination, is sent to the applicant, whether the report arose from the full examination under section 48 or from a modified examination.

Where an applicant withdraws a request for modified examination and requests the full examination, the period for acceptance is 12 months from the date of sending the first report arising from the full examination.

The Commissioner may extend the 12 months' period to a maximum of 21 months from the date of sending the report on payment of fees.

Opposition

The period for opposition (three months from the date of advertisement of acceptance), and the grounds, are unchanged (s. 59), but a new subsection (2A) has been inserted to the effect that an opponent citing an Australian application in respect of which no request for examination has been made, must, if he is a party to the cited application, request examination of that application within three months after lodging the notice of opposition. If the cited application is a third party's, the opponent must, within the same period, give notice to the Commissioner requiring him to direct the third party to make a request for examination. Failure to meet the relevant requirement will result in the notice of opposition so far as it relates to that ground, being deemed to have been withdrawn, and a further notice of opposition on that ground is not receivable.

The periods for the various stages in the opposition procedure have each been reduced from three months to two months. These stages are the lodging of evidence in support, the lodging of evidence in answer and the lodging of evidence in reply. It will still be possible, however, on payment of a fee, to extend these periods. The reduced periods do not apply to any case where the previous stage of the proceedings was completed before January 1, 1970.

Where an opponent or an applicant does not intend to lodge evidence at any particular stage, he may within the period serve on the applicant or the opponent, as the case may be, a written notice to that effect and shall lodge a copy of that notice at the Patent Office. Where evidence has not been served, the party concerned with the next stage of the proceedings may lodge his evidence within two months after expiry of the previous period or within two months after notice has been served on him, whichever is the earlier.

Common Informer

After a complete specification has been laid open to public inspection, *i.e.* at the latest 18 months from the date of filing the complete specification, and before acceptance, any person may give written notice to the Commissioner of any document:

(*a*) that has been published in Australia before the priority date of a claim of the complete specification as open to public inspection; and

(*b*) that the person asserts would, if a patent were granted in respect of the invention claimed in that claim, affect the validity of the patent by reason of obviousness and lack of inventive step, prior claiming or lack of novelty.

The Commissioner must inform the applicant of the document relied on, which may also be formally cited by the examiner.

Any document formally notified and supplied to the Commissioner becomes open to public inspection.

By a new section, 159C, a common informer may obtain, subject to important limitations, a compulsory licence, on terms settled by the Commissioner, if

(*a*) a claim of a complete specification has been amended; and

(*b*) he gave notice under section 57 prior to the amendment; and

(c) between the date of notice and the date of amendment he availed himself, or took steps to avail himself, of the invention as claimed in that claim on the basis that a valid patent could not be granted for the claim.

The limitations are:

(1) A licence will not be granted if the amendment was lodged with reasonable diligence after the applicant had received notice under section 57; and

(2) The licence will not cover any claim included in the complete specification before amendment and in respect of which a patent has been validly granted.

When application is made for a licence by a common informer, a copy thereof must be served on the applicant for patent who may, within three months, give notice of opposition to the application for licence and must then serve on the applicant for licence a copy of the notice. Thereafter, the Commissioner will hear both parties, if they wish to be heard, and will decide whether or not to grant a licence.

Restoration of Patents

Section 97 has been amended to include application for restoration by a beneficial owner who is not the patentee.

International Convention

Sections 141, 142, 142AA and 158 of the Act have been amended to bring them into line with the Stockholm Amendment to Article 4 of the International Convention, so that a claim to priority may be based on an application for an inventor's certificate.

Division of Applications

Where, in response to an examiner's report, an applicant excludes, or proposes to exclude, an invention from his application, he may file a divisional application in respect of the excluded invention but it must be limited to an invention falling within the scope of a claim which has been or will be excluded (s. 49A).

Documents, Specifications and Drawings

With one exception there are no fundamental changes in the general formal requirements for documents or for specifications and drawings. These are contained in regulations 6, 7, 7A, 7B and 7C. The detailed requirements appear in Parts I, II and III of the Third Schedule to the Regulations.

Both in the former regulations and the new regulations, where there is non-compliance with the general or the detailed requirements, the Commissioner is empowered to return a document, specification or drawings with a statement of the requirements which have not been complied with; and he may treat the document or specification as not having been lodged or, alternatively, he may treat it as having been lodged but require alterations to bring it into compliance with the requirements. The exception mentioned above relates to provisional specifications. It would appear from the new regulations that where a provisional specification does not meet the general or detailed requirements the Commissioner is not empowered to treat the specification as having been lodged but may only treat it as not having been lodged and return it, with the application and any other document lodged, to the person from whom the papers were received with a statement indicating the offending matters. In the case of complete specifications, the Commissioner does have the alternative power but if he decides to treat the complete specification as having been filed he must return it within three months with a direction to the applicant to bring it into conformity with the requirements. If appropriate action is not taken by the applicant within six months of the direction, the application will lapse and this fact will be advertised in the *Official Journal*. Within three months of that advertisement, the applicant may apply for restoration. If the Commissioner is satisfied that

(*a*) the failure to comply with the requirements was unintentional and resulted from an error or omission on the part of the applicant or his agent or attorney, or from circumstances beyond the control of the applicant;
(*b*) the applicant has complied with the direction; and
(*c*) there has been no undue delay in making the application for restoration,

the Commissioner will restore the application. If he is not so satisfied, he must refuse the application for restoration. There is no provision for opposition to an application for restoration on the grounds set out, but there is an appeal to the Patents Appeal Tribunal from any decision by the Commissioner.

The detailed formal requirements in relation to documents (other than specifications and drawings) are contained in Part I of the Third Schedule to the Regulations and show no important change from the former requirements. It may be noted, however, that there is no reference to the size of paper to be used as there is for specifications (although presumably the size should be A4 or foolscap), and that it is permitted to make interlineations, alterations, erasures or amendments in a document before it is lodged in the Patent Office provided each is initialled in the margin by the signatory to the document.

On the other hand there are important changes in the detailed formal requirements in relation to specifications and drawings, which are contained in Parts II and III of the Third Schedule. These changes may be set out as follows:

(1) specifications must not contain any interlineations, alterations or erasures;

(2) specifications and drawings may be prepared on paper of foolscap folio size (13″ × 8″) or of International Standards Organisation size A4 (29·7 cm. × 21 cm.). Drawings must, however, be on the same size of paper as used for the specification;

(3) the contents of the specification must be set out in an area not exceeding $9\frac{7}{8}$ inches in depth by $6\frac{3}{4}$ inches in width. Drawings must be contained in an area of the same size;

(4) both specifications and drawings must have the following margins: (*a*) head margin—not less than one inch; (*b*) bottom margin—not less than three-quarters of an inch; and (*c*) left-hand margin—not less than one and one-half inches;

(5) the description of the invention must commence at the head of the second sheet of the specification;

(6) the contents of the specification shall be typewritten or otherwise reproduced on one side of the paper only;

(7) except with the permission of the Commissioner, the specification shall be typewritten or otherwise reproduced (*a*) in sharp black characters suitable for reproduction by photographic means; and (*b*) either in letters not smaller than pica type face, with double spacing between lines, or in some other form approved by the Commissioner.

(8) at least each tenth line of each sheet must be numbered in the left-hand margin.

It will be apparent that unless there is full compliance with the requirements concerning the documents, specifications and drawings and in view of the Commissioner's powers, particularly to treat the document or specification as not having been lodged, applicants may find themselves in serious difficulties. On the other hand, it may be that what appear to be very stringent regulations will be interpreted liberally and that, as under the former regulations, the Commissioner will not exercise his power to treat documents or specifications as not having been lodged.

It will be noted that the requirement for pica size type remains.

Fees

The fee for lodging a complete specification in the first instance is reduced to $20.00, and that for a complete specification following a provisional specification to $16.00. New fees have been introduced in respect, at the time of filing, of the length of complete specifications and the number of claims.

When a complete specification, including drawings, as lodged, exceeds ten sheets, there is payable an additional fee of $1.00 in respect of each sheet in excess of ten. Also, if the number of claims exceeds ten, there is payable an additional fee of $2.00 for each claim in excess of ten.

The fee for sealing a patent is increased to $30.00. But if the patent application is one in which the Examiner's first report on the complete specification was sent to the applicant before January 1, 1970, the fee will be $15.00. The fee for extension of the period for acceptance of an application from the twelfth to the twenty-first month is $8.00 per month.

The fees referred to in this note are in Australian dollars.

Continuation Fees

These are payable on the expiration of the second year from the date of lodgment of the complete specification and annually thereafter while the application is pending. Those for the third and fourth years are $8.00 and $10.00 respectively. For subsequent years they are equal in amount to the renewal fees payable for the corresponding year of the patent, namely $12.00 to $50.00 for the fifth to the sixteenth years. Thus, the continuation fees merge into renewal fees, but presumably will be referred to as continuation fees until sealing takes place.

For complete specifications lodged prior to January 1970, the continuation fees will be assessed as though the complete had been lodged on the anniversary of its filing date first occurring after January 1, 1970.

Extensions of time of up to six months are obtainable on payment of fines.

Renewal Fees

The new scale of renewal fees is as follows:

Year of Patent	*Fee—Australian dollars*
5th	12.00
6th	15.00
7th	18.00
8th	21.00
9th	24.00
10th	27.00
11th	30.00
12th	34.00
13th	38.00
14th	42.00
15th	46.00
16th	50.00

The fee for extension of the period for paying a renewal fee will be Australian $5.00 per month.

This scale will be effective for renewal fees due on or after January 1, 1971.

In respect of any complete specification lodged before January 1, 1970, but on which a patent is not sealed until January 1, 1970, or later *and* where the patent is then in its fifth, or a later, year, the renewal fees payable will be that for the year first expiring after sealing together with any back fees, on the appropriate scale. From this total will be deducted the sum of continuation fees paid if the complete specification was filed earlier than January 1, 1969; if the complete was filed in 1969 the deduction will be the sum of continuation fees paid for the fourth and subsequent years.

Where prior to January 1, 1970, fees under the old scale were paid in advance, the patentee must pay up the difference between the old scale and the new scale, for any year of the patent running on or after January 1, 1971; and if that difference is not paid, the Commissioner will appropriate it from any remaining balance of the fees paid in advance. A patentee may, however, before expiration of that patent year, obtain from the Commissioner repayment of any balance less the amount necessary to cover the increased fee for the current year.

Hungary

The new Hungarian patent law, which came into force on January 1, 1970, contains many innovations, including provisions for a system of deferred examination, early publication, inventors' remuneration, and the protection of new plant varieties and new animal breeds.

Form and Scope of Protection

Patents of Addition have been abolished and there is now only one form of protection, namely independent patents granted for a term of 20 years from the date of filing, subject to payment of annual renewal fees.

The scope of protection is determined by the claims. The description and drawings may be used only for purposes of interpretation of the claims and not for determination of scope.

Provisional patent protection is established on publication of the patent application, but the effect of the protection is retroactive to the date of application. This protection becomes definitive on grant of the patent. During the period of provisional protection infringement proceedings may be instituted but will be deferred until grant.

The patentee has the exclusive right to work the invention or to grant licences.

Where a patent is granted for a process, its effects extend to products obtained directly by means of the process.

Rights of prior use exist in favour of any third party who, within the state and before the priority date of the patent, had systematically manufactured or used the invention or had made serious preparation to do so. This right of prior use is transferable only with the undertaking to which it belongs.

Rights and Obligations

The right to patent protection belongs to the inventor or his successor in title. However, in the case of an " employee-invention," that is to say an invention made by a person who on the basis of his employment or other contract has the duty to work on problems within the technical field of his invention, the right belongs to the employer or other person entitled by contract. If the employer or other person does not claim the right to the patent or the invention, but gives his consent, the inventor or his successor in title may dispose of the invention. The inventor of an employee-invention is entitled to remuneration for use of the invention, which remuneration is calculated on the basis of special regulations.

Patentability

A patent may be granted for any invention which provides a solution which is (*a*) new; (*b*) represents progress; (*c*) of a technical nature; and (*d*) capable of practical application.

The Act defines these requirements as follows:

(*a*) an invention is new if it has not been made available to the public to such an extent that it can be carried out by a person skilled in the art;

(*b*) progress is present when the invention, as compared with the prior art, satisfies needs which remained unsatisfied or if it satisfies needs more advantageously;

(*c*) technical nature is present if the invention results in a change in a product or in a manufacturing process;

(*d*) practical application is present if the invention can be carried out repeatedly with the same result.

Plant varieties and animal breeds, and processes for obtaining them, are patentable if the variety or breed is new, homogeneous and relatively stable.

The following are specifically excluded from patent protection:

(*a*) pharmaceuticals, chemical products, and food for human or animal consumption (but this exemption does not include processes, plant varieties and animal breeds);

(*b*) inventions of which the use would be contrary to law or morality, unless trade in the products is merely restricted by law; and

(*c*) an invention of which the subject-matter is identical with that of a patent of earlier priority; if identity is only partial, a patent may be granted with appropriate limitations.

Examination

Under the former law each patent application was automatically fully examined to ensure compliance with the law. According to the new law patent applications filed after January 1, 1970, will be examined initially only as to formal requirements and the following criteria contained in Article 45 (*a*)–(*e*) of the Act:

(*a*) whether the subject of the application is of a technical nature and capable of practical application;

(*b*) whether the subject of the application relates to a pharmaceutical, chemical product, or food for human or animal consumption, or whether its use would be contrary to law or morality;

(*c*) whether the description and patent claims comply with legal requirements;

(*d*) whether the invention is unitary; and

(*e*) whether the application is entitled to the claimed priority.

Further examination relating to novelty, technical advance and prior rights will not be taken up unless:

(*a*) the applicant requests complete examination when filing the application; or

(*b*) the subject-matter of the application comes within a patent class which is subject to obligatory complete examination; or

(*c*) the applicant or a third party requests the subsequent examination within four years from the day when the application has been laid open to public inspection and this fact has been published in the *Official Gazette*.

After the initial examination, if the application complies with the requirements of Article 45 (*a*)–(*e*) it will be laid open to public inspection and this fact will be announced in the *Official Gazette*. The application remains open to the public for four years, during which time anyone may inspect the documents and obtain photocopies thereof. At this stage of the examination procedure no opposition can be entered, but anyone may file evidence with the National Invention Office showing that the invention claimed is unpatentable and setting out the grounds for the allegation. This evidence is not considered as an opposition but will be taken into account if the complete examination procedure is effected.

The applicant or a third party may request subsequent examination within four years from publication in the *Official Gazette* of the fact that the application has been laid open to public inspection.

Within three months from the announcement in the *Official Gazette* that the complete examination has been ordered, anyone may enter opposition against the application on the basis of Article 45 (*a*)–(*g*). After expiry of the opposition period the subsequent examination will be carried out in respect of the remaining criteria of Article 45, namely:

(*f*) whether the subject of the application is new and represents progress; and

(*g*) whether there is no other Hungarian patent application or patent relating to the same invention and having an earlier priority right.

If opposition has been entered, the documents cited by the opposer will be taken into consideration in the course of the subsequent examination procedure. The National Invention Office decides on the merits of the subsequent examination and the opposition procedure in the same official action.

If complete examination is requested when filing the application the procedure will be substantially the same as previously, comprising several official actions under the requirements of Article 45 with fixed periods for reply. If the application meets all the requirements for patentability it will be laid open to public inspection and remain open to opposition for a period of three months from the date of publication.

Thus applications are laid open to public inspection after either the initial examination or after the complete examination, but opposition may be entered only if the application has been subjected to complete examination or subsequent examination has been requested and ordered.

Postponement of Publication

An applicant may request postponement of publication for a period of not more than one year. The first request for postponement must be filed within 30 days from delivery of the official action ordering publication. This term cannot be extended. Further requests for postponement, up to the maximum, may be filed before expiry of a term already granted.

Abstracts

It is now required to file an abstract comprising 50–150 words, which may take the form required under U.S. practice. The abstract serves for technical information concerning the essence of the invention. In the case of applications directed to the preparation of pharmaceutically active new compounds, the general formula of the desired end-products, the definition of the substituents and the utility are to be disclosed.

Japan

The Japanese Law No. 91, which was promulgated on May 22, 1970, and came into force on January 1, 1971, contains important amendments to the patent and utility model laws, which may be summarised as follows:

1. early publication;
2. deferred examination;
3. broader interpretation of prior applications;
4. re-examination prior to appeal; and
5. time limits for amendment, division and conversion.

1. Early publication

On the expiry of 18 months from the filing date, or, if convention priority is being claimed, from the earliest priority date, patent and utility model applications will be laid open to public inspection. In the case of patents, the laying-open takes the form of printed publication in the *Patent Gazette* of the full text of the specification, claims and drawings (with amendments if any). In the case of utility models, only the claim, drawings and a brief explanation of the drawings will be printed in the *Utility Model Gazette*, but the full specification, claims and drawings will be available for public inspection in the Patent Office.

The procedure is subject to two provisos, namely,

(*a*) that the contents of an application do not offend against public order or morality; and

(*b*) that the application has not previously been published in the *Gazette* as a result of the official examination.

After laying-open to public inspection, an applicant obtains a certain measure of provisional protection. Thus, he has the right to claim compensation from any third party who is working the invention, and the right, where such working is taking place, to request the office to give examination of his application priority over other pending applications.

A claim for compensation cannot be made until publication of the application after full examination and the applicant must give advance warning to the third party or must be able to prove that the third party has worked the invention in the knowledge that it is the invention claimed in the application laid-open to public inspection. The amount of compensation will be equivalent to what the applicant would normally receive in royalties if the invention were patented and a licence granted. The period of unauthorised working which will rank for compensation will run from the date of receipt of the warning letter up to the date of publication of the application after examination. Where an applicant receives compensation and a patent is not granted on the application, or if the working by the third party is outside the scope of the claim of the patent, the applicant will be liable to pay damages to the third party.

It may be noted that as soon as an application has been *published after examination*, the applicant may institute action to obtain an injunction and payment of damages or return of undue profits.

2. Deferred examination

Applications will not be examined unless the applicant, or a third party, makes written request accompanied by the official fee of Yen 7,000 plus Yen 1,000 per claim for a patent application, or Yen 4,500 for a utility model application.

For patents, the period for requesting examination is seven years, and for utility models four years, from the date of filing in Japan. A request for examination cannot be withdrawn, although the application itself may be withdrawn. Failure to file the request within the appropriate period will result in the application being treated as withdrawn. The request for examination will be published in the *Gazette*. The applicant will be notified if a request is lodged by a third party.

With regard to

(*a*) a divisional application; or
(*b*) an application converted to or from a utility model application; or
(*c*) a new application incorporating new matter rejected in the original application;

a request for examination may be made within a maximum period of 30 days from the date on which such an application is filed even after the lapse of the relevant 7/4 years' period. It should be noted that the period of 7/4 years runs from the filing date in Japan of the parent or original application in the case of a divisional or a converted application, and from the date of filing the amendment introducing new matter in the case of a new application incorporating such new matter.

There are no substantive changes in the existing procedure for examination, publication and opposition.

3. Broader interpretation of prior application

The complete disclosure in the specification or drawings as filed with an earlier application may form a basis for rejection of a later application. Thus, an earlier application which was not available to the public on the filing date of a later application but which is subsequently laid-open to public inspection may be used as a basis for rejection of the later application in so far as the invention claimed in the later application is identical to what is shown or described anywhere in the earlier application. Under the law prior to amendment, it was basically the claim of an earlier application that could become a bar to a later application.

An earlier application will not become a bar to a later application if the inventor or inventors are identical in both applications, or if the applicants in both applications are identical at the time of filing the later application.

4. Re-examination prior to appeal

If an appeal is lodged with the Appeal Board of the Patent Office against an examiner's final rejection and if an amendment is timeously filed, the application will be returned to the examiner for re-examination.

Amendments to the specification, claims or drawings must be made simultaneously with the filing of the appeal or within a maximum period of 30 days from the date of filing the appeal.

Where an appeal is lodged from an examiner's final rejection based on a published application, for example as a result of opposition proceedings, there can be no re-examination by the examiner because in this case the filing of an amendment is not permissible.

The general procedure on re-examination is as follows:

(*a*) If the examiner considers that the application is allowable in view of the amendments, he may issue a decision for publication. If, thereafter, no opposition is entered and if no new ground for rejection is found to exist, the examiner may then issue a decision to grant a patent by cancelling his previous rejection.

(*b*) If the examiner finds a ground for rejection different from that forming the basis of his previous rejection, he may give the applicant the opportunity to file an argument or make further amendment. Should the examiner be satisfied with the applicant's response he may issue a decision for publication. The procedure for grant is then as above.

(*c*) If opposition is entered but the examiner finds that the opposition is not well-founded and that there is no new ground for rejection, he may issue a decision dismissing the opposition and also a decision to grant a patent.

(*d*) With the exception of those cases where the examiner issues a decision to grant a patent, he must report to the Director-General of the Patent Office his findings on re-examination. Thereafter the application proceeds to the appeal judges.

5. Time limits for amendment, division and conversion

(a) *Amendment before decision for publication*

Prior to issuance of the decision for publication of an application, amendment of the specification, claims or drawings, may be made provided no new matter is introduced:

(i) at any time during a period of 15 months from the filing date or the earliest priority date where Convention priority has been claimed;

(ii) simultaneously with the filing by the applicant of a request for examination;

(iii) within a maximum period of three months from the date of receipt of notification that a third party has requested examination;

(iv) within the period of three months, extensible by one month, set for filing a response to an official action giving reasons for rejection;

(v) within the maximum period of 30 days from the date of filing an appeal.

(b) *Amendment after decision for publication*

After issuance of the decision for publication of an application, amendments intended to reduce the scope of claims, to correct clerical errors or to clarify indistinct statements may be made:

(i) Within the period of three months, extensible by one month, set for filing a reply to an opposition.

(ii) Within the period of three months, extensible by one month, set for filing a reply to an official action setting out new reasons for rejection.

(c) *Division*

The time limits for filing a divisional application are identical to those set out above for making amendments.

(d) *Conversion*

(i) *Patent application to utility model application.* Conversion can be effected within a period of four years from the filing date of the patent application; but if a notice of rejection is issued conversion can be effected only within a period of 30 days (extensible by two months) from the date of the examiner's first notice of rejection.

(ii) *Utility model application to patent application.* Conversion can be effected within a period of seven years from the filing date of the utility model application; but if a notice of rejection is issued conversion can be effected only within a period of 30 days (extensible by two months) from the date of the examiner's first notice of rejection.

6. Transitional measures

(i) An application pending at the time of enforcement of the new law will be governed by the former law until a decision or judgment on such an application becomes finally binding.

(ii) The grounds for invalidation provided in the former law remain effective in invalidating a patent, or a registered utility model, matured from an application filed under the former law.

All periods referred to herein apply only to non-resident applicants.

India

The Indian Patents Act 1970 came into force on April 20, 1972, with the exception of section 12 (2) relating to the period within which the Examiner must report to the Controller; section 13 (2) which provides for the novelty search of literature other than Indian applications and patents; section 28 which relates to mention of the inventor as such; section 68 which provides that unregistered assignments and licences shall be invalid; and sections 125–132 which relate to the registration of Patent Agents.

Although the provisions of the Act are based generally on those of the United Kingdom Patents Act 1949, certain provisions give to Government far-reaching powers, particularly in relation to the use of patented articles, medicines and drugs.

The more significant innovations contained in the Act are summarised below.

Patentability

Invention means any new and useful

(i) art, process, method or manner of manufacture;
(ii) machine, apparatus or other article;
(iii) substance produced by manufacture,

and includes any new and useful improvement of any of them, and an alleged invention.

The following are not inventions within the meaning of the Act:

(*a*) an invention which is frivolous or which claims anything obviously contrary to well-established natural laws;
(*b*) an invention the primary or intended use of which would be contrary to law or morality or injurious to public health;
(*c*) the mere discovery of a scientific principle or the formulation of an abstract theory;
(*d*) the mere discovery of any new property or new use for a known substance or of the mere use of a known process, machine or apparatus unless such known process results in a new product or employs at least one new reactant;
(*e*) a substance obtained by a mere admixture resulting only in the aggregation of the properties of the components thereof or a process for producing such substance;
(*f*) the mere arrangement or re-arrangement or duplication of known devices each functioning independently of one another in a known way;
(*g*) a method or process of testing applicable during the process of manufacture for rendering the machine, apparatus or other equipment more efficient or for the improvement or restoration of the existing machine, apparatus or other equipment or for the improvement or control of manufacture;
(*h*) a method of agriculture or horticulture;

(*i*) any process for the medicinal, surgical, curative, prophylactic or other treatment of human beings or any process for a similar treatment of animals or plants to render them free of disease or to increase their economic value or that of their products.

Also, inventions relating to atomic energy are not patentable. In the case of inventions:

(*a*) claiming substances intended for use, or capable of being used, as food, medicine or drug; or

(*b*) relating to substances prepared or produced by chemical processes (including alloys, optical glass, semi-conductors and inter-metallic compounds),

claims to the substances themselves are not allowable, but claims to the methods or processes of manufacture will be allowed.

"Food" is defined as any article of nourishment and includes any substance intended for use of babies, invalids or convalescents as an article of food or drink.

"Medicine or drug" is defined as including:

(i) all medicines for internal or external use of human beings or animals;

(ii) all substances intended to be used for or in the diagnosis, treatment, mitigation or prevention of diseases in human beings or animals;

(iii) all substances intended to be used for or in the maintenance of public health, or the prevention or control of any epidemic disease among human beings or animals;

(iv) insecticides, germicides, fungicides, weedicides and all other substances intended to be used for the protection or preservation of plants;

(v) all chemical substances which are ordinarily used as intermediates in the preparation or manufacture of any of the medicines or substances above referred to.

Novelty

Novelty is destroyed by:

(*a*) prior publication, before the priority date of applicant's complete specification, in any specification filed in pursuance of an Indian patent application and dated on or after January 1, 1912;

(*b*) prior claiming in any complete specification published on or after the priority date of applicant's complete specification, and being a specification filed in pursuance of an Indian patent application dated before, or claiming a priority date earlier than, that date;

(*c*) prior publication in India or elsewhere in any document other than one referred to in (*a*) and (*b*) above, before the priority date of applicant's complete specification;

(*d*) prior public knowledge or public use in India before the priority date of applicant's complete specification.

Applicant

An application for a patent may be made by any of the following persons:

(*a*) the true and first inventor;

(*b*) the assignee of the true and first inventor;

(*c*) the applicant for protection in a convention country;

(*d*) the assignee of the applicant in a convention country;

(*e*) the legal representative of any deceased person who immediately before his death was entitled to make the application.

An application, other than a convention application, by any person qualifying under paragraph (*a*), (*b*) or (*e*), may be made by that person either alone or jointly with any other person.

The term "true and first inventor" does not include either the first importer of an invention into India, or a person to whom an invention is first communicated from outside India.

Information to be Furnished

(a) Applications:

An applicant will be required to furnish the following information in respect of any corresponding application (whether filed in his name alone or jointly with another person, or by anyone from whom he claims title):

(i) A statement on Form 4, to be filed with the application setting out:

(*a*) names of countries where corresponding applications have been filed, with details of the application numbers and filing dates;

(*b*) whether any of the applications has been accepted, refused, abandoned or withdrawn;

(*c*) whether a patent has been granted on any of the applications;

(*d*) name and address of anyone to whom the rights in any of the applications have been assigned; and

(ii) An undertaking that, up to the date of acceptance of his Indian application, he will keep the Controller informed in writing, from time to time, of similar information in respect of every other corresponding application filed outside India subsequent to filing the statement referred to, the information to be supplied within three months from the date of filing each such application.

The Controller is also empowered to call for details relating to any objections, made against any corresponding application, on the ground of lack of novelty or patentability, the amendments effected and the claims allowable.

Failure to disclose the information required, or the furnishing of false information, is a ground of opposition and of revocation.

(b) Patents:

The Controller may require a patentee or licensee to furnish him with information or periodical statements as to the extent to which the patented invention has been commercially worked in India.

Refusal or failure to furnish the Controller with any information required is punishable with a fine of up to 1,000 rupees; the supply of false information is punishable with imprisonment up to six months, or with a fine, or with both.

The statements are to be set out on Form 58, which calls for the following particulars:

(i) the manner and the extent to which the patent has been worked;

(ii) the licences and sub-licences granted during the year;

(iii) details regarding the undertaking through which the invention has been worked;

(iv) the details of collaboration, if any;

(v) difficulties faced in working the invention;

(vi) other particulars, if any.

The statements are to be furnished in respect of every calendar year within three months of the end of each year, and the Controller has power to publish them.

Term of Patents

Patents will be dated as of the day of filing the complete specification, and the terms will be:

(*a*) for a patent for a method or process of manufacture of a substance intended for use, or capable of being used, as a food, or medicine or drug:
5 years from the date of sealing, or
7 years from the date of the patent
whichever period is shorter.

(*b*) for all other patents:
14 years from the date of the patent.

In respect of those presently pending applications relating to food or medicine or drugs for which grant has been delayed by operation of section 78C of the former Act, any eventual patent will be dated as of the date of filing the complete specification or the date of commencement of the new Act, whichever is later.

There is no change in the term of existing patents, that is, 16 years from the date of application or priority date, if any.

Renewal fees will be payable as in the past, but a six-month period of grace will be available.

Government Rights of Use

In respect of patents granted under the new Act the Government has the right to use any patented process, or make or import any patented machine, apparatus or other article, merely for its own use. In the case of a patent in respect of a medicine or drug, the medicine or drug may be imported by the Government merely for its own use or for distribution in any dispensary, hospital or other medical institution maintained by or on behalf of the Government or specified by it. There is no provision for payment of any compensation to the patentee.

It would also appear that so far as concerns existing patents, as well as applications filed and patents granted under the new Act, the Government has similar powers, and can also give written authority to any person to use the invention for Government purposes. The terms for such use are to be settled between the parties or, failing settlement, by the High Court. Where the use is in respect of any medicine or drug or article of food, however, the royalty or other remuneration shall not exceed 4 per cent. of the net ex-factory sale price in bulk of the patented article.

Licences of Right

At any time after the expiration of three years from the date of sealing a patent the Government may apply for endorsement of the patent "Licences of Right" on the ground that the reasonable requirements of the public with respect to the patented invention have not been satisfied or that the patented invention is not available to the public at a reasonable price.

Every patent in force at the commencement of the Act, in respect of inventions relating to foods, medicines, drugs and chemical substances, shall be deemed to be endorsed "Licences of Right" from the commencement of the Act or from the expiration of three years from the date of sealing the patent. Similarly, every patent granted after commencement of the Act in respect of any invention within the fields mentioned will be deemed to be endorsed from the expiration of three years from the date of sealing. The licence royalty or other remuneration under any endorsed patent relating to foods, medicines or drugs will in no case exceed 4 per cent. of the net ex-factory sale price in bulk of the patented article.

The Controller may, before settlement of licence terms, permit an applicant for a licence under an endorsed patent to work the patent on such terms as the Controller thinks fit.

Acquisition of Inventions and Patents

The Government may, if it considers it necessary for public interest, acquire all the rights in an invention or patent, by publishing a notice of acquisition in the official Gazette. The applicant or patentee, as well as any party having a registered interest in the patent, will be informed and compensation will be payable on terms agreed between the parties; failing agreement the terms will be settled by the High Court.

Bolivia

The Bolivian Decree No. 09364 dated August 27, 1970, prohibits the patenting of pharmaceutical processes and products.

The Decree contains the following provisions:

(1) As of the date of the Decree there are declared as non-patentable chemical and biological products for pharmaceutical use, as well as all compositions or pharmaceutical formulae, and methods, processes and systems used in their preparation. Also declared non-patentable are dietetic or nutrient formulae in general,

methods, processes and systems for their formulation, and their industrial uses.

(2) No renewal fees will be accepted on patents already granted for the prohibited subject-matter, nor will extensions of working terms be granted.

(3) The Patent Office will give preferential treatment to applicants for compulsory licences, or may expropriate patents for the prohibited subject-matter, or may declare their lapsing for lack of exploitation.

(4) Those patents that for any of the reasons for lapsing listed in the law, or those that lapse by virtue of this Decree, and pass therefore into the public domain, may be given by the Patent Office to the public or to the Chambers of Industry for their use and exploitation.

Nigeria

The Patents and Designs Decree 1970, which came into force on December 1, 1971, provides, *inter alia*, for an independent system of patents and repeals the earlier legislation whereby patent protection was obtainable only by registration of a United Kingdom patent.

The repealed legislation includes the Registration of United Kingdom Patents Act and the Patent Rights (Limitation) Decree 1968.

A patent registered in Nigeria under the former law and which was in force immediately before the commencement of the new Decree will be treated in Nigeria as if it had been granted under the Decree but will expire at the end of the term granted under the former law. An action for infringement will lie under the Decree only if the alleged infringement occurred on or after the commencement of the Decree; otherwise the action will lie under the former law.

Within twelve months after commencement of the Decree, further transitional or saving provisions may be made.

Patentability, Novelty and Inventive Step

The new provisions are based on the Strasbourg Convention on Substantive Law. Thus, an invention is patentable if it is:

(*a*) new, and

(*b*) results from inventive activity, and

(*c*) is capable of industrial application; or

(*d*) if it constitutes an improvement upon a patented invention and also is new, results from inventive activity and is capable of industrial application.

An invention is new if it does not form part of the state of the art, which is defined as everything, concerning the art or field of knowledge to which the invention relates, which has been made available to the public anywhere by written or oral description, by use or any other means, prior to the filing date of the application in Nigeria or any foreign priority date validly claimed.

Novelty is not destroyed through publication at an official or officially recognised international exhibition by the inventor or his successor in title, provided that the Nigerian application is filed within six months of such disclosure.

"Inventive activity" is present if the invention does not obviously follow from the state of the art.

An invention is capable of industrial application if it can be manufactured or used in any kind of industry, including agriculture.

The following are specifically excluded from protection:

(*a*) Plant or animal varieties, or essentially biological processes for the production of plants or animals (other than microbiological processes and their products);

(*b*) Inventions whose publication or exploitation would be contrary to public order or morality. (The exploitation of an invention is not contrary to public order or morality merely because its exploitation is prohibited by law.)

(*c*) Principles and discoveries of a scientific nature.

Right to Patent

The right to obtain a patent is vested in the statutory inventor, that is to say the person who is the first to file, or validly to claim a foreign priority for, a patent application in respect of the invention. The true and first inventor is, however, entitled to be named as such in the patent.

Where the essential elements of a patent application have been obtained by the applicant from the invention of another person, or his successor, the rights in the application and in any patent granted thereon shall be deemed to be transferred to that person, or his successor.

The right to a patent on an invention made in the course of employment, or in execution of a contract for the performance of specified work, is vested in the employer or the person who commissioned the work. Where the inventor is an employee he is entitled to fair remuneration, taking into account his salary and the importance of the invention, if:

(*a*) his contract of employment does not require him to exercise any inventive activity but in making the invention he has used data or means that his employment has put at his disposal, or

(*b*) the invention is of exceptional importance.

Specification and Claims

The Decree requires an application to be accompanied by a description of the invention, with drawings where appropriate, and a claim or claims. The description must disclose the invention in a manner sufficiently clear and complete for the invention to be put into effect by a person skilled in the art, and the claims should define the protection sought and should not go beyond the limits of the description.

Each application should relate to one invention only, but may include

(*a*) claims
- (i) for any number of products,
- (ii) for any number of manufacturing processes for those products, and
- (iii) for any number of applications of those products, and

(*b*) claims
- (i) for any number of processes, and
- (ii) for the means of working those processes, for the resulting product or products and for the application of those products.

Examination

Applications will be examined only for formalities and unity of invention.

If the application documents are not in accord with official requirements the Registrar has power to reject the application.

If the application relates to more than one invention, the applicant may restrict it to one invention and may, within three months from the official objection, lodge separate applications for any excluded inventions, with preservation of priority.

Applications will not be examined for patentability nor to determine whether the description and claims satisfy the requirements of the law. Neither will there be any examination to determine whether a prior application, or an application benefiting from a foreign priority has been made in Nigeria in respect of the same invention, nor whether a patent has been granted as a result of such an application.

Publication

Documents relating to a patent application will not be available to the public until grant of a patent thereon.

Form and Scope of Patent

There is only one form of patent, namely, an independent patent; the law makes no provision for the grant of patents of addition.

Patents are granted for a term of twenty years from the date of filing the relevant patent application, subject to the payment of annual fees. A period of grace of six months is allowed for payment of the annual fees.

The patentee is entitled to prevent others from exploiting the invention for industrial or commercial purposes, and the scope of protection will be determined by the terms of the claims which will be interpreted by the description and the plans or drawings if any. A process patent covers also the direct product of the process.

If:

(*a*) the patent covers a process for the manufacture of a new product, and

(*b*) the same product is manufactured by a third party

the product will, in the absence of proof to the contrary, be presumed to have been manufactured by that process.

Third party rights are reserved in favour of anyone who, at the date of filing a patent application, or at the date of a validly claimed foreign priority date, was, in Nigeria and in good faith, manufacturing the patented product or applying the patented process or had made serious preparations with a view to doing so. These rights are personal to the third party.

A patentee may surrender his patent in respect of any or all of the claims, with the written consent of the registered licensee under any contractual licence or licence of right.

In the absence of any provision to the contrary among themselves, joint owners of a patent may separately transfer their shares or exploit the patented invention. A licence, however, may not be granted by joint owners otherwise than jointly.

Nullity

There is no provision for opposition, but any person having a material interest, or a public officer in the exercise of his functions, may institute an action for nullity of a patent either in its entirety or in part on any of the following grounds:

(*a*) The subject of the patent is not patentable under the law;

(*b*) The description of the invention or the claim does not conform with the legal requirements;

(*c*) A Nigerian patent has been granted on a prior application or on an application benefiting from an earlier foreign priority.

In an action for nullity, the court may require the patentee to produce in evidence any of the following:

(*a*) A list of any publications or earlier patents referred to in connection with a corresponding foreign patent application;

(*b*) Any proceedings relating to the said foreign application or to any patent granted thereon;

(*c*) Any publications or patents mentioned in any report sent to the patentee by a governmental or inter-governmental investigation institute.

Where a declaration of nullity is made the patent will be deemed to have been null and void since grant, but it will be unnecessary to repay licence royalties unless the court so orders.

International Convention

An application under the International Convention must be filed within twelve months from the filing date of the earliest application filed in a country which has been declared to be a convention country. The request for priority must be made when filing the application and within three months thereafter a certified copy of the basic application must be filed.

The Patents and Designs (Convention Countries) Order 1971 declares to be convention countries all present members of the

Convention, including the German Democratic Republic, but excluding Rhodesia and South Africa.

Assignments

Rights in a patent application or in a patent may be assigned, transferred by succession or held in joint ownership. An assignment must be in writing and signed by the parties. Assignments and transfers by succession must be registered or they will have no effect against third parties.

Licences

A patentee may grant a licence in writing to any person, and in the absence of any contrary provision the licensee will be entitled to exploit the patent as fully as the patentee.

Licences are not effectual against third parties unless registered: a registration may be cancelled at the request of the licensor if the Registrar is satisfied that the licence has been terminated.

Any clause in a licence will be null and void if it imposes restrictions not derived from the patent rights or unnecessary for safeguarding those rights. The following are not restrictions of this kind:

(*a*) limitations of scope, extent, territory or duration, or of quality or quantity of products;

(*b*) obligations on the licensee to abstain from acts capable of prejudicing the validity of the patent; and

(*c*) limitations justified by the licensor in the technically efficient exploitation of the invention.

In the absence of any provision to the contrary

(*a*) the licence will not prevent the licensor from granting further licences nor from exploiting the patent himself;

(*b*) the licence is not assignable by the licensee; and

(*c*) the licensee will not be entitled to grant further licences.

The Commissioner is empowered to order that licence clauses involving the payment of royalties outside Nigeria shall be invalid unless they have official approval.

A licensee may himself institute infringement proceedings if the licensor unreasonably refuses, or neglects, to institute proceedings.

Licences of Right

A patentee may request endorsement of his patent "Licences of Right," provided he is not precluded by the terms of any previously registered licence from granting a further licence.

On endorsement:

(*a*) any person has the right to obtain a licence to exploit the patent. Failing agreement between the parties, terms will be settled by the court; and

(*b*) annual fees payable thereafter are reduced by half.

A licensee is not entitled to assign the licence or grant further licences under it.

An endorsement may be cancelled on the request of the patentee provided there is agreement by the holders of any licences granted under this section and subject to payment of the balance of all fees paid at the half-rate.

Compulsory Licences

At any time after the expiration of four years after the filing of a patent application or three years after the grant of a patent, whichever period last expires, a person may apply to the court for the grant of a compulsory licence on one or more of the following grounds:

(*a*) that the patented invention, being capable of being worked in Nigeria, has not been so worked;

(*b*) that the existing degree of working of the patented invention in Nigeria does not meet on reasonable terms the demand for the product;

(*c*) that the working of the patented invention in Nigeria is being hindered or prevented by the importation of the patented article; and

(*d*) that, by reason of the refusal of the patentee to grant licences on reasonable terms, the establishment or development of industrial or commercial activities in Nigeria is unfairly and substantially prejudiced.

The owner of a patent which cannot be worked without infringing a patent of earlier date or priority, may obtain a compulsory licence to the extent necessary for the working of his invention, provided it serves industrial purposes different from those served by the invention of the earlier patent, or constitutes substantial technical progress over that invention.

If the two inventions serve the same industrial purposes, the compulsory licence will be granted only if a cross-licence is granted to the patentee of the earlier patent if he so requests.

Working comprises:

(*a*) the manufacture of a patented article, or

(*b*) the application of a patented process, or

(*c*) the use in manufacture of a patented machine,

by an effective and serious establishment existing in Nigeria on a scale which is adequate and reasonable in the circumstances.

A compulsory licence will not entitle the licensee to grant further licences, will be non-exclusive, and will be transferable only with the industrial undertaking in which the invention is used and then only with the consent of the court.

A compulsory licence may be cancelled if its terms are not complied with or if the conditions which justified its grant cease to exist; the terms may also be varied.

Orders may be made by the Federal Commissioner for Trade providing for the grant of compulsory licences before expiry of the normal working period in respect of patented products and processes declared to be of vital importance for the defence or the economy of Nigeria or for public health.

Use of Patents for Service of Government Agencies

Part II of Schedule 1 contains the provisions of the now-repealed Patent Rights (Limitation) Decree 1968 and empowers any Federal or State Commissioner, who is satisfied that it is in the public interest to do so, to authorise any person to purchase, make, exercise or vend any patented article or invention for the service of a Government agency. A Commissioner's authority may be exercised before or after the relevant patent is granted, before or after the doing of the acts for which authority is given, and may be given to any person whether or not he is authorised directly or indirectly by the patentee in respect of the article or invention. Further, the Government, authorised persons, suppliers of the Government or authorised persons and agents of the suppliers are exempt from liability for infringement of any relevant patent and from liability to make any payment, whether by royalty or otherwise, to the patentee.

Patentees may be furnished with such information as they require as to the extent of any acts done under a Commissioner's authority.

There are also rendered nugatory the provisions of any licence, assignment or agreement, of whatever date, between a patentee and any person other than the Government or a Ministry in so far as the provisions restrict or regulate the use of a patented article or invention or provide for the making of payments in respect of any such use or are calculated by reference thereto.

During any period of emergency, the powers are available for any purpose which appears to a Commissioner necessary or expedient.

Specific "articles" coming within the scope of the Decree include:

(a) any drugs or pharmaceutical preparations, substances or materials, and

(b) any plant, machinery or apparatus, whether fixed to the land or not after importation.

Peru

Peruvian Law No. 18350 and the Rules of Practice came into force on January 27, 1971, and cover Industrial Property generally. The following is a resumé of the law in so far as it relates to patents.

Forms of Protection

There are two forms of protection of inventions, namely:

(a) Patents of Invention, which are granted for a maximum term of 10 years from the date of grant. There are no annual renewal fees payable;

(b) Limited Patents, which may be granted only to persons domiciled in Peru, for an invention which is under study or experiment and where the inventor requires to carry out further experiments or requires the construction of apparatus, which may lead to broadening of the invention. The Limited Patent expires at the end of one year from application if the inventor does not file formal application for a Patent of Invention within that term.

Patentability

Patents of Invention are granted to the inventor or assign without guarantee of novelty, priority, or utility, for inventions, discoveries or improvements of practical application and use.

The following are specifically excluded from patent protection:

(1) Discoveries of elements existing in nature;
(2) Purely scientific theories and principles;
(3) Commercial, financial and accounting, and simple publicity combinations, systems and plans;
(4) Foreign inventions on the expiry of two years from the date of filing the first foreign application.

Although pharmaceutical compounds are not specifically excluded by the new Law, it is believed that the Patent Office will refuse claims to such compounds, but will allow claims to processes for producing them.

Novelty

Novelty is destroyed if the invention has, prior to the date of application, been known or used by third parties in Peru, or if it has been described in a printed publication in Peru or elsewhere.

Publication

Apart from publication of the resumé of the invention for opposition purposes, the Registers and Files are not open to the public until grant.

Examination

Applications are examined for formalities, suitability for patenting and unity of invention.

When there is any informality the applicant is given a period of 30 days within which to remove the informality.

If the Office alleges that the claims cover more than one invention the applicant is given a period of 60 days to limit the claims and, if he wishes, to lodge a divisional application in respect of any excluded invention, with preservation of priority. Failure to comply with the official requirement will result in the application being treated as abandoned. Where an invention relates to the manufacture of a new product, the application may include claims to the process and to the product, or only to one of these.

Opposition

The applicant must advertise a resumé of the description within 30 days after filing the application. The advertisement consists of one insertion in the Industrial Property Gazette and, for opposition purposes, one insertion for six consecutive days in the Official Journal "El Peruano." Within 10 days following the last advertisement in "El Peruano" the applicant must lodge in the Patent Office copies of the first and last journals containing the advertisement.

The owner of any Industrial Property may oppose an application for patent, within 30 working days from the last advertisement, by lodging a considered statement. The opposition is communicated by the Patent Office to the applicant who is entitled to lodge a reply within 20 working days from the Office notification. This reply is communicated by the Office to the opponent, who is also given a term of 20 working days to reply. The opponent's reply is in turn communicated to the applicant who is again given 20 working days wherein to file a further reply. A technical and legal Report on the case is then prepared by the Office within a term of 60 days from receipt of the applicant's final reply or if there has been no final reply from the end of the term therefor. The Office is then required to issue a decision within 15 days from issue of the Report. Appeal from the decision lies to the Director General of Industries within 15 working days, each party having a period of 10 days to present arguments. A decision on the appeal should be made within 60 days from the date of appeal.

Specification and Claims

The law calls for a descriptive specification with clearly defined claims and drawings when required. Protection is accorded only to claims presented and approved.

Documents

Any document executed abroad requires consular legalisation, for example, Powers of Attorney and Assignments.

Where a foreign application has been filed, the Peruvian application must be filed within two years of the first filing date and must be accompanied by a legalised certified copy of the basic specification. A period of 30 days is allowed for filing this document.

Working

Working must be commenced within two years, with the possibility of a single extension of two years, from the date of grant, and the patentee must report the date of commencement of working to the Patent Office for official recordal. A patentee is required to sell the patented product, if it is being commercially worked, to anyone wishing to purchase for industrial use. Refusal to sell, or the fixing of an unjustifiably high price, may lead to annulment of the patent.

Compulsory Licences

1. Lack of exploitation

Compulsory licences may be granted when exploitation of the invention in Peru is impeded or obstructed by importation of the patented product by the patentee, or if the exploitation does not satisfy public demand. On receipt of an application for a compulsory licence, the Patent Office will determine its merits according to the following criteria:

(*a*) Can the patent be exploited in Peru without delay and to a sufficient extent;

(*b*) Is the applicant's technological knowledge and experience sufficient to ensure adequate exploitation; and

(*c*) Will the patentee receive reasonable compensation.

A compulsory licence will be refused if these criteria are not met or if the patentee can offer a legitimate excuse for his failure to exploit. Importation does not rank as a legitimate excuse.

2. Dependent patents

The owner of a junior patent which cannot be worked without infringing an earlier patent may obtain a licence to the extent necessary to enable him to work his own patent provided that it serves a different industrial purpose or represents an outstanding technical advance. If both inventions serve the same industrial purpose the licence will be granted only on condition that the owner of the earlier patent may, if he so wishes, obtain a cross-licence.

3. General

In all applications for compulsory licences, the applicant must prove that he has previously sought a licence from the patentee but has been unable to secure one on reasonable conditions.

Compulsory licences may be exclusive but a licensee is not allowed to grant sub-licences.

A licence may be transferred only with the licensee's firm or that part of the firm using the invention, and the transfer is in any case subject to approval by the Patent Office.

The holder of a compulsory licence must exploit the patent within a term of six months from the date of grant of the licence and must not cease exploitation for more than six months, on penalty of revocation of the licence.

Mauritius

The Mauritius Act No. 29 of 1971 repeals the United Kingdom Patents Registration Ordinance so that protection is now available only by independent patenting under the Patents Ordinance (Title XXVIII—Chapter 406). The Act also consequentially amends section 25 of the Patents Ordinance by limiting the acts destructive of novelty to acts occurring in Mauritius, and repeals the provisions of sections 41 and 42 relating to International and Intercolonial Arrangements.

Colombia

Colombian Decree No. 410 of 1971, which came into force on January 1, 1972, covers Industrial Property generally. The following is a resumé of the Law in so far as it relates to patents.

Patentability, Novelty and Inventive Step

An invention is patentable if it is:

(*a*) new; and
(*b*) results from inventive activity; and
(*c*) is capable of industrial application; or
(*d*) if it constitutes an improvement upon a patented invention and also is new and capable of industrial application.

An invention is not new, if prior to the date of filing the patent application, or prior to a priority date validly claimed, it has become available to the public anywhere by commercial or industrial working, by oral or written description, by use or by any other means, sufficient to enable the invention to be put into practice.

Novelty is not destroyed by the disclosure of an invention within six months prior to filing the patent application if such disclosure resulted, directly or indirectly from:

(*a*) An evident act of bad faith in contravention of the rights of the applicant or the owner of the rights in the invention; or (*b*) Exhibition of the invention by the applicant or the owner of the rights at an officially recognised trade fair in Colombia.

"Inventive activity" is present if the invention does not obviously follow from the state of the art.

An invention is capable of industrial application if it can be manufactured or used in any kind of industry, including agriculture and cattle-raising.

The following are specifically excluded from patent protection:

(*a*) Plant or animal varieties, or essentially biological processes for the production of plants or animals (other than microbiological processes and their products);

(*b*) Pharmaceutical preparations and active ingredients therefor, medicines, beverages or foodstuffs for human or animal consumption or for plant use. However, patents will be granted for processes of manufacture of such substances, but only if the applicant can, within one year from filing the application, show that he is exploiting, in Colombia, the process the subject of the application and that he is able to supply the market under reasonable conditions of quantity, quality and price;

(*c*) Inventions whose application or exploitation is contrary to public order or morality. (An invention is not contrary to public order or morality merely because its exploitation is prohibited by law.)

Right to Patent

The right to obtain a patent belongs to the first applicant or the person owning his rights.

In the absence of contractual provisions to the contrary, an invention made by an employee or an agent, employed to invent, belongs to the employer or principal. The same provision applies when an employment contract does not require the employee to exercise any inventive activity but when he has made the invention using data or means that his employment has put at his disposal. In this case, however, the employee will have a right to remuneration taking into account his salary, the importance of the invention, the benefits obtained by the employer, and other similar factors.

If the invention forming the subject of a patent application has been stolen from the inventor, or from his attorneys, or if the application is the result of default in a contractual or legal obligation, the person harmed may claim the invention and all rights in the application. Similar action is available after grant of the patent.

The inventor is entitled to be named as such in the patent; he may, however, oppose such nomination.

Specification and Claims

The Decree calls for a complete specification, with drawings if applicable, describing the invention in a manner sufficiently clear and complete to enable any person skilled in the art to carry it out, and one or more claims setting out the scope of novelty and the industrial application of the invention. An abstract containing at least one claim characterising the invention must also be lodged.

Each application should relate to one invention only, or to a group of interrelated inventions provided there is unity of invention. Applications not complying with these requirements may be divided or limited, within a period of six months from the official requirement, and divisional applications will take the priority of the parent application.

Priority

An applicant who wishes to avail himself of the priority of an earlier application made in another country is required to file his Colombian application within six months following the date of the earlier application and must indicate in his application the number and date of the earlier application and the country in which it was filed. Within three months of filing the Colombian application there must be lodged a certified copy of the earlier application.

Examination and Opposition

Applications will be examined initially only for formalities and unity of invention, and a period of six months will be allowed for removing objections on these grounds. Thereafter the abstract will be published and the application will be laid open to public inspection. Within 60 days from the publication, opposition may be entered on the ground of lack of novelty. When the opposition period has expired there will be an official preliminary examination of novelty and industrial application, as well as of any opposition entered. The report of this examination, which will also indicate whether there is a conflicting Colombian application or patent of earlier date, will be transmitted to the applicant who will be given a period of 30 days within which to present arguments or amended claims. Thereafter a final report will be issued. If the final report is favourable (or the preliminary report if there was no opposition) the patent will be granted; if only partially favourable, the patent will be granted with a limitation of claims; if entirely unfavourable, or if the applicant will not accept limitation of the claims, the application will be rejected.

The grant of a patent is published in the Official Gazette with the characteristic claims, and the patent file is open to inspection.

There may later be introduced provisions for complete examination as to patentability in relation to specific technical fields.

Form and Scope of Protection

There are two forms of protection, namely:

(*a*) Patents of Invention which are granted for a maximum period of 12 years from the date of grant. There will be an initial grant for eight years, but the patentee has the right to an extension of four years if he can prove that the invention is being exploited in Colombia or that it has been exploited there during the eighth year of the original term;

(*b*) Patents of Improvement, which may be granted only to the owner of the original patent and are coterminous therewith.

The scope of protection will be determined by the terms of the claims; the specification, drawings and reports will be used to interpret the claims.

The patent will confer on the registered owner the right to preclude third parties from the following acts:

(1) Making the product of the patented invention;

(2) Using, importing, transferring, offering for sale or placing on the market in any manner whatsoever, the patented product, as well as stocking such product for the purpose of using or offering for sale;

(3) Using or carrying out, transferring or offering for sale the process or means which are the subject of the patented invention;

(4) Doing any of the acts set out in (2) in relation to products obtained by means of the patented process.

The patent right also precludes third parties from granting, permitting or promising to those who are not licensees, the process or means to put a patented invention into practice.

Acts carried out exclusively for scientific purposes will not be considered infringement of the patent rights.

In the absence of any provision to the contrary among themselves, joint owners of a patent may separately exploit the patented invention and take action against infringement; but they may only grant licences with the consent of the other joint owners, or through a court order, and they may transfer their shares but subject to a preferential right of the other joint owners to acquire such shares within a period of three months from notification.

A patentee may surrender his patent in respect of any or all of the claims, with the written consent of the owners of any rights under the patent.

Nullity

The Public Ministry or any person may institute an action for nullity of a patent either in its entirety or in part on the ground that the invention covered by the patent does not comply with the requirements for patentability (novelty, inventive step or industrial application) or that the specification does not describe the invention in a manner sufficiently clear and complete to enable any person skilled in the art to carry it out. If the patent is found to be partially invalid the claims will be limited to those found valid.

Licences

The Decree provides for three forms of licence, namely Contractual, Compulsory and Authority.

1. Contractual licences

The applicant or the owner of a patent may by written contract grant to some other person a licence to exploit the invention.

In the absence of any provision to the contrary in the licence contract, the grant of a licence will not prevent the licensor from granting further licences to third parties nor from exploiting the invention himself, and the licensee will be entitled to exploit the invention during the whole duration of the patent and in the entire territory of the country, through any application of the invention. Again in the absence of any provisions to the contrary, a licence will not be assignable to third parties and the licensee will not be entitled to grant sub-licences.

Clauses in a contractual licence will be null and void if they impose upon the licensee, in the commercial or industrial field, restrictions not deriving from the rights conferred by the patent. The following will not be deemed to constitute such restrictions:

(1) Limitations concerning the extent or duration of exploitation of the subject of the patent;

(2) Limitations preventing marketing of a patented product unless it meets certain standards of quality.

2. Compulsory licences

At any time after the expiration of four years after the filing of the patent application or three years after the grant of the patent, whichever period last expires, any person may apply to the court for the grant of a compulsory licence upon one or more of the following grounds:

(*a*) That the patented invention has not been worked in Colombia, or its working has been suspended for more than one year;

(*b*) That the working of the patented invention within Colombia does not meet on reasonable terms the national demand in respect of quality, quantity or price;

(*c*) That the owner of the patent has not granted contractual licences which would enable a licensee to meet on reasonable terms the national demand in respect of quality, quantity or price.

An application for a compulsory licence may be opposed by the owner of the patent.

A compulsory licence will not be granted if the owner of the patent justifies himself by legitimate reasons. Importation will not constitute a legitimate reason.

Working of a patented invention means the permanent and continuous use of the patented process or the manufacture of the patented product, in Colombia, so as to meet the market demands on reasonable conditions.

Compulsory licences will be non-exclusive, and will not imply the right to import, nor to assign the licence, nor to grant sub-licences.

The court will determine the duration of the licence, its conditions, its field of application, and the royalties to be paid to the owner of the patent.

3. Licences of Authority

At any time the Ministry of Public Health, or other appropriate Ministry, may apply to the court for an order subjecting a patent to licensing on any of the following grounds:

(*a*) The patent is of interest for public health;

(*b*) The patent is of importance in the economic development of the country;

(*c*) The patented product has not been made available to the public in sufficient quality and quantity for normal consumption, or the price is excessive;

(*d*) The patent hinders working of another patent.

Once an order has been made, any person who can show ability to work the invention, or any public entity, may apply to the Patent Office for grant of a licence.

This form of licence, which is referred to as a Licence of Authority, is non-exclusive and the licensee cannot assign it nor grant sub-licences.

The licence will contain provisions as to the conditions under which it is granted, and the duration and field of application, but will not include royalty terms. These will be determined by agreement between the parties, with the approval of the Patent Office. In the absence of agreement the terms will be settled by the court.

4. General

The conditions of a Compulsory licence or a Licence of Authority may be varied by the court on the request of the owner of the patent or the licensee, if circumstances justify such variation. One such circumstance would arise if the owner of the patent grants a licence on conditions more favourable than those contained in an existing Compulsory licence or a Licence of Authority.

A Compulsory licence or a Licence of Authority may be terminated if the licensee fails to meet the conditions of the licence.

The owner of a patent and any licensee thereunder may jointly or separately institute legal actions for the defence of their rights.

Licences must be recorded.

Expropriation

Patents relating to public health or national defence are to be considered of social interest or public utility, and may be expropriated when considered necessary by the appropriate Ministry.

Infringement

The owner of a patent or a licensee may apply to the court and may obtain relief in the form of a " precautionary measure " which may require an infringer to procure a bond guaranteeing discontinuance of the infringing acts, and which may result also in seizure of infringing goods and an embargo on any machinery used in their manufacture as well as an embargo on advertising.

A suit for damages may be instituted independently of the action for a precautionary measure.

Rhodesia

The Patents Act No. 26 of 1971, which consolidates and amends Rhodesian patent law, came into force on February 1, 1972. The earlier legislation is repealed, with the savings that patents and licences granted, or directions made prior to that date and then in force, have force and effect in terms of the new Act; similarly any matters pending before the Patent Office, Patent Tribunal or court may continue in terms of the new Act. Specifically, the earlier provisions for prolongation of the terms of patents will continue in respect of patents granted under the former Southern Rhodesian legislation.

The principal changes introduced by the Act involve the term of patents and prolongation thereof, restoration of lapsed patents, disputes concerning inventions, novelty, infringement and revocation, registration of assignments and licences, and Convention applications. The earlier Acts were based substantially on the British Patents Act 1949, and it is of interest that most of those changes are in accord with recommendations made in the Report of the Bank's Committee set up to examine the patent system and patent law of the United Kingdom.

Term of Patents

The term of patents granted under the amended Act or under the former Patents Act 1957 is now 20 years from the date of lodging the complete specification. For patents granted under the former Southern Rhodesian legislation of 1939, or under the

Transitional Provisions of 1958, the term is 14 years from the date of application. This means that patents based on applications filed on or after April 1, 1958, have a 20-year term, and that those based on applications filed prior to April 1, 1959, have a 14-year term.

Prolongation of Term

The provisions for prolongation of the term of a patent on the ground of inadequate remuneration or war loss have been repealed, so that the 20-year term will be a maximum one. However, the provisions continue to apply to any patents granted under the former Southern Rhodesian legislation, that is patents applied for prior to April 1, 1958.

Restoration of Lapsed Patents

Where a patent has lapsed by reason of failure to pay any renewal fee, restoration may be sought within a maximum period of three years from the date on which the patent lapsed. The applicant for restoration must show that the failure to pay the fee was not intentional and that there has been no undue delay in making the application. Where the patent was held by two or more persons jointly the application may, with leave of the Registrar, be made by one or more of those persons without joining the others.

Disputes as to Inventions

In addition to his power to settle disputes between an employer and an employee, the Registrar is now empowered also to determine disputes as to the rights in inventions between any persons in respect of an invention made by those persons jointly. In such cases the Registrar may apportion the invention and any patent between the parties or two or more of the parties in such manner as he considers just.

The former provisions for the settlement by the Registrar of a dispute between an employer and an employee as to the rights in an invention have been amended by removal of the power of apportionment.

Novelty

The provisions concerning novelty have been widened to include publication anywhere in writing or in any other way, at the effective date of the application, as being destructive of novelty.

Thus an invention is not new if, on or before the effective date of the application the invention was:

(1) known or used in Rhodesia by anyone other than the applicant or his agent or the person from or through whom the applicant has derived his right or title. Secret knowledge or secret user otherwise than on a commercial scale is to be disregarded;

(2) worked in Rhodesia, otherwise than by way of reasonable technical trial or experiment by the applicant or the person from or through whom the applicant derived his right or title;

(3) described in a patent specification available to public inspection under any repealed legislation or under the present Act;

(4) described in writing or in any other way in any publication of which a copy was available in or outside Rhodesia;

(5) claimed in an unpublished Rhodesian complete specification of earlier effective date.

Infringement/Revocation

The amended Act provides for the consolidation of an infringement action and an application for revocation, which formerly took in different courts, and that no action for infringement of a patent may now be instituted more than three years after the date on which the patent expired or lapsed.

The earlier Act contained provision for the protection of "innocent infringers"; that is to say, damages would not be awarded against a defendant who proved that at the date of the infringement he was not aware, and had no reasonable ground for making himself aware that the patent existed; and the application to an article of any patent marking unaccompanied by the number and year of the patent did not constitute such grounds. However, in awarding damages, the court is now empowered to take into account any dilatory conduct on the part of the patentee or plaintiff in making the infringer aware of the patent.

Assignments/Licences

Where there has been a change of ownership of a patent, or an exclusive licence has been granted, no damages will be recoverable by the new owner or the Licensee in respect of infringement during the period from the date of the change of ownership or grant of exclusive licence up to registration of the change or licence, unless such registration was effected within six months of the change of ownership or grant of licence.

International Convention

Hitherto, an applicant claiming Convention priority was required to be one who qualified under Article 2 or Article 3 of the Convention, that is he had to be a national of a Convention country, or one who had a domicile or a real and effective industrial establishment in a Convention country. This restriction has been removed so that a Convention application may now be made by anyone who has made application in a Convention country, or by the legal representative or assignee of such a person, not more than 12 months prior to the date of filing in Rhodesia.

Brazil

The Brazilian Law No. 5772 of December 21, 1971, which came into force on December 31, 1971, represents a complete revision of the patent law, including introduction of a system of deferred examination and reintroduction of Utility Models. A provision of great importance to foreign applicants is that filing of a patent application *without claiming Convention priority* will preclude payment of royalties under any licence. The provisions of the law apply to all pending applications. Patents and Utility Models granted previously remain in force for the periods established by the earlier legislation under which they were granted, but they are subject to the new system of renewal fees.

Form and Scope of Protection

There are now two forms of protection, namely:

(*a*) Patents of Invention, granted for a period of 15 years from the date of filing, and

(*b*) Utility Models granted for a period of 10 years from the date of filing.

Both forms are subject to payment of annual renewal fees from the beginning of the third year from filing. The fees must be paid within the first 180 days of the yearly period. Restoration is possible if sought within a period of 30 days from expiry of the grace period.

Pending applications of whatever filing date are subject to payment of renewal fees, the first fee payable being that corresponding to the first complete year of life of the application after December 31, 1971, and reckoned from the filing date. They are also subject to the deferred examination system, so that requests for examination must be made within two years from December 31, 1971, or from their filing date, whichever is the later. The only exceptions to this are applications previously granted or rejected but now under appeal.

Patents granted, since promulgation of the new law, on applications then pending will have a term of 15 years from their filing date and will be subject to the new system of renewal fees. For Utility Models in this category, the term will be 10 years subject to payment of renewal fees.

Utility Models are defined as any new arrangement or form introduced or obtained in known objects, provided they serve a practical work or use.

Objects comprise tools, instruments of work or implements. Protection is granted in respect only of new arrangements or forms which result in improved utilisation of the function to be performed by the object. Protection will not be granted to anything patentable as an invention nor to works of sculpture, architecture, painting, engraving, enamelling, embroidery, photographs or any other models or designs of a purely artistic character.

Patentability and Novelty

Inventions or utility models are patentable if they are new and capable of industrial application.

An invention is considered as new when it is not comprised in the state of the art which is defined as embracing everything that has been made available or disclosed to the public, either by written or oral description, by use or by any other means, including disclosure in patents, anywhere prior to the filing date in Brazil.

An invention is considered capable of industrial application if it can be manufactured or used in industry.

Novelty is not destroyed by communication of an invention to a learned society, or by publication or display at an official or officially recognised exhibition or fair, provided the patent application is filed within one year. Application should be made to the Patent Office for a guarantee of priority by lodging a detailed description, with drawings, of the invention. The Office will issue a certificate of filing and the grace period runs from the date of the certificate. For utility models the grace period is six months. If the application for patent or utility model is not filed within the grace period, the guarantee of priority will be automatically cancelled and the invention or model will pass to the public domain.

The following are not patentable:

(*a*) inventions whose purposes are contrary to law, morality, health, public safety, religious worship and to sentiments worthy of respect and veneration;

(*b*) substances, materials, or products obtained by chemical processes or means. (New processes of production or modification of such are patentable.)

(*c*) substances, materials, admixtures, food products, chemical pharmaceutical products and medicines of any kind, as well as processes of production or modification of such.

(*d*) metallic admixtures and alloys in general (but there are patentable those having specific intrinsic qualities, which are precisely characterised by their qualitative composition, quantitatively defined, or by a special treatment to which they have been subjected, provided they do not come within the prohibited period in sub-paragraph (*c*) above).

(*e*) the juxtaposition of known procedures, means or elements, the simple change of form, proportions, dimensions or of materials unless there results a new or different effect which is not otherwise unpatentable.

(*f*) the use or utilisation of discoveries, including the use of varieties or species of micro-organisms, for specified purposes.

(*g*) surgical or therapeutic techniques (but devices, apparatus or machinery used therewith may be patented).

(*h*) systems and programming, plans or schemes of commercial book-keeping, calculating of credit and financing, lotteries, speculation or advertising.

(*i*) purely theoretical concepts.

(*j*) substances, materials, admixtures, elements or products of any kind, as well as the modification of their physical-chemical properties and of the respective processes of their production or modification, when resulting from the transformation of atomic nucleus.

Right to Patent

The author of an invention or a utility model is entitled to obtain a patent which guarantees him ownership and the exclusive use thereof. The patent may be applied for by the author or his heirs or successors, by authorised legal entities or by assignees of the rights. If the applicant is not the author proof of title must be filed. The first applicant is presumed to be the author of the invention. Where there is a joint authorship, the patent may be applied for by all or any of the co-authors, their respective rights being reserved by recital of data concerning all the inventors.

The authorisation or declaration from the inventor authorising filing of the application must be submitted with the application. It does not require legalisation. Although the Patent Office might accept the document if filed within 60 days, there is no certainty as to acceptance because the law explicitly calls for submission with other application papers.

Inventions made by an employee during the period of validity of a service contract agreement, and improvements thereof, belong to the employer when the service requires the exercise of inventive activity or when such activity derives from the essential nature of the work performed. If the service contract does not provide otherwise, compensation is limited to the agreed salary. In the absence of an agreement to the contrary, inventions and improvements will be treated as having been made during the employment period if the employee files a patent application within one year after cessation of the service contract.

Patent protection for any invention resulting from a service contract must be applied for in Brazil, and the name of the inventor must be mentioned in the application and patent.

Inventions made outside the scope of the service contract or without utilising the resources of the employer, belong exclusively to the employee.

In the absence of an agreement to the contrary, inventions made outside the scope of a service contract by the personal contribution of an employee but utilising the resources of his employer will be owned jointly, the employer having the exclusive right of working and the employee the right to compensation. If the employer does not commence working of the invention within one year after the date of issue of the patent, the rights will revert entirely to the employee.

Specification and Claims

The law calls for a description and claims, drawings if any, and an abstract. The claims, based on the description, must refer to the characteristic features of the invention, establishing and limiting the rights of the inventor.

Priority

Brazil is a member of the International Convention, having ratified the text of The Hague, also of the Buenos Aires Pan-American Convention of 1910.

Applications claiming priority must be filed within 12 months from the filing date of the earliest application filed in a convention country. The claim must be supported by filing a certified copy of the basic application containing its number, date, title, description and claims. A maximum period of 180 days from the date of filing in Brazil is allowed for submission of the certified copy together with a sworn translation thereof.

If the applicant requests examination, he will be requested by the Patent Office to file the priority documents within a term of 90 days, but this term cannot extend beyond the 180 days period. It is important to note that the grant of a patent licence by anyone domiciled or established outside Brazil will not be effective so far as royalties are concerned if the patent application did not claim convention priority.

Examination and Publication

When an application is lodged it will be subjected only to a preliminary formal examination and accepted for filing if the application documents are in order. The application will not be published until 18 months after the earliest priority date, unless the applicant requests earlier publication.

A system of deferred examination has been adopted. The applicant must request examination within two years from the date of publication. The request may be made by a third party. In the case of applications pending on December 31, 1971, the two-year period runs from that date. If examination is not sought within the stipulated period, the application will be regarded as withdrawn.

On publication, the application will be open to opposition for a period of 90 days. If the applicant wishes to reply to an opposition, he may do so within 60 days of his being notified of the opposition.

The examination will be directed to ensuring that the legal requirements have been met, that the application is technically properly defined, and to suitability for patenting, novelty and capability of industrial use. Objections will be notified to the applicant who will be given a period of 90 days to reply.

If an official action is neither complied with nor contested, the application will be treated as abandoned. If the applicant's reply is not acceptable to the Office, the application will be shelved.

Appeals against decisions to grant, reject or shelve applications may be lodged within 60 days from the date of the decision.

If an application carries a claim to priority, the applicant may be called on to report any objections, the results of novelty searches or examinations, made in connection with any corresponding applications in other countries.

Amendment

An applicant is entitled voluntarily to amend his specification, claims, drawings and abstract only in the following instances:

(1) to correct typographical errors;

(2) to clarify, specify or restrict the application, if this is essential, but only up to the date of request for examination;

(3) in response to official actions.

Infringement

When the patent has issued, the patentee may take action for infringement committed during pendency of his application.

Assignments and Licences

Assignments or other transfers of ownership and licences, must be recorded before they become effective against third parties.

Licences covering patents or patent applications must recite the conditions of payment and for working the invention, as well as referring specifically to the patent or application being licensed.

A licence must not contain any restrictions as to the marketing or export of products manufactured under the licence, nor to the importation of materials necessary for their manufacture.

Any improvements made in a licensed process or product shall belong to the licensee.

Payments to be made must comply with regulations of the monetary and exchange authorities, but recordal of a licence will not be effective so far as concerns payment of royalties if the licence concerns:

(*a*) a patent not granted in Brazil;
(*b*) a patent granted to a person domiciled or established abroad who did not claim convention priority;
(*c*) an expired patent or one under invalidation or cancellation proceedings;
(*d*) a patent whose previous owner had no right to receive royalty payments.

Working and Compulsory Licences

Actual working is defined as the proved, continuous and regular use of an invention on an industrial scale by manufacture by the patentee or some duly authorised third party. Importation does not rank as working. Under certain circumstances a patentee may be called on to prove working either by himself or by a duly authorised third party.

Compulsory licences may be granted in the following cases:

(1) If at the expiry of three years after the date of grant, the patentee has not actually worked the patent, or has interrupted working for more than one year, unless he can prove *force majeure*.
(2) If it is in the public interest, when there is lack of actual working or when the working does not meet market demands.

A request for a compulsory licence must be accompanied by evidence of the conditions offered to the patentee. The patentee will be notified of the request and will be allowed a term of 60 days to reply and will be required to file evidence of actual working. If the patentee does not file a reply, the request will be allowed. If the patentee replies, the necessary investigation will proceed, and a report will be issued within 60 days. When a licence is granted, it will contain the royalty terms. The licensee must commence actual working of the invention within one year from the date of the licence and must not discontinue working for longer than one year. He will be given power to take administrative or legal action in defence of the patent. The patentee will be entitled to control manufacture, volume of sales and proper use of the invention. The licence may be cancelled if there is a breach of conditions by the licensee.

Patents are subject to forfeiture, *ex officio*, or at the instance of a third party, unless *force majeure* is proved, when:

(*a*) working in Brazil has not started within four years (or five if a licence has been granted) from the date of grant;

(*b*) working has been discontinued for more than two consecutive years.

Any proposal as to forfeiture will be communicated to the patentee who must, within 60 days, prove that the grounds of forfeiture have not been met or that *force majeure* applies. A decision on forfeiture will be rendered after expiry of the 60-day period; appeal lies within 60 days of the decision.

Secrecy and Expropriation

When the subject-matter of a patent application is deemed to be of interest to National Security, it will be kept secret but will be submitted to the National Security Council who may delegate technical examination to the Armed Forces Ministries. If it is decided that the application is not of interest to National Security, secrecy will be removed. A patent may be granted on a secret application but the patent likewise will be kept secret although copies will be sent to the National Security Council and to the General Staff of the Armed Forces.

An invention may, by decision of the National Security Council, be expropriated if it is considered to be of interest to national defence, or that it should be put into the public domain, or when the national interest demands its exclusive working by a Government entity or one in which the Government participates.

Powers of Attorney

The law requires that powers granted by foreign applicants must be valid for the whole life of the application and any patent granted thereon. Further, they must include power to the attorney to receive service of summons in matters relating to industrial property.

For new applications, the power must be filed with the application, or if *force majeure* can be proved, within 60 days from the filing date.

The power requires neither notarial attestation nor consular legalisation.

No term has been fixed for the filing of powers in pending applications. For granted patents, a term expiring on June 28, 1972, has been fixed, and if the power is not filed by that date the patent will be cancelled.

Bangladesh

On April 10, 1972, the Bangladesh Government issued the "Laws Continuation and Enforcement Order" whereby all laws in force in the former territory of East Pakistan on March 25, 1971, remain in force subject to such consequential changes as may be necessary on account of the creation of the new State of Bangladesh. Thus, patents granted in Pakistan prior to March 25, 1971, will be regarded as continuing to be operative in Bangladesh, subject of course to payment of renewal fees.

Although it seems likely that eventually the holders of patent rights in Bangladesh will be required formally to record them, such action is not presently required.

The present position may be summarised as follows:

(1) Patents already granted in Pakistan should be renewed separately in both countries, if it is desired to keep them in force. In the case of Bangladesh, it may for the present be possible only to tender fees so as to ensure proof of the taking of timely action to renew. Further, it would seem advisable when renewing in Bangladesh to tender the fees for two years, in view of the declaration of Independence as from March 25, 1971.

(2) Any new patent applications will require to be filed in both Bangladesh and West Pakistan if protection for the whole of the former Pakistan is required.

(3) With regard to patent applications pending in Pakistan on March 25, 1971, or filed in Pakistan since that date, it would be advisable to file new applications in Bangladesh if protection is desired there.

APPENDICES

APPENDIX 1

Chemical and Pharmaceutical Inventions

ALLOWABLE CLAIMS

While it is believed that the position as regards allowable patent claims in the field of chemical and pharmaceutical inventions is as stated below, practice is very uncertain in some countries, even varying from Examiner to Examiner. It also varies with time. There is a trend to increase protection in industrial countries and to decrease it in the developing countries. A positive indication has been given where possible in the belief that this will be more helpful to practitioners with difficult or borderline cases.

		Process Claims		*Product Claims*		*Composition Claims*		*Use Claims*
Country		Processes for making chemical compounds	Whether more than one process can be covered in one patent	Chemical compounds which are pharmaceuticals	Chemical compounds if non-pharmaceutical (*e.g.* intermediates, or compounds directed to other purposes)	Pharmaceutical compositions [1]	Methods of making pharmaceutical compositions [1]	Methods for therapeutically treating humans with pharmaceuticals
Aden	R	Yes	Yes	Yes	Yes	Yes	Yes	No
Afghanistan		No Patent Law						
African and Malagasy Union		Yes	Yes	No	Yes	No	Yes	No
Algeria		Yes	Yes	Yes	Yes	Yes	Yes	No
Andorra		No Patent Law						
Antigua		Yes	Yes	Yes	Yes	Yes	Yes	No
Argentina		Yes	No [3]	No	Yes	No	No	No
Ascencion		No Patent Law						
Australia		Yes	Yes	Yes	Yes	Yes	Yes	No
Austria		Yes	No	No	No	No	No	No
Bahamas		Yes	Yes	Yes	Yes	Yes	Yes	No
Bahrein	R	Yes	Yes	Yes	Yes	Yes	Yes	No
Bangladesh		Yes	Yes	No	No	Yes	Yes	No
Barbados		Yes	Yes	Yes	Yes	Yes	Yes	No
Belgium		Yes	Yes	Yes	Yes	Yes	Yes	Yes
Bermuda		Yes	Yes	Yes	Yes	Yes	Yes	No
Bolivia		Yes [11]	No ?	No	No	No	Yes [11]	No
Botswana		Covered by British Patent						

British Honduras		Yes	Yes	Yes	Yes	Yes	Yes	No
British Solomon Islands	R	Yes	Yes	Yes	Yes	Yes	Yes	No
British Virgin Islands		Yes	Yes	Yes	Yes	Yes	Yes	No
Brunei	R	Yes	Yes	Yes	Yes	Yes	Yes	No
Burundi		Yes	Yes	Yes	Yes	Yes	Yes	Yes
Bulgaria		Yes	No	No	No	No [4]	Yes [10] ?	No ?
Burma		Covered by Indian Patent						
Cambodia		Yes	Yes	No	Yes	No	Yes ?	No
Cameroon		See African and Malagasy Union						
Canada		Yes	Yes	No	Yes	Yes [5]	Yes [5] ?	No
Central African Republic		See African and Malagasy Union						
Chad		See African and Malagasy Union						
Chile		Yes	Yes	No	Yes	No	No	No
China (People's Republic) [6]		Yes	Yes ?	No	No	No	No	No
Colombia		Yes [13]	Yes	No	Yes	No	Yes [13]	No
Congo		See African and Malagasy Union						
Costa Rica		Yes	Yes	Yes	Yes	Yes	Yes	Yes
Cuba		Yes	Yes	Yes	Yes	Yes	Yes	Yes
Cyprus	R	Yes	Yes	Yes	Yes	Yes	Yes	No
Czechoslovakia		Yes	No	No	No	No [4] ?	Yes [7] ? [10] ?	No
Dahomey		See African and Malagasy Union						
Denmark		Yes	Yes [12]	No	Yes [9]	No	Yes [7] ?	No
Dominica		Yes	Yes	Yes	Yes	Yes	Yes	No
Dominican Republic		Yes	Yes	Yes [14]	Yes [14] ?	Yes [14]	Yes [14]	Yes
Ecuador		Yes	Yes	No	Yes	No	No	No
Ethiopia		No Patent Law						
Falkland Islands	R	Yes	Yes	Yes	Yes	Yes	Yes	No
Fiji		Yes	Yes	Yes	Yes	Yes	Yes	No
Finland		Yes	Yes	No	Yes [9]	No	Yes [7] ?	No
France		Yes	Yes	Yes	Yes [15]	Yes [15]	Yes	No
Gabon		See African and Malagasy Union						
Gambia	R	Yes	Yes	Yes	Yes	Yes	Yes	No

Country		Process Claims: Processes for making chemical compounds	Process Claims: Whether more than one process can be covered in one patent	Product Claims: Chemical compounds which are pharmaceuticals	Product Claims: Chemical compounds if non-pharmaceutical (*e.g.* intermediates, or compounds directed to other purposes)	Composition Claims: Pharmaceutical compositions [1]	Composition Claims: Methods of making pharmaceutical compositions [1]	Use Claims: Methods for therapeutically treating humans with pharmaceuticals
E. Germany		Yes	Yes	No	No	No	No	No
W. Germany		Yes	Yes	Yes	Yes	Yes [15] ?	No	No
Ghana	R	Yes	Yes	No	Yes	No ?	No	No
Gibraltar	R	Yes	Yes	Yes	Yes	Yes	Yes	No
Gilbert & Ellice Islands	R	Yes	Yes	Yes	Yes	Yes	Yes	No
Greece		Yes	Yes	No	Yes	No	Yes	No
Grenada		Yes	Yes	Yes	Yes	Yes	Yes	No
Guatemala		Yes	Yes	Yes	Yes	Yes	Yes	No
Guernsey	R	Yes	Yes	Yes	Yes	Yes	Yes	No
Guinea [16]		Yes	Yes	No	Yes	No	Yes ?	No
Guyana		Yes	Yes	Yes	Yes	Yes	Yes	No
Haiti		Yes	Yes	Yes	Yes	Yes	Yes	Yes
Honduras		Yes	Yes	Yes	Yes	Yes	Yes	Yes
Hong Kong	R	Yes	Yes	Yes	Yes	Yes	Yes	No
Hungary		Yes	Yes	No	No	No	Yes [7]	No
Iceland		Yes	Yes	No	Yes	No	Yes	No
India		Yes [17]	No	No	No	No	No	Yes [19] ?
Indonesia		No Patent Law						
Iran		Yes	Yes	No	Yes	No	Yes ?	No
Iraq		Yes	Yes	No	Yes	No	Yes ?	No
Ireland		Yes	Yes	Yes	Yes	Yes	Yes	No
Israel		Yes	Yes	Yes	Yes	Yes	Yes	No
Italy		Yes [2]	Yes	No	Yes	No	No	No
Ivory Coast		See African and Malagasy Union						
Jamaica		Yes	Yes	Yes	Yes	Yes	Yes	No
Japan		Yes	Yes [18]	No	No	No	No	No
Jersey	R	Yes	Yes	Yes	Yes	Yes	Yes	No
Jordan		Yes	Yes	Yes	Yes	Yes	Yes	No
Kenya	R	Yes	Yes	Yes	Yes	Yes	Yes	No
Kuwait		Yes	Yes ?	No	Yes	No	Yes [10]	No
Laos		Yes	Yes	No	Yes	No	Yes ?	No
Lebanon		Yes	Yes	No	Yes	No	Yes ?	No

		Covered by British Patent						
Libya		Yes	Yes ?	No	Yes	No	Yes [10]	Yes
Liberia		Yes	Yes	Yes	Yes	Yes	Yes	Yes
Liechtenstein		Covered by Swiss Patent						
Luxembourg		Yes	Yes ?	No	No	No	Yes ?	No
Malagasy		See African and Malagasy Union				No		
Malawi		Yes	Yes	Yes	Yes	Yes	Yes	No
Malaya	R	Yes	Yes	Yes	Yes	Yes	Yes	No
Maldive Islands		No Patent Law						
Mali [16]		Yes	Yes	No	Yes	No	Yes ?	No
Malta		Yes	Yes	Yes	Yes	Yes	Yes	No
Mauritania		See African and Malagasy Union						
Mauritius		Yes	Yes	Yes	Yes	Yes	Yes	No
Mexico		Yes	No	No	No	No	Yes [8]	No
Monaco		Yes	Yes	No	Yes	No	Yes ?	No
Montserrat		Yes	Yes	Yes	Yes	Yes	Yes	No
Morocco		Yes	Yes	No	Yes	No	Yes ?	No
Muscat and Oman		No Patent Law				No		
Nauru	RA	Yes	Yes	Yes	Yes	Yes	Yes	No
Netherlands		Yes	Yes	No	No	No	Yes	No
Netherlands Antilles		Covered by Dutch Patent						
New Guinea		Covered by Australian Patent						
New Zealand		Yes	Yes	Yes	Yes	Yes	Yes	No
Nicaragua		Yes	Yes	Yes	Yes	Yes	Yes	No
Niger		See African and Malagasy Union						
Nigeria		Yes	Yes	Yes	Yes	Yes	Yes	No
Norfolk Island		Covered by Australian Patent						
Norway		Yes	Yes [12]	No	Yes [9]	No	Yes [7]	No
Pakistan		Yes	Yes	No	No	Yes	Yes	No
Panama		Yes	Yes	Yes	Yes	Yes	Yes	Yes
Papua		Covered by Australian Patent						
Paraguay		Yes	Yes	No	Yes	No	Yes ?	No
Peru		Yes	Yes	No	Yes	No	No ?	No
Philippines		Yes	Yes	Yes	Yes	Yes	Yes	Yes
Poland		Yes	Yes [12]	No	No	No [4] ?	No	No [4] ?
Portugal		Yes	Yes	No	No	No	Yes	Yes ?
Qatar		No Patent Law						
Rhodesia		Yes	Yes	Yes	Yes	Yes	Yes	No
Rwanda		Yes	Yes	Yes	Yes	Yes	Yes	Yes

Country		Process Claims		Product Claims		Composition Claims		Use Claims
		Processes for making chemical compounds	Whether more than one process can be covered in one patent	Chemical compounds which are pharmaceuticals	Chemical compounds if non-pharmaceutical (*e.g.* intermediates, or compounds directed to other purposes)	Pharmaceutical compositions [1]	Methods of making pharmaceutical compositions [1]	Methods for therapeutically treating humans with pharmaceuticals
Roumania		Yes	Yes	Yes [20] ?	Yes [20] ?	Yes [20] ?	Yes [20] ?	No
St. Christopher		Yes	Yes	Yes	Yes	Yes	Yes	No
St. Helena	R	Yes	Yes	Yes	Yes	Yes	Yes	No
St. Lucia		Yes	Yes	Yes	Yes	Yes	Yes	No
St. Vincent		Yes	Yes	Yes	Yes	Yes	Yes	No
Sabah	R	Yes	Yes	Yes	Yes	Yes	Yes	No
Salvador		Yes	Yes	Yes	Yes	Yes	Yes	Yes
San Marino		Covered by Italian Patent						
Sarawak	R	Yes	Yes	Yes	Yes	Yes	Yes	No
Saudi Arabia		No Patent Law						
Senegal		See African and Malagasy Union						
Seychelles		Yes	Yes	Yes	Yes	Yes	Yes	No
Sierra Leone	R	Yes	Yes	Yes	Yes	Yes	Yes	No
Singapore	R	Yes	Yes	Yes	Yes	Yes	Yes	No
Somali Republic [21]		Yes	Yes	Yes	Yes	Yes	Yes	No
South Africa		Yes	Yes	Yes	Yes	Yes	Yes	Yes
South Korea		Yes	Yes	No	Yes	No	No	No
South West Africa		Yes	Yes	Yes	Yes	Yes	Yes	Yes
Spain		Yes	Yes [22]	No	No	No	Yes	No
Sri Lanka		Yes	Yes	Yes	Yes	Yes	Yes	No
Sudan		No Patent Law						
Surinam		Covered by Dutch Patent						
Swaziland		Covered by British Patent						
Sweden		Yes	Yes [12]	No	Yes [9]	No	No	No
Switzerland		Yes	No	No	No	No	No	No
Syria		Yes	Yes	No	Yes	No	Yes ?	No
Taiwan		Yes	Yes	No	No	No	Yes ?	No
Tanzania	R	Yes	Yes	Yes	Yes	Yes	Yes	No
Thailand		No Patent Law						
Togo		See African and Malagasy Union						
Tongan Islands		No Patent Law						
Trinidal & Tobago		Yes	Yes	Yes	Yes	Yes	Yes	No

Trucial States		No Patent Law						
Tunisia		Yes	Yes	No	Yes	No	Yes ?	No
Turkey		Yes [2]	Yes	No	Yes	No	No	No
Uganda	R	Yes	Yes	Yes	Yes	Yes	Yes	No
U.A.R.		Yes	Yes	No	Yes	No	Yes	No
U.K.		Yes	Yes	Yes	Yes	Yes	Yes	No
U.S.A.		Yes	Yes ?	Yes	Yes	Yes	Yes	Yes
U.S.S.R.		Yes	No	No	No	No [4]	Yes [12] ? [4]	No [4]
Upper Volta		See African and Malagasy Union						
Uruguay		Yes	Yes	No	No	No	Yes ?	No
Vatican City		Covered by Italian Patent						
Venezuela		Yes	Yes	No	No	No	Yes	No
Vietnam		Yes	Yes ?	No	Yes	No	Yes ?	No
Yemen-Arab Republic		No Patent Law						
Yemen-People's Democratic Republic		No Patent Law Except Aden						
Yugoslavia		Yes	Yes	No	No	Yes [23] ?	Yes [23] ?	No
Zaïre		Yes	Yes	Yes	Yes	Yes	Yes	Yes
Zambia		Yes	Yes	Yes	Yes	Yes	Yes	No

1 These compounds do not include compositions which are mixtures of known ingredients possessing only the aggregate of the known properties of the ingredients.
2 Not allowable if products are pharmaceutical.
3 Practice varies; in some cases more than one compound can be covered.
4 But Author's Certificate available.
5 Only if active ingredient is known.
6 Strictly there is no Patent Law, but inventions are protected for practical purposes similarly to Author's Certificates.
7 If synergistic effect is shown.
8 If a special effect is shown by the active ingredient.
9 Claims to chemical compounds are limited by stated use.
10 Special methods only.
11 If the products incorporate a new invention or application.
12 In some circumstances.
13 For pharmaceutical inventions the applicant has to show that he is exploiting the process in Colombia, and that he is in a position to supply the market under reasonable conditions of quantity, quality and price.
14 Approval by Medical Board of Republic needed.
15 Patentable even if compound known, when presented for first medical use. In Germany the President of the German Patent Office's Rules indicate this may be so.
16 Situation uncertain.
17 Pharmaceutical inventions include agrochemical ones and all necessary intermediates, and patents have very short life.
18 Multiple processes are now allowed under recent change of practice.
19 As India uses American definition of invention, such claims are not apparently excluded under the new Act.
20 Patents are granted only to Roumanian State enterprises.
21 Registration of British patent in case of former British Somaliland; separate patent application necessary in case of former Somalia.
22 But validity is then questionable.
23 According to the Supreme Court such patents should be allowed but in practice the Patent Office refuses them.
R Registration of British Patent.
RA Registration of Australian Patent.

APPENDIX 2

1. *International* (*Paris*) *Convention* for the Protection of Industrial Property (Lisbon Act, October 31, 1958)

2. *Buenos Aires Convention* on Inventions, Patents, Designs and Industrial Models (August 20, 1910)

3. *Montevideo Convention* on Patents of Invention (January 16, 1889)

4. *Caracas Convention* on Patents and Privileges of Invention (July 18, 1911)

5. *European Convention* relating to the formalities required for patent applications (December 11, 1953)

6. *European Convention* on the International Classification of Patents for Invention (December 19, 1954)

7. *European Convention* on the Unification of Certain Points of Substantive Law on Patents for Invention (November 27, 1963)

8. *Agreement* concerning the Establishment of an International Patents Bureau (June 6, 1947)

9. *Agreement* revising the 1947 Agreement concerning the Establishment of an International Patents Bureau (February 16–December 31, 1961)

INTERNATIONAL (PARIS) CONVENTION FOR THE PROTECTION OF INDUSTRIAL PROPERTY

Lisbon, October 31, 1958

Article 1

(1) The countries to which the present Convention applies constitute themselves into a Union for the protection of industrial property.

(2) The protection of industrial property is concerned with patents, utility models, industrial designs, trademarks, service marks, trade names, and indications of source or appellations of origin, and the repression of unfair competition.

(3) Industrial property shall be understood in the broadest sense and shall apply not only to industry and commerce proper, but likewise to agricultural and extractive industries and to all manufactured or natural products; for example, wines, grain, tobacco leaf, fruit, cattle, minerals, mineral waters, beer, flowers, and flour.

(4) The term " patents " shall include the various kinds of industrial patents recognised by the laws of the countries of the Union, such as patents of importation, patents of improvement, patents and certificates of addition, etc.

Article 2

(1) Nationals of each of the countries of the Union shall, as regards the protection of industrial property, enjoy in all the other countries of the Union the advantages that their respective laws now grant, or may hereafter grant, to nationals, without prejudice to the rights specially provided by the present Convention. Consequently, they shall have the same protection as the latter, and the same legal remedy against any infringement of their rights, provided they observe the conditions and formalities imposed upon nationals.

(2) However, no condition as to the possession of a domicile or establishment in the country where protection is claimed may be required of persons entitled to the benefits of the Union for the enjoyment of any industrial property rights.

(3) The provisions of the laws of each of the countries of the Union relating to judicial and administrative procedure and to jurisdiction, and to the election of domicile or the designation of an agent, which may be required by the laws on industrial property, are expressly reserved.

Article 3

Nationals of countries not forming part of the Union, who are domiciled or have real and effective industrial or commercial establishments in the territory of one of the countries of the Union, are treated in the same manner as nationals of the countries of the Union.

Article 4

A.—(1) A person who has duly filed an application for a patent, or for the registration of a utility model, or of an industrial design, or of a trademark, in one of the countries of the Union, or his successors in title, shall enjoy, for the purpose of filing in the other countries, a right of priority during the periods hereinafter stated.

(2) Every filing that is equivalent to a regular national filing under the domestic law of any country of the Union or under bilateral or multilateral treaties concluded between countries of the Union shall be recognised as giving rise to a right of priority.

(3) By a regular national filing is meant any filing that is adequate to establish the date on which the application was filed in the country concerned, whatever may be the outcome of the application.

B.—Consequently, the subsequent filing in any of the other countries of the Union before the expiration of those periods shall not be invalidated through any acts accomplished in the interval, as, for instance, by another filing, by publication or exploitation of the invention, by the putting on sale of copies of the design or model, or by use of the mark, and these acts cannot give rise to any right of third parties, or of any personal possession. Rights acquired by third parties before the date of the first application which serves as the basis for the right of priority are reserved under the domestic legislation of each country of the Union.

C.—(1) The above-mentioned periods of priority shall be twelve months for patents and utility models, and six months for industrial designs and for trademarks.

(2) These periods shall start from the date of filing of the first application; the day of filing shall not be included in the period.

(3) If the last day of the period is an official holiday, or a day when the Office is not open for the filing of applications in the country where protection is claimed, the period shall be extended until the first following working day.

(4) A subsequent application for the same subject as a previous first application within the meaning of paragraph (2) above and filed in the same country of the Union, shall be con-

sidered as the first application, of which the filing date shall be the starting point of the period of priority, provided that, at the time of filing the subsequent application, the previous application has been withdrawn, abandoned or refused, without being open to public inspection and without leaving any rights outstanding, and has not served as a basis for claiming a right of priority. The previous application may not thereafter serve as a basis for claiming a right of priority.

D.—(1) Any person desiring to take advantage of the priority of a previous filing shall be required to make a declaration indicating the date of such filing and the country in which it was made. Each country will determine the latest permissible date for making such declaration.

(2) These particulars shall be mentioned in the publications issued by the competent authority, and in particular in the patents and the specifications relating thereto.

(3) The countries of the Union may require any person making a declaration of priority to produce a copy of the application (specification, drawings, etc.) previously filed. The copy, certified as correct by the authority which received the application, shall not require any authentication, and may in any case be filed, without fee, at any time within three months of the filing of the subsequent application. They may require it to be accompanied by a certificate from the same authority showing the date of filing, and by a translation.

(4) No other formalities may be required for the declaration of priority at the time of filing the application. Each of the countries of the Union shall decide what consequences shall follow the omission of the formalities prescribed by the present Article, but such consequences shall in no case go beyond the loss of the right of priority.

(5) Subsequently, further proof may be required.

A person who avails himself of the priority of a previously filed application shall be required to specify the number of that application, which shall be published under the conditions provided for by paragraph (2) above.

E.—(1) Where an industrial design is filed in a country by virtue of a right of priority based on the filing of a utility model, the period of priority shall be only that fixed for industrial designs.

(2) Furthermore, it is permissible to file a utility model in a country by virtue of a right of priority based on the filing of a patent application, and vice versa.

F.—No country of the Union may refuse a priority or a patent application on the ground that the applicant claims multiple priorities, even originating in different countries, or on the ground that an application claiming one or more priorities contains one or more elements that were not included in the original application or applications whose priority is claimed, provided that, in both cases, there is unity of invention within the meaning of the law of the country.

With respect to the elements not included in the original application or applications whose priority is claimed, the filing of the later application shall give rise to a right of priority under the usual conditions.

G.—(1) If examination reveals that an application for a patent contains more than one invention, the applicant may divide the application into a certain number of divisional applications and preserve as the date of each the date of the initial application and the benefit of the right of priority, if any.

(2) The applicant may also, on his own initiative, divide a patent application and preserve as the date of each divisional application the date of the initial application and the benefit of the right of priority, if any. Each country of the Union shall have the right to determine the conditions under which such division shall be authorised.

H.—Priority may not be refused on the ground that certain elements of the invention for which priority is claimed do not appear among the claims formulated in the application in the country of origin, provided that the application documents as a whole specifically disclose such elements.

Article 4*bis*

(1) Patents applied for in the various countries of the Union by persons entitled to the benefits of the Union shall be independent of patents obtained for the same invention in other countries, whether members of the Union or not.

(2) This provision is to be understood in an unrestricted sense, in particular, in the sense that patents applied for during the period of priority are independent, both as regards the grounds for invalidation and for forfeiture and as regards their normal duration.

(3) The provision shall apply to all patents existing at the time when it comes into effect.

(4) Similarly, it shall apply, in the case of the accession of new countries, to patents in existence on either side at the time of accession.

(5) Patents obtained with the benefit of priority shall have in the various countries of the Union a duration equal to that which they would have had if they had been applied for or granted without the benefit of priority.

Article 4ter

The inventor shall have the right to be mentioned as such in the patent.

Article 4^{quater}

The grant of a patent shall not be refused and a patent shall not be invalidated on the ground that the sale of the patented product or of a product obtained by means of the patented process is subject to restrictions or limitations resulting from the domestic law.

Article 5

A.—(1) The importation by the patentee into the country where the patent has been granted of articles manufactured in any of the countries of the Union shall not entail forfeiture of the patent.

(2) Each country of the Union shall have the right to take legislative measures providing for the grant of compulsory licences to prevent the abuses which might result from the exclusive rights conferred by the patent, for example, failure to work.

(3) Forfeiture of the patent shall not be prescribed except in cases where the grant of compulsory licences would not have been sufficient to prevent such abuses. No proceeding for the forfeiture or revocation of a patent may be instituted before the expiration of two years from the grant of the first compulsory licence.

(4) An application for a compulsory licence may not be made on the ground of failure to work or insufficient working before the expiration of a period of four years from the date of filing of the patent application or three years from the date of the grant of the patent, whichever period last expires; it shall be refused if the patentee justifies his inaction by legitimate reasons. Such a compulsory licence shall be non-exclusive and shall not be transferable, even in the form of the grant of a sub-licence, except with that part of the enterprise or goodwill using such licence.

(5) The foregoing provisions shall be applicable, *mutatis mutandis*, to utility models.

B.—The protection of industrial designs shall not, under any circumstances, be liable to any forfeiture either by reason of failure to work or by reason of the importation of articles corresponding to those which are protected.

C.—(1) If, in any country, the use of a registered trademark is compulsory the registration shall not be cancelled until after a reasonable period, and then only if the person concerned cannot justify his inaction.

(2) The use of a trademark by the proprietor in a form differing in elements which do not alter the distinctive character of the mark in the form in which it was registered in one of the countries of the Union, shall not entail invalidation of the registration and shall not diminish the protection granted to the mark.

(3) The concurrent use of the same mark on identical or similar goods by industrial or commercial establishments considered as co-proprietors of the mark according to the provisions of the national law of the country where protection is claimed shall not prevent the registration or diminish in any way the protection granted to the mark in any country of the Union, provided the use does not result in misleading the public and is not contrary to the public interest.

D.—No indication or mention of the patent, of the utility model, of the registration of the trademark, or the deposit of the industrial design shall be required upon the product as a condition or recognition of the right to protection.

ARTICLE 5*bis*

(1) A period of grace of not less than six months shall be allowed for the payment of the prescribed fees for the maintenance of industrial property rights, subject to the payment of a surcharge, if the domestic law so provides.

(2) The countries of the Union shall have the right to provide for the restoration of patents which have lapsed by reason of non-payment of fees.

ARTICLE 5*ter*

In each of the countries of the Union the following shall not be considered as infringements of the rights of a patentee:

1. The use on board vessels of other countries of the Union of devices forming the subject of his patent in the body of the vessel, in the machinery, tackle, gear and other accessories, when such vessels temporarily or accidentally enter the waters of a country, provided that such devices are used there exclusively for the needs of the vessel.
2. The use of devices forming the subject of the patent in the construction or operation of aircraft or land vehicles of other countries of the Union, or of accessories to such aircraft or land vehicles, when those aircraft or land vehicles temporarily or accidentally enter the country.

Article 5quater

When a product is imported into a country of the Union where there exists a patent protecting a process of manufacture of the said product, the patentee shall have all the rights, with regard to the imported product, as are accorded to him by the domestic law of the country of importation, on the basis of the process patent, with respect to products manufactured in that country.

Article 5quinquies

Industrial designs shall be protected in all the countries of the Union.

Article 6

(1) The conditions for the filing and registration of trademarks shall be determined in each country of the Union by its domestic law.

(2) However, an application for the registration of a trademark filed by a national of a country of the Union in any country of the Union may not be refused nor may a registration be cancelled on the ground that filing, registration or renewal has not been effected in the country of origin.

(3) A mark duly registered in a country of the Union shall be regarded as independent of marks registered in the other countries of the Union, including the country of origin.

Article 6bis

(1) The countries of the Union undertake, either administratively if their legislation so permits, or at the request of an interested party, to refuse or to cancel the registration and to prohibit the use of a trademark which constitutes a reproduction, imitation or translation liable to create confusion of a mark considered by the competent authority of the country of registration or use to be well-known in that country as being already the mark of a person entitled to the benefits of the present Convention and used for identical or similar goods. These provisions shall also apply when the essential part of the mark constitutes a reproduction of any such well-known mark or an imitation liable to create confusion therewith.

(2) A period of at least five years from the date of registration shall be allowed for seeking the cancellation of such a mark. The countries of the Union may provide for a period within which the prohibition of use must be sought.

(3) No time limit shall be fixed for seeking the cancellation or the prohibition of the use of marks registered or used in bad faith.

Article 6ter

(1) (*a*) The countries of the Union agree to refuse or to invalidate the registration, and to prohibit by appropriate measures the use, without authorisation by the competent authorities, either as trademarks or as elements of trademarks, of armorial bearings, flags and other State emblems of the countries of the Union, official signs and hall-marks indicating control or warranty adopted by them and all imitations thereof from a heraldic point of view.

(*b*) The provisions of sub-paragraph (*a*) above apply equally to armorial bearings, flags and other emblems, abbreviations or titles of international intergovernmental organisations of which one or more countries of the Union are members, with the exception of armorial bearings, flags and other emblems, abbreviations or titles that are already the subject of existing international agreements intended to ensure their protection.

(*c*) No country of the Union shall be required to apply the provisions of sub-paragraph (*b*) above to the prejudice of the owners of rights acquired in good faith before the entry into force in that country of the present Convention. The countries of the Union shall not be required to apply the said provisions when the use or registration covered by sub-paragraph (*a*) above is not of such a nature as to suggest to the public that a connection exists between the organisation concerned and the armorial bearings, flags, emblems, abbreviations or titles, or if such use or registration is clearly not of a nature to mislead the public as to the existence of a connection between the user and the organisation.

(2) The prohibition of the use of official signs and hall-marks indicating control and warranty shall apply solely in cases where the marks which contain them are intended to be used on goods of the same or of a similar kind.

(3) (*a*) For the application of these provisions the countries of the Union agree to communicate reciprocally, through the International Bureau, the list of State emblems and official signs and hall-marks indicating control and warranty which they desire, or may thereafter desire, to place wholly or within certain limits under the protection of the present Article and all subsequent modifications of this list. Each country of the Union shall in due course make available to the public the lists so communicated.

Nevertheless, this communication is not obligatory so far as the flags of States are concerned.

(*b*) The provisions of sub-paragraph (*b*) of paragraph (1) of this Article shall only apply to armorial bearings, flags and other emblems, abbreviations or titles of international intergovernmental organisations that the latter have communicated to the countries of the Union through the International Bureau.

(4) Any country of the Union may, within a period of twelve months from the receipt of the communication, transmit through the International Bureau its objections, if any, to the country or international intergovernmental organisation concerned.

(5) In the case of State flags, the measures prescribed by paragraph 1 above shall apply solely to marks registered after November 6, 1925.

(6) In the case of State emblems other than flags, and of official signs and hall-marks of the countries of the Union and in the case of armorial bearings, flags and other emblems, abbreviations or titles of international intergovernmental organisations, these provisions shall be applicable only to marks registered more than two months after the receipt of the communication provided for in paragraph (3) above.

(7) In cases of bad faith the countries shall have the right to cancel the registration of marks that contain State emblems, signs or hall-marks even though registered before November 6, 1925.

(8) Nationals of each country who are authorised to make use of State emblems, signs or hall-marks of their country, may use them even though they are similar to those of another country.

(9) The countries of the Union undertake to prohibit the unauthorised use in trade of the State armorial bearings of the other countries of the Union, when the use is of such a nature as to be misleading as to the origin of the goods.

(10) The above provisions shall not prevent the countries from exercising the power given in paragraph (3) of Article $6^{quinquies}$ B, to refuse or to cancel the registration of marks containing, without authorisation the armorial bearings, flags, and other State emblems or official signs or hall-marks adopted by a country of the Union as well as the distinctive signs of international intergovernmental organisations mentioned in paragraph (1) of this Article.

Article 6^{quater}

(1) When in accordance with the law of a country of the Union, the assignment of a mark is valid only if it takes place at the same time as the transfer of the business or goodwill to which the mark belongs, it shall suffice for the recognition of this validity that the portion of the business or goodwill situated in that country be transferred to the assignee, together with the exclusive right to manufacture or sell there the goods bearing the mark assigned.

(2) This provision does not impose upon the countries of the Union any obligation to regard as valid the assignment of any mark the use of which by the assignee would, in fact, be of such a nature as to mislead the public, particularly as regards the origin, nature or material qualities of the goods to which the mark is applied.

Article 6*quinquies*

A.—(1) Every trademark duly registered in the country of origin shall be accepted for filing and protected in its original form in the other countries of the Union, subject to the reservations indicated in the present Article. These countries may, before proceeding to final registration, require the production of a certificate of registration in the country of origin, issued by the competent authority. No authentication shall be required for this certificate.

(2) The country of the Union where the applicant has a real and effective industrial or commercial establishment, or, if he has not such an establishment within the Union, the Union country where he has his domicile or if he has no domicile in the Union, the country of his nationality if he is a national of a Union country, shall be considered his country of origin.

B.—Trademarks under the present Article may not be denied registration or invalidated except in the following cases:

1. when they are of such a nature as to infringe rights acquired by third parties in the country where protection is claimed;
2. when they are devoid of distinctive character, or consist exclusively of signs or indications which may serve in trade to designate the kind, quality, quantity, intended purpose, value, place of origin of the goods or time of production, or have become customary in the current language or in the bona fide and established practices of the trade in the country where protection is claimed;
3. when they are contrary to morality or public order and, in particular, of such a nature as to deceive the public. It is understood that a mark may not be considered contrary to public order for the sole reason that it does not conform to a provision of the law relating to trademarks, except where such provision itself relates to public order.

The above is, however, subject to Article 10*bis*.

C.—(1) To determine whether a mark is eligible for protection, all the circumstances of the case must be taken into consideration, particularly the length of time the mark has been in use.

(2) Trademarks shall not be refused in the other countries of the Union for the sole reason that they differ from the marks protected in the country of origin only by elements that do not alter the distinctive character and do not affect the identity of the marks in the form in which these have been registered in the said country of origin.

D.—No person may benefit from the provisions of the present Article if the mark for which he claims protection is not registered in the country of origin.

E.—However, in no case shall the renewal of the registration of a mark in the country of origin involve the obligation to renew the registration in the other Union countries where the mark has been registered.

F.—The benefits of priority shall be accorded to applications for the registration of marks filed within the period fixed by Article 4, even when registration in the country of origin does not occur until after the expiration of such period.

Article 6*sexies*

The countries of the Union undertake to protect service marks. They shall not be required to provide for the registration of such marks.

Article 6*septies*

(1) If the agent or representative of the person who is the proprietor of a mark in one of the countries of the Union applies, without such proprietor's authorisation, for the registration of the mark in his own name in one or more Union countries, the proprietor shall be entitled to oppose the registration applied for or demand its cancellation or, if the law of the country so allows, the assignment in his favour of the said registration, unless such agent or representative justifies his action.

(2) The proprietor of the mark shall, subject to the reservations of paragraph (1) above, be entitled to oppose the use of the mark by his agent or representative if he has not authorised such use.

(3) Domestic laws may provide an equitable time limit within which the proprietor of a mark must assert the rights provided for in the present Article.

Article 7

The nature of the goods to which a trademark is to be applied shall in no case form an obstacle to the registration of the mark.

Article 7bis

(1) The countries of the Union undertake to accept for filing and to protect collective marks belonging to associations the existence of which is not contrary to the law of the country of origin, even if such associations do not possess an industrial or commercial establishment.

(2) Each country shall be the judge of the particular conditions under which a collective mark shall be protected and may refuse protection if the mark is contrary to the public interest.

(3) Nevertheless, the protection of these marks shall not be refused to any association the existence of which is not contrary to the law of the country of origin, on the ground that such association is not established in the country where protection is sought or is not constituted according to the law of the latter country.

Article 8

A trade name shall be protected in all the countries of the Union without the obligation of filing or registration, whether or not it forms part of a trademark.

Article 9

(1) All goods unlawfully bearing a trademark or trade name shall be seized on importation into those countries of the Union where such mark or name has a right to legal protection.

(2) Seizure shall likewise be effected in the country where the unlawful application occurred or in the country into which the goods have been imported.

(3) Seizure shall take place at the request either of the public prosecutor or of any other competent authority or of any interested party, whether a natural or a juridical person, in conformity with the domestic law of each country.

(4) The authorities shall not be bound to effect seizure in transit.

(5) If the law of a country does not permit seizure on importation, such seizure shall be replaced by prohibition of importation or by seizure within such country.

(6) If the law of a country permits neither seizure on importation nor prohibition of importation nor seizure within the country, then, until such time as the law is modified accordingly, these measures shall be replaced by the actions and remedies available in such cases to nationals under the law of such country.

Article 10

(1) The provisions of the preceding Article shall apply in cases of direct or indirect use of a false indication of the source of the product or the identity of the producer, manufacturer or trader.

(2) Any producer, manufacturer or trader, whether a natural or juridical person, engaged in the production or manufacture of, or trade in such goods and established either in the locality falsely indicated as the source or in the district where this locality is situated, or in the country falsely indicated, or in the country where the false indication of source is used, shall in any case be deemed an interested party.

Article 10bis

(1) The countries of the Union are bound to assure to persons entitled to the benefits of the Union effective protection against unfair competition.

(2) Any act of competition contrary to honest practices in industrial or commercial matters constitutes an act of unfair competition.

(3) The following in particular shall be prohibited:

1. all acts of such a nature as to create confusion by any means whatever with the establishment, the goods, or the industrial or commercial activities of a competitor;
2. false allegations in the course of trade of such a nature as to discredit the establishment, the goods, or the industrial or commercial activities of a competitor;
3. indications or allegations the use of which in the course of trade is liable to mislead the public as to the nature, the manufacturing process, the characteristics, the suitability for their purpose or the quantity of the goods.

Article 10ter

(1) The countries of the Union undertake to assure to nationals of the other countries of the Union appropriate legal remedies to repress effectively all the acts referred to in Articles 9, 10 and 10bis.

(2) They undertake, further, to provide measures to permit syndicates and associations which represent the industrialists, producers or traders concerned and the existence of which is not contrary to the laws of their countries, to take action in the Courts or before the administrative authorities, with a view to

the repression of the acts referred to in Articles 9, 10 and 10bis, in so far as the law of the country in which protection is claimed allows such action by the syndicates and associations of that country.

Article 11

(1) The countries of the Union shall in conformity with their domestic law, grant temporary protection to patentable inventions, utility models, industrial designs and trademarks, in respect of goods exhibited at official or officially recognised international exhibitions held in the territory of one of them.

(2) This temporary protection shall not extend the periods provided by Article 4. If later the right of priority is invoked, each country may provide that the period shall start from the date of introduction of the goods into the exhibition.

(3) Each country may require, as proof of the identity of the article exhibited and of the date of its introduction, such evidence as it considers necessary.

Article 12

(1) Each of the countries of the Union undertakes to establish a special industrial property service and a central office for the communication to the public of patents, utility models, industrial designs, and trademarks.

(2) This agency shall publish an official periodical journal. It shall publish regularly:

(*a*) the names of the proprietors of patents granted, with a brief description of the inventions patented;
(*b*) reproductions of trademarks registered.

Article 13

(1) The international office established under the name International Bureau for the Protection of Industrial Property is placed under the high authority of the Government of the Swiss Confederation, which regulates its organisation and supervises its operation.

(2) (*a*) The French and English languages shall be used by the International Bureau in performing the tasks provided for in paragraphs (3) and (5) of this Article.

(*b*) The conferences and meetings referred to in Article 14 shall be held in the French, English and Spanish languages.

(3) The International Bureau centralises information of every kind relating to the protection of industrial property and com-

piles and publishes it. It undertakes studies of general utility concerning the Union and edits, with the help of documents supplied to it by the various Administrations, a periodical journal dealing with questions relating to the objects of the Union.

(4) The issues of this journal, as well as all the documents published by the International Bureau, shall be distributed to the Administrations of the countries of the Union in proportion to the number of contributing units mentioned below. Additional copies as may be requested, either by the said Administrations or by companies or private persons, shall be paid for separately.

(5) The International Bureau shall at all times hold itself at the disposition of the countries of the Union, to supply them with any special information they may need on questions relating to the international industrial property service. The Director of the International Bureau shall make an annual report on his administration, which shall be communicated to all the countries of the Union.

(6) The ordinary expenditure of the International Bureau shall be borne by the countries of the Union in common. Until further authorisation, it shall not exceed the sum of 120,000 Swiss francs per annum. This sum may be increased, when necessary, by a unanimous decision of one of the conferences provided for in Article 14.

(7) Ordinary expenditure does not include expenses relating to the work of conferences of plenipotentiaries or administrative conferences nor the expenses caused by special work or publications effected in conformity with the decisions of a conference. Such expenses, the annual total of which may not exceed 20,000 Swiss francs, shall be divided among the countries of the Union in proportion to their contributions towards the operation of the International Bureau in accordance with the provisions of paragraph (8) below.

(8) To determine the contribution of each country to this total expenditure, the countries of the Union and those which may afterwards join the Union are divided into six classes, each contributing in the proportion of a certain number of units, namely:

First class	25	units
Second class	20	,,
Third class	15	,,
Fourth class	10	,,
Fifth class	5	,,
Sixth class	3	,,

These coefficients are multiplied by the number of countries in each class, and the sum of the products thus obtained gives the number of units by which the total expenditure is to be divided. The quotient gives the amount of the unit of expense.

(9) Each of the countries of the Union shall, at the time it becomes a member, designate the class in which it wishes to be placed. However, any country of the Union may declare later that it desires to be placed in another class.

(10) The Government of the Swiss Confederation will supervise the expenditure of the International Bureau and its accounts and will make the necessary advances.

(11) The annual account rendered by the International Bureau shall be communicated to all the other Administrations.

Article 14

(1) The present Convention shall be submitted to periodical revision with a view to the introduction of amendments designed to improve the system of the Union.

(2) For this purpose conferences shall be held successively in one of the countries of the Union between the delegates of the said countries.

(3) The Administration of the country in which the conference is to be held shall make preparations for the work of the conference, with the assistance of the International Bureau.

(4) The Director of the International Bureau shall be present at the meetings of the conferences, and take part in the discussions, but without the right of voting.

(5) (*a*) During the interval between the Diplomatic Conferences of revision, Conferences of representatives of all the countries of the Union shall meet every three years in order to draw up a report on the foreseeable expenditure of the International Bureau for each three-year period to come and to consider questions relating to the protection and development of the Union.

(*b*) Furthermore, they may modify, by unanimous decision, the maximum annual amount of the expenditure of the International Bureau, provided they meet as Conferences of Plenipotentiaries of all the countries of the Union, convened by the Government of the Swiss Confederation.

(*c*) Moreover, the Conferences provided for in paragraph (*a*) above may be convened between their triennial meetings by either the Director of the International Bureau or the Government of the Swiss Confederation.

Article 15

It is understood that the countries of the Union reserve the right to make separately between themselves special arrangements for the protection of industrial property, in so far as these arrangements do not contravene the provisions of the present Convention.

Article 16

(1) Countries which are not parties to the present Convention shall be permitted to accede to it at their request.

(2) Any such accession shall be notified through diplomatic channels to the Government of the Swiss Confederation, and by it to all the other Governments.

(3) Accession shall automatically entail acceptance of all the clauses and admission to all the advantages of the present Convention and shall take effect one month after the despatch of the notification by the Government of the Swiss Confederation to the other countries of the Union, unless a subsequent date is indicated in the request for accession.

Article 16*bis*

(1) Any country of the Union may at any time notify in writing the Government of the Swiss Confederation that the present Convention is applicable to all or part of its colonies, protectorates, territories under mandate or any other territories subject to its authority, or any territories under its sovereignty, and the Convention shall apply to all the territories named in the notification one month after the dispatch of the communication by the Government of the Swiss Confederation to the other countries of the Union unless a subsequent date is indicated in the notification. Failing such a notification, the Convention shall not apply to such territories.

(2) Any country of the Union may at any time notify in writing the Government of the Swiss Confederation that the present Convention ceases to be applicable to all or part of the territories that were the subject of the notification under the preceding paragraph and the Convention shall cease to apply in the territories named in the notification twelve months after the receipt of the notification addressed to the Government of the Swiss Confederation.

(3) All notifications sent to the Government of the Swiss Confederation in accordance with the provisions of paragraphs (1) and (2) of the present Article shall be communicated by that Government to all the countries of the Union.

Article 17

Any country party to this Convention undertakes to adopt, in accordance with its constitution, the measures necessary to ensure the application of this Convention.

It is understood that at the time an instrument of ratification or accession is deposited on behalf of a country, such country will be in a position under its domestic law to give effect to the provisions of this Convention.

Article 17*bis*

(1) The Convention shall remain in force for an indefinite time, until the expiration of one year from the date of its denunciation.

(2) Such denunciation shall be addressed to the Government of the Swiss Confederation. It shall affect only the country in whose name it is made, the Convention remaining in operation as regards the other countries of the Union.

Article 18

(1) The present Act shall be ratified and the instruments of ratification deposited in Berne not later than May 1, 1963. It shall come into force, between the countries in whose names it has been ratified, one month after that date. However, if before that date it is ratified in the name of at least six countries, it shall come into force between those countries one month after the deposit of the sixth ratification has been notified to them by the Government of the Swiss Confederation,[7] and for countries in whose name it is ratified at a later date, one month after the notification of each such ratification.

(2) Countries in whose names no instrument of ratification has been deposited within the period referred to in the preceding paragraph shall be permitted to accede under the terms of Article 16.

(3) The present Act shall, as regards the relations between the countries to which it applies, replace the Convention of Paris of 1883 and the subsequent Acts of revision.

(4) As regards the countries to which the present Act does not apply, but to which the Convention of Paris revised at London in 1934 applies, the latter shall remain in force.

(5) Similarly, as regards countries to which neither the present Act nor the Convention of Paris revised at London apply, the Convention of Paris revised at The Hague in 1925 shall remain in force.

[7] The Convention came into force on January 4, 1962.

(6) Similarly, as regards countries to which neither the present Act nor the Convention of Paris revised at London, nor the Convention of Paris revised at The Hague apply, the Convention of Paris revised at Washington in 1911 shall remain in force.

ARTICLE 19

(1) The present Act shall be signed in a single copy in the French language, which shall be deposited in the archives of the Government of the Swiss Confederation. A certified copy shall be forwarded by the latter to each of the Governments of the countries of the Union.

(2) The present Act shall remain open for signature by the countries of the Union until April 30, 1959.

(3) Official translations of the present Act shall be established in the English, German, Italian, Portuguese and Spanish languages.

CONVENTION ON INVENTIONS, PATENTS, DESIGNS AND INDUSTRIAL MODELS

Entered into at Buenos Aires on August 20, 1910

Between

Argentina	Ecuador	Peru
Brazil	Guatemala	Salvador
Chile	Haiti	Uruguay
Colombia	Honduras	U.S.A.
Costa Rica	Mexico	Venezuela
Cuba	Nicaragua	
Dominican Republic	Panama	
	Paraguay	

ARTICLE I

The subscribing nations enter into this Convention for the protection of patents of invention, designs and industrial models.

ARTICLE II

Any persons who shall obtain a patent of invention in any of the signatory states, shall enjoy in each of the other states all the advantages which the laws relative to patents of invention, designs and industrial models concede. Consequently they shall have the right to the same protection and identical legal remedies against any attack upon their rights, provided they comply with the laws of each State.

Article III

Any person who shall have regularly deposited an application for a patent of invention or design or industrial model in one of the contracting states shall enjoy, for the purposes of making the deposit in the other states, and under the reserve of the rights of third parties, a right of priority during a period of twelve months for patents of invention, and of four months for designs or industrial models.

In consequence the deposit subsequently made in any other of the signatory states before the expiration of these periods, cannot be invalidated by acts performed in the interval, especially by other deposits, by the publication of the invention or its working, or by the sale of copies of the design or of the model.

Article IV

When, within the terms fixed, a person shall have filed applications in several States for the patent of the same invention the rights resulting from patents thus applied for shall be independent of each other.

They shall also be independent of the rights arising under patents obtained for the same invention in countries not parties to this Convention.

Article V

Questions which may arise regarding the priority of patents of invention, shall be decided with regard to the date of the application for the respective patents in the countries in which they are granted.

Article VI

The following shall be considered as inventions: A new manner of manufacturing industrial products; a new machine or mechanical or manual apparatus which serves for the manufacture of said products; the discovery of a new industrial product; the application of known methods for the purpose of securing better results; and every new, original and ornamental design or model for an article of manufacture.

The foregoing shall be understood without prejudice to the laws of each State.

Article VII

Any of the signatory states may refuse to recognise patents for any of the following causes:

(*a*) because the inventions or discoveries may have been published in any country prior to the date of the invention by the applicant;
(*b*) because the inventions have been registered, published, or described in any country more than one year prior to the date of the application in the country in which the patent is sought;
(*c*) because the inventions have been in public use, or have been on sale in the country in which the patent has been applied for, one year prior to the date of said application;
(*d*) because the inventions or discoveries are in some manner contrary to morals or laws.

Article VIII

The ownership of a patent of invention comprises the right to enjoy the benefits thereof, and the right to assign or transfer it in accordance with the laws of the country.

Article IX

Persons who incur civil or criminal liabilities, because of injuries or damage to the rights of inventors, shall be prosecuted and punished, in accordance with the laws of the countries wherein the offence has been committed or the damage occasioned.

Article X

Copies of patents certified in the country of origin, according to the national law thereof, shall be given full faith and credit as evidence of the right of priority, except as stated in Article VII.

Article XI

The treaties relating to patents of invention, designs or industrial models, previously entered into between the countries subscribing to the present Convention, shall be superseded by the same from the time of its ratification in so far as the relations between the signatory states are concerned.

Article XII

The adhesions of the American nations to the present Convention shall be communicated to the Government of the Argentine Republic in order that it may communicate them to the other states. These communications shall have the effect of an exchange of ratifications.

Article XIII

A signatory Nation that sees fit to retire from the present Convention, shall notify the Government of the Argentine Republic, and one year after the receipt of the communication the force of this Convention shall cease, in so far as the nation which shall have withdrawn its adherence is concerned.

CONVENTION ON PATENTS OF INVENTION

Entered into at Montevideo on January 16, 1889

Between Argentina, Bolivia, Paraguay, Peru, Uruguay.

Article 1

Anyone obtaining a patent for invention in any of the signatory countries enjoys inventor's rights in the others, if within the maximum term of *one year* he registers his patent in the manner laid down by the laws of the country in which he applies for its recognition.

Article 2

The term of the privilege will be determined by the local laws. This period may be limited to that indicated by the laws of the country in which the patent was originally granted, should it be shorter.

Article 3

Any disputes arising as to the priority of the invention shall be settled taking into account the date of the application for the relevant patents in the countries in which they were granted.

Article 4

An invention or discovery is considered to be a new method, mechanical or manual apparatus serving to manufacture industrial products, the discovery of a new industrial product, and the application of improved means for the purpose of achieving results superior to those already known.

A patent may not be obtained for:

1. Inventions and discoveries which have had publicity in any of the signatory countries, or in others not bound by this agreement;
2. Those contrary to morals or the laws of the country in which the patents for invention are to be issued or recognised.

ARTICLE 5

The inventor's right covers the power to benefit from his invention and to transfer it to others.

ARTICLE 6

Any civil or criminal responsibilities which may be incurred by those infringing the inventor's right will be pursued and punished in accordance with the laws of the country in which the prejudice has been caused.

ARTICLE 7

This agreement does not for its validity require the simultaneous ratification of all signatory countries. A country approving it will notify the Governments of the Republics of Argentina and of Uruguay, so that they may notify the other contracting countries. This procedure will take the place of exchange.

ARTICLE 8

Exchange having been effected in the manner of the preceding article, this agreement will come into force henceforth for an indefinite period.

ARTICLE 9

If any of the signatory countries should think it desirable to secede from the Agreement or to introduce modifications into it, the others are to be notified, but the secession will take place only two years after the announcement, during which time an attempt will be made to reach a new agreement.

ARTICLE 10

Article 7 is extended to cover countries which though they have not attended this Congress may wish to adhere to the present Agreement.

CONVENTION ON PATENTS AND PRIVILEGES OF INVENTION

Entered into at Caracas on July 18, 1911

Between Bolivia, Colombia, Ecuador, Peru, Venezuela.

ARTICLE 1

Anyone obtaining a patent or privilege of invention for the first time in any of the signatory countries will enjoy the rights of inventor in the others, if in the maximum period of *two years* he should register his patent in the manner laid down by the laws of the country in which its recognition is applied for.

ARTICLE 2

The number of years of the privilege will be that fixed by the laws of the country in which he applies to have it made effective.

ARTICLE 3

An invention or discovery for the purposes of this agreement will be considered to be a new method, mechanical or manual apparatus, serving to manufacture industrial products; the discovery of a new industrial product, the application of improved means for the purpose of achieving results superior to those already known.

Patents may not be obtained or those already obtained be registered:

1. If the inventions or discoveries to which they refer have already been published in any of the signatory countries, or in others which are not bound by this agreement;
2. If the inventions or discoveries are devoted to public health in accordance with the laws of the country where the patents of invention are to be issued or recognised.

ARTICLE 4

The inventor's right comprises the power to enjoy his invention or to transfer it to others.

ARTICLE 5

The civil and criminal responsibilities incurred by those infringing the rights of an inventor will be pursued and punished in accordance with the laws of the country in which the prejudice has been caused.

The signatory countries undertake to maintain in their legislation a penalty against infringers of this right.

EUROPEAN CONVENTION RELATING TO THE FORMALITIES REQUIRED FOR PATENT APPLICATIONS

Paris, December 11, 1953

ARTICLE 1

1. An application for a patent in any Contracting State
   (*a*) may be required to accord with the provisions of Article 2 of this Convention;

(*b*) shall not be denied its date of filing on formal grounds if it complies with the requirements specified in Article 3 of this Convention;

(*c*) shall, if it otherwise complies with the law of that Contracting State, not be refused, so long as the requirements specified in Articles 4 to 6 of this Convention are satisfied.

2. The Contracting States shall make no other formal requirements than those set out in this Convention, but a Contracting State may dispense with any of the requirements contained herein.

ARTICLE 2

1. The applicant for a patent may be required to submit:

(*a*) an application form; a Contracting State may, however, require this form in duplicate;

(*b*) a specification of the invention in duplicate; a Contracting State which makes use of a system of examination for novelty may, however, require this specification in triplicate;

(*c*) drawings necessary for the understanding of the specification, in duplicate, or, if the law of the country in which the application is made requires it, in triplicate;

(*d*) such samples as the law of the country in which the application is made requires;

(*e*) if an agent is employed, a document proving his authorisation to act as such, and, if the law of the country in which application is made requires it, his acceptance of the authorisation; no legalisation or certification shall be necessary for this document;

(*f*) if the applicant is not himself the inventor according to the law of the country in which the application is made, and if such law requires it, a document proving his status, such as assignee of the inventor, or the assent of the inventor to the making of the application by an assignee;

(*g*) the fees required for an application or proof that they have been paid.

2. The application form and the accompanying documents shall be written in the language of, or in a language recognised for the purpose by, the country in which the application is made. The specification filed in support of an application for a patent or certificate of addition may be required to be in the same language as the application for the main patent.

Article 3

1. An application shall not be denied its date of filing on formal grounds if the application form, though it does not comply with the requirements of Article 4, is filed accompanied by:

(*a*) one copy of a specification of the invention in the language of, or in a language recognised for the purpose by, the country in which the application is made, even though that specification does not comply with the requirements of Article 5;

(*b*) one copy of the drawings where necessary for the understanding of the specification, even though those drawings do not comply with the requirements of Article 6;

(*c*) the amount of the fees or proof that they have been paid.

2. The law of the country in which application is made may fix time-limits within which the other documents mentioned in Article 2 shall be filed or the documents already filed shall be regularised.

3. The Contracting States shall permit applications to be sent by post, provided that nothing in this paragraph shall affect the validity of any laws of any Contracting State relating to the requirement of an agent or of an address for service.

Article 4

1. The application form shall be regarded as formally in order, as regards its size and the kind of paper used, if it is made on strong white paper of a size of 29 to 34 cms. by 20 to 22 cms.

2. The application form shall be regarded as formally in order as regards its contents if it is properly made on one of the standard application forms annexed to this Convention, or if it complies with the provisions of paragraph 2 of Article 2 and contains:—

(*a*) the surname and first names (or in the case of a body corporate, the name), nationality, domicile or registered office and complete address of the applicant;

(*b*) the full name and address of the agent, if there is one;

(*c*) a short and precise title for the invention, without any fancy names;

(*d*) if the law of the country in which application is made requires it, a declaration stating that the applicant is the true and first inventor or the assignee thereof;

(*e*) a statement whether the applicant requires an independent patent, a patent of importation, a patent for an improvement or a patent or certificate of addition or whether his application is a divisional application. There shall also be given the number of the patent, or of the application for the patent, to which the application for a patent for an improvement, or for a patent or certificate of addition or the divisional application relates;

(*f*) if there are several applicants and no common agent, the name of the person to whom official communications are to be addressed;

(*g*) the signature of the applicant or that of his agent, if, under the law of the country in which the application is made, the latter is empowered by the applicant to sign. If two application forms are required, only one need be signed;

(*h*) if the law of the country in which application is made requires it, a list of the documents accompanying the application as set out in Article 2;

(*i*) an address for service in the country in which the application is made, if the applicant's address is outside the country and its law does not require that there be an agent therein.

Article 5

The specification shall be regarded as formally in order if it complies with the provisions of paragraph 2 of Article 2 and with the following conditions:—

(*a*) it is written on one side only of one or more sheets of strong white paper, 29 to 34 cms. long and 20 to 22 cms. wide; the sheets are connected together in such a way that they can be separated and re-united without causing any difficulty to the reader; and the pages are numbered;

(*b*) it is handwritten, typed, lithographed or printed, and easily legible, the ink being dark and indelible;

(*c*) a margin of about 3 or 4 cms. is left on the left-hand side of each sheet as well as spaces of about 8 cms. at the head of the first page and foot of the last;

(*d*) a space sufficient to permit the interlineation of corrections is left between the lines;

(*e*) the specification does not contain drawings other than graphic chemical and mathematical formulae;

(*f*) units of weight and measures are in accordance with the metric system, temperatures in degrees centigrade, and density as specific gravity: for electrical units the rules agreed by international practice are observed and for chemical formulae the symbols, atomic weights and molecular formulae in general use in the country in which the application is made are employed;

(*g*) the specification is reasonably free from erasures, alterations or overwritings, and any which do occur in the originally filed document are mentioned in the margin or recited at the end of the description and initialled, and are made in the same manner on all the copies;

(*h*) the heading recites the surname and first names of the applicant (or in the case of a body corporate, its name) and the title of the invention;

(*i*) one or more copies of the specification is or are signed by the applicant or his agent, according to the law of the country in which the application is made.

ARTICLE 6

The drawings shall be regarded as formally in order if they comply with the following conditions:

(*a*) one of the copies of the drawings is made on one or more sheets of strong, non-shiny, flexible, transparent material. Not more than two other copies, exact replicas of the first, are supplied on strong, white, smooth, non-shiny paper; these copies may be good quality lithographs. If the copy on flexible, transparent material is made by means of a printing press, the other copies may be printed from the same block. Any Contracting State may, however, require that one of these latter copies shall bear no reference signs;

(*b*) each sheet is 29 to 34 cms. long by 21 cms. wide, or, exceptionally, 42 cms. wide. With sheets 21 cms. wide, the surface used is no more than 25·7 cms. by 17 cms.;

(*c*) all parts of the drawings are executed in durable, dark (if possible, black) markings without colours or colour washes and lend themselves to simple photographic reproduction or to reproduction without any intermediary steps on a stereotype;

(*d*) sections are indicated by oblique hatching which does not impede the clear reading of the reference signs and leading lines;

(*e*) the scale of the drawings is such that, depending on the degree of complexity of the figure, a photographic reproduction with a linear reduction in size to two-thirds allows all the detail to be seen without difficulty; and, if the scale is shown on the drawings, it is drawn and not indicated in writing;

(*f*) the different figures are clearly separated one from another, arranged on as few sheets as possible and numbered continuously and independently of the number of sheets;

(*g*) all numbers, letters and reference lines appearing on the drawings are simple and clear, the letters and numbers being at least 0·32 cms. high; and each item depicted in the figures, insofar as the understanding of the specification requires it, is denoted by the same reference letter or number throughout and these agree with those used in the specification;

(*h*) the drawings do not contain explanatory matter, with the exception of such terms as "water," "steam," "section on AB," "open," "shut," and, in the case of electric block schematic diagrams and flow sheet diagrams, explanatory matter sufficient to enable them to be understood, when such terms and explanatory matter appear in the language of, or in a language recognised for the purpose by, the country in which the application is filed;

(*i*) each sheet carries in the margin the name of the applicant, the total number of sheets with the number of each sheet, and the signature of the applicant or his agent;

(*j*) the drawings are filed in such a way as to be free from creases or cracks unfavourable to photographic reproduction.

Article 7

1. In each Contracting State any person desiring to take advantage, under the Convention of Paris for the Protection of Industrial Property, of the priority of a previous application shall enjoy a period of at least two months, starting from the subsequent application, to make a declaration to this effect. Each Contracting State, however, reserves the right to prescribe that this declaration should be made within the priority period laid down by that Convention.

2. When a declaration of priority is made in accordance with paragraph 1 of this Article, the applicant may be required to submit a certified copy of the specification and drawings of the original application and such other documents as the law of the country in which the subsequent application is made may require.

3. Insofar as the documents referred to in paragraph 2 of this Article are drawn up in English, French or German or accompanied by an officially certified translation in one of these languages, it shall not be necessary to provide a translation in the language of, or in a language recognised for the purpose by, the country in which application is made, unless the competent authority requires it.

Article 8

1. This Convention shall be open to the signature of the Members of the Council of Europe. It shall be ratified. Instruments of ratification shall be deposited with the Secretary-General of the Council of Europe.

2. This Convention shall come into force [6] on the first day of the month following the date of deposit of the fourth instrument of ratification.

3. As regards any Signatory ratifying subsequently, the Convention shall come into force on the first day of the month following the date of the deposit of its instrument of ratification.

Article 9

1. After it has come into force, this Convention shall be open to accession by all States which are Members of the International Union for the Protection of Industrial Property.

2. Accession shall be effected by the deposit of an instrument of accession with the Secretary-General of the Council of Europe, which shall take effect on the first day of the month following the date of deposit.

Article 10

The Secretary-General of the Council of Europe shall notify to the Members of the Council, to any States which may have acceded to this Convention and to the Director of the International Bureau for the Protection of Industrial Property at Berne:

(*a*) the date of entry into force of this Convention and the names of any Members of the Council which ratify it;

(*b*) the deposit of any instruments of accession in accordance with Article 9;

(*c*) any notification received in accordance with Article 11.

Article 11

1. This Convention shall remain in force for an unlimited time.

2. Any Contracting State may denounce this Convention by giving one year's notice to this effect to the Secretary-General of the Council of Europe.

[6] June 1, 1955.

ANNEX I

Application for Patent

I/We the undersigned [1]..

acting { in my/our own name.. / on behalf of [2]..

hereby make application for a patent for the invention described in the accompanying specification (and drawings) and entitled ....

I/We the applicant {
- claim(s) to be the true (and first) inventor(s) of the invention
- claim(s) the following of us (them), namely to be the true and first inventor(s)
- believe(s)..to be the true and first inventor(s)
- claims(s) to be the { Assignee(s) / Personal Representative(s) } of the inventor
- by virtue of [3]..

I/We request that the patent may be granted as a [4]..................

....

to Patent [5] { No. .... / Application No.............dated.............................. }

[6]..

....

Dated this...........day of...................., 19......

List of documents accompanying this application.

....

N.B.—Delete where not applicable or required.

INSTRUCTIONS

1 Give the following particulars:

(a) When this form is signed by the applicant(s), here insert his/their first names, surname(s), full address(es) and nationality(ies), or the name and full address where the applicant is not a physical person;

(b) When the form is signed by a nominee of the applicant(s) here insert the first names, surname and full address of the nominee. *Note*: Nominees cannot apply in certain countries.

2 In the case [1] (*b*), insert here the particulars at [1] (*a*).

3 Here insert particulars of the assignment or other document.

4 Here indicate the nature of the protection applied for, *e.g.*, independent patent, patent of importation, patent for an improvement, patent or certificate of addition.

5 In the case of a divisional application or where otherwise applicable, insert here the number of the related patent, or, where the related patent application is still pending, the number and date of such application.

6 Insert here, where necessary, any other relevant particulars such as the authorisation of an agent in the country in which the application is made, or, if no such agent is appointed, an address for service in that country.

ANNEX II

Convention Application for Patent

I/We the undersigned [1]

acting { in my/our own name..
{ on behalf of [2]..

Hereby declare that (an) application(s) for protection for an invention or inventions has(ve) been made in the following country(ies) on the following date(s), namely:—

in..................................on..................................
by..
in..................................on..................................
by..

and that the said application or each of the said applications was the first application in a Convention country.

I am/We are the assignee(s) of the said ....
or the personal representative(s) of the said ....
by virtue of ([3]) ....

I/We request that a patent may be granted with priority founded on the above-mentioned application(s) in a Convention country(ies) for the invention described in the accompanying specification (and drawings) and entitled ....
....

I/We request that the patent may be granted as a ([4]) ....
....

to Patent ([5])

No. ....

Appn. No. ....dated ....

([6])..

....

Dated this........day of...................., 19.....

List of documents accompanying this application:

....

N.B.—Delete where not applicable or required.

INSTRUCTIONS

[1] Give the following particulars:

(*a*) When this form is signed by the applicant(s), here insert his/their first names, surname(s), full address(es) and nationality(ies), or the name and full address where the applicant is not a physical person;

(*b*) When the form is signed by a nominee of the applicant(s) here insert the first names, surname and full address of the nominee. *Note*: Nominees cannot apply in certain countries.

[2] In the case [1] (*b*), insert here the particulars at [1] (*a*).

[3] Here insert particulars of the assignment or other document.

[4] Here indicate the nature of the protection applied for, *e.g.*, independent patent, patent of importation, patent for an improvement, patent or certificate of addition.

[5] In the case of a divisional application or where otherwise applicable, insert here the number of the related patent, or, where the related patent application is still pending, the number and date of such application.

[6] Insert here, where necessary, any other relevant particulars such as the authorisation of an agent in the country in which the application is made, or, if no such agent is appointed, an address for service in that country.

EUROPEAN CONVENTION ON THE INTERNATIONAL CLASSIFICATION OF PATENTS FOR INVENTION

Paris, December 19, 1954

with amended form of Annex which entered into force on December 16, 1961.

European Convention on the International Classification of Patents for Invention

Article 1

1. Subject to the provisions of this Convention, each Contracting Party shall adopt the system of classification of patents for inventions set out in the Annex hereto, together with any elaborations or modifications which shall have entered into force in accordance with paragraph 2 of Article 2. This system, including the said elaborations and modifications, is hereinafter referred to as the " International Classification."

2. Each Contracting Party shall be at liberty to apply the International Classification either as a principal or as a subsidiary system.

Article 2

1. The Committee of Experts on Patents of the Council of Europe shall be responsible for the further elaboration of the International Classification and shall give its opinion to the Contracting Parties on any modification thereof which may be proposed by any of them.

2. Any elaboration or modification approved by that Committee shall enter into force six months after all the Contracting Parties have been notified of such approval, unless two at least of the Parties have informed the Secretary-General of the Council of their objection to the proposed elaboration or modification not less than one month before the expiry of the said period of six months.

Article 3

1. The printed patent specifications issued by the Contracting Parties or, in their absence, any extract or similar document which may be issued by a Contracting Party as a substitute for such a printed specification shall, after the expiry of a period of six months from the date on which this Convention enters into force, be marked by the national authorities with the complete symbols of the International Classification.

2. Any signatory or acceding Government which does not classify patents for the purpose of examining the novelty of inventions may, when signing this Convention or when depositing its instrument of ratification, or when notifying its accession, declare that it does not undertake to mark the printed patent specifications, extracts or similar documents with all or some of the symbols relating to the elaborations of the classification system referred to in Articles 1 and 2. No such reservation may be made in connection with the Annex to this Convention or any modification thereof which does not constitute an elaboration.

3. The symbols of the International Classification, preceded by the words: " International Classification " or an abbreviation thereof, shall be printed in heavy type in the heading of the document.

4. The provisions of the preceding paragraphs shall not prejudice the right of any Contracting Party to require that the printed documents issued by their national authorities shall bear other symbols.

Article 4

1. This Convention shall be open for signature by the Members of the Council of Europe. It shall be ratified. Instruments of ratification shall be deposited with the Secretary-General of the Council of Europe.

2. Subject to the provisions of Article 6, this Convention shall enter into force on the first day of the month following the date of deposit of the fourth instrument of ratification.[6]

3. Subject to the provisions of Article 6, this Convention shall enter into force, for any signatory Government which subsequently ratifies it, on the first day of the month following the date of the deposit of its instrument of ratification.

Article 5

1. After its entry into force, this Convention shall be open to accession by any Member of the International Union for the Protection of Industrial Property which is not a Member of the Council of Europe.

2. Accession shall be effected by notifying the Government of the Swiss Confederation through the diplomatic channel, in accordance with the corresponding Article of the Convention for the Protection of Industrial Property. That Government shall notify such accessions to all other Members of the International Union for the Protection of Industrial Property and to the Secretary-General of the Council of Europe. Accession shall take

[6] August 1, 1955.

effect one month after the date of the notification by the Government of the Swiss Confederation.

Article 6

Any signatory or acceding Government may, when signing this Convention or when depositing its instrument of ratification, or when notifying its accession, declare that this Convention shall not come into force, so far as the said Government is concerned, until it has been ratified by the Governments of the Federal Republic of Germany, the Kingdom of the Netherlands and the United Kingdom of Great Britain and Northern Ireland.

Article 7

1. The Secretary-General of the Council of Europe shall notify the Members of the Council and the Director of the International Bureau for the Protection of Industrial Property at Berne:—

(*a*) of the date of entry into force of this Convention and the names of any Members of the Council which ratify it;

(*b*) of the approval of any elaborations or modifications of the kind referred to in paragraph 2 of Article 2, of any objections thereto, and of the entry into force of any such elaborations or modifications;

(*c*) of any notification received in accordance with paragraph 2 of Article 8.

2. He shall inform the Members of the Council of Europe who are not Members of the International Union for the Protection of Industrial Property of each accession notified pursuant to Article 5, and of any notice of denunciation given in accordance with paragraph 3 of Article 8.

Article 8

1. This Convention shall remain in force indefinitely.

2. Any Member of the Council of Europe which has signed and ratified this Convention may denounce it by giving one year's notice to this effect to the Secretary-General of the Council.

3. Any acceding Government may denounce this Convention by giving one year's notice to this effect to the Government of the Swiss Confederation through the diplomatic channel, in accordance with the corresponding Article of the Convention for the Protection of Industrial Property. That Government shall notify such denunciations to all other Members of the International Union for the Protection of Industrial Property and to the Secretary-General of the Council of Europe.

ANNEX (AMENDED)—SYSTEM OF CLASSIFICATION OF PATENTS FOR INVENTION

This Document replaces the text contained in the Annex to the European Convention on the International Classification of Patents for Invention.

Preliminary Note

This classification scheme is devised only for the purpose of classifying inventions which are the subjects of patents, and the requirements of Articles 3 (1) and 3 (3) are intended to be applied only to such symbols of the classification as are necessary to classify the invention of any particular patent. These symbols will usually relate only to one sub-class and one place in the elaborations thereof, but in certain cases they may extend to two or more sub-classes and/or places.

There is, however, no bar to the use of additional symbols of the classification for any other purpose (for example, for classifying subject-matter which may be disclosed in a patent specification without forming part of the invention thereof) provided that, if such additional symbols are placed on the documents referred to in Article 3 (1), these symbols are distinguished from those which relate to the invention as stated in the paragraph above, for example, by being printed in lighter type. It is not necessary for the additional symbols to include any symbols relating to groups or sub-groups of the classification system (which are not yet included in the Annex to the Convention), and they may, if desired in any case, indicate only the class concerned.

Interpretation of the Classification System

In interpreting this system of classification it should be noted that the wording describing the subject-matter of a classification unit [2] normally designates either a product or a process or both, the words "product" and "process" being used here in their widest possible senses, as indicated by the examples given below. Wording in other terms, *e.g.*, designating a use or application of a process or material, is used in some cases.

Examples of products are:

Chemical compounds, compositions, wire, films, fabrics, articles, apparatus, tools, machines, transport means, structures, assemblies, electric circuits, and systems composed of any of these.

Examples of processes are:

Polymerisation, fermentation, separation, shaping, conveying, treatment of textiles, transfer and transformation of energy, building, preparation of foodstuffs, testing, methods and modes of operation of machines, and processing and transmitting information.

In many cases the subject-matter of a classification unit is not confined to the product or process designated, but should be understood as follows:

1. A classification unit designating a product includes the processes used in the manufacture of the product, unless these processes are covered elsewhere in the system by a classification unit or units designating a process. In so far as the unit thus includes a process, paragraph 2 also applies to it. A classification unit designating a product also includes any parts of the product not covered by other such units.

2. A classification unit designating a process includes any apparatus,

[2] In this note, the term "classification unit" is used to mean a class which has no sub-classes, a sub-class or any sub-division which has a classification symbol and which is to form part of an elaboration of this system.

tools, machines, devices or materials used in the process, unless the apparatus, tools, machines, devices or materials are covered in the system by units designating products; and also includes any product produced by the process, unless it is covered in the system by a unit designating a product.

System of Classification
of Subject-Matter
for Patents of Invention

SECTIONS AND SUB-SECTIONS

A—Human necessities

Sub-sections: *Agriculture; Foodstuffs; Apparel; Medicine and hygiene.*

B—Performing operations

Sub-sections: *Separating and mixing; Shaping; Printing; Transporting.*

C—Chemistry and metallurgy

Sub-sections: *Chemistry; Metallurgy.*

D—Textiles and paper

Sub-sections: *Textiles; Paper.*

E—Fixed constructions

Sub-sections: *Building; Mining.*

F—Mechanics, lighting and heating

Sub-sections: *Engines; Lighting and heating.*

G—Physics

Sub-sections: *Instruments; Nucleonics.*

H—Electricity

Sub-section: *Electricity.*

System of Classification
of Subject-Matter
for Patents of Invention

CLASS HEADINGS

Section A.—Human necessities

classes

Agriculture

A 01 Agriculture; Forestry; Animal husbandry; Hunting; Trapping; Fishing.

Foodstuffs

A 21 Baking; Edible doughs.

A 22 Butchering; Meat treatment.

A 23 Foodstuffs and their treatment not included in other classes.

A 24 Tobacco; Cigars; Cigarettes; Smokers' requisites.

Apparel

A 41 Wearing apparel.

A 42 Headwear.

A 43 Footwear.

A 44 Haberdashery; Jewellery.

A 45 Hand and travelling articles.

A 46 Brushware.

A 47 Furniture; Household articles and appliances (ladders A 64).

Medicine and Hygiene

A 61 Medical and veterinary science; Hygiene.

A 62 Life-saving; Fire-fighting (ladders A 64).

A 63 Sports; Games; Amusements.

A 64 Ladders (ship ladders B 63 b; ladders for aircraft B 64 d; scaffolding E 04 g).

Section B.—Performing operations

classes

Separating and Mixing

B 01 Physical and chemical processes and apparatus (general).

B 02 Milling grain; Preparatory treatment of grain for milling; Crushing; Disintegrating; Pulverising; Sifting.

B 03 Washing and separating of ores, fuels, garbage, ashes and slag.

B 04 Centrifuges.

B 05 Spraying and atomising in general; Spreading liquids on surfaces in general.

B 06 Methods and apparatus for generating and/or transmitting mechanical vibrations of subsonic, sonic or supersonic frequency for performing mechanical work for general use (generation of electrical oscillations H 03 b).

Shaping

- B 21 Sheet metal; Metal tubes; Wire.
- B 22 Metal casting.
- B 23 Mechanical working of metal; Working of other materials by the same machines.
- B 24 Grinding; Polishing.
- B 25 Hand tools; Pneumatic tools.
- B 26 Hand cutting tools and thrusting weapons; Cutting machines and devices not specially adapted for particular materials or purposes.
- B 27 Working and preserving wood and similar material.
- B 28 Working cement, clay and stone; Clay and briquette presses.
- B 29 Working (mechanical part) plastic materials, rubber and horn-like substances, not otherwise provided for.
- B 30 Presses.
- B 31 Making paper articles; Working paper.

Printing

- B 41 Printing; Lining machines; Typewriters; Stamps.
- B 42 Bookbinding; Albums; Files; Special printed matter.
- B 43 Writing and drawing appliances.
- B 44 Sculpture; Painting; Decorative art.

Transporting

- B 61 Railways.
- B 62 Rail-less vehicles.
- B 63 Ships; Shipbuilding; Shipping.
- B 64 Aircraft; Aviation; Astronautics.
- B 65 Conveying; Packing; Storing.
- B 66 Hoisting (lifting devices).
- B 67 Liquid handling.
- B 68 Saddlery; Upholstery.

Section C.—CHEMISTRY AND METALLURGY

CLASSES

Chemistry

- C 01 Inorganic chemistry.
- C 02 Water; Treating water, waste water and sewage (distilling, filtering, separating B 01).
- C 03 Glass; Mineral and slag wool.
- C 04 Cements; Mortars; Ceramics; Artificial stone; Treatment of stone (chemical part); Sound and/or thermal insulating materials (chemical part); Kilns.
- C 05 Manufacture of fertilisers.
- C 06 Explosives; Matches.
- C 07 Organic chemistry (such compounds as the oxides, sulphides and oxysulphides of carbon, cyanogen, phosgene, hydrocyanic acid and salts thereof C 01; dyes C 09; macromolecular compounds C 08; fermentation products C 12).
- C 08 Macromolecular compounds, including their preparation and chemical working-up; Compositions based thereon (production of artificial threads, fibres, bristles and ribbons D 01).
- C 09 Dyes; Paints; Polishes; Natural resins; Adhesives; Miscellaneous substances and compositions.
- C 10 Fuels; Lubricants; Bitumen.
- C 11 Animal and vegetable oils, fats, fatty substances and waxes; Fatty acids therefrom; Detergents; Candles.
- C 12 Fermentation industry; Beer; Spirits; Wine; Vinegar; Yeast.
- C 13 Sugars; Starches; Like carbohydrates.
- C 14 Skins; Hides; Pelts; Leather.

Metallurgy

- C 21 Metallurgy of iron.
- C 22 Metallurgy (non-ferrous); Alloys, including ferrous alloys.

C 23 Working and treatment of metals, other than by mechanical means.

Section D.—Textiles and paper

CLASSES

Textiles

D 01 Natural and artificial threads and fibres (glass fibres, mineral wool, slag wool C 03; metal threads B 21).
D 02 Spinning.
D 03 Weaving.
D 04 Braiding; Lace-making; Machine knitting; Trimmings; Non-woven fabrics.
D 05 Sewing; Embroidery.
D 06 Bleaching, washing, dyeing, finishing and printing of textiles; Dyeing and bleaching of leather; Bed feathers; Wallpaper; Floor coverings.
D 07 Ropes; Cables (non-electric).

Paper

D 21 Paper making; Production of cellulose.

Section E.—Fixed constructions

CLASSES

Building

E 01 Construction of roads, railways and bridges.
E 02 Hydraulic engineering; Foundations.
E 03 Water supply; Sewerage.
E 04 Building.
E 05 Locks; Keys; Window and door fittings; Safes.

Mining

E 21 Mining.

Section F.—Mechanics, lighting and heating

CLASSES

Engines

F 01 Steam engines; Steam accumulators.
F 02 Internal combustion engines; Air and special vapour engines; Spring and weight motors.
F 03 Wind and water motors.
F 04 Compressors; Blowers; Air pumps.
F 05 Pumps; Other apparatus for lifting liquids.
F 06 Engineering elements and units; General measures for producing and maintaining effective functioning of machines or installations.
F 07 Arms; Ammunition.

Lighting and Heating

F 21 Lighting; Distribution and utilisation of gas.
F 22 Steam generation.
F 23 Furnaces and related features.
F 24 Heating and ventilating plants in buildings.
F 25 Refrigeration; Manufacture and storage of ice; Heat exchange; Liquefying gases not readily condensed by mechanical means.
F 26 Drying; Drying plants; Kilns; Coffee roasters.

Section G.—Physics

CLASSES

Instruments

G 01 Measuring.
G 02 Optics.
G 03 Photography; Cinematography.
G 04 Horology.
G 05 Regulating; Controlling.
G 06 Calculating; Accounting.
G 07 Checking devices.
G 08 Signalling.
G 09 Education; Advertising.
G 10 Musical instruments; Acoustics.

Nucleonics

G 21 Nucleonics.

Section H.—Electricity

CLASSES

Electricity

H 01 Electrotechnical elements.
H 02 Generation, conversion and distribution of electric power.
H 03 Electric oscillation and pulse technique.
H 04 Electric communication technique.
H 05 Special electrical techniques.

DIVISION OF THE CLASSES

A 01—*Agriculture; Forestry; Animal husbandry; Hunting; Trapping; Fishing.*

b Soil working (making and/or covering furrows or holes for sowing, planting, or manuring A 01 c).
c Planting; Sowing, Fertilising (combined with general working of soil A 01 b).
d Harvesting.
f Processing of harvested produce; Hay and straw presses; Devices for storing fruit; Machines for peeling and cutting vegetables and fruit in bulk.
g Culture of vegetables, flowers, fruit, vines, and hops; Forestry; Watering; Spraying.
h New plants.
j Manufacture of dairy products (mechanical part).
k Breeding animals; Aquaria; Installations for transporting live fish; Fishing.
l Shoeing of animals.
m Catching and trapping of animals; Apparatus for the destruction of noxious animals and noxious plants.
n Preservation of, and preserved, animals and plants; Chemical treatment of soil; Destruction of noxious animals and noxious plants (chemical).

A 21—*Baking; Edible doughs*

b Ovens; Machines and equipment for baking.
c Machines and equipment for making and processing doughs.
d Processes for preparing dough; Baking; Baking powders; Baking aids; Biscuits; Pastry.

A 22—*Butchering; Meat treatment*

b Slaughtering.
c Processing of meat (preserving A 23 b); Meat products.

A 23—*Foodstuffs and their treatment, not included in other classes*

b Preserving and canning of, and preserved and canned meat, fish, eggs, fruit, vegetables, flour and bread.
c Milk; Milk products; Manufacturing, pasteurising, sterilising and preserving same (chemical part).
d Artificial butter; Edible oils and fats (obtaining, refining and preserving C 11).
f Coffee; Tea; Their substitutes; Manufacture, preparation and infusion thereof.
g Cocoa; Chocolate; Confectionery; Ice cream.
h Other non-alcoholic beverages.
j Proteins; Concentrated foods.
k Fodder; Apparatus for preparing same.
l Preparation and preservation of foodstuffs, and prepared and preserved foodstuffs not otherwise included (cutting and peeling A 47 j, A 01 f).
m Vessels for cooking and preserving foodstuffs (domestic apparatus A 47 j).

A 24—*Tobacco; Cigars; Cigarettes; Smokers' requisites*

b Manufacture and preparation of tobacco for smoking and chewing; Tobacco; Snuff.
c Machines for making cigars and cigarettes.
d Cigars; Cigarettes.
f Smokers' requisites; Lighters.

A 41—*Wearing apparel*

b Underwear.
c Corsets.
d Outerwear; Accessories.
f Garment fastenings; Suspenders.
g Artificial flowers and feathers; Wigs; Masks.
h Appliances for the tailoring trade (sewing machines D 05 b).

A 42—*Headwear*

b Hats; Head coverings.
c Manufacturing and trimming hats and other head coverings.

A 43—*Footwear*

b Footwear.
c Fastenings; Laces; Attachments; Spurs, etc.
d Machines; Tools; Equipment; Methods.

A 44—*Haberdashery; Jewellery*

b Buttons, pins, buckles, slide fasteners, etc.
c Jewellery, bracelets, etc.

A 45—*Hand and Travelling articles*

b Walking sticks; Umbrellas; Sunshades; Fans.
c Purses; Travelling bags and baskets; Suitcases.
d Toilet requisites.
f Travelling and camp equipment.

A 46—*Brushware*

b Brushes.
c Handles; Their attachments.
d Manufacture of brushes.

A 47—*Furniture; Household articles and appliances (ladders A 64)*

b Tables; Desks; Wardrobes; Cabinets; Drawers.
c Chairs; Sofas; Beds (upholstery in general B 68 g).
d Furniture specially adapted for children.
f Special furniture and fittings for shops, stores, offices, bars, etc.; Devices for drawing off and cutting paper from a roll.
g Household and table equipment (knives B 26 b).
h Furnishing for windows and doors (fittings E 05).
j Kitchen and other domestic appliances not included in A 47 g.
k Household toilets; Toilet fittings (connecting to water supply E 03 c; wash-basins connected to the wastepipe E 03 c; sinks E 03 c).
l Washing and cleaning the house or household articles (brushes A 46 b; laundry D 06 f).

A 61—*Medical and veterinary science; Hygiene*

b Instruments, implements and processes for diagnostic and surgical purposes, including obstetrics; Instruments for cutting corns; Vaccination instruments.
c Dentistry; Artificial teeth; Cleaning of teeth (toothbrushes A 46 b); Toothpicks; Apparatus for rinsing the mouth; Instruments for oral and dental hygiene.
d Veterinary instruments; implements and tools.
f Prosthesis (artificial teeth A 61 c); Splints; Bandages; Fomentation; Protection of the eyes and ears.
g Transport and accommodation for patients; Operating tables and chairs; Chairs for dentistry; Burial devices.
h Medical and respiratory gymnastics; Artificial respiration; Massage; Bath and washing devices for special purposes and specific parts of the body.
j Pharmaceutical appliances and implements; Devices for administering medicines; Feeding bottles and teats; Sputum flasks.
k Medicinal methods (non-surgical); Medicines; Dentistry (chemical part); Beauty preparations.
l Disinfection and sterilisation methods and apparatus; Material for dressings; Preservation of corpses.
m Suction, pumping, spraying and atomising devices for medical use (cups, breast relievers, irrigators, sprays, powder insufflators, atomisers, inhalers); Apparatus for local and general anaesthetics; Catheters; Dilators; Apparatus for introducing medicines into cavities of the body.

A 62—*Life-saving; Fire-fighting (ladders A 64)*

b Devices, apparatus and methods for life-saving (at sea B 63 c).
c Fire-fighting equipment.
d Fire-extinguishing preparations; Methods of fighting fire or poisonous gases by chemical means.

A 63—*Sports; Games; Amusements*

b Apparatus for physical training,

gymnastics, swimming, climbing and fencing; Ball games; Training equipment.
c Skates; Skis; Watershoes; Roller skates; Physical training wheels; Courts; Rinks.
d Bowling-alleys; Bagatelle; Billiards.
f Card games; Dice; Roulette; Patience; Horseracing; Similar games.
g Merry-go-rounds; Swings; Rocking-horses; Chutes; Switchbacks; similar devices for public amusement.
h Toys, *e.g.*, tops, dolls, hoops, building blocks.
j Devices for theatres, circuses, etc.; Conjuring appliances and the like.
k Race-tracks; Equipment and accessories therefor.

A 64—*Ladders (ship ladders B 63 b; ladders for aircraft B 64 d; scaffolding E 04 g)*

b Free movable ladders.
c Other ladders (construction of ladders in general A 64 b).

B 01—*Physical and chemical processes and apparatus (general)*

b Boiling; Boiling apparatus.
c Calcining; Fusing; Muffle furnaces for chemical purposes.
d Separation, *e.g.*, evaporation, distillation, crystallisation, filtration, absorption, adsorption; Separating apparatus (sifting B 02 f; centrifuges B 04).
f Mixing, *e.g.*, dissolving, emulsifying, dispersing.
g Solidifying.
h Siphons; Receptacles for acids; Feed devices; Feed and outlet regulating devices.
j Chemical and/or physical processes; Their relevant apparatus (catalysis, colloid chemistry).
k Electro-chemical processes and apparatus; Electrophoresis.

B 02—*Milling grain; Preparatory treatment of grain for milling; Crushing; Disintegrating; Pulverising; Sifting*

b Preparing grain for milling; Refining granular fruit to commercial products by working the surface (making dough from cereals direct A 21 c; preservation or sterilisation of cereals A 23 b; cleaning fruit A 01 f; preparation of malt C 12 c).
c Crushing, pulverising or like disintegrating in general; Milling grain; Dressing mill discs or rollers (working stone B 28 d).
d (Sub-class cancelled. Subject-matter transferred to B 02 c).
f Screening; Sifting; Sorting.
g (Sub-class cancelled. Subject-matter transferred to B 01 f).
h (Sub-class cancelled. Subject-matter transferred to B 01 d).

B 03—*Washing and separating of ores, fuels, garbage, ashes and slag*

b Washing and separating other than magnetic and electric separation and flotation.
c Magnetic and electric separation.
d Flotation; Differential sedimentation.

B 04—*Centrifuges*

b Centrifuges.
c Cyclones.

B 05—*Spraying and atomising in general; Spreading liquids on surfaces in general*

B 06—*Methods and apparatus for generating and/or transmitting mechanical vibrations of subsonic, sonic or supersonic frequency for performing mechanical work for general use (generation of electrical oscillations H 03 b)*

B 21—*Sheet metal; Metal tubes; Wire*

b Rolling of metal (manufacture of special objects by rolling, *e.g.*, screws, wheels, rings, barrels, balls, B 21 h; bending by rolling B 21 d).

c Manufacture of metal sheets, wire, rods, tubes and profiles otherwise than by rolling.

d Working and processing of sheet metal and metal tubes, rods and profiles (operations involved in the manufacture of such materials *per se* B 21 b, c).

f Working and processing of wire (reducing diameter by rolling B 21 b; by drawing B 21 c).

g Manufacture of pins, needles and nails.

h Manufacture of special objects by rolling, *e.g.*, screws, wheels, rings, barrels, balls.

Explanatory note:

This sub-class includes only rolling operations which are specially adapted for use in the manufacture of particular objects and which, so far as the invention is concerned, are not combined with any separate metal-working operation.

B 22—*Metal casting*

b Smelting and other furnaces.

c Moulding machines for moulds and cores.

d Casting and moulding in general.

B 23—*Mechanical working of metal; Working of other materials by the same machines*

b Turning; Boring.

c Milling.

d Planing; Slotting; Shearing; Punching; Broaching; Sawing; Filing; Scraping; Sorting; Feeding.

f Manufacture of gears and toothed racks.

g Thread cutting; Working of screws, bolt heads and nuts.

h Making files and rasps.

j Hammers; Forging presses; Riveting machines.

k Forging; Pressing; Bending; Soldering; Welding; Flame-cutting; Furnaces relating thereto.

l Manufacture of forged and pressed products, *e.g.*, horse-shoes, rivets, bolts, wheels and the like.

m Manufacture of chains.

n Metallic powder; Articles made therefrom.

p Other working of metal; Combined operations; Universal machine tools.

B 24—*Grinding; Polishing*

b Machines, devices and methods for grinding and polishing different articles, surfaces and substances; Truing of grinding stones; Safety devices for grinding and polishing machines; Feeding of grinding agents.

c Sandblasting devices.

d Grinding tools, *e.g.*, grinding and polishing discs and knife sharpeners; Manufacture of grinding agents.

B 25—*Hand tools; Pneumatic tools*

b Tools for fastening or connecting, disengaging and holding; Vices.

c Nailing and stapling tools.

d Hammers; Picks.

f Combined or universal tools.

g Handles for tools; Tool boxes.

h Work benches.

B 26—*Hand cutting tools and thrusting weapons; Cutting machines and devices not specially adapted for particular materials or purposes*

b Cutting tools.

c Thrusting weapons.

d Cutting and perforating machines or devices so far as they are not specially adapted for materials or purposes fully provided for in one other class.

B 27—*Working and preserving wood and similar material*

b Saws.

c Planing, drilling, milling, turning and universal machines.

d Working of veneer; Grinding; Polishing; Manufacture of frames and mitres.

f Dovetailed work; Tenons, Slotting machines; Nailing and stapling machines (hand nailing and stapling tools B 25 c); Manufacture of cases, trunks and boxes.

g Accessory machines and apparatus; Tools; Safety devices, including those for saws.
h Bending; Cooperage; Wheelmaking.
j Mechanical working of cane, cork and similar materials.
k Methods and apparatus for impregnating (with or without drying), including preserving, fireproofing, staining and dyeing.
l Removing bark; Manufacture of veneer, wood shavings and wood fibre.
m Methods and machines for special purposes, *e.g.*, manufacture of shingles, compressed wood, dowels.
n (Sub-class cancelled. Subject-matter transferred to B 29 and C 08).

B 28—*Working cement, clay and stone; Clay and briquette presses*

b Pressing briquettes, clay and similar materials.
c Working cement and clay.
d Working stone.

B 29—*Working (mechanical part) plastic materials, rubber and horn-like substances not otherwise provided for*

b Preparation and pre-treatment of the material to be shaped.
c Shaping in general, *e.g.*, moulding, bending, cutting, joining.
d Processes and apparatus to produce special articles.
f Processes and apparatus specially adapted for thermoplastic substances.
g Processes and apparatus specially adapted for thermosetting substances.
h Processes and apparatus specially adapted for natural and synthetic rubbers.
j Processes and apparatus specially adapted for materials not provided for above, *e.g.*, horn, ivory, sulphur.

B 30—*Presses*

b Fluid-operated presses.
c Mechanical presses.

B 31—*Making paper articles; Working paper*

b Making boxes, cartons, envelopes and bags.
c Making wound articles, *e.g.*, tubes.
d Making other paper articles.
f Auxiliary equipment; Cutting; Trimming.

B 41—*Printing; Lining machines; Typewriters; Stamps*

b Machines and accessories for making, setting and distributing type; Type.
c Processes for the manufacture and reproduction of printing surfaces (except photomechanical or photoelectrical).
d Apparatus for reproducing printing surfaces (except galvanoplastic).
f High-speed cylinder presses; Rotary machines; Office printing machines and platen presses; Printing methods in so far as they relate to the use of special machines.
g Auxiliary equipment and apparatus for folding, perforating, bronzing and edging.
h Lining machines.
j Typewriters and accessories.
k Stamps; Stamping and numbering devices.
l Manifolding devices.
m Printing, duplicating and copying methods; Colour printing (printing textiles D 06 q).
n Printing plates and foils; Materials for surfaces used in printing machines for printing, inking, damping, or the like; Preparing such surfaces for use and conserving them.

B 42—*Bookbinding; Albums; Files; Special printed matter*

b Stitching methods, tools and equipment (hand stapling tools B 25 c).
c Bookbinding methods, tools and equipment, including tools with cutting elements.
d Books; Book covers; Loose leaves; Postcards; Forms.

f Apparatus and devices for filing and classifying, *e.g.*, card indexes.

B 43—*Writing and drawing appliances*

b Pencils; Styles; Chalks; Pencil or chalk holders; Attaching writing appliances to wearing apparel or objects; Combinations of writing appliances.

c Nibs; Nib holders; Pens; Reservoir pens; Pen caps; Filling devices; Devices for removing or wiping nibs (combinations of writing appliances, including multicolour and other multiple pens, B 43 b).

d Ink receptacles; Ink stands.

f Blotters; Fixing seals on documents; Supports for attachment to hands or arms for facilitating writing and drawing; Devices for inserting documents into envelopes; Devices for opening or closing envelopes; Paperweights; Hand or desk devices of the office or personal type for applying liquid by contact to surfaces.

g Repeatedly-usable boards or tablets for writing or drawing; Blackboard or slate cleaning devices; Erasers, rubbers or erasing devices; Writing or drawing underlays; Drawing-pins; Writing or drawing appliance receptacles functioning as or combined with writing or drawing appliances; Sharpeners for pencils or leads.

h Drawing boards; Rulers; Curve-drawing instruments; Continuously-adjustable nibs; Drawing instruments or writing or drawing appliances, *e.g.*, pantographic, not otherwise provided for; Drawing accessories.

B 44—*Sculpture; Painting; Decorative art*

b Machines, apparatus and tools for sculpturing, modelling, copying, engraving, guilloching, carving and embossing (embossing leather C 14 b).

c Processes for the production of decorations; Mosaics; Tarsia work.

d Painting; Decorating; Paint and metal sprayers.

f Special designs and pictures.

B 61—*Railways*

b Various railway systems (atmospheric, pneumatic, sliding, platform, rack, elevated, aerial, rope and transport railways, underground railways and town tramways), including equipment in so far as this equipment does not come under B 61 c to f.

c Locomotives; Motors; Railcars (non-electric devices thereof, also non-electric devices of electric locomotives).

d Cars; Lorries; Trolleys; Velocipede trolleys (railroad velocipedes); Railway furniture; Buffer cars as a safety device in case of collisions.

f Underframe (understructure); Axles; Devices for the adjustment of axles; Journal bearings; Wheels; Supporting axles; Safety devices.

g Couplings; Draught and buffing appliances.

h Brakes, in so far as they are fitted in the cars; Electrically-operated air brakes.

j Traversers; Turn-tables; Water cranes (columns); Buffer stops; Shunting devices; Cars for transporting cars; Means for transferring passengers to and from trains; Shifting devices and the like.

k Auxiliary equipment for railways (devices to indicate the overheating of components, devices on locomotives and cars to indicate bad sections in the track, measuring devices for wheel rims, car moving devices, energy storing brakes, track brakes, stop blocks, apparatus for placing cars on the track and taking them off the track, car haulage apparatus, devices for washing cars, mailbag catchers, etc.).

l Points (switches except trolley wire switches); Gates for railway crossings; Signals (including station indicators); All types of safety measures for railway traffic.

m Electric railways (in so far as they do not come under the construction of railways in general); Devices on rails and rail joints for carrying current and for insulation; Overhead and underground trolley wires or contact lines; Section line systems; Safety devices against earth currents; Erecting and scaffold cars (construction of electric insulators other than section insulators H 01 b).

n Electrical equipment for railways; Electric or mixed electric (with other sources of energy) systems of rail transport; Power pick-up devices; Motors, including the control of the motors for individual cars or entire train units; Dynamic braking; Electric or mixed electric brakes.

B 62—*Rail-less vehicles*

b Hand carts; Perambulators; Sledges.

c Vehicles drawn by animals.

d Motor vehicles (undercarriages, driving mechanisms, attachment of the engine, steering devices, etc.); Trucks; Trailers.

f Wheels, axles and axle bearings for vehicles and bicycles.

g Tyres, air pumps and valves for motor cars, bicycles and other vehicles.

h Bicycle stands; Devices for hanging up bicycles; Bicycle locks; Devices for learning to ride.

j Bicycle saddles and other accessories (alarm and signal devices, if they form part of the construction of the bicycle, luggage carriers, chain-guards, mudguards).

k Bicycle frames; Tube connections; Handlebars; Steering devices; Chainguards (as part of the frame).

l Brakes for bicycles.

m The propulsion of cycles (one and two-wheeled) and sledges by the driver and by engines, as well as of vehicles with three or more wheels by the driver.

B 63—*Ships; Shipbuilding; Shipping*

b Shipbuilding; Ships; Equipment and shipping (rigging, signalling and buoys); Ship's furniture and closets; Apparatus for observing and measuring the rolling, resistance and movement of ships; Submarines; Towing; Diving apparatus; Subduing of waves.

c Devices on slip-ways and in dry-docks; Launching and hauling out devices for building and repairing ships; Floating docks; Salvage vessels; Life-saving at sea; Life belts and jackets.

d Boats and other vessels, including vessels driven by human or animal power.

f Torpedoes; Mines.

g Armouring and armament of ships.

h Marine propulsion (paddle wheels, propellors and other propulsion devices); arrangement of propulsion plant.

j Auxiliary machines.

B 64—*Aircraft; Aviation; Astronautics*

b Airships; Balloons.

c Aeroplanes; Helicopters; Air-cushion vehicles.

d Equipment for aircraft; Arrangement of propulsion plant.

f Ground installations, *e.g.*, lay-outs for airfields and beacons.

g Vehicles and equipment for astronautics.

B 65—*Conveying; Packing; Storing*

b Machines, implements and methods for packing (nailing and stapling tools B 25 c).

c Labelling machines and apparatus.

d Packings, containers and accessories, *e.g.*, cases, crates, barrels, bags, mail boxes, hose reels and racks, wrappers, cartons, packing material, holders for articles, loose binding means and fastening seals.

f Removal of refuse.

g Transport of storage devices, *e.g.*, conveyors for loading and tipping (truck loaders B 66 f), tanks, means for preventing spontaneous combustion in storage depots, shop conveyor systems, pneumatic tube conveyors, postal sorting and distributing.

B 66—*Hoisting* (*lifting devices*)

b Elevators.

c Cranes.

d Capstans; Winches; Tackles (pulley blocks and hoists).

f Lifting devices, *e.g.*, truck loaders, rack and pinion jacks, devices for lifting sacks, lifting loads, lifting and pushing by means of hydraulic or pneumatic power.

B 67—*Liquid handling*

b Receptacles; Tins; Bottles; Closure and opening devices for same; Stoppers; Preserving cans; Drink registers; Mats for beer glasses; Corkscrews; Tin openers.

c Cleaning, filling and emptying of bottles, glasses and tubes.

d Beer pumps; Devices for drawing up for retail sales; Syphons; Valves and the like.

B 68—*Saddlery; Upholstery*

b Harness; Devices to prevent animals from bolting, and for rapid harnessing, for training and tethering horses and other traction animals; Rein holders; Horse protectors; Whips and the like.

c Saddles; Stirrups.

d Equipment and machines for saddle making.

f Making leather, canvas and like articles.

g Methods, equipment and machines for use in upholstering; Upholstery not otherwise provided for.

C 01—*Inorganic chemistry*

b Non-metallic elements, metalloids and their compounds, except those mentioned under C 01 c (arsenic, antimony C 22 b).

c Ammonia and cyanogen and their compounds (C 01 b takes precedence in respect of salts of oxyacids of halogens, peroxides, persalts, azides, imido and amido compounds other than cyanamide and its salts, nitrites, phosphides, salts of oxyacids of phosphorus, silicates, compounds containing selenium, tellurium, arsenic, antimony or boron).

d Compounds of alkali metals (lithium, sodium, potassium, (rubidium, caesium). (C 01 f and C 01 g take precedence; metal hydrides, salts of oxyacids of halogens, salts of peracids, metal peroxides, sulphides, thiosulphates, hyposulphites, polythionates, compounds containing selenium or tellurium, nitrides, azides, imido or amido compounds, nitrites, phosphides, salts of oxyacids of phosphorus, carbides, compounds containing arsenic, antimony, silicon or boron C 01 b; cyanides, salts of cyanamide, thiocyanates C 01 c).

f Compounds of the metals beryllium, magnesium, aluminium, calcium, strontium, barium, radium, thorium, and of the rare earth metals (metal hydrides, salts of oxyacids of halogens, salts of peracids, metal peroxides, sulphides of magnesium, calcium, strontium or barium, thiosulphates, hyposulphites, polythionates, compounds containing selenium or tellurium, nitrides, azides, imido or amido compounds, nitrites, phosphides, carbides, salts of oxyacids of phosphorus, compounds containing arsenic, antimony, silicon or boron C 01 b; Cyanides, salts of cyanamide, thiocyanates C 01 c).

Explanatory note:

Compounds containing at least two different metals are classified in the last appropriate place in C 01 f or g.

g Compounds of metals not provided for above (metal hydrides, salts of oxyacids of halogens, salts of peracids, metal peroxides, thiosulphates, hyposulphites, polythionates, compounds containing selenium or tellurium, nitrides, azides, imido or amido compounds, nitrites, phosphides, salts of oxyacids of phosphorus, carbides, compounds containing arsenic, antimony, silicon or boron C 01 b; Cyanides, salts of cyanamide, thiocyanates C 01 c).

C 02—*Water; Treating water, waste water and sewage* (*distilling, filtering, separating B 01*)

b Treatment of water, including apparatus, processes and the use of reagents; Agents for preventing and removing scale (adding materials to water to prevent corrosion of metals C 23 f).

c Treatment of sewage and waste water (C 02 b takes precedence).

d Water impregnated with carbon dioxide (soda water) or other gases.

C 03—*Glass; Mineral and slag wool*

b Manufacture, shaping and supplementary processes.

c Chemical composition of glasses, glazes or vitreous enamels; Surface treatment of glass; Joining glass to glass or other materials.

C 04—*Cements; Mortars; Ceramics; Artificial stone; Treatment of stone* (*chemical part*); *Sound and/or thermal insulating materials* (*chemical part*); *Kilns*

b Cements; Mortars; Refractories; Ceramics; Glazing thereof; Artificial stone; Preserving, colouring, hardening and other treatment of natural and artificial stone and of the starting materials therefor; Sound and/or thermal insulating materials.

c Kilns for baking, glazing, annealing or burning of bricks, earthenware, porcelain and the like; Kilns for the baking of bricks, burning of cement, lime, gypsum and the like; Drying kilns if they form a single unit with the baking kiln.

C 05—*Manufacture of fertilisers*

Explanatory note:

An ingredient in a mixture of fertilisers, or a single fertiliser which contains more than one of the chemical elements on which the division into sub-classes is based, is classified only in the first of the appropriate sub-classes. Thus a nitrophosphate or an ammoniated superphosphate is classified in C 05 b but not in C 05 c, magnesium phosphate is classified in C 05 b but not in C 05 d, and calcium cyanamide in C 05 c but not in C 05 d. A mixture of fertilisers is classified in the places appropriate to each of the ingredients, insignificant amounts, *e.g.*, of impurities in an ingredient, being disregarded. Mixtures containing superphosphates are classified in C 05 b and in the places appropriate to the other ingredients.

b Phosphatic fertilisers.

c Nitrogenous fertilisers.

d Other inorganic fertilisers; Fertilisers producing carbon dioxide.

f Other organic fertilisers, including fertilisers from waste or refuse.

C 06—*Explosives; Matches*

b Explosives; Manufacture of explosive compositions and compounds of indefinite structure (pure compounds C 01, C 07, or C 08; Detonating or priming compositions C 06 c).

c Ignition devices and compositions (including detonators, ignition pills and pneumatic igniters); Percussion caps; Fuses; Explosive charges; Methods of blasting; Pyrophoric compositions.

d Fireworks; compositions therefor; Means for generating smoke or mist; Fulminating parts of flashlights; Gas-attack compositions; Generation of gas for blasting or propulsion (chemical part) (fuels C 10).

f Matches; Manufacture of matches.

C 07—*Organic chemistry (such compounds as the oxides, sulphides and oxysulphides of carbon, cyanogen, phosgene, hydrocyanic acid and salts thereof C 01; Dyes C 09; Macromolecular compounds C 08; Fermentation products C 12)*

Explanatory note:

Salts of a compound, unless specially provided for, are classified as that compound, *e.g.*, aniline hydrochloride is classified as containing C, H and N only, sodium oxalate is classified as oxalic acid, and a mercaptide is classified as the mercaptan. Similarly alcoholates and phenates are classified in C 07 c and not in C 07 f. In the absence of a reference to the contrary, a compound is always classified in the last appropriate place in the classification, *e.g.*, a compound containing an acyclic chain and a hetero-cyclic ring is classified only as a heterocyclic compound, and a sterol is classified only as cyclopentanophenanthrene compound. Where a compound exists in tautomeric forms, it is classified according to the form which appears last in the system, unless another form is specifically mentioned earlier.

Albumens, proteins, alkaloids of unknown structure, glucosides of unknown structure are examples of compounds to be found under C 07 g.

b General methods and apparatus of organic chemistry.

c Acyclic and carbocyclic compounds.

d Hetero-cyclic compounds.

f Acyclic, carbocyclic and heterocyclic compounds containing, outside any ring, elements other than hydrogen, halogen, oxygen, nitrogen, sulphur, selenium and tellurium, with or without the latter specified elements (acetylides C 07 c; metal-containing porphyrins C 07 d).

g Compounds of unknown constitution.

C 08—*Macromolecular compounds, including their preparation and chemical working-up; Compositions based thereon (production of artificial threads, fibres, bristles and ribbons D 01)*

b Polysaccharides and their derivatives (production of cellulose D 21; Production of starch, sugar and like carbohydrates C 13; Paints, lacquers C 09 d; Textile-treating compositions D 06; Lubricating compositions C 10 m; Explosive compositions C 06).

c Natural rubbers and their derivatives.

d Synthetic rubbers.

Explanatory note:

For the purpose of this classification system the term "synthetic rubbers" is restricted to rubbery vulcanisable products obtained by the polymerisation of a conjugated diene, if desired together with one or more other unsaturated monomers. Thus polyisobutylene, which is not vulcanisable, will not be found here but in C 08 f, and silicone rubbers, polyalkylene polysulphides and isocyanate-modified polyamides will be found in C 08 g, factice in C 08 h, and liquid polymers of conjugated dienes in C 08 f.

f Polymerisation products, excluding synthetic rubbers, but including polymerised unsaturated condensation products (polymerised drying oil C 09 f).

g Polycondensation and polyaddition (two groups reacting) products.

h Macromolecular compounds not otherwise provided for; Compositions based thereon.

j General methods for preparing and working up.

k Additives for general use.

C 09—*Dyes; Paints; Polishes; Natural resins; Adhesives; Miscellaneous substances and compositions*

b Organic dyes and closely related compounds for producing dyes; Mordants; Lakes.

c Preparation of inorganic pigments and/or fillers not in fibrous form; Treatment of materials not in fibrous form to enhance their pigmenting or filling properties.

d Inks; Paints; Varnishes; Lacquers; Chemical paint removers; Pastes and solids for colouring and printing.

f Natural resins; French polish; Drying oils; Driers (siccatives); Turpentine.

g Polishing compositions other than French polish; Ski waxes.

h Preparation of glue.

j Adhesives other than glue; Adhesive processes in general.

Explanatory note:

Organic macromolecular adhesive substances or compositions based essentially thereon are always classified with the substance or composition in C 08, but the use of substances or compositions for adhesive purposes is classified here.

k Miscellaneous substances and compositions.

C 10—*Fuels; Lubricants; Bitumen*

b Destructive distillation of carbonaceous materials for production of gas, coke, tar and similar materials (cracking oils C 10 g).

c Tar and working tar; Pyroligneous acid.

d Briquettes; Fire-lighters; Solidifying fluid fuels; Solid fuels and the improving thereof.

f Cutting, drying and working-up of peat.

g Transformation, *e.g.*, cracking, destructive hydrogenation, polymerising, isomerising, reforming, cracking and polymerising, of hydrocarbons, carbonaceous material and other carbon containing substances including bitumen and waxes, to give indefinite mixtures of gaseous, liquid or solid hydrocarbons, other than C 10 b; Extracting (winning) oils and fractions (mixtures only) from hydrocarbon bearing substances, including natural products and the aforesaid transformation products; Refining and blending of hydrocarbon fuels; Mineral waxes and the blended products.

h Production of acetylene by wet methods; Its purification.

j Production of water-gas, air-gas, producer gas, and their mixtures.

k Purifying coal gas, water-gas, air-gas, and producer gas.

l Fuels not otherwise provided for.

m Lubricants; Mineral oil dispersions.

C 11—*Animal and vegetable oils, fats, fatty substances and waxes; Fatty acids therefrom; Detergents; Candles*

b Production (pressing, extraction), refining and preserving fats, fatty substances (*e.g.*, lanolin), fatty oils and waxes, including extraction from waste materials; Essential oils; Perfumes (drying oils C 09 f).

c Fatty acids from fats, oils and waxes; Candles; Fats, oils and fatty acids by chemical modification of fats, oils, or fatty acids obtained therefrom.

d Detergents in general; Soap and soap making (including resin soap for paper sizing); Glycerol.

C 12—*Fermentation industry; Beer; Spirits; Wine; Vinegar; Yeast*

b Fermentation processes, apparatus, media and starting materials of general use.

c Malt; Wort; Hops; Ethanolic fermentation (ethanol, beer, yeast).

d Production of chemical substances, other than ethanol, by microbiological processes, *e.g.*, fermentation, biosynthesis.

f Distillation and rectification of fermented solutions; Recovery of by-products; Denaturing of, and denatured alcohol.
g Wine; Other alcoholic beverages (except beer); Preparation thereof.
h Pasteurisation; Sterilisation; Preservation; Purification; Clarification; Ageing.
j Vinegar; Its preparation.
k Methods and apparatus for microbiological research; Isolation, identification and preparation of micro-organisms, including viruses; Microbiological materials and apparatus.
l Cleaning of casks; Pitching and depitching machines; Cask burners; Brewing devices; Cellar tools.

C 13—*Sugars; Starches; Like carbohydrates*

b Washing raw materials before extracting sugar, starch, or like carbohydrate (storing agricultural produce on the farm A 01 f; away from the farm B 65 g).
c Cutting mills; Shredding knives; Pulp presses.
d Production and purification of sugar juices.
f Preparation and processing of raw sugar, sugar and syrup.
g Evaporation apparatus; Boiling pans.
h Cutting machines for sugar; Combined cutting, sorting and packing machines for sugar.
j Extraction of sugar from molasses.
k Glucose; Invert sugar; Lactose; Maltose; Other sugars (chemical synthesis of sugars C 07 c).
l Starch; Dextrine; Similar carbohydrates (biological synthesis of starch or dextran C 12; compositions based on starch or its derivatives or its degradation products, *e.g.*, dextrine, C 08 b).

C 14—*Skins; Hides; Pelts; Leather*

b Mechanical treatment and processing of skins, hides and leather in general; Pelt-shearing machines; Manufacture of driving belts; Intestine-splitting machines; Devices for the manufacture of leather.
c Chemical treatment of hides, skins and leather, *e.g.*, tanning, impregnating, finishing; Apparatus therefor; Compositions for tanning (dyeing and bleaching of leather and furs D 06).

C 21—*Metallurgy of iron*

b Manufacture of iron and steel, including the pre-treatment of ores, production of pig-iron, direct process, blast furnaces and air heaters.
c Processing of pig-iron (refining, manufacture of wrought iron and steel).
d Hardening and annealing of steel and iron (also of objects such as tools and the like); Making malleable by decarburisation, tempering, and other treatments (cementation by diffusion processes C 23 c).

C 22—*Metallurgy (non-ferrous); Alloys including ferrous alloys*

b Production and refining of metals other than C 22 d; Pre-treatment of ores; Processing of slag (slagwool C 03).
c Alloys; Ferrous alloys.
d Electrolytic and electrothermic production and refining of metals.
f Changing of physical structure of metals and alloys other than of iron and steel.

C 23—*Working and treatment of metals, other than by mechanical means*

b Electrolytic surface treatment (electroplating); Electro-forming; Coating by electro-phoresis.
c Apparatus and processes for which provision is not made elsewhere for covering materials with metals; Diffusion processes for surface treatment of metals.
d Enamelling of and applying a vitreous layer to metals (chemical composition of the enamels C 03 c).

f Chemical surface treatment not included in C 23 b–d; Inhibiting corrosion of metals by means not otherwise provided for (painting B 44; by softening and purifying water C 02).
g Cleaning and de-greasing of metallic objects by chemical methods other than electrolytic (detergents in general C 11 d; polishing compositions C 09 g).

D 01—*Natural and artificial threads and fibres (glass fibres, mineral wool, slag wool C 03; Metal threads B 21)*

b Mechanical treatment of natural fibrous material to obtain fibres for spinning.
c Chemical treatment of natural fibrous material to obtain fibres for spinning; Carbonising.
d Mechanical methods and apparatus in the manufacture of artificial threads, fibres, bristles and ribbons.
f Chemical features in the manufacture of artificial threads, fibres, bristles and ribbons.

D 02—*Spinning*

b (Sub-class cancelled. Subject-matter transferred to D 01 b).
c Preliminary treatment of spinning fibres.
d Fine spinning and twisting; Yarns.
f Winding, making up and packing of yarns.

D 03—*Weaving*

b Machines for the preparatory stages.
c Devices for forming the shed (shaft and Jacquard machines).
d Weaving without pile; Non-pile fabrics.
f Weaving pile fabrics; Velvet; Plush; Chenille.
g Cane, straw and slat weaving.
h Wire weaving.
j Tools; Implements.
k Accessory machines used in weaving (crossing the warp threads, twisting in, tying on and looming warp threads, pattern and card making).

D 04—*Braiding; Lace making; Machine knitting; Trimmings; Non-woven fabrics*

b Knitting, including machine knitting.
c Braiding and manufacture of lace, including bobbinet or carbonised lace; Braiding machines.
d Trimmings.
f Tapestry (carpet making and the like).
g Net-making (wire netting B 21 f).
h Felts.
j Other non-woven fabrics.

D 05—*Sewing; Embroidery*

b Sewing.
c Embroidery.

D 06—*Bleaching, washing, dyeing, finishing and printing of textiles; Dyeing and bleaching of leather; Bed feathers; Wallpaper and floor coverings*

Note.—The words " (mechanical part) " or " (chemical part) " refer to the whole of the sub-class title in each case.

b Bleaching, dyeing, mercerising, impregnating, washing of spinning fibres, yarns, fabrics and other textiles; Fulling of fabrics and the like; Dyeing and bleaching of leather (mechanical part).
c Refining and decorating of yarns, fabrics and knitted materials (mechanical part).
d Printing of yarns, fabrics, knitted materials, floor coverings and wall coverings (mechanical part).
f Laundry, including finishing (mechanical part).
g Cleaning sacks; Machines for cleaning and conditioning bed feathers; Preparation of bed feathers.
h Folding, laying, doubling, measuring, winding, cutting, making-up, packing of yarns, woven fabrics, etc. (mechanical part).
j Pleating, Ruching.
k Floor and wall coverings, *e.g.*, linoleum, lincrusta, oil cloth,

leather-cloth, wallpaper (mechanical part).

l Bleaching, including optical bleaching, dry-cleaning and washing fibres, threads, yarns, fabrics, feathers or made-up fibrous goods; Bleaching leather or furs (chemical part) (chemical treatment of fibrous material to obtain fibres for spinning D 01; treatment of threads or fibres of glass, mineral wool or slag wool C 03; bleaching paper, pulp or cotton linters D 21).

m Treatment, not otherwise provided for, of fibres, threads, yarns, fabrics, feathers, or fibrous goods made from such materials (chemical part).

n Wall, floor and like covering materials, *e.g.*, linoleum, oilcloth, artificial leather, roofing felt, consisting of a fibrous web coated with a layer of macromolecular material (chemical part).

p Dyeing and printing textiles; Dyeing leather, furs or solid macromolecular substances in any form (chemical part) (dyeing paper D 21; dyeing glass fibres C 03 c; mordanting D 06 m; printing on surfaces of materials other than textiles B 41 m).

q Decorating textiles (chemical part) (dyeing and printing D 06 p).

r (Sub-class cancelled. Subject-matter transferred to D 06 m).

D 07—*Ropes; Cables (non-electric)*

D 21—*Paper making; Production of cellulose*

b Fibrous raw materials and their mechanical treatment.

c Production of cellulose by removing non-cellulosic substances from cellulose-containing materials; Regeneration of pulping liquors; Apparatus therefor.

d Treatment of the digested materials before passing to the paper-making machine; Addition of substances to the formed web on the paper-making machine.

f Paper-making machines; Methods of producing paper on them.

g Accessories for paper-making machines.

h Cardboard; Paper; Their manufacture other than D 21 f.

j Manufacture of articles from cellulosic fibrous suspensions; papier-mâché.

E 01—*Constructions of roads, railways and bridges*

b Permanent way; Permanent way tools; Machines for making railways of all kinds.

c Construction of and surfaces for roads, sports grounds, etc.; Machines and auxiliary tools for construction and repair.

d Construction of bridges and viaducts; Assembly of bridges.

f Additional work, such as equipping roads and the construction of platforms, signs, snow fences, etc.

g Construction of tunnels.

h Street cleaning; Cleaning of permanent ways.

E 02—*Hydraulic engineering; Foundations*

b Hydraulic engineering, *e.g.*, correction of streams, coast protection, weirs, dykes, dams, harbour and marine engineering, canals, water gratings, reclamation.

c Ship-lifting devices and mechanisms.

d Foundations.

f Dredging; Soil-shifting (winning peat C 10 f).

E 03—*Water supply; Sewerage*

b Installations and methods for obtaining, collecting and distributing water.

c Domestic water installations.

d Water-closets and urinals with flushing and disinfecting devices, including the valves of same.

f Sewers; Ventilation and emptying of cesspools.

E 04—*Building*

b General building constructions; Walls; Roofs; Ceilings; Insulation and other protection of buildings (border constructions of openings for doors, windows or the like E 04 f).

c Structural elements; Building materials (for insulation E 04 b; elements used as building aids E 04 g; for bridges E 01 d; for tunnels E 01 g; for mining E 21; structural elements with broader range of application than for building engineering F 06).

d Roof coverings; Dormer windows; Skylights; Gutters; Roof-working tools.

Explanatory note:

This sub-class includes not only roof coverings but as well any similar kind of water-tight covering against rain, snow, hail, etc., for other parts of buildings (coverings of outer walls by plaster or other porous material E 04 f).

f Finishing work on building, *e.g.*, stairs, floors, windows, doors.

g Scaffolding; Forms; Shuttering; Building implements and other building aids and their use; Handling building materials on the site; Repairing, breaking up and other work on existing buildings.

Explanatory note:

In this sub-class the word "scaffolding" includes other supports for like purposes.

h Special types of buildings (foundations E 02 d).

E 05—*Locks; Keys; Window and door fittings; Safes*

b Locks and accessories; Keyless locks; Handcuffs.

c Bolts and fastening devices, specially for doors and windows.

d Hinges and other suspension devices for doors and windows.

f Door and window closers, checks, furniture, etc.

g Safes; Safe hinges.

E 21—*Mining*

b Deep-drilling.

c Machinery for, and methods of, mining and quarrying.

d Shafts; Sinking shafts; Galleries; Lining galleries.

f Ventilation; Safety devices; Transport; Filling up; Rescue.

F 01—*Steam engines; Steam accumulators*

b Reciprocating piston engines.

c Rotary or oscillating piston engines.

d Steam and air turbines; Details common to turbines in general.

f Distributing and expansion slide and piston valve-gear.

g Distributing and expansion rotary valve-gear.

h Distributing and expansion poppet valve-gear.

j Accessories to steam engines in so far as they affect the operation of the engine.

k Special devices for utilising steam energy; Steam accumulators.

F 02—*Internal combustion engines; Air and special vapour engines; Spring and weight motors*

b Internal combustion piston engines.

c Internal combustion turbine engines.

d Controlling; Regulating.

f Component parts.

g Hot gas and compressed air piston engines; Combustion piston engines with external combustion; Utilisation of waste gases of combustion engines.

h Special vapour engines.

j Spring, weight and animal-driven motors; Solar energy engines.

k Jet propulsion plant (reaction principle).

l Combined engines and plants.

F 03—*Wind and water motors*

b Hydraulic turbines; Water wheels.

c Other water machines, *e.g.*, water pressure machines, tide and wave motors.

d Wind motors.

F 04—*Compressors; Blowers; Air pumps*

b Bellows.
c Reciprocating piston compressors and air pumps.
d Rotary compressors, blowers and air pumps.
f Jet-type vacuum pumps and compressors.
g Displacement compressors and vacuum pumps not included in F 04 b or c.

F 05—*Pumps; Other apparatus for lifting liquids*

b Pumps with reciprocating pistons; Diaphragm pumps; Flexible tube pumps.
c Centrifugal and other turbine pumps.
d Pulsometers; Pumps operated by compressed air; Jet pumps; Hydraulic rams.
f Scoop devices (bucket apparatus); Scoop wheels; Other water-lifting devices.
g Pumps not included in F 05 b to f.

F 06—*Engineering elements and units; General measures for producing and maintaining effective functioning of machines or installations*

b Devices for fastening and securing machine parts together, *e.g.*, nails, bolts, circlips, wedges (ornamental heads for nails, screws, etc., A 47 g).
c Shafts; Bearings.
d Couplings; Clutches; Brakes.
f Springs; Shock absorbers; Means for damping vibration.
g Chains; Belts.
h Gearing.
j Pistons; Cylinders; Packing.
k Valves; Taps; Cocks; Actuating-floats.
l Pipes; Pipe joints; Means for insulation and anti-corrosion.

Explanatory note:

In this sub-class the word "pipes" is understood to include all pipes and tubes not specially adapted to purposes other than that of conveying fluids, materials, or objects.

m Frames; Engine beds.
n Lubricating (special modifications of devices or systems for use in particular machines or apparatus are classified with the machines or apparatus).
p Safety devices in general (safety devices adapted to machines or apparatus for special purposes are classified with the machines or apparatus).
q Elements used for fine mechanics.
r Fluid dynamics, *i.e.*, means for influencing the flow of gases or liquids.

Explanatory note:

This sub-class comprises boundary-layer control and other arrangements and methods, not provided for in other classes, for influencing the flow of fluids relative to constraining surfaces and after leaving these surfaces, *e.g.*, producing or removing turbulence, deflecting jets, guiding flow through bends in conduits, affecting distribution of fluid in a conduit, reducing fluid friction.

F 07—*Arms; Ammunition*

b Hand fire-arms other than those included in F 07 c and k; Accessories.
c Air, spring-loaded and toy guns; Devices for producing reports; Bows and arrows; Devices for throwing and hurling missiles.
d Ordnance; Guns and their mountings and carriages (flame-throwers F 07 j).
f Ammunition; Ammunition transport and packing.
g Targets; Target stands; Bullet catchers.
h Sighting devices and mechanism; Aiming guns.
j Armour; Armoured turrets, cars and cover; Means of attack and defence in general.
k Automatic small arms; Machine guns; Automatic guns.
l Fuses for projectiles.

F 21—*Lighting; Distribution and utilisation of gas*

b Lanterns; Torches; Miners' lamps; Lamp attachments.

c Intensification and distribution of light; Reflectors; Searchlights; Black-out devices.
d Combinations of dissimilar light sources.
f Gasholders; Distribution of gas; Gas pipes and taps; Gas pressure regulators; Gas mixers and compressors.
g Gas lighters; Arrangements for lighting and extinguishing gas lamps.
h Incandescent mantles, etc.
j Wick light burners (other burners F 23 d, f).

F 22—*Steam generation*

b Steam boilers (domestic heating F 24 d).
c Special methods of steam production; Firing of boilers with preheated substances; Closed combustion devices.
d Pre-heating and mechanical purification of feed water; Feeding; Regulation of circulation.
f Gauge glasses; Signal devices; safety apparatus.
g Steam lines; Drying and superheating of steam; Steam traps.
h Cleaning of steam boilers and boiler tubes.
j Fitting and sealing tubes.

F 23—*Furnaces and related features*

b Combustion-apparatus for solid fuels.
c Combustion-apparatus for powdered fuels.
d Combustion-apparatus for liquid fuels.
f Combustion-apparatus for gaseous fuels and for metallurgical furnaces.
g Cremation and refuse-consuming furnaces.
h Grates, including cleaning and raking.
j Flue devices; Cleaning flues and furnace tubes; Removal of ashes; Precipitation of particles from smoke.
k Feeding fuel to furnaces.
l Air-feed and draught devices.
m Fire boxes; Accessories.
n Regulating and controlling combustion.
p Special processes for generating heat.

F 24—*Heating and ventilating plants in buildings*

b Stoves and ranges for solid fuels.
c Other stoves and ranges.
d Central heating.
f Air-conditioning; Ventilation.
g Heating of water (geysers); Installation of hot water supply.

F 25—*Refrigeration; Manufacture and storage of ice; Heat exchange; Liquefying gases not readily condensed by mechanical means*

b Refrigerating machines.
c Manufacture of ice and ice cream (refrigerating machines F 25 b).
d Refrigerators; Cold-rooms; Ice-boxes.
f Steam or vapour condensers.
g Open-heat exchange apparatus.
h Enclosed-heat exchange apparatus.
j Liquefying gases; Separation of liquefied gas mixtures; Gas-bottles for storing gases at high pressure and their filling.

F 26—*Drying; Drying plants; Kilns; Coffee roasters*

b Drying machines, methods and apparatus; Kilns (malt kilns C 12 c).
c Roasters (coffee and the like).

G 01—*Measuring*

b Devices for measuring length and thickness; Dividers; Calipers; Measuring devices for the workshop; Gauges and the like.
c Measuring instruments for geodetical, nautical, aeronautical and geo-physical purposes; Photogrammetry.
d Indicating and recording apparatus for measuring in general.
f Volume, flow and liquid-level meters.
g Scales; Weighing machines.
h Measurement and analysis of infrasonic, sonic or supersonic

vibrations; Combined generation and measurement of supersonic vibrations.

j Measurement and analysis of infra-red, visible or ultra-violet light, *e.g.*, photometers and colorimeters.

k Thermometers, *e.g.*, bolometers and optical pyrometers; Meteorological instruments; Calorimeters; Temperature-responsive elements.

l Instruments for measuring power, *e.g.*, dynamometers, pressure gauges, indicators, apparatus for measuring strength and fluid tightness.

m Testing of machines, *e.g.*, balancing parts of machines.

n Testing chemical and/or physical properties, including laboratory apparatus.

p Speedometers.

q Counting mechanisms; Revolution counters; Pedometers; Taximeters.

r Measuring electric values.

G 02—*Optics*

b Optical elements and systems, *e.g.*, lenses, prisms, optical mirrors.

c Spectacles.

d Optical apparatus.

G 03—*Photography; Cinematography*

b Cameras; Cinematographic cameras, projectors and accessories.

c Photographic processes; Light-sensitive surfaces, plates, films and papers; Colour photography; X-ray photography and cinematography in relief; Photo-sculpture.

d Photographic requisites; Dark rooms.

f Photomechanical reproduction.

G 04—*Horology*

b Clocks and watches (non-electric); Calendar clocks; Clockwork calendars.

c Electric clocks.

d Machines and tools for watch-making.

f Short time-interval measuring, including precision systems.

G 05—*Regulating; Controlling*

b Basic systems and constructional parts, *e.g.*, sensitive elements and servomotors.

c Speed regulating and power control devices for prime movers and engines.

d Regulators for regulating any non-electrical value not included in G 05 c.

f Regulators for electrical values and electric machines.

g Control devices.

G 06—*Calculating; Accounting*

b Construction elements.

c Mechanical digital machines (adding, subtracting, multiplying and dividing).

d Electric digital machines (electronic G 06 f).

f Electronic calculating machines, including machines controlled by punched sheets or by sheets provided with magnetic or other markings.

g Mechanical and electric calculating apparatus and computing scales.

h Cash registers.

j Accounting and bookkeeping machines.

k Statistical machines; Devices for marking of, segregating of, and compiling from cards, sheets, etc., with statistical representations; Data records.

G 07—*Checking devices*

b Ticket printing and issuing apparatus; Fare-registering apparatus; Franking apparatus.

c Time and attendance registers; Registering and indicating the working of machines; Voting and lottery apparatus.

d Coin changers and sorters.

f Coin-freed and such-like apparatus.

G 08—*Signalling*

b Domestic and hotel signalling and alarm devices; Ringing tower bells.

c Remote indicating of conditions and measured values.

d Order telegraphs; Fire and police telegraphs.

f Acoustic and optical signalling; Whistles; Sirens; Fog-horns, etc.

G 09—*Education; Advertising*

b Educational appliances (for music G 10 g); Planetaria; Globes; Maps.

c Coding and ciphering apparatus.

d Railway and like guides; Perpetual calendars (clock-work-driven G 04 b).

f Movable acoustical and optical advertising and displaying (in the nature of shop furniture A 47 f).

g Other advertising and displaying (in the nature of shop furniture A 47 f).

G 10—*Musical instruments; Acoustics*

b Organs; Harmoniums.

c Pianos.

d Orchestral instruments; Stringed instruments; Mouth organs; Accordions.

f Mechanical instruments (automatic).

g Teaching appliances and aids for music.

h Electrophonic musical instruments (tones generated by electrical means).

j Sound recording and reproducing.

k Acoustics not otherwise included.

G 21—*Nuclear physics*

H 01—*Electrotechnical elements*

b Cables, Conductors; Insulators (waveguides H 01 p).

c Resistances.

d Ferromagnetic cores; Inductive or magnet coils; Magnets; Magnetizing or de-magnetizing.

f Inductances; Transformers (transformers, reactors, and choke coils for use with mains or similar power supply systems and operation at mains frequency H 02 1; ferromagnetic cores and inductive or magnet coils in general H 01 d).

g Capacitors; Capacitors, rectifiers, detectors, switching devices, and light-sensitive devices, of the electrolytic type.

h Relays.

j Electric discharge tubes and discharge lamps (arc lamps with consumable electrodes H 05 b; particle accelerators H 05 h; spark-gap arresters H 02 d).

Explanatory note:

This sub-class deals only with devices for producing, influencing, or utilising a flow of electrons and/or ions, *e.g.*, for controlling, indicating, or switching of electric current, counting electric pulses, producing light or other electromagnetic oscillations such as X-rays, and having a closed casing containing a chosen gas, vapour, or vacuum, upon the pressure and nature of which the characteristics of the device depend.

k Electric incandescent lamps.

l Semi-conductor devices (electrolytic devices H 01 g or H 01 m; thermoelectric elements H 01 m).

Explanatory note:

Semi-conductor devices as interpreted in this sub-class comprise inherently at least one potential-jump barrier which is essential to the desired operation of the devices and which separates regions of different conductivity type, at least one region having P, P^+, N, N^+, I or S type conductivity.

m Batteries; Accumulators; Thermoelectric elements.

n Casings for electric apparatus.

p Waveguides; Resonators, lines or other devices of the waveguide type (aerials H 04 d).

Explanatory note:

In this sub-class, the term "waveguide type" as applied to transmission lines includes only high-frequency coaxial cables and Lecher lines, and as applied to resonators, delay lines and other devices includes all devices having distributed inductance and capacitance.

H 02—*Generation, conversion and distribution of electric power*

b Switch-boards; Distribution gear.
c Switches.
d Emergency protective means, *e.g.*, fuses and spark-gap arresters.
f Line connectors; Current collectors.
g Installation of electric cables and lines.
h Protecting living beings from electric shock.
j Relative disposition of machines and apparatus and lines.
k Dynamo-electric machines.
l Transformers, reactors and choke coils for use with mains or similar power supply systems and operation at mains frequency (transformers and inductances in general H 01 f; ferromagnetic cores and inductive or magnet coils in general H 01 d).
m Apparatus for conversion between AC and AC, between AC and DC, and between DC and DC (with moving parts H 02 n).
n Other generators, motors and converters.
p Controlling generators, motors and converters.

H 03—*Electric oscillation and pulse technique*

b Generation of oscillations.
c Modulation; Keying.
d Demodulations and transference of modulations from one carrier to another.
f Amplifiers.
g Regulation of generation and amplification.
h Impedance networks; Resonance circuits; Resonators (except cavity or like resonators H 01 p).
j Tuning of resonators
k Pulse technique.

H 04—*Electric communication technique*

b Transmission characterised by the transmitting medium; Interference and noise suppression or limitation.
c Transmission characterised by the method of modulation.
d Aerials.
f Synchronised systems of transmission.
g Directive transmission.
h Broadcast transmission.
j Multiplex transmission.
k Secret transmission; Jamming of transmission.
l Telegraphic communication.
m Telephonic communication.
n Pictorial communication; Television.
p Radio direction-finding, locating, distance and velocity measuring; Radio navigation systems.

H 05—*Special electric techniques*

b Electric heating and welding; Electric lighting not otherwise included.
c Electrified wire fencing.
d Detection of hidden masses; Geological exploration.
f Atmospheric electricity; Static electricity; Earth currents.
g Electro-, radio-, and magneto-therapy; X-ray technique.
h Production of accelerated electrically-charged particles and of neutrons.
j (Sub-class cancelled. Subject-matter transferred mainly to H 01 j).

CONVENTION ON THE UNIFICATION OF CERTAIN POINTS OF SUBSTANTIVE LAW ON PATENTS FOR INVENTION

Strasbourg, November 27, 1963

Article 1

In the Contracting States, patents shall be granted for any inventions which are susceptible of industrial application, which are new and which involve an inventive step. An invention which does not comply with these conditions shall not be the subject of a valid patent. A patent declared invalid because the invention does not comply with these conditions shall be considered invalid *ab initio*.

Article 2

The Contracting States shall not be bound to provide for the grant of patents in respect of

(*a*) inventions the publication or exploitation of which would be contrary to " *ordre public* " or morality, provided that the exploitation shall not be deemed to be so contrary merely because it is prohibited by a law or regulation;

(*b*) plant or animal varieties or essentially biological processes for the production of plants or animals; this provision does not apply to microbiological processes and the products thereof.

Article 3

An invention shall be considered as susceptible of industrial application if it can be made or used in any kind of industry including agriculture.

Article 4

1. An invention shall be considered to be new if it does not form part of the state of the art.

2. Subject to the provisions of paragraph 4 of this Article, the state of the art shall be held to comprise everything made available to the public by means of a written or oral description, by use, or in any other way, before the date of the patent application or of a foreign application, the priority of which is validly claimed.

3. Any Contracting State may consider the contents of applications for patents made, or of patents granted, in that State, which have been officially published on or after the date referred

to in paragraph 2 of this Article, as comprised in the state of the art, to the extent to which such contents have an earlier priority date.

4. A patent shall not be refused or held invalid by virtue only of the fact that the invention was made public, within six months preceding the filing of the application, if the disclosure was due to, or in consequence of:

(*a*) an evident abuse in relation to the applicant or his legal predecessor, or

(*b*) the fact that the applicant or his legal predecessor has displayed the invention at official, or officially recognised, international exhibitions falling within the terms of the Convention on international exhibitions signed at Paris on 22nd November 1928 and amended on 10th May 1948.

Article 5

An invention shall be considered as involving an inventive step if it is not obvious having regard to the state of the art. However, for the purposes of considering whether or not an invention involves an inventive step, the law of any Contracting State may, either generally or in relation to particular classes of patents or patent applications, for example patents of addition, provide that the state of the art shall not include all or any of the patents or patent applications mentioned in paragraph 3 of Article 4.

Article 6

Any Contracting State which does not apply the provisions of paragraph 3 of Article 4 shall nevertheless provide that no invention shall be validly protected in so far as it includes matter which is or has been validly protected by a patent in that State which, though not comprised in the state of the art, has, in respect of that matter, an earlier priority date.

Article 7

Any group of Contracting States who provide for a common patent application may be regarded as a single State for the purposes of paragraph 3 of Article 4, or of Article 6.

Article 8

1. The patent application shall contain a description of the invention with the necessary drawings referred to therein and one or more claims defining the protection applied for.

2. The description must disclose the invention in a manner sufficiently clear and complete for it to be carried out by a person skilled in the art.

3. The extent of the protection conferred by the patent shall be determined by the terms of the claims. Nevertheless, the description and drawings shall be used to interpret the claims.

Article 9

1. This Convention shall be open for signature by the member States of the Council of Europe. It shall be subject to ratification or acceptance. Instruments of ratification or acceptance shall be deposited with the Secretary-General of the Council of Europe.

2. This Convention shall enter into force three months after the date of deposit of the eighth instrument of ratification or acceptance.

3. In respect of a signatory State ratifying or accepting subsequently, the Convention shall come into force three months after the date of deposit of its instrument of ratification or acceptance.

Article 10

1. After the entry into force of this Convention, the Committee of Ministers of the Council of Europe may invite any Member of the International Union for the Protection of Industrial Property which is not a Member of the Council of Europe to accede thereto.

2. Such accession shall be effected by depositing with the Secretary-General of the Council of Europe an instrument of accession which shall take effect three months after the date of its deposit.

Article 11

1. Any Contracting Party may at the time of signature or when depositing its instrument of ratification, acceptance or accession, specify the territory or territories to which this Convention shall apply.

2. Any Contracting Party may, when depositing its instrument of ratification, acceptance or accession or at any later date, by notification addressed to the Secretary-General of the Council of Europe, extend this Convention to any other territory or territories specified in the declaration and for whose international relations it is responsible or on whose behalf it is authorised to give undertakings.

3. Any declaration made in pursuance of the preceding paragraph may, in respect of any territory mentioned in such declara-

tion, be withdrawn according to the procedure laid down in Article 13 of this Convention.

ARTICLE 12

1. Notwithstanding anything in this Convention, each Contracting Party may, at the time of signature or when depositing its instrument of ratification, acceptance or accession, temporarily reserve, for the limited period stated below, the right:

(*a*) not to provide for the grant of patents in respect of food and pharmaceutical products, as such, and agricultural or horticultural processes other than those to which paragraph (*b*) of Article 2 applies;

(*b*) to grant valid patents for inventions disclosed within the six months preceding the filing of the application, either apart from the case referred to in paragraph 4 (*b*) of Article 4, by the inventor himself, or, apart from the case referred to in paragraph 4 (*a*) of Article 4, by a third party as a result of information derived from the inventor.

2. The limited period referred to in paragraph 1 of this Article shall be ten years in the case of sub-paragraph (*a*) and five years in the case of sub-paragraph (*b*). It shall start from the entry into force of this Convention for the Contracting Party considered.

3. Any Contracting Party which makes a reservation under this Article shall withdraw the said reservation as soon as circumstances permit. Such withdrawal shall be made by notification addressed to the Secretary-General of the Council of Europe and shall take effect one month from the date of receipt of such notification.

ARTICLE 13

1. This Convention shall remain in force indefinitely.

2. Any Contracting Party may, in so far as it is concerned, denounce this Convention by means of a notification addressed to the Secretary-General of the Council of Europe.

3. Such denunciation shall take effect six months after the date of receipt by the Secretary-General of such notification.

ARTICLE 14

The Secretary-General of the Council of Europe shall notify the member States of the Council, any State which has acceded to this Convention and the Director of the International Bureau for the Protection of Industrial Property of:

(*a*) any signature;

(*b*) any deposit of an instrument of ratification, acceptance or accession;

(*c*) any date of entry into force of this Convention;
(*d*) any declaration and notification received in pursuance of the provisions of paragraphs 2 and 3 of Article 11;
(*e*) any reservation made in pursuance of the provisions of paragraph 1 of Article 12;
(*f*) the withdrawal of any reservation carried out in pursuance of the provisions of paragraph 3 of Article 12;
(*g*) any notification received in pursuance of the provisions of paragraph 2 of Article 13 and the date on which denunciation takes effect.

AGREEMENT CONCERNING THE ESTABLISHMENT OF AN INTERNATIONAL PATENTS BUREAU

The Hague, 6 June, 1947

Article 1

An International Patents Bureau is established to provide the Governments of the States Parties to this Agreement with reasoned opinions regarding the novelty of inventions in respect of which applications for patents have been filed with the respective national industrial property services. The International Patents Bureau may also provide these services with opinions regarding the novelty of inventions in respect of which applications for patents have not been filed.

Article 2

To enable the Bureau to carry out its duties, the Government of each of the States Parties to this Agreement will communicate to it the originals or certified photographic or microphotographic copies of such relevant documentary material as it possesses or can produce or collect, and in particular the texts of patents already issued and applications for patents filed with it. This material will be communicated as soon as possible.

Article 3

The work of the Bureau shall be directed by a Board of Administration, composed of one member appointed by the Government of each State Party to this Agreement.

The Board shall elect its chairman annually.

Article 4

The Board of Administration decides on all matters connected with the general work of the Bureau. It shall appoint by a two-thirds majority, and determine the functions of, the Director, who must be a national of a State Party to this Agreement. It shall draw up the annual budget and any necessary amending or additional budgets of receipts and expenditure. It shall inspect and approve the Director's accounts. It shall draw up the rules of procedure and financial regulations of the Bureau.

Article 5

A special provision of the rules of procedure shall determine the relations of the International Patents Bureau with the International Bureau for the Protection of Industrial Property established at Berne.

The financial regulations will, in particular, lay down the procedure by which control shall be exercised over the budget.

Article 6

Any State Party to this Agreement may in case of need empower the representative of another Contracting State to represent it on the Board of Administration; but no representative may have more than two votes.

Article 7

Decisions of the Board of Administration shall be taken by a majority of votes. In the case of a tie, the Chairman shall have the casting vote.

Article 8

The Bureau is under the high patronage of the Governments of the States Parties to this Agreement and under the permanent protection of the Royal Government of the Netherlands.

The Headquarters of the Bureau is situated at The Hague.

Article 9

The income of the Bureau is constituted as follows:

(*a*) by an initial contribution and an annual contribution from each State Party to the present Agreement. The amount of these contributions will be fixed on a scale identical with that provided for in Article 13, paragraphs 8 and 9, of the Union Convention of Paris for the Protection of Industrial Property;

(*b*) a fee for each opinion communicated at the request of the special industrial property service of any State.

The opinions of the Bureau will as a rule be communicated only to these services.

The Board of Administration may also authorise the collection of all sums in payment of services rendered to the official institutions concerned and in exceptional cases to private groups or individuals.

ARTICLE 10

This Agreement will be ratified. It will enter into force as soon as the instruments of ratification of the four signatory States have been deposited with the Ministry of Foreign Affairs at The Hague.[6]

ARTICLE 11

After the entry into force of this Agreement, any non-signatory State which is a member of the International Union for the Protection of Industrial Property may at any time adhere to it.

Such adhesion will be notified through diplomatic channels to the Royal Government of the Netherlands and by that Government to all the other Contracting States.

ARTICLE 12

The States signatory to this Agreement and States adhering to it subsequently may not denounce it before five years have elapsed from the date of its entry into force with respect to them. A denunciation will take effect one year after the date of its receipt by the Royal Government of the Netherlands.

ARTICLE 13

If the number of the States Parties to this Agreement is reduced by denunciations to less than four, the Bureau will be dissolved automatically and its property will vest in the last Contracting Parties in shares proportionate to the total amounts contributed by each in initial and annual contributions.

ARTICLE 14

This Agreement will be revised periodically with the purpose of introducing into it amendments likely to improve the services rendered by the Bureau in the matter of industrial property, and of developing and extending, if need be, its field of activity.

[6] The Agreement entered into force for these States on 10 June, 1949.

AGREEMENT REVISING THE AGREEMENT SIGNED AT THE HAGUE ON JUNE 6, 1947, CONCERNING THE ESTABLISHMENT OF AN INTERNATIONAL PATENTS BUREAU

(with Protocol and Resolution)
The Hague, 16 February–31 December, 1961

Article 1

1. The International Patents Bureau, founded by The Hague Agreement of 6 June, 1947 under the name Institut International des Brevets, shall be responsible for providing expert opinions on the novelty of inventions forming the subject of patent applications received or patents granted by the national government of each Member State or by any international intergovernmental organisation which is a member of the Institute, as defined in Article 2.

For the present agreement, applications lodged with the national government of a Member State solely for transmission to the government of another State or to an international intergovernmental organisation are not considered as patent applications received by that government.

2. Opinions of a different kind from those provided for in paragraph 1 of this Article may also be given by the Institute on the inventions referred to in that paragraph, subject to preliminary consent from the Administrative Council set up under Article 6.

3. In addition, the Institute may, on behalf of any applicant, undertake any documentary search on the state of the art.

Article 2

Any international intergovernmental organisation responsible for granting patents of invention which places in the hands of the International Patents Institute the formulation of expert opinions on the novelty of inventions, as provided for in Article 1, paragraphs 1 or 2, may become a member of the Institute through an agreement with the Institute as provided for in Article 9, paragraph 1, with the rights and obligations set out in Articles 5, 6, 8, 9, 12, 13, 14 and 17 of the present Agreement and in Article 1 of the Protocol.

The Protocol forms an integral part of the present Agreement.

Article 3

The expert opinion referred to in Article 1, paragraph 1, shall be in documentary form and based on a search, the nature and extent of which are laid down in Article 1, paragraphs 1, 2 and 3, of the Protocol.

Article 4

The Member States undertake to make provision, either in their national legislation or through international agreements, for all or some of the applications for patents, or the patents, effective in their territory to be obligatorily the subject of an expert opinion as referred to in Article 1, paragraph 1.

Article 5

In order to be able to carry out its task, the Institute is entitled to free copies from States or Member Organisations of patent specifications and published patent applications as issued by the governments of these States or by these Organisations.

Article 6

1. The Institute is governed by a Board of Administration composed of representatives of States or Organisations which are members, there being one representative from each State or Organisation.
2. Any Member State may, in case of need, be represented on the Board by another Member State. No member of the Board may, however, represent more than two States.
3. The Board shall draw up its standing orders and appoint its Chairman every year. It shall meet on the initiative of its Chairman, on that of one-third of the members, or, in an emergency, on that of the Director of the Institute.

Article 7

Apart from the tasks within its competency by virtue of other provisions of the present Agreement the Board of Administration shall lay down the general policy of the Institute, regulate and supervise the activity of the latter, and in particular:

(1) draw up the regulations necessary for carrying out the present Agreement and supervise their application;
(2) vote annually the budget, and, if necessary, modifying or additional budgets, and supervise their implementation;
(3) audit and approve the annual accounts and inventory;
(4) approve the annual report on the work of the Institute;
(5) appoint the Director and the Auditor of the Institute from nationals of Member States, decide their respec-

tive salaries and additional benefits, and exercise disciplinary power over them;

(6) give the necessary general instructions to the Director and any instructions useful to the Auditor and ensure their implementation;

(7) draw up the list of managerial posts and, after consultation with the Director, appoint the holders of these offices, decide their salaries and additional benefits, and exercise disciplinary powers over them;

(8) draw up the conditions of service of the staff;

(9) decide the complement of staff and their salary scales, and the nature and conditions regulating the additional benefits they receive;

(10) authorise the Director to exercise the juridical capacity of the Institute in accordance with the provisions of Article 11.

Article 8

1. For every decision of the Board of Administration which requires a vote, polling shall take place on the basis of one vote per representative of a Member State or Organisation.

In matters relating to the annual contribution of a Member State or Organisation, however, whatever the result of the vote may be, the representative of any Member State or Organisation may demand a fresh vote in which the allocation of votes is governed by the provisions of paragraphs 2, 3 and 4 of the present Article. The decision shall depend on this fresh vote.

2. In this fresh vote, the representative of each Member State or Organisation shall have 10 votes to which shall be added an additional number of votes equal to the quotient of the division of the amount of the annual contribution of this State or Organisation, as defined in Article 13, paragraph 3, by the unit of account defined in sub-paragraph 3 of this paragraph.

The number of votes thus allocated shall be rounded off to the nearest higher whole number. However, the total number of votes allocated to the representative of a Member State or Organisation may not exceed five times the total number of votes possessed by the representative of another Member State or Organisation.

The unit of account shall equal the quotient of the division of the sum of the annual contributions of Member States and Organisations by the number obtained by multiplying by ten the number of Member States and Organisations.

3. The number of votes allocated to the representative of each Member State or Organisation shall be determined at the

beginning of every year on the basis of the contributions agreed for the penultimate year.

4. For the period following the accession of a State or Organisation, during which the provisions of paragraph 3 of the present Article cannot be applied, the number of votes possessed by the representative of that Member State or Organisation shall be decided by the Board.

Article 9

1. Decisions of the Board of Administration on the following matters shall require a two-thirds majority of the total votes possessed by the representatives of Member States and Organisations:

(*a*) the conclusion of agreements with States or international intergovernmental organisations and the adoption or modification of the regulations necessary for the application of these agreements;

(*b*) the adoption or modification of the regulations necessary for the application of the present agreement, including those relating to the conditions of service of the different categories of staff;

(*c*) the drawing up of the opinions referred to in Article 1, paragraph 2;

(*d*) the appointment of the Director;

(*e*) the modification of the budget provided for in Article 13, paragraph 2;

(*f*) the creation of the supplementary services referred to in Article 17.

2. Other decisions shall require a simple majority of the total votes cast for or against.

In case of an equal division, a second vote shall be held: any second equal division shall be equivalent to the rejection of the proposed decision.

Article 10

The Director shall be responsible for the management of the Institute in accordance with the provisions of the Protocol, with the regulations drawn up by the Board of Administration, and with the general instructions of the Board.

Article 11

1. The Institute shall have legal status. In each Member State it shall possess the widest legal capacity admitted to legal entities by the national legislation of that State.

2. This juridical capacity of the Institute is embodied in the Director within the limits fixed by the Protocol.

ARTICLE 12

1. Member States and Organisations shall pay an initial contribution.

2. The initial contribution of States shall be determined by the number of units of the class in which they are placed in application of the provisions set out in Article 13, paragraphs 8 and 9, of the Convention for the Protection of Industrial Property signed in Paris on 20 March, 1883, and last revised in Lisbon on 31 October, 1958. The amount of a unit is equal to the exchange value of two kilograms of pure gold by the exchange rate of the country in which the Institute is located on the date of accession.

3. The initial contribution of Organisations shall be determined by the agreement concluded with the Institute referred to in Article 2.

ARTICLE 13

1. The annual expenses of the Institute shall be met by:

(*a*) the annual contributions of the Member States and Organisations;

(*b*) payment received for the services mentioned in Article 1, paragraph 3;

(*c*) all other receipts, in particular revenues derived from the property of the Institute.

2. The annual expenses of the Institute shall be divided into running expenses and examination expenses.

The distribution of expenses is made in accordance with a budget voted by the Board of Administration by simple majority and, in case of need, amended by the qualified majority referred to in Article 9, paragraph 1. This budget shall be drawn up on the basis of a report submitted by chartered accountants appointed by the Board.

On the basis of this accountancy scheme (budget) the Board shall determine the percentage of running expenses. This percentage shall be fixed every 5 years for the following 5-year period.

3. The annual contributions of Member States and Organisations cover the amount of the annual expenses, deducting the payments received and the receipts referred to in paragraph 1 (*b*) and (*c*) of the present Article.

The share of the budget covering the running expenses shall be divided among the Member States and Organisations proportionately to co-efficients which, for each of them, shall be equal to the quotient, rounded up to the next higher unit, of the division by one thousand of the number of patent applications received by the government of each State or each Organisation in the course of the financial year concerned.

The share of the budget covering examination expenses shall be divided proportionately to the number of opinions mentioned in Article 14 requested from the Institute in the course of the financial year concerned.

4. The Board shall decide before the beginning of each financial year the provisional amount of contributions covering the running expenses that each Member State or Organisation must pay in the course of that financial year, and also the contractual fee applicable during this period to the applications for opinions mentioned in Article 14.

The payments thus made shall constitute advances on the annual contributions of Member States or Organisations due by virtue of the budget in question.

5. With regard to the fixing of the annual contributions referred to above, the Board shall lay down, for the opinions provided for in Article 1, paragraph 2 of the present Agreement, and in Article 1, paragraphs 2 and 3 of the Protocol, co-efficients proportional to the amount of work needed to draw up such opinions, in relation to the work required by opinions founded on the search as defined in Article 1, paragraph 1 of the Protocol.

6. The Board shall fix the amount of the payments to be made for the services referred to in Article 1, paragraph 3: this amount may not be less than the sum of the running costs and examination expenses made necessary by the provision of such services.

Article 14

1. In determining the sharing of the annual contributions of each Member State provided for in Article 13, paragraph 3, part 3:

(*a*) the expert opinions referred to in Article 1, paragraphs 1 and 2, demanded from or transmitted by the national administration of that State shall be taken into account;

(*b*) subject to notification to the Institute, expert opinions as envisaged in Article 1, paragraphs 1 and 2, demanded by physical persons or legal entities in accordance with conditions determined by that State, may also be taken into consideration.

2. With regard to Member Organisations, only the expert opinions as envisaged in Article 1, paragraphs 1 and 2, demanded by these Organisations shall be taken into account in calculating

the share of the annual contribution as laid down in Article 13, paragraph 3, sub-paragraph 3.

Article 15

1. The Institute may participate in the preparation or execution of international agreements on the protection of industrial property in so far as these agreements are connected with its activity.

2. It may be represented on the organisations created by these agreements.

Article 16

1. The Institute is located at The Hague.

2. The Institute is placed under the protection of the Government of the Netherlands.

Article 17

1. When the drawing up of opinions applied for by a Member State or Organisation calls for documentary research in a language other than German, English, French and Dutch, the Institute may, for this task, create supplementary services; the additional costs are to be borne by the State or Organisation in question.

2. Similar powers are open to the Institute to meet any particular needs of Member States or Organisations.

Article 18

1. The present agreement is open for signature, up to 31 December, 1961, by any State party to the Convention for the Protection of Industrial Property signed in Paris on 20 March, 1883, and last revised in Lisbon on 31 October, 1958.

2. It shall be ratified and the instruments of ratification shall be deposited with the Ministry for Foreign Affairs of the Netherlands.

Article 19

1. The present Agreement shall enter into force one month after the deposit of all the instruments of ratification of the signatory States which are parties to the Agreement of 6 June, 1947.

2. With regard to any signatory State which was not a party to the Agreement of 6 June, 1947, the present Agreement shall come into force on the date provided for in paragraph 1 of the present Article if the deposit of the instrument of ratification preceded that of the last of the instruments of ratification

referred to in that paragraph, or if the deposit of the instrument of ratification is effected subsequently, one month after such deposit.

ARTICLE 20

1. Any non-signatory State which is party to the Convention referred to in Article 18 may accede to the present Agreement.

2. Instruments of accession shall be deposited with the Ministry for Foreign Affairs of the Netherlands.

3. Accession shall take effect on the date of entry into force of the present Agreement. If the instrument of accession is deposited after that date, the accession shall take effect one month after this deposit, unless a later date shall be specified in the instrument of accession.

ARTICLE 21

Any State party to the present Agreement may denounce it by written notification addressed to the Ministry for Foreign Affairs of the Netherlands. The denunciation shall take effect on 31 December of the second year following that in which the Ministry for Foreign Affairs of the Netherlands shall have received the notification.

ARTICLE 22

1. The present Agreement shall be subject to periodic revision, especially with a view to introducing modifications tending to improve the services rendered by the Institute and to develop, if the need arises, its field of activity.

2. In the interval between such revisions, the Protocol and its Annex may be amended by a conference of representatives of the Member States with immediate effect, unless this conference fixes a later date for implementing the amendments. These amendments shall be adopted by unanimous decision of the States represented.

ARTICLE 23

The Netherlands Ministry for Foreign Affairs shall notify signatory or acceding States of:

(1) signatures and the deposit of instruments of ratification;

(2) the deposit of instruments of accession and the date on which such accessions take effect;

(3) the date on which the present Agreement enters into force in accordance with the provisions of Article 19;

(4) denunciations provided for in Article 21 and the dates on which they take effect;

(5) the text of amendments made to the Protocol and to its Annex in accordance with the conditions set out in Article 22, paragraph 2.

PROTOCOL

Article 1

1. For the search referred to in Article 3 of the Agreement, the documents mentioned in the Annex to this Protocol shall be the minimum documentation to be consulted. The documents held in the subdivisions of the system of classification in use at the Institute to which the invention submitted for examination belongs by virtue of its nature, and the documents held in the related subdivisions shall be consulted.

2. Any Member State or Member Organisation shall have the right to require opinions based on a more limited search than that defined in paragraph 1 of this Article.

However, except in the case of a unanimous decision to the contrary taken by the Board of Administration, this right may not be exercised in regard to patent applications or patents which, by virtue of a claim for priority right, relate to the same invention as a different patent application or a different patent that has been the subject of a previous opinion based on a search as defined in paragraph 1 of this Article.

3. Subject to the previous agreement of the Board of Administration, any Member State or Member Organisation may obtain opinions based on a more extensive search than that defined in paragraph 1 of this Article.

Article 2

Within limits of the authority vested in him by Article 10 of the Agreement, the Director:

(1) shall draw up and implement the budget;

(2) shall submit the annual accounts and inventory to the Board of Administration;

(3) shall recruit and appoint the members of the staff with the exception of those covered by Article 7, sections (5) and (7), of the Agreement;

(4) shall take decisions on the promotion of the members of staff he appoints, and shall exercise disciplinary power over them;

(5) shall submit annually to the Board of Administration a report on the work of the Institute;
(6) shall have the right to attend the meetings of the Board of Administration, except in the instances provided for in Article 7, section (5), of the Agreement, and where the proceedings concern the members of the Board only.

Article 3

The permission of the Board of Administration, vouched for by the signature of its Chairman, shall be required for the exercise of the legal capacity of the Institute in the following cases:

(1) actions at law, except for those having the character of conservation;
(2) deeds concerning the purchase and transfer of real estate, those affecting the property of such estate, and those relating to the construction of buildings;
(3) any other deeds relating to transactions for amounts exceeding the exchange value of twenty kilograms of pure gold.

Article 4

In the event of prolonged absence of the Director, or in the event of vacancy of his post, the powers provided for in Article 10 of the Agreement and in Article 2 of this Protocol shall be exercised by the member of staff appointed to do so by the Board of Administration.

ANNEX TO THE PROTOCOL

List of documents referred to in Article 1, paragraph 1, of the Protocol which are to be included in the documentation used by the Institut International des Brevets:

A. *Patents*

1. German Patents	from the year	1877
2. U.S. Patents	... ...	1921
3. Belgian Patents	... ...	1926
4. British Patents	... ...	1909
5. French Patents	... ...	1902
6. Luxembourg Patents	... ...	1947
7. Netherlands Patents	... ...	1912
8. Swiss Patents	... ...	1940

B. *Published Patent Applications*

1. German Patent Applications
   from the year ... 1957
2. Netherlands Patent Applications ... 1912
3. Swiss Patent Applications 1961

C. *Periodical Publications and Technical Books*

Periodical publications and technical books written in the German, English, French or Dutch languages, selected from among the most prominent.

All the documentation mentioned in A, B and C above shall be continuously kept up to date.

INDEX OF COUNTRIES

GENERAL INDEX